MICROSOFT WORD FOR WINDOWS MADE EASY, THIRD EDITION

Paul Hoffman

Osborne **McGraw-Hill**

Berkeley New York St. Louis San Francisco
Auckland Bogotá Hamburg London Madrid
Mexico City Milan Montreal New Delhi Panama City
Paris São Paulo Singapore Sydney
Tokyo Toronto

Osborne **McGraw-Hill**
2600 Tenth Street
Berkeley, California 94710
U.S.A.

For information on translations or book distributors outside of the U.S.A., please write to Osborne **McGraw-Hill** at the above address.

Microsoft Word for Windows Made Easy, Third Edition

Copyright © 1994 by McGraw-Hill, Inc. All rights reserved. Printed in the United States of America. Except as permitted under the Copyright Act of 1976, no part of this publication may be reproduced or distributed in any form or by any means, or stored in a database or retrieval system, without the prior written permission of the publisher, with the exception that the program listings may be entered, stored, and executed in a computer system, but they may not be reproduced for publication.

1234567890 DOC 9987654

ISBN 0-07-881955-5

Information has been obtained by Osborne **McGraw-Hill** from sources believed to be reliable. However, because of the possibility of human or mechanical error by our sources, Osborne **McGraw-Hill**, or others, Osborne **McGraw-Hill** does not guarantee the accuracy, adequacy, or completeness of any information and is not responsible for any errors or omissions or the results obtained from use of such information.

CONTENTS

INTRODUCTION

Microsoft Word for Windows Made Easy, Third Edition will help you master Microsoft Word for Windows version 6. It discusses both the essential and unique features of the program and provides practical suggestions for putting Word for Windows to work for you. This book supplements the documentation, the Word for Windows *User's Guide,* by showing you, in step-by-step fashion, how to use Word. (Throughout this book, Word for Windows will be referred to simply as Word.)

Even though a few of Word's features appear complex, they are relatively easy to master once you understand the concepts behind them. This book is arranged to teach you these concepts in a logical order, and it reinforces the concepts with many practical examples. The examples demonstrate the numerous word processing functions performed in a typical business office, although they are just as useful in any situation that requires word processing capabilities.

Each chapter is divided into lessons that are fully illustrated with pictures of the Windows screen so you will know what to expect as you use the program. There are also review exercises at the end of each chapter.

For those of you who have never used a word processing program before, this book explains basic concepts when they first appear in the text. Even if you have used other word processing programs, you will find that some of Word's features are unique. (For example, Word can display several parts of a file simultaneously.) These features, too, are explained in full to help you completely understand the power of Word. You need to know only the basics of using Windows to use this book; you do not need to be familiar with any other word processing program.

If you already have Microsoft Word for Windows or are thinking of buying it, this book is for you. As a beginning user, you will find that the lessons are easy to follow, and succeeding lessons build on concepts learned earlier in the book. If you are an intermediate user, you will find that topics mentioned only briefly in different parts of the documentation are described fully in one location in this book. All users will find that the real-world examples in this book are more helpful than the terse step-lists in the Word manual.

What Is Microsoft Word?

A word processing program is a computer program that lets you type and save any text (such as memos, letters, reports, and books). Word processing programs such as Microsoft Word let you easily enter text for a document, revise the text once it has been entered (called editing), and print the text out on your printer in a professional form (called formatting).

There is a wide variety of word processing software available for many different computers. Some software gives you the bare minimum of capabilities, while other programs, such as Word, give you many more useful features that make word processing easier.

Word is useful for all types of word processing, such as writing memos, business letters, financial statements, articles, books, and long reports. It is generally easy to use and has many advanced features that you can use or ignore, depending on the type of document you are writing. For example, many people use Word to create attractive brochures and advertisements. The more you use Word, the less you need to worry about what your text will look like; this lets you spend more time concentrating on what you want to say.

Advantages of Using Word

If you have compared Word to word processing packages that do not run under Windows, you know that it has many features that others do not. Of course, having a plethora of features does not make a word processor good—you have to be able to use these features easily. Three outstanding features of Word are mentioned briefly here and described fully in this book.

See Exactly How Your Document Looks

You always know precisely how your document will look as you type it into Word. You see the margins, page headings, and so on. If you have put art in your document, such as a letterhead at the top of a letter, you see that as well.

Help Feature

If you are ever unsure of what you are doing in Word, the program can always offer help. This feature prevents you from having to look up information in the reference manual (or in this book) when you just want to know a small bit of information. The help that Word gives you is often more useful than the help you get from other programs. It first gives you help on what you are currently doing and then makes it easy to ask for more information if you need it. If you are currently a WordPerfect for DOS user, you will be pleasantly surprised how good Word's help for you is.

Windows

One problem with many word processing programs is that you can see only a small portion of your document at a time. With Word, you can see many parts of the text at the same time in different windows. You can also see two parts of a document in one window. This feature is very useful when you are writing a long document: you can look at what you wrote earlier while you write new text. You can also use Word to look at different files on the screen at the same time and to move text between files.

Using Word in Business

You have probably heard of the many advantages that word processing offers over normal typing for a business. Since Word has many more features than most other word processing programs, it lets you do more work more easily. For example:

- Most businesses have form letters (standard letters for which the computer fills in different names and addresses), and many word processing packages let you write simple form letters. Word allows you to integrate other information into your form letters so the letters look more personalized. Word can also read the names and addresses from data files stored by other programs, such as data management systems, and integrate these names and addresses into letters. This feature is called *print merge*.
- Word's advanced formatting lets you make reports that look professionally typeset. With Word, you can design each page to your

specifications and not worry about what it will look like if you change some of the text. Word works well with all printers that work with Windows.

- With Word, newsletters and other bulletins can be printed with many columns on one page, giving your writing a professional look. You can also use many different type styles (such as boldface or italics) and different type sizes that make your headlines stand out from your text.
- Many of Word's features are especially useful in certain professions. For example, Word's ability to number lines on a page is very helpful for lawyers' pleadings and depositions.
- You can use Word to make an outline and then use that outline to prepare a business document. You can have Word automatically number the headings in your outline and change those numbers as you move or delete headings.

As you read this book, remember that you can always try out the information that is presented to you. Use the files that the book tells you to type, or create your own. The more you use Word for your own files, the more quickly you will master Microsoft Word.

New Features in Version 6

If you are using Microsoft Word for Windows version 2, you should upgrade your copy to version 6. Version 6 has many more features than version 2, and many features are easier to access. Contact Microsoft to determine how you can upgrade to version 6.

Version 6 also has many significant new features and improvements to the user interface, which make Word easier to use and allow you to prepare business documents in a more natural way. This book has been completely revised to incorporate these new features (as well as dozens of minor ones).

- Word corrects common typing errors for you automatically. For instance, if you type "teh" instead of "the", Word automatically fixes that as you type. It also catches other common typing mistakes, such as double capital letters ("WOrd", for example).
- Tables are now easier to create and modify. You can change the way header rows look, add consistent formatting to text in the table, and quickly change the lines between rows and columns.
- You now have better control over the look of your screen. You can choose which toolbars appear at different times, and the tools in the toolbars are more useful. You can even create your own toolbars that work just the way you want.

- A major improvement is the ability to edit text while in print preview mode. This means that you no longer have to keep switching between view modes as you are performing the final steps of creating a document.
- You can automatically add captions to your drawings and have the captions automatically numbered (such as "Figure 4").
- Styles have been improved again. There are now character styles so you can format words in a consistent fashion (such as italicizing all book titles). Creating new styles is also easier, and Word comes with more examples of standard styles you might want to use in your document.
- Word's Undo command is now much more powerful. You can undo not only the previous change, but any change you have recently made to the document. This makes it much easier to fix problems as you are entering or changing your text and formatting.
- It is now incredibly easy to create mail merge documents. The Mail Merge command walks you through the required steps, giving you hints along the way.
- Word's help features have expanded so that the help commands meet the requirements of all levels of users. You even get a "tip of the day" each time you start Word.

All of these new features, and everything from the basics to advanced commands, are described in this book.

PART 1

WORD BASICS

C H A P T E R

1 GETTING STARTED

This chapter explains the few steps you need to follow before you can begin to use Word for Windows and shows you how to start up the program. After following the installation instructions, you can start to edit and format documents immediately; in fact, you will start using Word in Chapter 2 to enter a business letter that is used throughout the next six chapters and in many other sections of the book as well.

If you have no word processing experience, the first lesson gives you a quick overview of many of the terms you will find in this book. If you are familiar with another word processor, you can probably skim the section.

Lesson 1: Word Processing Terms

Word processing programs give you two major capabilities: editing and formatting of text. *Editing* is the ability to enter text into the program, make corrections, save the text on disk, and later change the text. *Formatting* is the ability to specify how the text will look when you print it out—for example, in boldface or italic in a specific type size and style. Formatting also allows you to add special features to the printout, such as page numbers on each page, and to specify the width of the left and right margins.

In order to make a word processing program work, you give it *commands,* which are instructions that tell the program what you want to do. In Word, you can give commands by using the mouse or by pressing the Ctrl key or the Alt key in combination with one or more other keys.

When you write a document, you *insert* text into a file. This is done by typing the text as you would on a typewriter. Once you have typed the text, you can use editing commands to correct mistakes or to rearrange the text. While you are editing, you can move around in the text so you can edit different parts. When you want to see text that is not on the screen, the word processing program *scrolls,* or moves, the screen to the desired location. When you are done with a file, you can *save* it on disk, and when you want to use the file later, you can tell the word processing program to *open* it from disk.

Lesson 2: Preparing for Word

Word for Windows comes on diskettes containing the programs and special files needed to run it. Since Word is such a large program, it takes up several diskettes. Follow the directions for copying the files from the Word distribution disks to your hard disk in the *Quick Results* guide that comes with Word for Windows. The installation program guides you through the choices you need to make when installing Word (such as deciding which directory it should go in).

When you install Word, the SETUP program asks if you want to use WordPerfect keyboard settings. Reply "No" to this prompt since Word's keyboard settings are easier to follow. If you have already installed Word and answered "Yes" to this, see Chapter 11 for more information on how to change this setting.

After you have installed Word, it is a good idea to store the distribution floppies in a safe place, preferably away from your computer. (Many people even keep their distribution floppies in a different room.) If the copy of Word that you have made on your hard disk or other floppies later becomes damaged or lost, you can reinstall the program from the original floppies.

Lesson 3: Starting the Word Program

You start Word in much the same way you start other Windows applications. Start Windows as you normally do. This leads you to the Windows Program Manager. To start Word, double-click the Word icon, which is shown here:

This is the method you will normally use for starting Word.

Another method for starting Word and editing an existing file is to double-click the Program Manager icon for that file. When you double-click a Word document, Windows starts Word and opens that file automatically. The Program Manager icon for Word files looks like this:

When you install Word, you are asked to personalize your copy. This puts your name and company name into the program; these names are shown each time you start the program. If you work for a company, they may have already personalized your copy for you.

After Word's initial screen comes up, you are presented with a small dialog box with the "tip of the day." For now, just click the OK button or press Enter to make this dialog box disappear. You will learn more about this feature later in this chapter.

When you start Word without opening a document, you see Word's main window, shown in Figure 1-1. (The items labeled on the figure are discussed throughout this and the following chapters.) The file is named Document1 until you save it to disk with a name of your choice. The next new file that you open during this session will be named Document2, and so on.

It is important to note the difference between Word's program window and its document windows. Word's *program window* is the outside window, the one with the menu at the top. When Word starts for the first time, the program window is *maximized,* that is, it is the full size of the screen. The

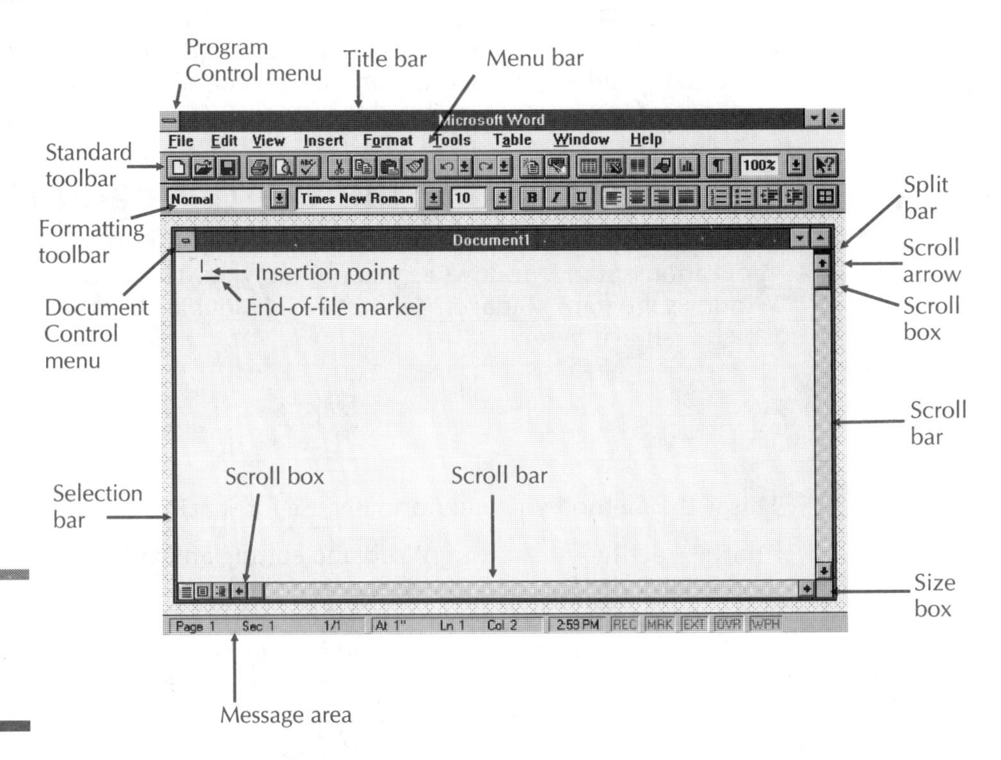

Features of Word's main window

Figure 1-1.

maximized program window has a *restore box* with two triangles in the upper-right corner of the screen:

Each document has its own *document window* that resides inside the Word program window. When a document window is maximized, it takes up the entire program window. When Word starts for the first time, the document window and the program window are both maximized. The maximized document window has a restore box that appears at the right side of the menu bar:

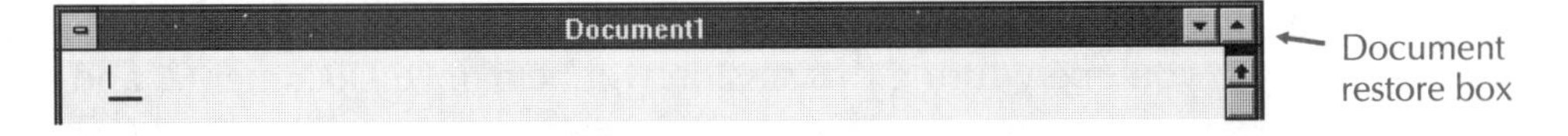

Note that the document's restore box is different from the program's restore box.

If you work on more than one document at a time, it is more convenient if the document windows are not maximized. However, when you work on just one document, it is better to have the document window maximized so that you can see more at one time. To maximize the document window, click the restore box for the document window. The result is shown in Figure 1-2. Note that when a document is maximized, its name appears in Word's *title bar*.

As you can see, many of the features of the Word window are the same as in other Windows programs, but some are unique to Word. Those features seen only in Word are described throughout this book.

One mark on the window that may interest you now is the horizontal line near the top of the document window. This is called the *end-of-file marker* because it shows you where the end of your document is. All text in your document appears above this mark.

The *toolbars* near the top of the window make accessing commands quick and easy:

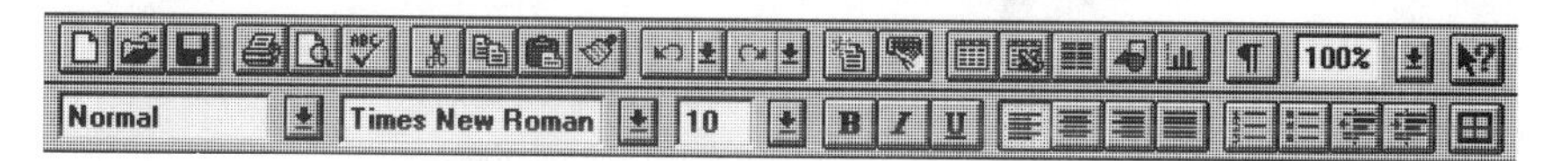

These toolbars have buttons that perform tasks such as opening files and printing. You can click these buttons instead of giving commands. The top toolbar is called the *Standard toolbar*; the lower one is called the *Formatting toolbar*. There are other toolbars that appear when you give certain Word commands. They are described throughout the book.

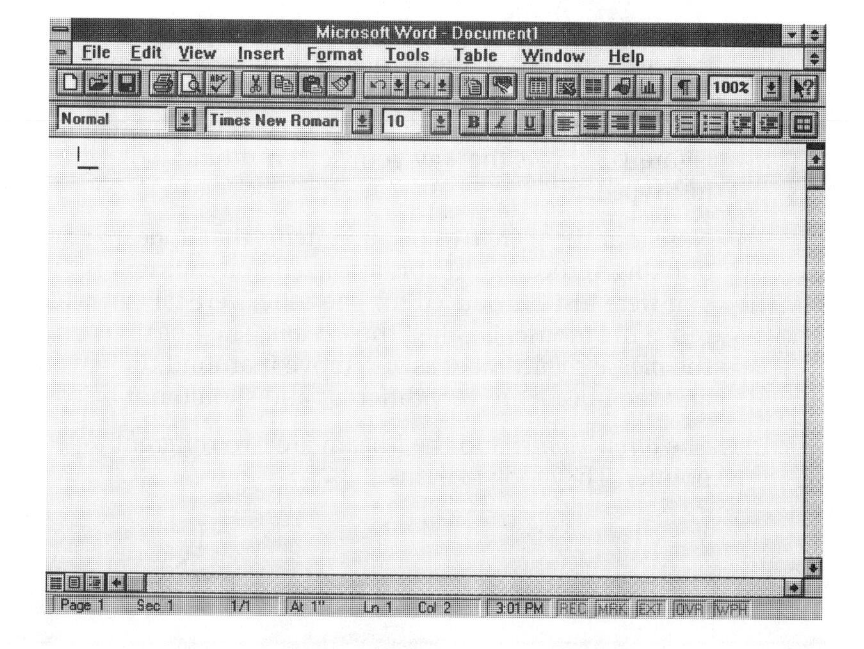

Word window with document window maximized
Figure 1-2.

You can even change the toolbars if you want to add different buttons yourself. This is covered in Chapter 24.

Lesson 4: Entering Text

As soon as Word is started, it is ready for you to start entering text. Near the upper-left corner of the document window, the blinking vertical bar is where the first letters you type will appear. This bar is called the *insertion point,* just as in other Windows programs. It indicates where you are in the text.

When you type text, you can correct typing mistakes by pressing the Backspace key, located in the upper-right corner of the main part of the keyboard, to erase the character to the left of the insertion point.

You can type just as you would on a typewriter. To start experimenting, type **This is just like a typewriter**. If you make a mistake as you type, you can press Backspace to erase the letter (or letters) you just typed. (In Chapter 2, you will learn other ways to delete text.)

Lesson 5: Selecting and Inserting Text

To tell Word to do something to some text in your document, you first specify the text you want to work on and then indicate the action. To specify the text on which you will work, you *select* it with the mouse or keyboard. If you want to insert text, you set the insertion point to the position where you want the new text.

While selecting and inserting text may sound easy, they are often confusing to beginning Word users, especially those who have not dealt much with computers. Even though selecting is basic to all Windows use, it requires you to use a few things at once and thus can be a bit daunting to beginners. Figure 1-3 shows the way your screen should look with the sentence that you just typed.

Note that there are two nontext items that appear as vertical bars. The blinking vertical bar that is at the end of your text is the insertion point that you were just introduced to. The other vertical bar, which moves when you move the mouse, is called the *I-beam*. The I-beam is one of a few shapes that the *mouse pointer* takes as you move it around the screen. The insertion point and the I-beam are very different and should not be confused.

The *arrow pointer* and the I-beam are two different aspects of the mouse pointer. They look like this:

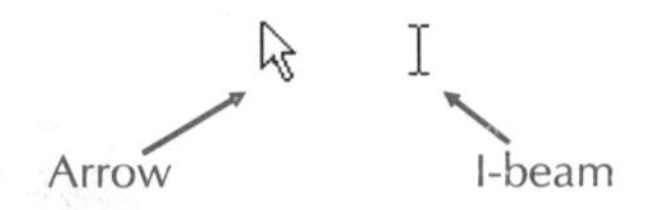

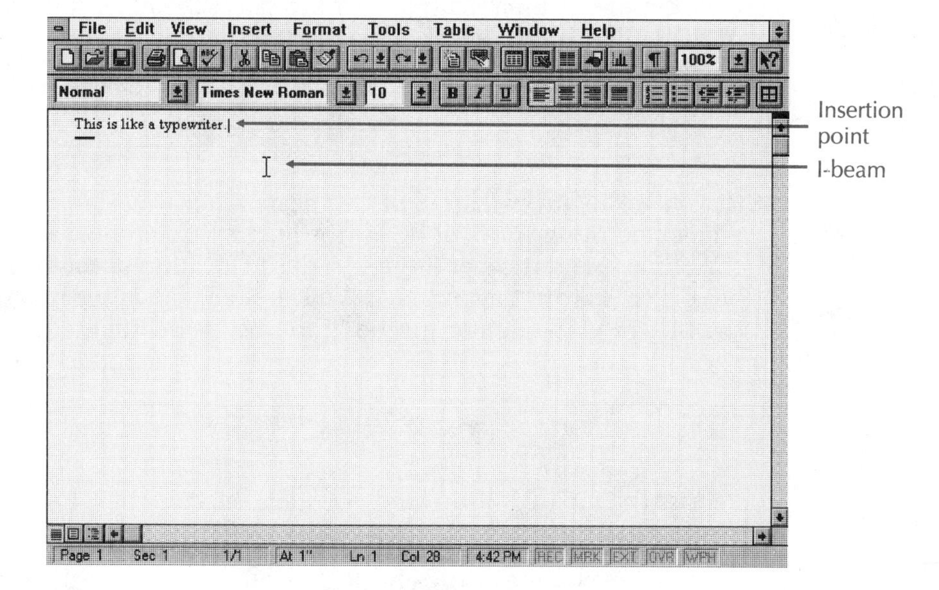

Screen after sentence is typed
Figure 1-3.

These are used to point at menus and parts of your document. The mouse pointer's shape is totally dependent on where you move the mouse. As you move from a command or window control area to the text area, the pointer changes from the arrow to the I-beam. The insertion point, however, is a specific location in your document that remains the same even when you move the mouse pointer. You can see this by moving the I-beam around and noting that the blinking insertion point remains stationary.

When you begin to type, the mouse pointer becomes invisible. This makes it easier to type because it prevents the mouse pointer from obscuring the text you are typing. The mouse pointer becomes visible again as soon as you move the mouse.

This chapter shows you the basics of selecting and inserting text. You will see more ways to select and insert text in the next chapter.

Selecting Text with the Mouse

To select text with the mouse, you click the I-beam at the beginning of the group of characters you want to select, hold down the left button on the mouse, move the I-beam to the end of the group of characters, and release the mouse button. This is known as *dragging* the mouse across the text. As you select text, it becomes *highlighted,* meaning that it appears as white letters on a black or colored background.

For example, assume that you want to select the letter "j" in the word "just" in the sentence you typed. Move the I-beam to just before the "j", as shown here:

This is just like a typewriter.

(If you see an arrow instead of an I-beam when you start to make a selection, you are pointing above or below the letters.) Hold down the mouse button; the blinking insertion point jumps to the location of the I-beam, but don't be concerned with that for now. While holding down the mouse button, drag the I-beam to the right until the "j" in "just" is highlighted, as shown here:

This is just like a typewriter.

Release the mouse button, and you have selected the letter.

You have now created a selection. Whenever you give Word commands that have an effect on text in your file, the effect is only on the selected text. You can select from one character to the whole document at any time. The text that is highlighted is the text that is currently selected (in this case, the letter "j").

You have just seen how to select a single letter by dragging the mouse. You can also select more than one letter by using the same technique. For example, to select the word "like" in the sentence, move the I-beam to just before the "l", hold down the mouse button, drag the I-beam to the right until the "e" is highlighted, and release the mouse button. You have now selected the entire word.

You can use the mouse to quickly select specific amounts of text. A common task is to select a whole word. Instead of having to drag over the word as you just did, you can double-click the word you want. To see this, move the I-beam to anywhere on the word "just" and double-click. The result is shown here:

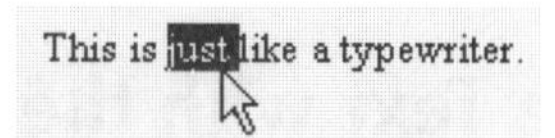

Note that Word also selects the space after the word.

You can also select a whole sentence quickly. If you hold down the Ctrl key at the same time that you click once anywhere on the sentence, Word selects the entire sentence, including the space after the period.

As you use Word more, you will find that most of your selections are more than one or two characters. Because of this, Microsoft designed Word to select whole words easily. If you select a space character before a word and continue to drag, Word selects whole words at a time. This prevents you from having to double-click to begin selecting words.

Inserting Text with the Mouse

You may be wondering, "If the insertion point disappears when I select text, why have an insertion point at all?" The insertion point tells you where the next letter that you type will appear—in other words, "where you are." As you can imagine, that can be pretty important. It allows you to quickly change the place where you insert text.

When you click the I-beam in the text area, Word puts the insertion point at the place where you click. If anything is selected when you click the I-beam, it becomes deselected when the insertion point is placed. You can now see that you will never have both a selection and an insertion point on the screen at the same time.

To see this, first select the word "just" by double-clicking it. Next, put the I-beam between the letter "r" and the period at the end of the sentence. When you click the mouse button, "just" becomes deselected and the insertion point appears between the "r" and the period:

This is just like a typewriter.

If you begin typing when the insertion point is between two characters, the text you type appears at that position. For example, type **but is much easier** and notice how these words appear between the "r" and the period. Every time you type a letter, the insertion point moves to the right:

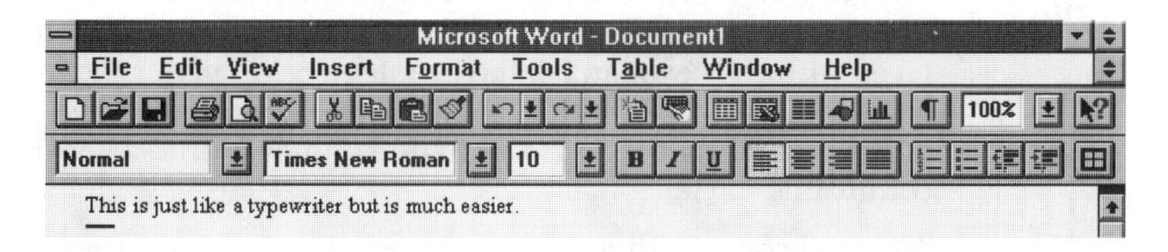

It may take some practice to get used to pointing with the mouse. A common mistake is to click the mouse button so hard that you move the mouse, with the result that the pointer is no longer exactly where you want it on the screen. If you press the mouse hard and move it as you are pressing, you make a selection instead of placing the insertion point. When you point at information on the screen, Word uses either the tip of the arrow or the middle of the I-beam (not the whole pointer) to indicate what you are pointing at.

Selecting and Inserting Text with the Keyboard

So far, you have only seen how to use the mouse to create selections or place the insertion point. Some people prefer to use the keyboard. Word lets you perform these tasks with the keyboard as easily as with the mouse.

To move the insertion point, use the arrow keys. These arrow keys, marked ←, →, ↑, and ↓, almost always appear below the right Shift key or between the main part of the keyboard and the numeric keys on the far right. Experiment with these keys to see how the insertion point moves in the sentence you have typed.

Making selections with the keyboard is just as easy as using the mouse. You move the insertion point to the beginning of the desired selection, hold down the Shift key, and use the arrow keys to move to the end of the desired selection. The selection (as indicated by the highlighting) moves as you press the arrow keys. Release the Shift key when you have finished making the selection.

For example, to select the word "typewriter" in the sentence you typed, use the ← or → key to move the insertion point to the left of the first "t". Hold down the Shift key and press the → key until the entire word is selected. If you go too far, keep the Shift key held down and press the ← key. You will learn more efficient ways of selecting in Chapter 2.

Lesson 6: Using Word Commands

Just as there are two ways to give commands in Windows, there are two ways to give Word commands: with the mouse and with the keyboard. Almost every command can be given with the mouse, and most can also be given with the keyboard. Some people strongly prefer the mouse over the keyboard; others prefer the keyboard over the mouse. Most Word users, however, find that they use a mixture of mouse and keyboard to give commands.

All Word commands appear in the *menus,* which are grouped in the *menu bar* at the top of the Word program window. The menus contain groups of similar commands. The menu bar looks like this:

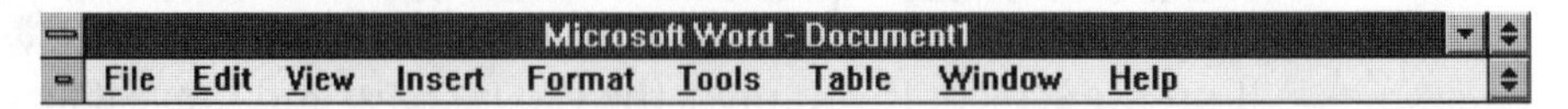

In this book, every command is identified by the command name and the menu name so that you can find it easily. For example, the Ruler command appears in the View menu; in this book, you would be told to "give the Ruler command from the View menu." Note that the first menu on the left, marked with a long horizontal line, is called the Word *program Control menu.* This is not to be confused with the menu marked with the short horizontal line in the document window, called the *document Control menu.*

To give a command with the mouse, you point at the desired menu, click and hold the mouse button, and then drag down to the desired command while still holding down the mouse button. When you release the button, the command executes. For example, give the Ruler command from the View menu. This command turns the ruler on and off. The *ruler* is a tool that helps you format your document, and is described in detail in Chapter 8. When the ruler is showing, there is a check mark next to the command name.

Many Word commands also have *keyboard equivalents*—keystrokes you can press instead of having to use the mouse. The keyboard equivalents are various combinations of the Ctrl key, Alt key, and Shift key with regular keyboard keys.

Keyboard equivalents of commands are sometimes listed on the menu, to the right of the name of the command. If a command does not have a keyboard equivalent listed in the menu, you can still access it by pressing the Alt key, then the letter that is underlined in the menu name, and then the letter that is underlined in the command name.

For example, here is the top of the File menu:

File	
New...	Ctrl+N
Open...	Ctrl+O
Close	
Save	Ctrl+S
Save As...	
Save All	
Find File...	
Summary Info...	
Templates...	
Page Setup...	
Print Preview	
Print...	Ctrl+P

To close a menu you have opened, press the Esc key.

The keyboard equivalent for the Open command from the File menu is Ctrl-O, the keyboard equivalent for the Save command is Ctrl-S, and so on. Another way to give the Open command is to press Alt-F-O (since "F" is underlined in the File menu name and "O" is underlined in the Open command). To press Alt-F-O, hold down the Alt key, press F, release both keys, and press O.

To see how to use keyboard equivalents, press Alt-V-R, the key combination for the Ruler command. (Press Alt-V-R using the same technique that you used with Alt-F-O.) This turns the ruler on and off just like the Ruler command did. Try these sequences to see the ruler turn on and off.

You can change the keys associated with any command, as you will see in Chapter 24. The keyboard equivalents discussed in this book are the ones that come assigned to the commands when you run Word for the first time. You can also add and remove commands from the menus. If you are using a copy of Word that someone else has used, the key equivalents and the commands you see in the menus may be somewhat different from what you see in this book.

Many Word commands act on a part of a document you specify. For example, you may want to make a word in your text bold. When you want a command to act on some specific text, you always select the text first and then give the command. This is true of all Windows programs: specify what you want to work on first and then give the command.

As you become more familiar with Word, you will find that you use particular commands over and over in certain situations. Word can predict what you are most likely to do at a given time, so it makes those commands easily accessible. If you prefer using the mouse, these commands are at your fingertips. Without moving the mouse from its present location, click the right button (not the left button as you normally use). Word pops up a miniature menu under the mouse pointer. To choose one of these commands, drag through the menu as you would in the regular menus at the top of the screen.

Lesson 7: Making Paragraphs in Word

In your text, each set of lines that is grouped as a unit is called a *paragraph.* Unfortunately, this is easy to confuse with the definition of a paragraph that you learned in grammar school, which is a group of sentences developing an idea. In Word, a paragraph is really just a line or a group of lines that ends with a press of the Enter key. For instance, in a business letter, the line with the date, the lines that show the recipient's address, and the line with the salutation are all paragraphs, as is each group of sentences in the letter. When you see the word "paragraph" in this book and the Word reference manual, it refers to Word's definition.

Word identifies the end of a paragraph by a special mark that it puts in your text when you press the Enter key. For this reason, you do not use the Enter key at the end of each line inside a paragraph, only at the end of the paragraph. One of Word's features that makes typing much easier is automatic *wordwrap,* which eliminates the need to decide where to end each line. As you type a paragraph, Word automatically figures out what will fit on a line and where to start a new line. You press Enter only at the end of the paragraph.

For example, continue typing after the sentence you have already typed. Use the mouse or keyboard to move the insertion point to follow the period, and type a second sentence: **As I type in this second sentence, I notice that Word goes to the next line without my pressing the Enter key.** Now press Enter, and notice that the insertion point moves to the beginning of the next line after the text.

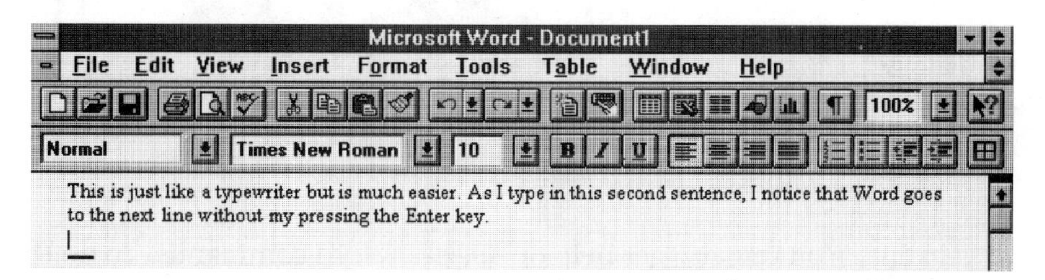

Lesson 8: Getting Help

The commands in the Help menu are a quick way to get information about a Word command or to figure out what is happening in the program. The Help program that comes with Word has a list of choices that you can use to get information about any command and all of its options.

To get help, give the Index command from the Help menu, the menu at the far right side of the menu bar. You see the dialog box shown in Figure 1-4 (your screen might look different, depending on its resolution and the size of your help window). Scroll through the list to select the topic you want help on. To quickly see the topics that start with a particular letter, click on that letter's button. When you find the topic in which you are interested, click on the topic name.

You can close the help windows like you do all other Word windows: press Ctrl-F4. Some Help windows also have Close buttons.

Some help topics have additional topics within them. You can keep clicking new topics until you have all the information you want. When you are finished, give the Exit command from the File menu in the Help window to continue with Word. You can also just click anywhere in the main Word window, and the Help window will move behind the Word window.

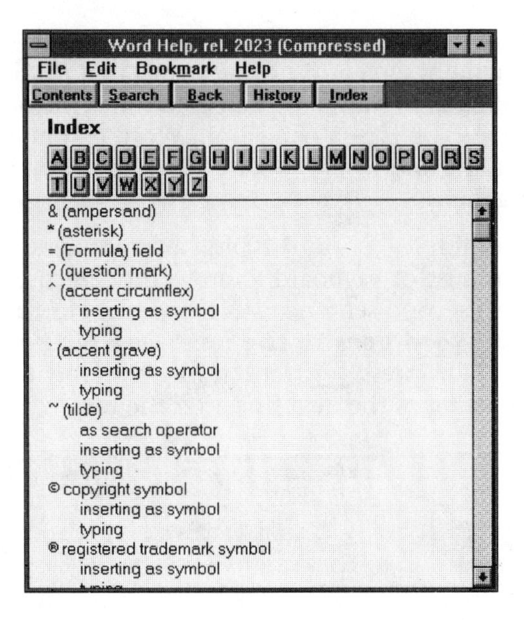

Index dialog box
Figure 1-4.

You can also get help on specific Word commands. To do this, press F1 at any time. For example, to find out the features of the Open dialog box, give the Open command from the File menu and press F1. Many commands also have a Help button in their dialog boxes that will take you to the appropriate help text.

The Help button on the Standard toolbar can make finding help faster. Click the Help button; the mouse pointer turns into the help pointer:

With the help pointer, choose the item that you want help on. For example, to find help on the Font command from the Format menu, click on the Help button, then use the help pointer to select the Font command from the Format menu as you normally would. When you use the help pointer, a Help window opens instead of the normal dialog box.

The toolbars have their own special kind of help. If you want to find out what a particular button on one of the toolbars is, simply move the mouse pointer over the button. After a moment, a label appears telling you what that button does. For example:

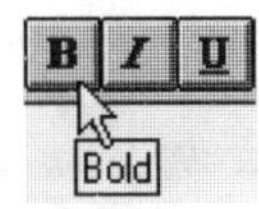

1

Lesson 9: More Help Options

The Help menu has many commands that make learning Word easy, even after you have been using it for a while. Microsoft recognizes that users learn at different speeds and have different backgrounds, so they provide many choices in getting help.

If you are just starting to use Word and don't have experience with other word processors, the Quick Preview command from the Help menu is a great place to start. This starts a guided tour of Word's basic features that you follow simply by clicking on buttons on the screen. If you have some experience with Word for Windows version 2 or with WordPerfect for DOS, this command is also useful. The first screen lets you decide which tour you want:

- Getting Started
- What's New
- Tips for WordPerfect Users

When you are finished, click the Return to Word button.

The Examples and Demos command in the Help menu holds another wealth of information. It contains a road map to dozens of other Word features, organized by subject. For instance, there are entries for Typing and Editing, Formatting Text, Working with Tables, and so on. Each entry has one or more screens with examples of the feature, and many of the screens have further screens that show step-by-step instructions. These are the same instructions you saw earlier by going through the Index command, but they also show the results of the command. For example, Figure 1-5 shows an example from the Overview of Formatting Text choice.

You probably already noticed the tip of the day when you started Word. You can get more tips just by choosing the Tip of the Day command from the Help menu. The dialog box looks like this:

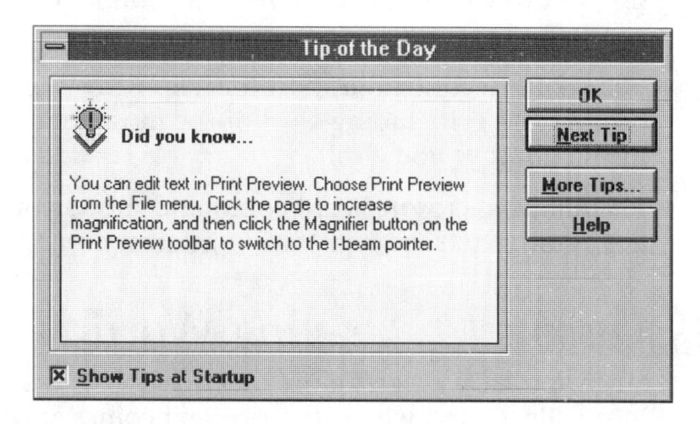

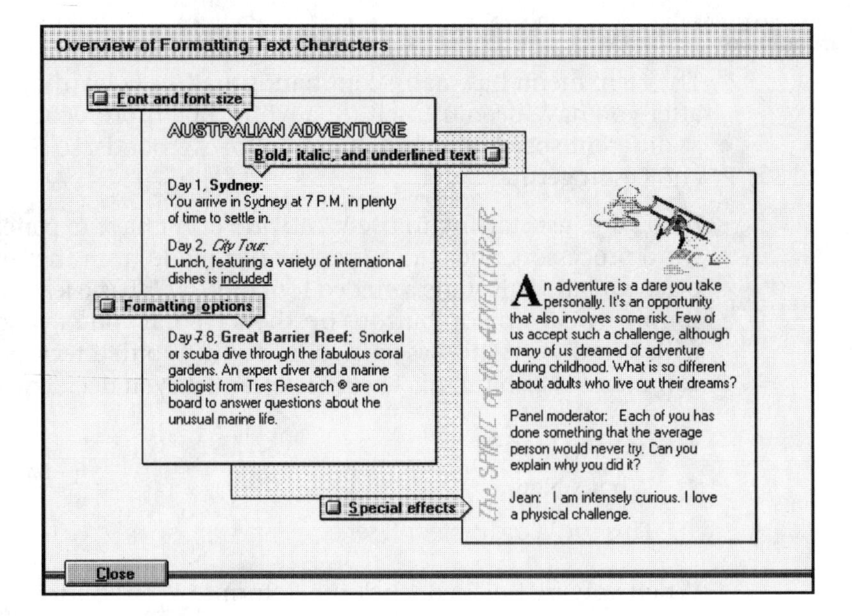

Sample of Examples and Demos command
Figure 1-5.

To see more tips, simply click on the Next Tip button. When you are finished, click the OK button. If you don't want to see this dialog box each time you start Word, click on the Show Tips at Startup choice to deselect it.

The WordPerfect Help command gives WordPerfect users all they need for moving to Word. Not only can you learn how to convert your old WordPerfect files; all the WordPerfect concepts and keyboard equivalents are fully explained.

Figure 1-6 shows the WordPerfect help dialog box. In the list at the left, choose the WordPerfect phrase or key for which you want to know the Word equivalent; the description appears on the right. For many of the actions, you can also click on the Demo button, and Word will show you the simplest way to give the equivalent command in Word.

The Technical Support command in the Help menu tells you how to contact Microsoft's technical support for help with Word. It also gives you a few tips before calling, including a list of the most commonly asked questions. These tips might save you a call.

The About Microsoft Word command shows you the version of Word you are running and the registration information.

Lesson 10: Leaving Word

Since you have entered only practice text, it is unlikely that you want to save it in a file. (Don't worry; the real text comes at the beginning of the next

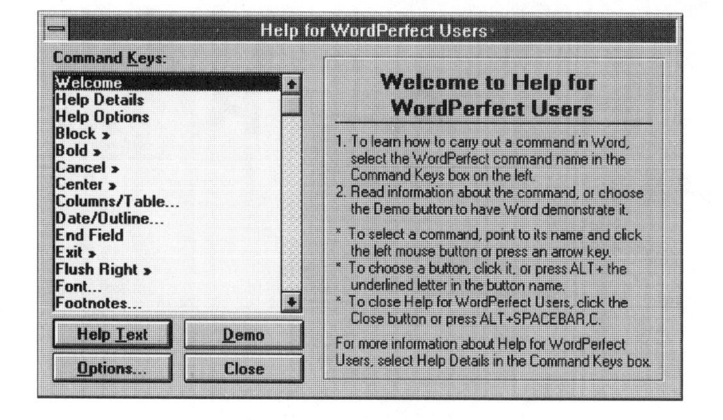

WordPerfect Help
Figure 1-6.

chapter.) When you leave Word, the program checks to see if you have saved your text in a file before it returns you to the Windows Program Manager. It is easy, however, to tell Word not to bother.

When you want to exit from Word and return to the Windows Program Manager, choose the Exit command from the File menu. If there is text that you have not saved on disk (you will learn how to save text in the next chapter), Word prompts you with the following dialog box:

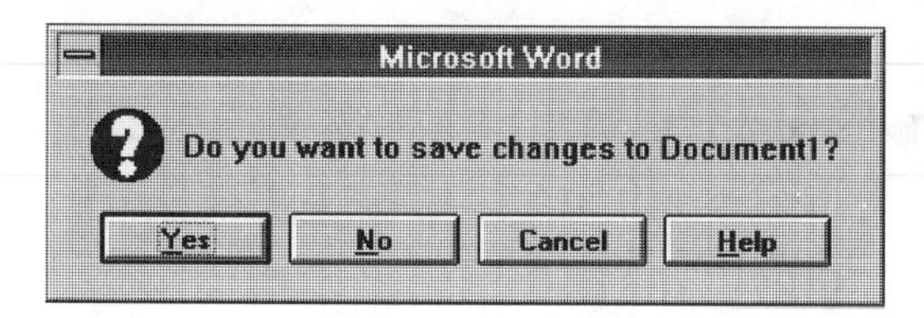

If you want to save your text, select the Yes button in the box. In this case, however, you can select the No button since the material is just for practice. If you realize that you want to do more editing or would like to save the file under a different name, select the Cancel button. You can also quit from Word with the Alt-F4 key.

Review

Start a new document and copy any two sentences from this book into the document. Select the first sentence by using the mouse. Then place the insertion point in the second sentence. Now select the first sentence by using the keyboard.

Type another sentence between the first and second sentences. Note how the text moves to the right as you do this.

C H A P T E R

2

BASIC EDITING WITH WORD

This and the next several chapters show you how to enter and edit a variety of documents, from short memos to long reports. The lessons in this chapter use the sample business letter that you type in the first lesson. You also see how to print the document at the end of the chapter.

Lesson 11: Typing Your First File

Now that you know how to start Word, how to enter text, and a bit about giving Word commands, you are ready to type your first exercise, the business letter shown in Figure 2-1. Type it using the rules you have learned so far; if you make mistakes, correct them with the Backspace key.

Note that this letter may be longer than one screen, depending on the size of your PC's monitor. If you reach the bottom of the screen as you are typing, just keep typing. Word scrolls the text up as you type.

Whenever you want to add text to the middle of text that you have already entered, simply move the I-beam to the desired location, click the mouse button to set the insertion point, and type. You can also move the insertion point with the arrow keys on the keyboard.

The next section explains how to save the letter you have just typed in a file on disk. This file will be used in many of the chapters in this book.

Lesson 12: Saving Your Text in a File

Now that you have text that you want to keep, you need to know how to tell Word to save it in a file. To do this, give the Save As command from the File menu. Word displays the dialog box shown in Figure 2-2. This is the same dialog box for saving that you see in almost every Windows program.

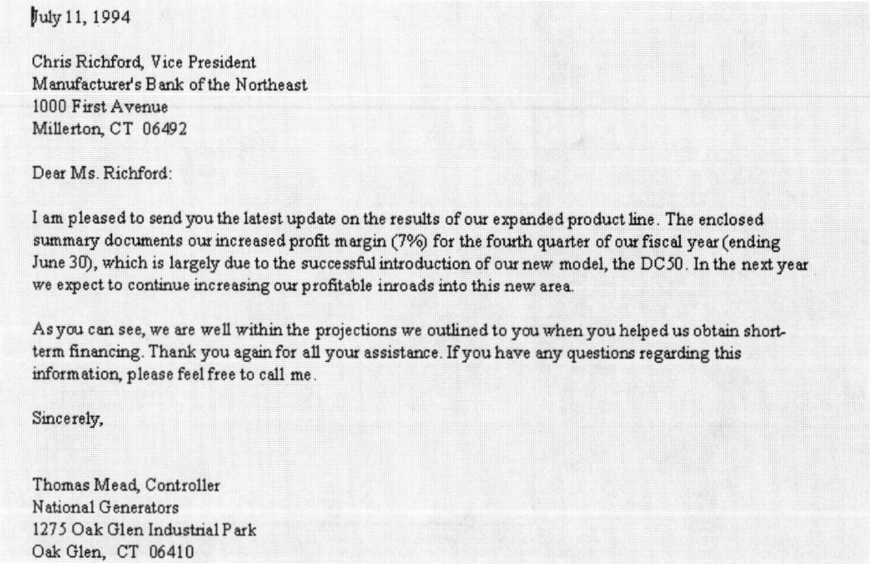

July 11, 1994

Chris Richford, Vice President
Manufacturer's Bank of the Northeast
1000 First Avenue
Millerton, CT 06492

Dear Ms. Richford:

I am pleased to send you the latest update on the results of our expanded product line. The enclosed summary documents our increased profit margin (7%) for the fourth quarter of our fiscal year (ending June 30), which is largely due to the successful introduction of our new model, the DC50. In the next year we expect to continue increasing our profitable inroads into this new area.

As you can see, we are well within the projections we outlined to you when you helped us obtain short-term financing. Thank you again for all your assistance. If you have any questions regarding this information, please feel free to call me.

Sincerely,

Thomas Mead, Controller
National Generators
1275 Oak Glen Industrial Park
Oak Glen, CT 06410

Text of SAMPLE1 file
Figure 2-1.

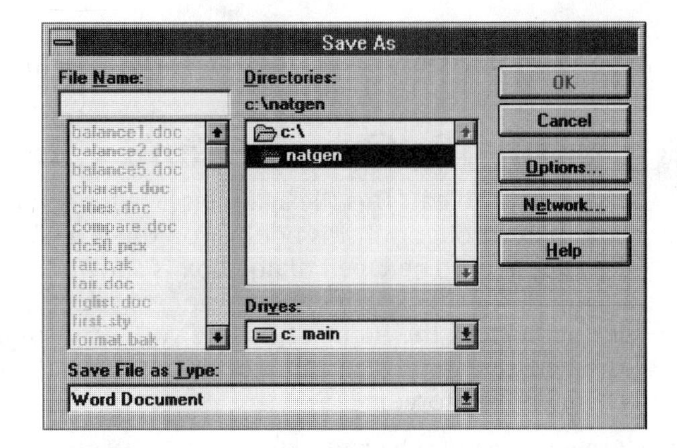

Save As dialog box
Figure 2-2.

You should first decide which directory you want to save your files in. In this book, a directory called "NATGEN" is used because the information all pertains to the business called "National Generators." You should have your own directories set up for the exercises in this book and for your own work. Use the File Manager program that comes with Windows to create directories for your files.

It is a good idea to save your file in a different directory than the one in which Word is saved. Although you may be tempted just to save all your Word files in the Word directory, this leads to difficulty later. It is best to create directories for your various projects and keep files for those projects in those directories.

Use the Drives and Directories options in the Save As dialog box to navigate to the directory in which you want to save the file. In the File Name option, type **SAMPLE1** and press Enter (or type **SAMPLE1** and click the OK button).

Word saves the file on disk. You can continue to edit the file if you wish, or you can leave Word with the Exit command from the File menu. If you are unfamiliar with dialog boxes, there is a lesson later in this chapter on that subject. For now, close the file by choosing the Close command from the File menu or pressing Ctrl-F4.

You have other choices in the Save As command that you will not use yet but that you should know about. The Options button brings up additional dialog boxes that let you change settings related to saving files; these are described in detail in Chapter 11. The Network button lets you connect to a network drive if your PC is on a network.

The list in the Save File as Type section of the Save As dialog box lets you select a type of file to save, for example, if you are creating a file to be read by another program. The types of files you can save are described in detail in Chapter 21; for now, you always want to save in Word format.

Lesson 13: Opening and Closing a File

If you want to edit this file again later (which you will, since it is used for examples throughout this book), you open it with the Open command from the File menu. The Open dialog box is shown in Figure 2-3. A list of files will appear. Either click the file you want (to select it) and select the OK button, or double-click the name of the file you want to open it. You may have to use the Drives and Directories options to find the directory in which the desired file is stored.

If you want to look at a file but not change it, select the Read Only choice in the lower-right corner of the dialog box. Although this isn't necessary, it is a useful way of preventing accidents. Also, if the file is on a network and you do not choose the Read Only option, no one else can open the file. Thus, everyone who is just reading the file should select Read Only.

Word can open many types of files, not just those that you created in Word. For instance, you can open files that were created with other word processors. Chapter 21 gives much more detail about the additional types of files you can open. If you are converting from other programs, Word performs most of those conversions automatically, but cannot always determine what program created a given file. If you want Word to tell you which conversion it is using, select the Confirm Conversions choice.

Word remembers the files that you have opened recently and adds their names to the bottom of the File menu. Instead of using the Open command and searching for the file, you can simply pick it from the bottom of the menu.

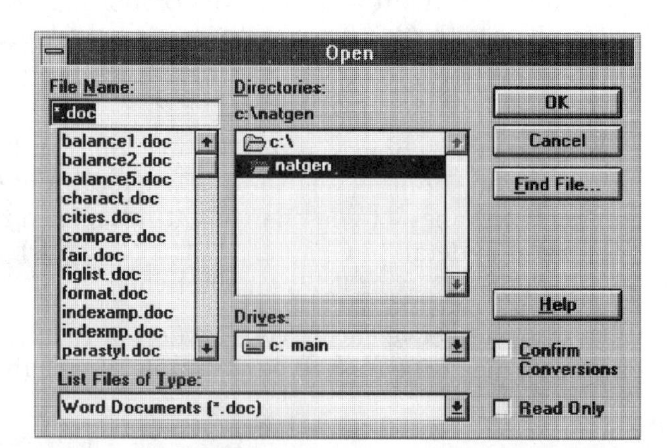

Dialog box for the Open command
Figure 2-3.

You can tell Word which directory you want it to start in when you give the Open command. This option is described in Chapter 11.

If you make editing changes in a file and you do not want to save those changes (for example, if you are experimenting with some Word commands and do not want to change the file on disk), use the Close command from the File menu; when the command prompt asks if you want to save your changes, select the No button.

Lesson 14: Starting New Files

When you start Word by double-clicking on its icon, it automatically starts with a new document. As you have already seen, that new document has no text in it.

You can start more new documents by choosing the New command from the File menu. The dialog box for the New command is shown in Figure 2-4. Simply make sure that the Normal template is chosen and that Document is selected, and click OK. This is what you will do for most of your work as you start to use Word. The New command has a few other interesting options, however, that may make your work easier.

As you can see, there are many templates other than Normal listed at the left side of the New dialog box. Templates are described in detail in Chapter 11, but for now you should know that a *template* is a special kind of document that lets you start with more than just a blank sheet of paper. The Normal template is, in fact, just like a blank piece of paper; other templates contain text that you can change after you have given the New command.

For example, choose the New command and choose the Faxcovr1 template from the list at the left side of the dialog box. Instead of being blank, the

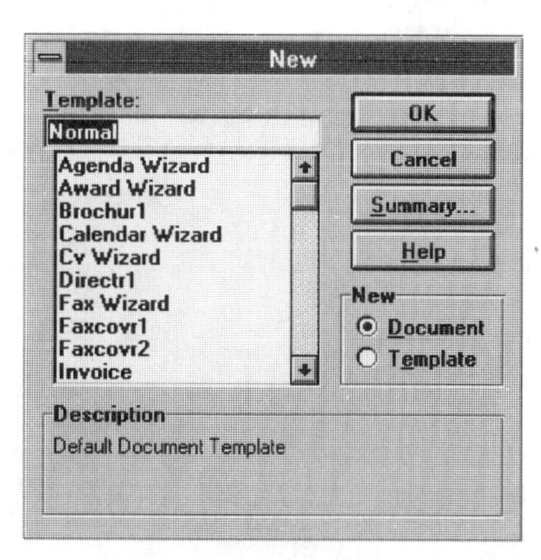

Dialog box for the New command
Figure 2-4.

new document looks similar to Figure 2-5. You can change any of the text in the new document, just as if you had opened a saved file.

Also note that some of the templates have the word "Wizard" in their names, such as Award Wizard. These are advanced Word files that are not really documents at all. Instead, when you start a new document that uses the Wizard feature, Word prompts you for information before the new document is started. For example, the Award Wizard asks you what kind of award you want to create (such as formal or jazzy), whether you want a border, whether you want the award to be horizontal or vertical, the name on the award, and so on.

When you finish answering the questions, Word creates the new document to your specifications. Of course, you can change any part of the new document, just as you can change any other Word document. In this way, a Wizard document is like a template, but you get a chance to specify how you want it to look before it is created so that you don't have to make as many changes afterwards.

As you can see, opening a template or a Wizard document is similar to opening an existing document, but with many advantages. You will see many more template features in Chapter 11. For now, assume that you always want to start new documents using the Normal template.

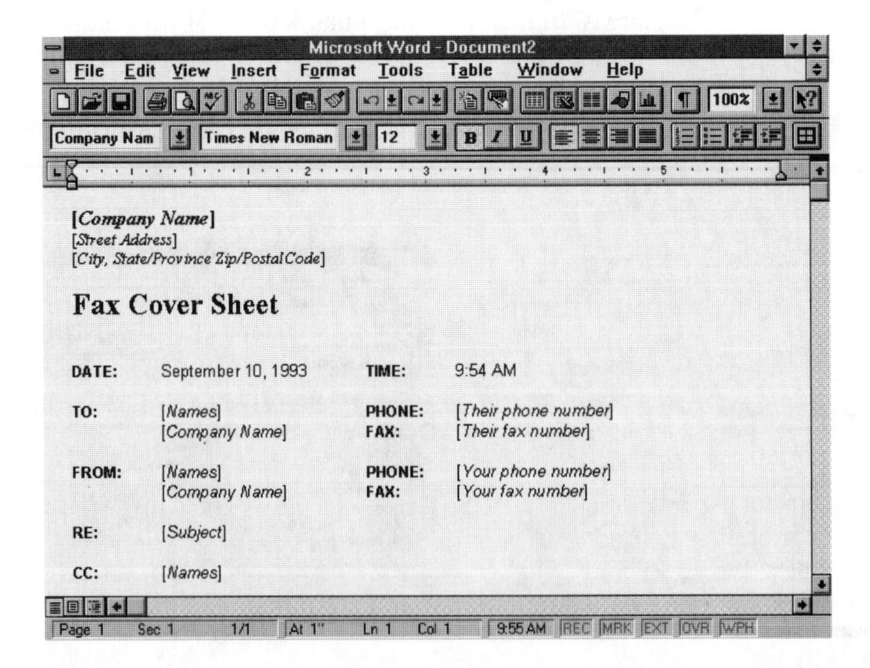

New document started with the Faxcovr1 template
Figure 2-5.

2

Lesson 15: Scrolling Around in Your Document

Word gives you many ways to move around in a file when you are editing. Since your file can be much longer than a single screenful of text, you need a way to find text that you want to change or add to. As you saw before, you always have either an insertion point or a selection in your text. However, that insertion point or selection may not be visible if you are looking at a different part of your text.

To start this lesson, move to the beginning of the SAMPLE1 file, as shown in Figure 2-6. If you have closed the file, open it with the Open command from the File menu. If you have quit Word, start Word and open the file.

If the insertion point is not already there, move to the beginning of the text by dragging the *scroll box* (on the right side of the screen) up to the top of the scroll bar. Click the I-beam before the first letter of the file to place the insertion point there. To move to the beginning of the document with the keyboard, simply press Ctrl-Home. (If pressing Ctrl-Home brings up the Go To dialog box instead of moving the insertion point to the beginning of the file, you have WordPerfect navigation turned on. Choose the WordPerfect Help command from the Help menu, choose the Options button, and deselect this choice.)

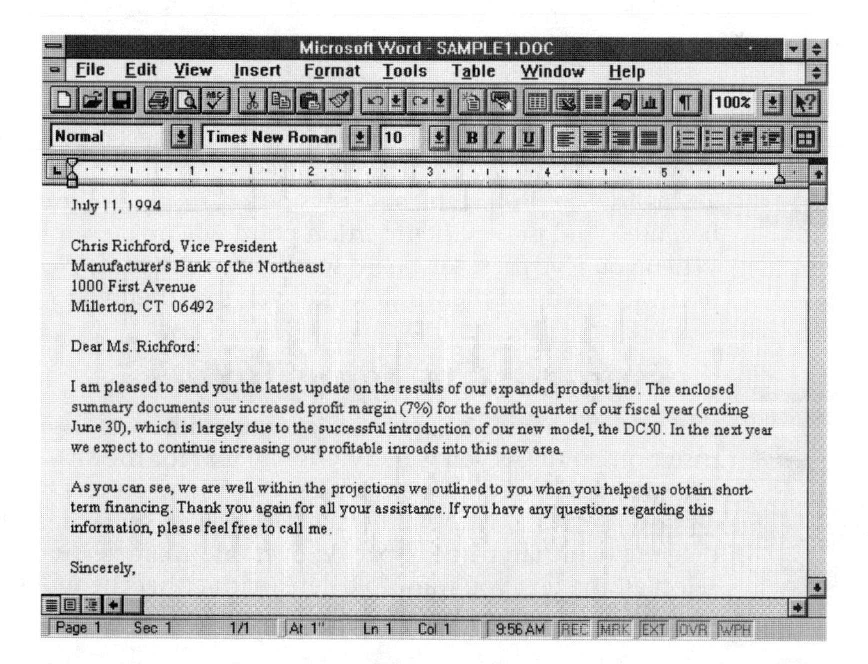

Top of SAMPLE1 document
Figure 2-6.

Scrolling with the Mouse

To see different parts of your text, use the scroll bar on the right border of the window (this is called the *vertical scroll bar*). For example, to scroll the screen down one line, click the arrow at the bottom right of the screen that is pointing down. If you point at this arrow and continue to hold down the button, the screen continues to scroll. The scroll bar on the bottom border of the window moves it left and right, which you rarely want to do.

To jump to a particular place in your text, you can drag the scroll box up and down the scroll bar and then release the mouse. This is sometimes called *thumbing,* since it is like thumbing through a book. To get to the end of a file, drag the box to the bottom of the bar; drag it to the top to get to the beginning of the file.

If you click above or below the scroll box in the scroll bar, Word jumps up or down by a full screen. In this case, that is not very useful, since the SAMPLE1 letter is short. In longer documents, it is very handy to click in the scroll bar if you are looking for particular information or skimming the information in a file.

When you scroll or jump by using the scroll box or the scroll bars, Word does not change the position of the insertion point or selection. You can see this by scrolling back to the top of the SAMPLE1 file. Notice that the insertion point is still blinking before the first letter. If you had made a selection and scrolled with the mouse, your selection would still be highlighted and in the same place.

Scrolling with the Keyboard

To scroll up or down a line at a time with the keyboard, press ↑ or ↓. To move up or down by a full screen, press the Pg Up or Pg Dn key on your keyboard. Scrolling with these keys differs from scrolling with the mouse because Word moves the insertion point when you scroll with the keyboard. When you give these keyboard scrolling commands, Word puts the insertion point at the top of the window that you see when you scroll.

Lesson 16: Changing Text

You saw in Chapter 1 how to select text and how to insert text at the insertion point. As you were typing the text for the SAMPLE1 file earlier in this chapter, if you made a mistake, you had to correct it by pressing the Backspace key, character by character. However, there are faster ways of deleting text than by backspacing over one character at a time. You can select all the text you want to delete (with either the mouse or keyboard) and choose the Clear command from the Edit menu or press Del.

Deleting text is a common practice, but replacing text with new text is even more common. For example, as you review what you have written, you often think of better words to use. To replace some text in a document with new words, simply select the text and begin typing. Word deletes the first text and starts inserting at that point.

To see this, assume that you want to replace the word "pleased" with the word "happy" in the first full sentence of the letter. Select "pleased" by double-clicking on it, and then type **happy**. Notice that when you type the "h", Word removes the selected text, replaces it with "h", and puts the insertion point at that spot. It is as if you had pressed Del and started typing.

You can also delete text with some other keyboard commands when there is no text selected and the insertion point is showing. To delete the character after the insertion point (instead of the one before it), press Del. You can also delete whole words at a time. Ctrl-Backspace deletes the word before the insertion point, while Ctrl-Del deletes the word after it.

Lesson 17: More Ways to Select Text

Most people prefer to use the mouse for moving the insertion point and selecting text. This is because using the mouse makes a very visual connection to the document; you do not have to remember which keys to use.

Selecting Text with the Mouse

You can choose from six different kinds of selections of fixed lengths: a character, a word, a sentence, a line, a paragraph, and the entire document. If you want to select a portion of text that is not included in the six choices (such as several words but not a sentence, several sentences but not a paragraph, or several paragraphs, but not an entire document), you can also make selections of varying lengths.

You already saw in the last chapter how to select a character, a word, and a sentence by dragging, double-clicking, and clicking with the Ctrl key, respectively. You also learned how to select varying amounts of text by clicking and dragging.

To review the steps, point at any letter in the word "update" in the first sentence. Double-click to select the entire word, press the Ctrl key, and hold down the mouse button to select the entire sentence. You can select a variable amount of text by clicking at the beginning of the desired selection and dragging to the end.

To select larger areas of text, move the mouse pointer into the *selection bar,* the blank column between the left window border and the text. When you point to the selection bar, the I-beam changes to an arrow that points up and to the right instead of to the left as it normally does. For example, point to the selection bar on the third line of the body of the letter, which begins with "June 30".

Clicking in the selection bar has a different effect than clicking in the text. Clicking once in the selection bar selects the entire line, double-clicking selects the entire paragraph, triple-clicking selects the whole document. Instead of triple-clicking, you can press the Ctrl key and then click in the selection bar to select the whole document. Experiment with each of these choices.

When selecting by dragging, if the text that you want to select is not completely on the screen, you can extend the selection by scrolling the screen. To do this, start your selection, hold down the mouse button, and briefly bring the pointer into the upper or lower screen border. Word then scrolls the screen, and you can continue to extend your selection. Sometimes Word scrolls more than you expect, so using this method takes a bit of practice. If you are still holding down the mouse button, you can back up to the proper spot and then release the button.

Selecting Text with the Keyboard

Word has many keyboard commands that allow you to move the insertion point and select parts of your document. The keyboard commands for selecting text are the same as the keyboard commands for moving the insertion point, except that the Shift key is held down. For example, the ↓ key moves the insertion point down a line, while Shift-↓ extends the selection down one line.

Table 2-1 shows the keys for moving the insertion point.

You may have noticed that many of these key combinations use keys that may be on the keypad, the area to the far right of your keyboard. Of course, you may want to use the keypad for its most obvious use, namely to type numbers. To do so, you must put Word in *numeric lock* mode by pressing the Num Lock key at the top of the keypad.

Lesson 18: The Undo Command

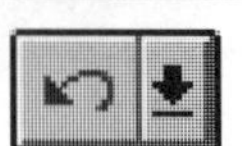

Now that you know how to select any text you want, you can experiment with selecting different amounts of text and deleting or replacing them. You might hesitate to experiment with important information, fearing that when you delete information, it is gone forever. With Word, however, you can give the Undo command from the Edit menu to undo the last change and restore the text that you deleted, replaced, or changed.

2

Movement	Key
Right one character	→
Left one character	←
Up one line	↑
Down one line	↓
To end of line	End
To beginning of line	Home
Up one screen	Pg Up
Down one screen	Pg Dn
Left one word	Ctrl-←
Right one word	Ctrl-→
Up one paragraph	Ctrl-↑
Down one paragraph	Ctrl-↓
To top of window	Ctrl-Pg Up
To bottom of window	Ctrl-Pg Dn
To beginning of document	Ctrl-Home
To end of document	Ctrl-End

Insertion Point Movement with the Keyboard
Table 2-1.

The Undo command restores your text to the way it was before your last edit. For example, if you select a paragraph of text and then delete it by choosing the Clear command from the Edit menu or pressing Del, you can use the Undo command from the Edit menu or use the Undo button from the Standard toolbar to bring the paragraph back, even if you have moved to a new selection.

As it is described here, the Undo command restores only the last editing command that you have given, such as Cut, or Copy, or pressing Backspace a few times (Cut and Copy are described in Chapter 4). You will see in Chapter 19 that you can also use the Undo command to undo earlier edits using an advanced feature called "multiple undo."

The Redo command can undo your last Undo command. This may seem strange, but it is useful if you are not sure that you want to restore an edit you have made. For example, if you delete a sentence but are not sure that you deleted the correct sentence, you can undo the deletion; and if it turns out that you did delete the correct sentence, give the Redo command from the Edit menu to cause Word to delete it again. The Redo command is only available after you have given the Undo command.

To experiment with the Undo command, delete the date from the letter:

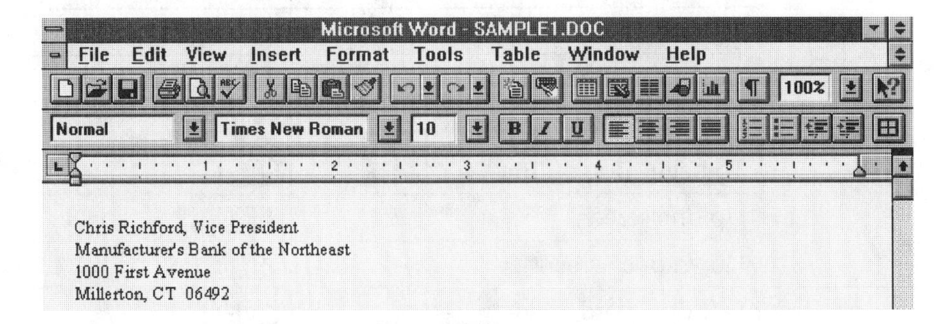

Now give the Undo command, and the date is restored:

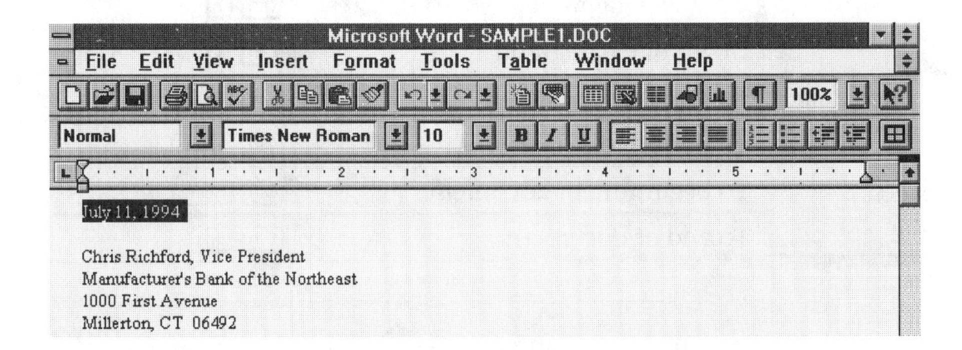

As you will see in later chapters, you can use the Undo command to reverse a number of different editing and formatting commands. You may well find it to be a safety net at a critical moment.

Lesson 19: Inserting Line Breaks Within Paragraphs

In Chapter 1, you saw how to type text into your document. You learned that to make paragraphs, you had to use the Enter key and that Word inserted a special paragraph mark into your document. There are other special characters in Word for other purposes, which are described in this lesson.

If you want to force Word to start a new line within a paragraph but not start a new paragraph, hold down the Shift key while you press the Enter key. This key combination is called a *newline,* and it lets you make lines of different lengths within a paragraph that are not like the lines of a paragraph made with wordwrap—you can start a new line without starting a new paragraph. You would use newline instead of starting a new paragraph because many Word formatting commands pertain to the whole paragraph. If you signal a paragraph with Enter, you have to format it separately from the preceding lines; if you use newline, you only need to format the whole paragraph once.

A good example of using newline is in typing the recipient's address in a letter. Later in this book you will learn how to see the difference between the end of a paragraph and a newline; for now, it is not important.

Look again at the SAMPLE1 letter. You used Enter characters at the end of each line in the addresses. Instead, it is better to use a newline (the Shift-Enter combination) in the two addresses since each address is really a single unit. You can change the Enter characters to newline characters by selecting each one and pressing Shift-Enter.

You can select Enter characters even though you can't see them by dragging over the blank character at the end of the paragraph. You will see the selection extend by an extra space, even though there isn't a space character at the end of the line. After you have made the changes, give the commands to select whole paragraphs; you will notice that the whole address is selected.

Lesson 20: Printing Your Document

Normally, the primary purpose of word processing is to obtain a finished printed document. At this point you have learned the basics of using Word to input and edit a document. Now that you have edited your text, it is likely that you want to see it on a printed page.

To print the file that you are editing, use the Print command from the File menu. When you give this command, you see a dialog box that is explained in detail in Chapter 10. To print a single copy of your document, you simply select the OK button. You will also see in Chapter 10 how to use the Options and Printer buttons, which help you set up printing parameters. Before printing, be sure that your printer is turned on and that it is properly connected to your PC.

Lesson 21: Making Choices in Dialog Boxes

The Word commands introduced so far have been quite simple. When you give some commands, however, you are offered a *dialog box* of items to choose from. Dialog boxes are common to all Windows programs. This lesson is a quick refresher on how to use the mouse and the keyboard to make dialog box choices. Note that Word's dialog boxes have some nonstandard features, so you may want to skim this lesson even if you are familiar with Windows.

The Find command from the Edit menu is a good example of a command that has a dialog box with many choices. When you give the Find command, Word presents you with the dialog box shown in Figure 2-7. Many of the dialog boxes that you see in Windows have only one or two buttons, such as OK or Cancel. Here you have many sets of buttons.

Making Dialog Box Choices with the Mouse

The Find Whole Words Only and Match Case buttons are on-off buttons that tell if you want a particular feature. If you click one of the square boxes (such as Match Case), an "X" appears in the box:

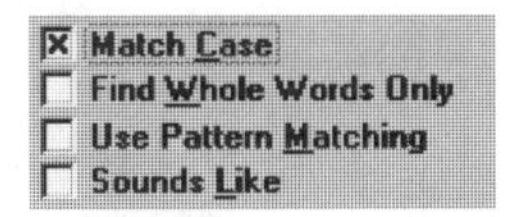

This indicates that the choice is selected. A list of square boxes, sometimes called *check boxes,* indicates that you can check more than one of the boxes at the same time. For example, the dialog box with both Find Whole Words Only and Match Case options selected looks like this:

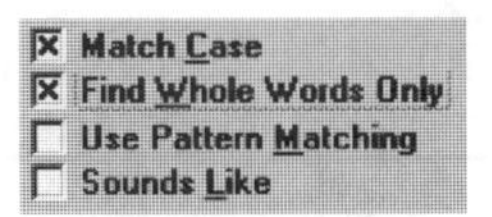

Some dialog boxes have *drop-down lists* that let you choose one item from a list. The Search choice in the Find dialog box is an example of this. You can

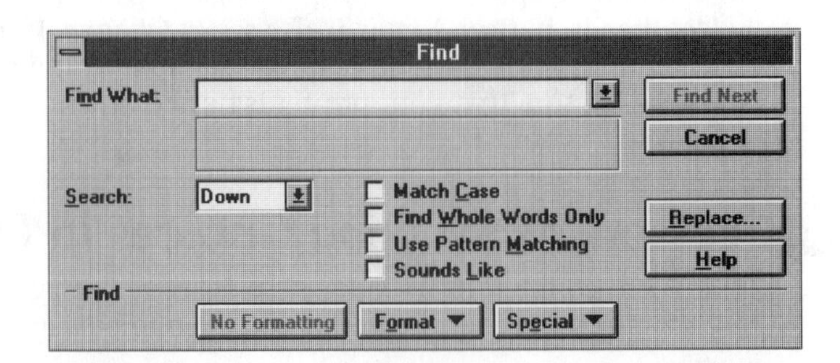

Find dialog box
Figure 2-7.

select from the list by clicking the name or the arrow and scrolling up or down the list while holding down the mouse button.

Some dialog boxes allow you to enter text or numbers; you have already seen this in the Save As dialog box. In the Find dialog box, you enter text by typing in the Find What box.

Many Word dialog boxes can be moved around on the screen while they are open. This lets you look at your document before you make your choices. You can click the title bar of any dialog box with a shaded title bar (like the Find dialog box shown earlier) and drag it to a new location.

Some Word dialog boxes have tabs at the top that make them look like file folders. Clicking on a tab brings up another panel of choices for that dialog box. For example, the Fonts command from the Format menu opens the dialog box shown in Figure 2-8. It has two tabs, Font and Character Spacing.

Making Dialog Box Choices with the Keyboard

Word lets you make dialog box choices with the keyboard. Only die-hard keyboard enthusiasts will want to do so because the method is somewhat convoluted.

To move to the next option in a dialog box, press Tab; to move to the previous option, press Shift-Tab. You can jump directly to an option by pressing Alt and the underlined letter in that option's name (this also works for dialog boxes with tabs). To select an option in a drop-down list, use the ↑ and ↓ keys, and then press Alt-↓ to close the list.

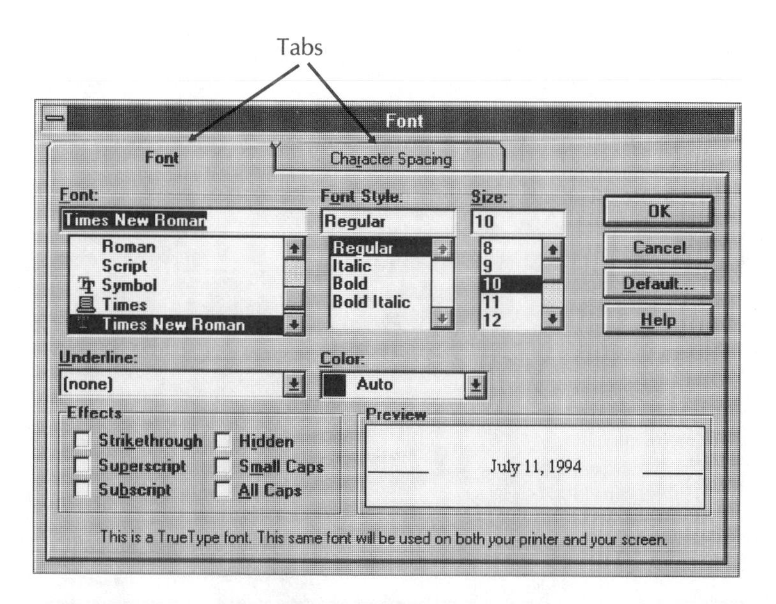

Font dialog box with tabs at the top
Figure 2-8.

Review

Start a new document and type a few paragraphs from a magazine article you have read recently. Make sure you type in more than one screenful of text, and don't worry about spelling. Save this text on disk as MAGAZINE. You will use this file in the review sections for many other chapters.

Practice moving the insertion point with the keyboard and practice scrolling with the mouse.

Change the first word in the second sentence to something else. Think about the many ways you can do this, and try them all. Each time you make a change, undo the change with the Undo command from the Edit menu, then redo the change with the Redo command.

Word For Windows
Word For Windows

CHAPTER

3

USING WORD'S WINDOWS

Using Word's windows effectively will probably save you more time than any of its editing features. Until now you have used only one window in Word. However, you can split the large window into two smaller ones with little effort. You can also have many separate windows in different files open at once. This may seem like a feature that only advanced users would want. However, it is possible to use windows in your everyday editing to meet a number of different needs.

For example, if you are editing the top of a letter and want to look at some information near the bottom, you do not need to take your attention away from either part if you split your window into two. If you are writing a memo and need to look at a report you wrote earlier, you can use one window for the memo and another window for the report.

Lesson 22: Splitting a Window in One File

To see how two windows can significantly help editing, start Word with the SAMPLE1 file in one window. In this lesson you learn how to split the window horizontally to get two views of the file. When you are looking at two parts of one file, it is common to make a split about halfway down the screen. Each half is called a *pane*.

One feature of the Word window you may notice that is different from windows in most other Windows programs is the black box near the top of the scroll bar, above the up scroll arrow on the right side of the window. This is called the *split box*:

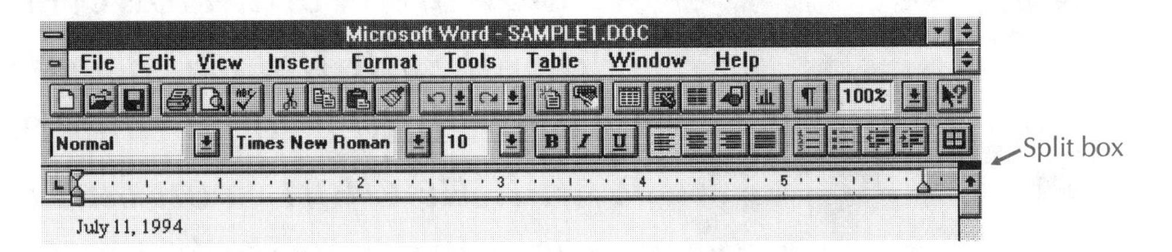

Splitting a window is straightforward. Point at the split box, and notice that the mouse pointer changes shape:

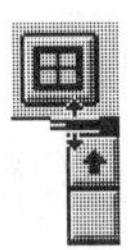

Hold down the mouse button and drag the split box down to where you want to divide the window; when you release the button, the window is split. If you have rulers showing before you split the panes, each pane will have its own ruler at the top.

When you press the mouse button, notice that Word draws a gray bar across the screen. It may be hard to see the bar at first. Look right below the title bar:

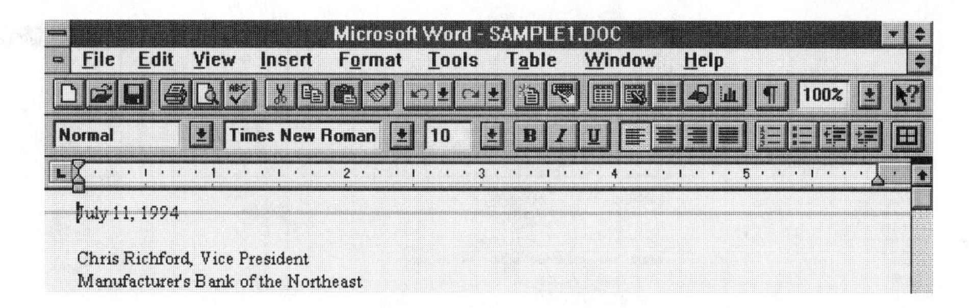

Now drag the split box down until the gray bar is below the line that begins "I am pleased...", as in Figure 3-1. When you release the button, Word creates the two halves of the window, each with its own separate vertical scroll bar on the right, as shown in Figure 3-2.

You can also split the window with the Split command from the Window menu. When you choose this command, Word shows the suggested split in the middle of the window. Use the mouse, or the ↑ or ↓ keys, to move the bar to the desired location, then press Enter.

To change the position of the split, drag the split box to a new location using the mouse. To go back to a single window, drag the split box all the

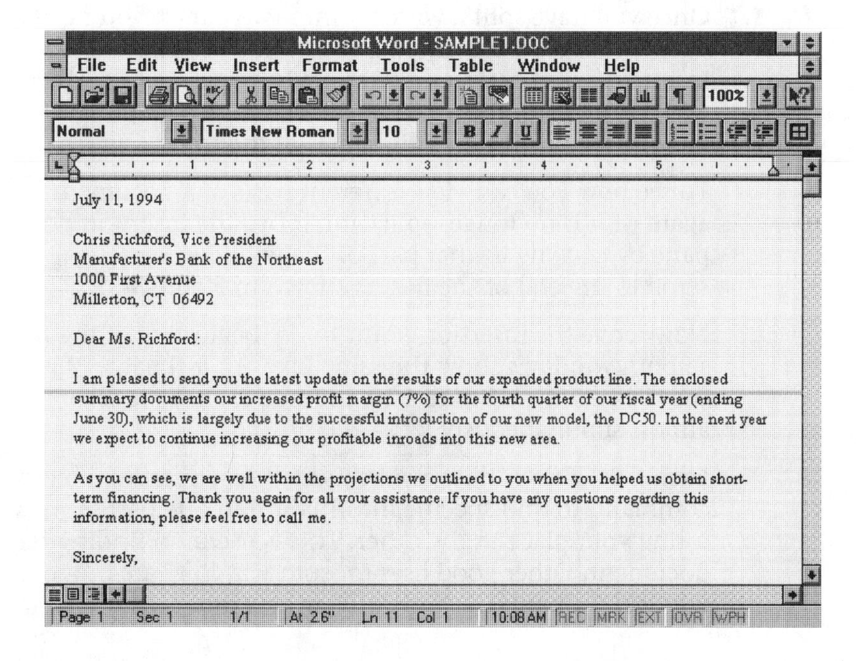

July 11, 1994

Chris Richford, Vice President
Manufacturer's Bank of the Northeast
1000 First Avenue
Millerton, CT 06492

Dear Ms. Richford:

I am pleased to send you the latest update on the results of our expanded product line. The enclosed summary documents our increased profit margin (7%) for the fourth quarter of our fiscal year (ending June 30), which is largely due to the successful introduction of our new model, the DC50. In the next year we expect to continue increasing our profitable inroads into this new area.

As you can see, we are well within the projections we outlined to you when you helped us obtain short-term financing. Thank you again for all your assistance. If you have any questions regarding this information, please feel free to call me.

Sincerely,

Gray bar positioned at desired point
Figure 3-1.

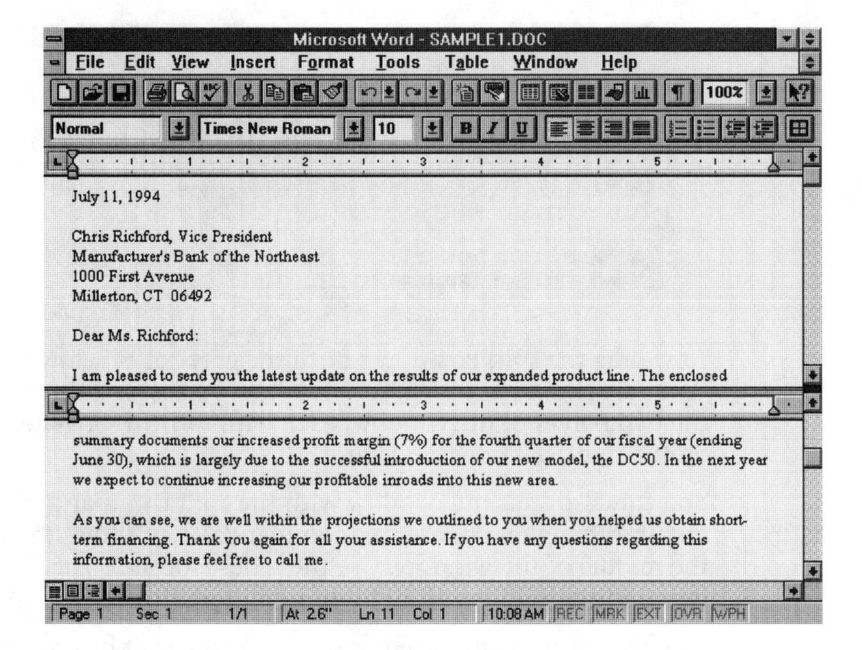

Window after splitting
Figure 3-2.

way to the top or bottom of the window, or double-click on the split box. You can also choose the Remove Split command from the Window menu.

Once you have split a window into two panes, you need only point to either part to move the insertion point from pane to pane. You can also move the insertion point between the panes by pressing F6. The text that you view in each part of a window can be scrolled independently. If you want, you can view the same text in both halves of the split window.

To see how you can view different parts of a document, split the window again (if it is no longer split) and move the insertion point to the bottom pane by clicking in that part of the window or pressing F6. You can now scroll to the end of the file, as shown in Figure 3-3.

Now move the insertion point to the beginning of the file in the lower half, so both windows show the same text. After the line "1000 First Avenue" in the top half, type **Suite 120** and notice that the second window is updated almost simultaneously.

Each half of a window can be used independently. You can use the Find command to find specific information in one part of the window without losing your place in the other. This is useful in finding related text in a long document. Other good uses for split windows are moving text (which you will see in Chapter 4) and comparing similar text.

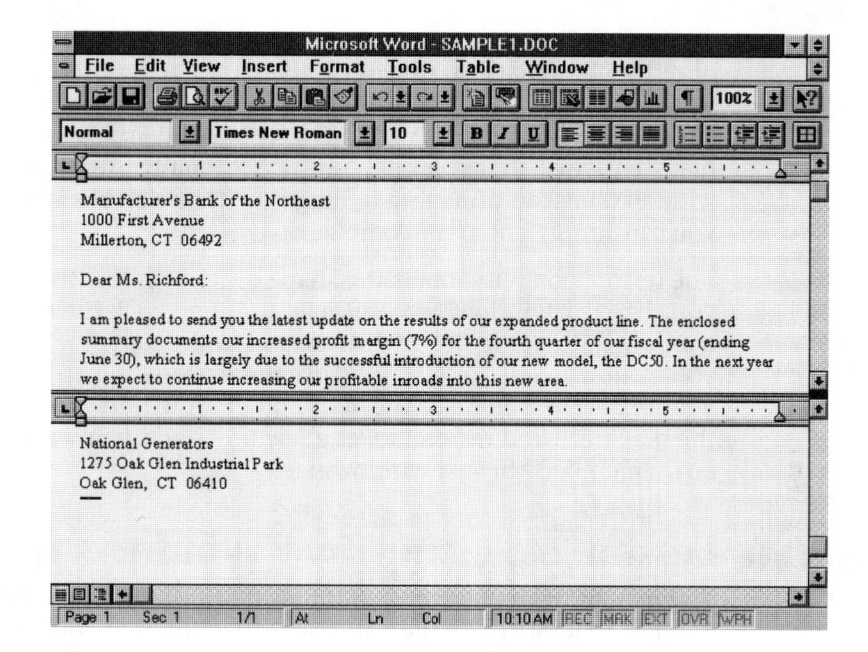

Top and bottom parts of file
Figure 3-3.

Lesson 23: Moving and Sizing Windows

You can change the location of a document window by dragging the title bar and change the size of a window by dragging its size box or one of the edges of the window. Like all Windows programs, you can also change the location and size of the Word program window in the same way. As you will see in the next lesson, it is convenient to change the locations and sizes of document windows when you have more than one document open in Word's program window.

To move a window, click its title bar—the shaded area at the top of the window—and drag the window while still holding down the mouse button. This is exactly like moving windows in all Windows programs. Note that you can move a window so that part of the window disappears off the side or bottom of the screen. You cannot move a window that is maximized.

The easiest way to change the size of a window is to click and drag the *size box,* the area at the lower-right corner of the window. This allows you to make the window narrow or short. You can also drag the horizontal or vertical border of any window. Again, this is like other Windows programs.

The keyboard commands to change the location and size of a window are in that window's Control menu. For all Windows programs, you use Alt-- (press the Alt key and the hyphen) to see the Control menu for a document window and Alt-Spacebar to see the Control menu for the program window.

You also can change the size of document windows by using the maximize or restore box that you saw in Chapter 1. Clicking this box causes the window to grow to the full size of Word's program window or, if it is already enlarged, to shrink to its previous size. Maximizing is handy if you have many windows that you open only occasionally. After you close these windows, instead of having to drag down the size box of your main window, you can simply click its maximize box.

The restore box remembers the shape of the window that you last used. If you change a window, maximize it, and then click the restore box, your window is the same size and shape and in the same location as it was before you maximized it. For example, use the size box to shrink the SAMPLE1 window to the middle of the Word program window, as in Figure 3-4. Click the maximize and restore boxes a few times and you'll see how the restore box remembers the last window size.

Lesson 24: Using Two Windows for Two Files

You may have already guessed the next step in using windows: using one window to look at one file and a second window to look at a different file. To look at two different files, use the Open command from the File menu to open a window for a second file. You can have many windows open at a time. On PCs with larger screens, you can work with four or more windows open at the same time. Word allows you to have over 20 documents open at one time, but it is unlikely that you would want to do so.

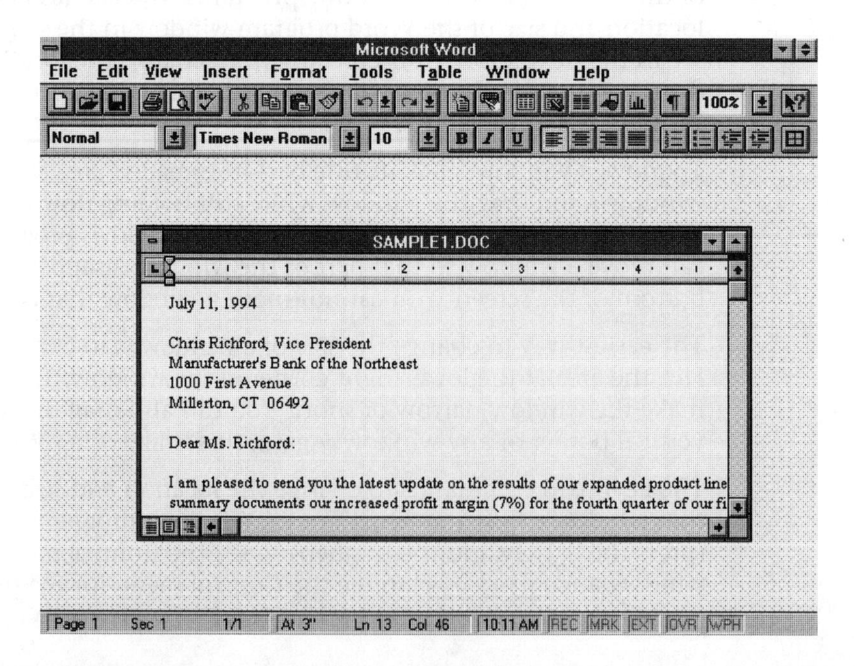

SAMPLE1 window shrunk
Figure 3-4.

To see how useful multiple windows are, close the SAMPLE1 window by giving the Close command from the File menu to clear your experimental modifications out of Word's memory (select No to the prompt of whether you want to save the changes). Give the New command from the File menu, and enter the short report shown in Figure 3-5. (Use the Tab key to line up the figures.) Save this on disk with the name REPORT1.

Use the Open command to open a window with the SAMPLE1 file. Word opens a document in the same location and at the same size as when you saved it, so the SAMPLE1 file hides the REPORT1 file.

Shrink both windows to about half the height of the screen by using their size boxes, and drag the SAMPLE1 window to the top of the screen and the REPORT1 window to the bottom. Your screen should look like the one in Figure 3-6.

You can now look at parts of each file independently. You can scroll each window so that you can see the relevant sections and compare the texts. In Chapter 4, you will see how you can quickly copy and move text from one window to another.

You may not want to have both windows fully showing since this reduces the amount of text you can see in each window. Instead, you may want both windows large, which forces you to switch from window to window. You can make a window come to the front and be completely visible by clicking

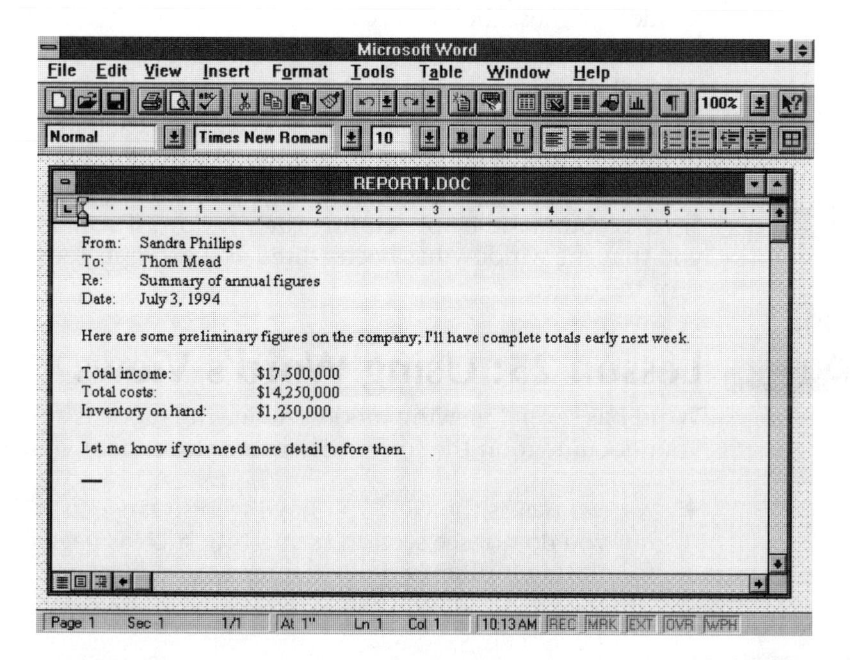

Text of REPORT1
Figure 3-5.

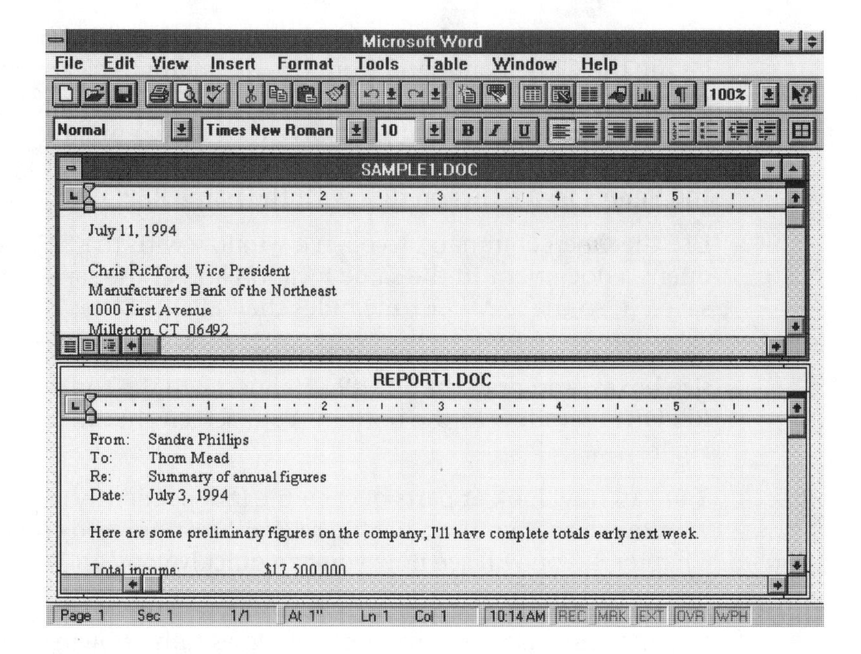

Both windows visible
Figure 3-6.

anywhere in that window. You can also bring the back window to the front by pressing Ctrl-F6 or by choosing the document name in the Window menu.

Use the size boxes of the SAMPLE1 and REPORT1 windows to make the windows almost the full size of the screen, and then move them so they are slightly offset, as in Figure 3-7. Experiment with switching back and forth between windows.

Of course, if you have more than two windows active, you can have that number of files open at the same time. If you have edited the text in a window and want to keep the changes, remember to save it with the Save or Save As command before closing the window. If you don't, Word reminds you that the window has been edited and prompts for whether you want to save the edits.

Lesson 25: Using Word's Views

Word has several viewing modes. A viewing mode is a way that you can see your document on the screen. There are three main views:

- *Normal view* is the view you have seen so far. This is the fastest to use, but you do not see section formatting such as page numbers (section formatting is described in Chapter 14).

✦ *Page layout view* is slightly slower to use than normal view, but you get the advantage of seeing section formatting.

✦ *Print preview* lets you see how your pages will look with all their formatting when printed, but at a reduced size.

(There is another view, outline view, described in Chapter 23.)

Page layout view and print preview let you see exactly how your document will look when it is printed. Even though what you see on the screen in normal view is generally what your document will look like when printed, it is not exact. For instance, you cannot see where the margins are positioned or how some special paragraphs will appear when you are looking at your document in normal view. If you specify the placement of a page number at the bottom of each page, you won't see the number on the screen in normal view; it will appear only on the printed page.

Using page layout view or print preview is faster than printing out your documents, and they don't waste paper. However, for your normal text entry and formatting, these views may be too slow, depending on your PC. You can use these views at any time, but most people only use them when they are doing document layout or previewing just before printing.

You select normal view and page layout view from the View menu; you select print preview from the File menu. You can also select normal view and page layout view from the left side of the horizontal scroll bar at the bottom of the window:

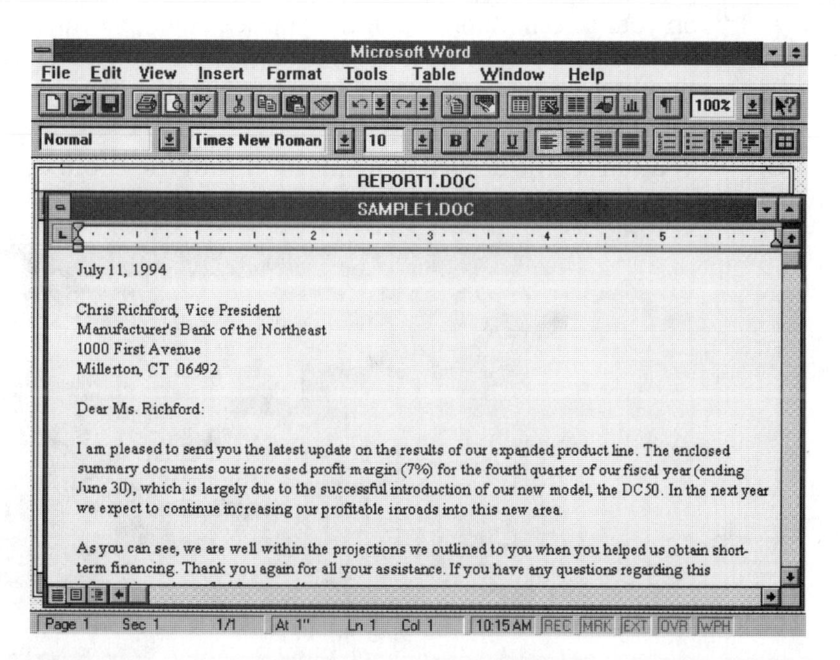

Two windows overlapping
Figure 3-7.

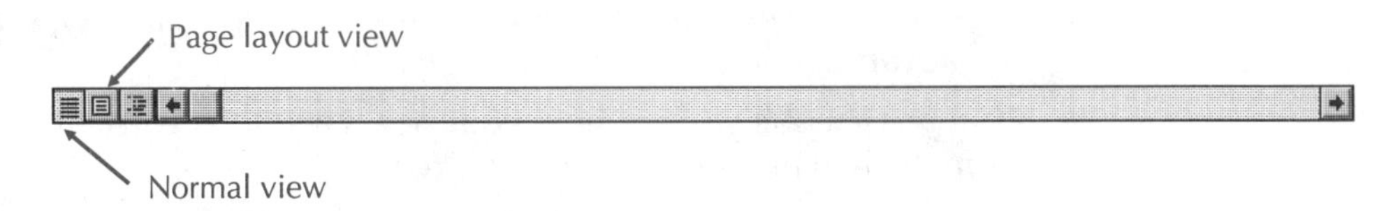

There is a button for print preview in the Standard toolbar:

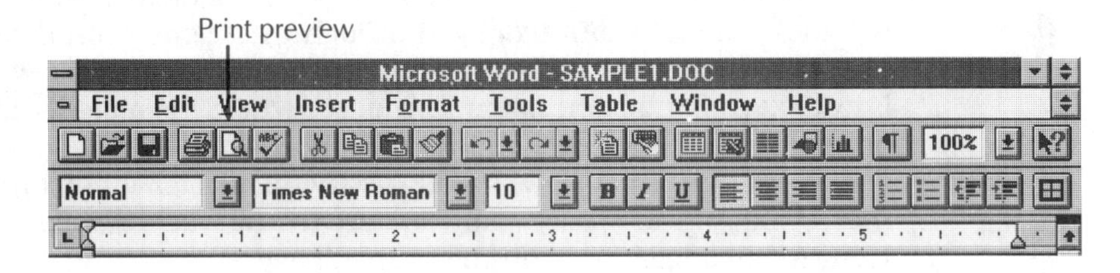

Lesson 26: Seeing More of Your Text

In any of the three views, you can see more of your document by going into full screen mode. *Full screen mode* removes all menus and toolbars from the screen, leaving you with just your document and a small button. To get out of full screen mode, click on the button. For instance, Figure 3-8 shows the SAMPLE1 document in normal view with full screen mode.

You can also zoom in or out of the text, making everything larger or smaller. Note that this does not change the size of the text when it is printed, only on your screen. Zooming in lets you see exact placement of items near each other. It can also be used by people with visual disabilities to read the text they are editing more easily. Zooming out gives you a quick overview of your text. Generally, you only zoom in.

You can set the desired magnification with the Zoom command in the View menu. The Zoom dialog box is shown here:

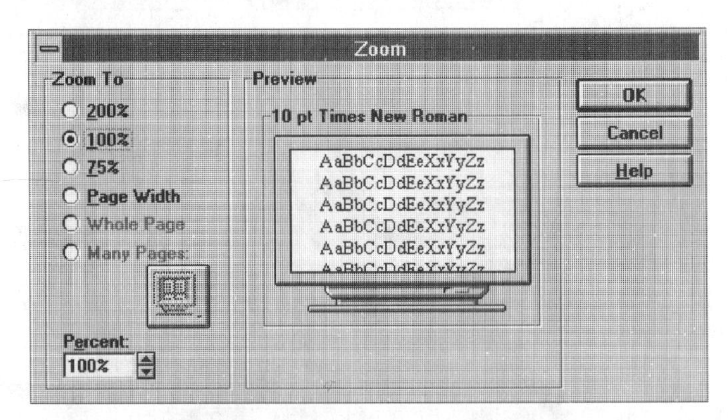

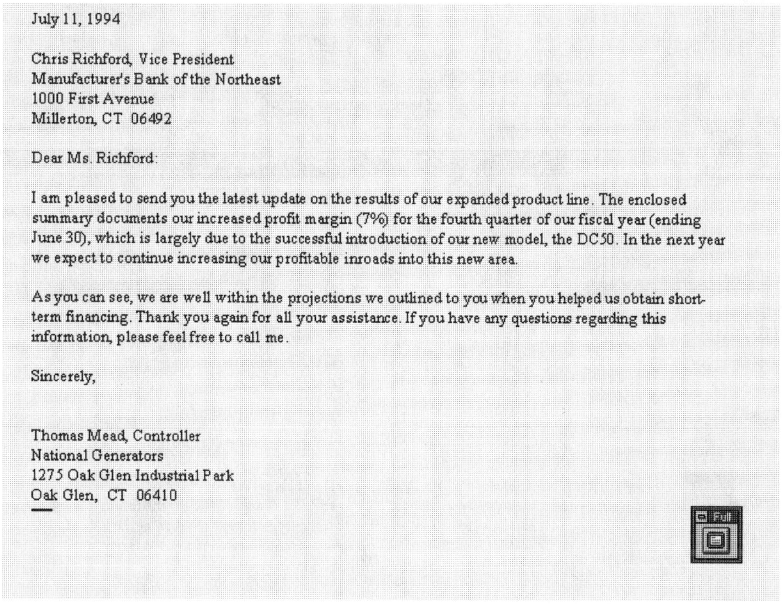

July 11, 1994

Chris Richford, Vice President
Manufacturer's Bank of the Northeast
1000 First Avenue
Millerton, CT 06492

Dear Ms. Richford:

I am pleased to send you the latest update on the results of our expanded product line. The enclosed summary documents our increased profit margin (7%) for the fourth quarter of our fiscal year (ending June 30), which is largely due to the successful introduction of our new model, the DC50. In the next year we expect to continue increasing our profitable inroads into this new area.

As you can see, we are well within the projections we outlined to you when you helped us obtain short-term financing. Thank you again for all your assistance. If you have any questions regarding this information, please feel free to call me.

Sincerely,

Thomas Mead, Controller
National Generators
1275 Oak Glen Industrial Park
Oak Glen, CT 06410

Full screen mode
Figure 3-8.

Choose a percentage from the Zoom To choices or specify an exact percent at the bottom of the dialog box. The preview area shows how your screen will change.

The Page Width choice specifies that the amount of zooming will make the page just fit on the screen from left to right. If you have a large screen or small pages, you can also choose Whole Page, which fits the entire page on your screen.

Lesson 27: Viewing in Page Layout View

If you want to see how a page will look as you edit it, page layout view is very useful, although it reduces Word's performance a bit (or a lot, depending on your computer and the complexity of your documents). This is because Word has to make many more calculations about placement of text and pictures as you edit or scroll. On fast PCs, this is not very noticeable, but page layout view is often difficult to use on slower PCs.

To switch from normal view to page layout view, give the Page Layout command from the View menu. This Page Layout window is similar to the normal view window. However, the few differences help you navigate easily around the pages in your document. Figure 3-9 shows the page layout view screen. If you have rulers showing when you go into page layout view, you will also get a vertical ruler along the left margin.

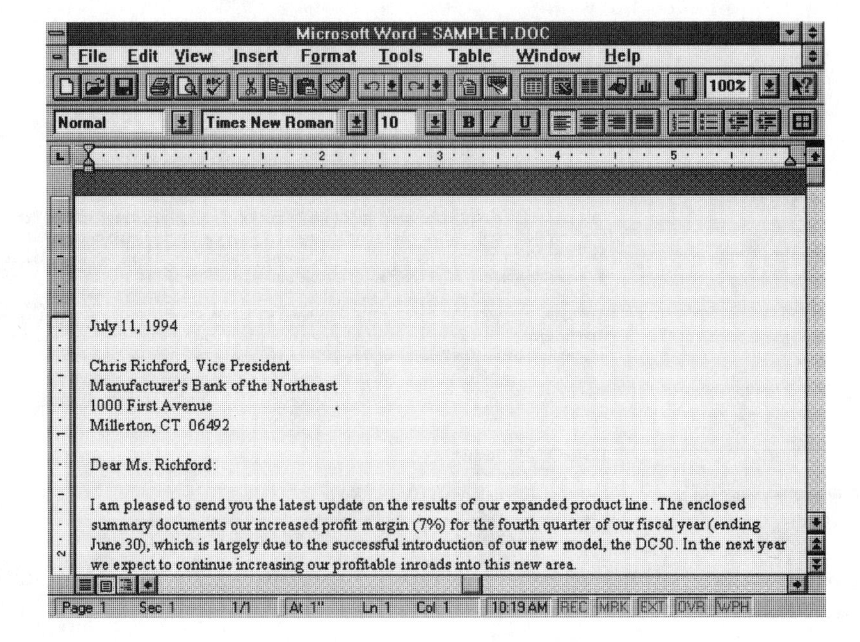

Page layout view
Figure 3-9.

In page layout view, you can edit your text as well as other parts of the page that you cannot see in normal view. For example, you can edit the headers and page numbers, which are described in Chapter 14. In addition, you can see where absolutely positioned paragraphs will appear when printed (these are special features for desktop publishing that are described in Chapter 20).

One major difference in page layout view is the addition of two double arrows on the right, near the bottom of the vertical scroll bar:

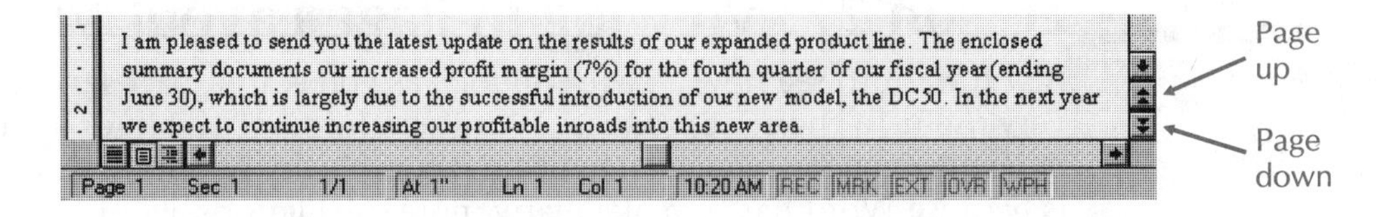

The double arrows let you quickly scroll up and down a full page.

If you have a large screen, you may find it useful to split the window into two panes, one in normal view and the other in page layout view. Splitting the window was covered earlier in this chapter. This can help you enter text quickly in the normal view pane but still see the exact results in the page layout view pane.

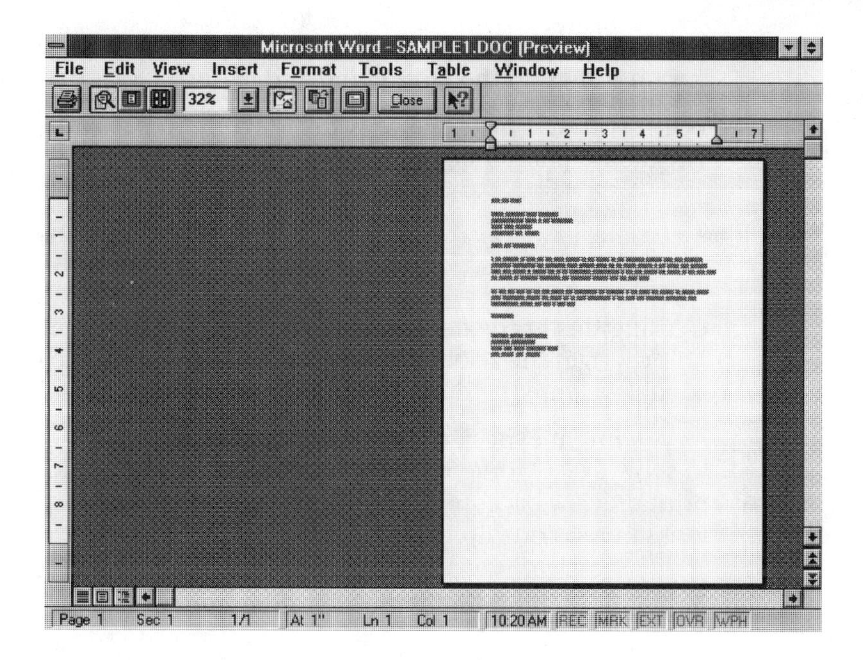

Print preview
Figure 3-10.

3

Lesson 28: Using Print Preview

Print preview gives you the most accurate view of your document, but it also takes more of your PC's power than the other views. If you have a fast PC, you may want to use print preview most of the time, using the other views only for entering text. On slower PCs, however, you will probably only use print preview when you have to see exactly how things will look on the printed page.

When you give the Print Preview command, Word changes the window, as shown in Figure 3-10. To close the Print Preview window, select the Close button to go to the previous view.

The toolbars change to the Print Preview toolbar. Because these tools are the ones that make the Print Preview command different from page layout view, a closer look at the Print Preview toolbar is worthwhile:

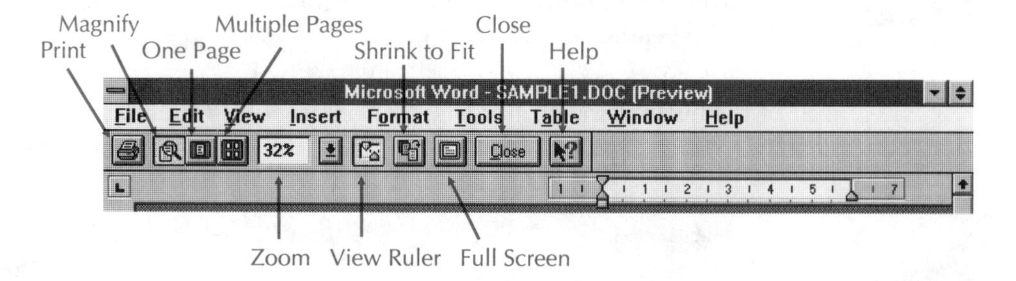

The Print button lets you print directly from the print preview. Selecting this button brings up the Print command dialog box, as described in Chapter 10.

When you start print preview, the Magnify tool is automatically selected. The mouse pointer becomes a magnifying glass with a "+" in it:

Clicking this in the document part of the window zooms into the document. This changes the Zoom drop-down list. If you prefer to choose an exact zoom level, use the drop-down list instead of the magnify cursor.

As you might expect, clicking the One Page button changes the zoom level to show exactly one page. This is also the default choice when you enter print preview because it is the fastest way to see how every item on a page looks in relationship to each other.

Use the Multiple Pages button to see more than one page at a time as *thumbnail* images. When you click the button, you see the following mini-dialog box:

By clicking on one of the rectangles, you specify how many pages you want to see at a time.

The View Ruler button adds the ruler to the print preview. This is not often used because the ruler has very little detail to it.

The Shrink to Fit button will reduce the size of the text in your document. It is unlikely you will use this option because it changes the sizes of fonts erratically. It is only useful if you have just one or two lines on the last page of a document.

The Full Screen button puts the print preview into full screen mode, as described earlier in this chapter.

To go back to the previous view, click the Close button. To get help with any of the buttons in print preview (or on any other topic), you can use the Help button.

Review

Open the MAGAZINE practice file that you made in the Review section of Chapter 2. Split the window in two. Show the beginning and end of that file at the same time. View the file in all of Word's different views.

C H A P T E R

4

MOVING AND COPYING TEXT

So far, the editing skills you have learned are how to enter text, how to move the insertion point and selection, and how to delete text from a document. This chapter explains how to use the Cut and Paste commands to move text from one part of a file to another, and how to copy text within a file with the Copy command. You will also see how to use the same procedures to move and copy text between files, and quick methods of moving and copying without using any commands.

The ability to move sections of text is one of the most useful features of word processing. For example, after writing a report you may decide you want to change the order of paragraphs or sentences. Since you can rearrange your ideas after seeing them on paper or on the screen, your finished writing will be much better organized. In this chapter, you will see that moving text is easy to do with Word.

Lesson 29: Using the Clipboard

Word uses the Windows Clipboard to hold information. You can imagine the Clipboard as a holder for a single chunk of text or a single picture. Every time you use the Copy or Cut command from the Edit menu in a Windows program, the contents of the Clipboard are replaced with the selected text or picture.

The Clipboard acts as a temporary holder of a single piece of information. It is most useful for moving text: you select the text, move it from its current location into the Clipboard, put the insertion point at the desired location, and copy it there from the Clipboard.

Many Windows programs, including Word, interact with the Clipboard by using three commands from the Edit menu:

- The Copy command places a copy of the selected text into the Clipboard, replacing its previous contents.
- The Cut command does the same thing as the Copy command, except that it removes the selected text from the document. This is like giving the Copy command followed by the Clear command.
- The Paste command inserts the contents of the Clipboard at the insertion point. If you have text selected when you give the Paste command, the contents of the Clipboard replace the selected text; this is similar to replacing text, as you saw in Chapter 2. Note that this does not "empty" the Clipboard; instead, the contents remain there until you replace them with another Copy or Cut command.

Windows includes a command you can use when you are using the Clipboard in Word. The Clipboard viewing program lets you look at the contents of the Clipboard but not edit them. This is a handy way to check what you have in the Clipboard. To run this program, choose it from your main Windows screen. To access the program directly from Word, choose the Run command from Word's program Control menu and enter CLIPBRD for the command name.

For example, be sure the SAMPLE1 file is open, select the word "latest" in the first paragraph, and copy it to the Clipboard with the Copy command from the Edit menu. Choose the Run command from Word's program Control menu and enter **clipbrd** in the Command line option. Word displays the Clipboard window:

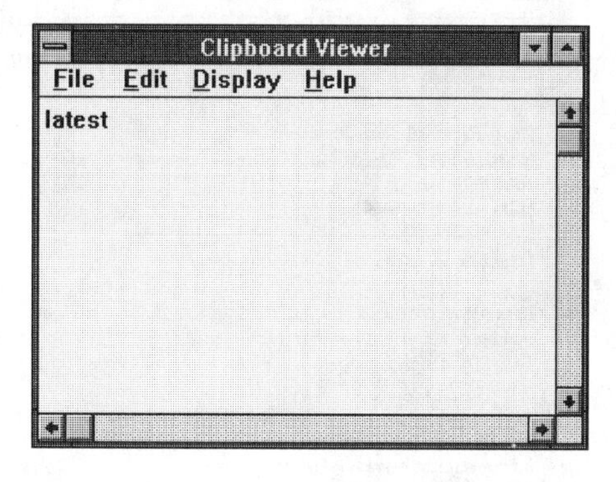

The Clipboard in Word acts just as it does in other Windows applications. Thus, if you now select another word from the file and give the Cut command, the Clipboard no longer contains the word "latest"; it contains the word you just selected. If you then give the Undo command from the Edit menu, you will find that the second word is back in the text, and if you then view the Clipboard, you'll find "latest" back in the Clipboard.

Notice that deleting characters with the Backspace key does not put the characters into the Clipboard; only the Cut command and the Copy command do. This chapter shows you the basic use of the Clipboard. You will also see the Clipboard used in many other chapters in the book with other Word commands.

Lesson 30: Moving and Copying Text Within a Document

The basic method for moving text within a document is quite simple:

1. Select the text that is to be moved.
2. Give the Cut command.
3. Set the insertion point at the desired location for the text.
4. Give the Paste command.

For example, try switching the second and third sentences of the first paragraph of the SAMPLE1 file. To do this, select the third sentence (which begins "In the next year..."), then delete the sentence with the Cut command. Your screen now looks like the one in Figure 4-1.

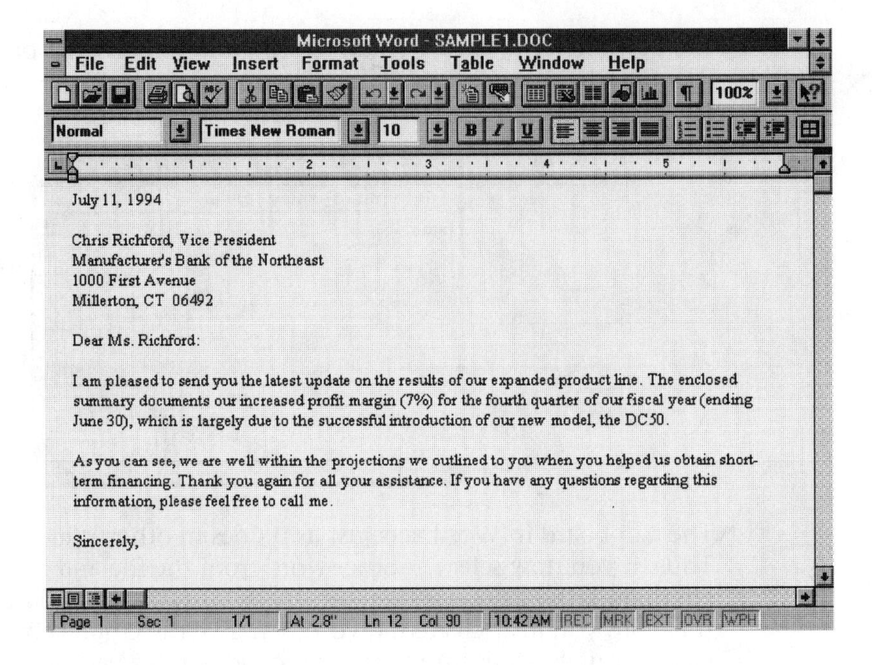

Third sentence cut
Figure 4-1.

Now set the insertion point at the beginning of the second sentence and give the Paste command. Press the Spacebar to separate the two sentences, as shown in Figure 4-2. Notice that Word automatically reformats the paragraph for you.

This is the way you most often use the Clipboard. Since it can hold any amount of information, you can use it to move large portions of your text, even whole chapters of books. This is also a convenient method for moving phrases around in a sentence to see different effects on the sound and meaning. Practice moving text around in your file by using the Clipboard and the Cut and Paste commands.

The Clipboard is also useful for making copies of parts of your text. Although copying text is not as common as moving text, you may find that a sentence or a line of text is used over and over in your document. If you copy the text, you do not have to retype it each time it is used.

To copy text, use the Copy command, which puts the contents of the selection in the Clipboard. The original text remains in your document. The contents even remain in the Clipboard when you leave Word and start another application.

The Copy, Cut, and Paste commands become even more powerful when they are used with split windows, since you can use the Clipboard to move text from one part of the window to the other without losing your place in

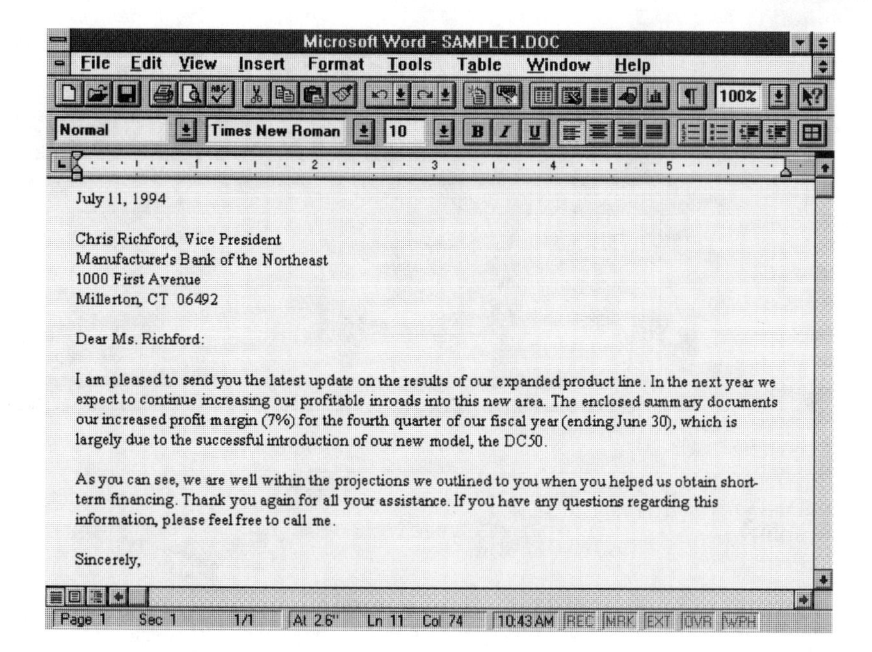

July 11, 1994

Chris Richford, Vice President
Manufacturer's Bank of the Northeast
1000 First Avenue
Millerton, CT 06492

Dear Ms. Richford:

I am pleased to send you the latest update on the results of our expanded product line. In the next year we expect to continue increasing our profitable inroads into this new area. The enclosed summary documents our increased profit margin (7%) for the fourth quarter of our fiscal year (ending June 30), which is largely due to the successful introduction of our new model, the DC50.

As you can see, we are well within the projections we outlined to you when you helped us obtain short-term financing. Thank you again for all your assistance. If you have any questions regarding this information, please feel free to call me.

Sincerely,

Sentence inserted from Clipboard

Figure 4-2.

either part of the file. This lets you instantly see the results of moving text as you perform the commands.

For example, you might want to see the effect of adding "From:" and the sender's name to the top of the letter. You can do this easily by leaving the end of the letter in the bottom part and showing the beginning of the letter in the top part.

With the window split into halves, position the text as shown in Figure 4-3. Type **From:** before the inside address (on the line above Chris Richford's name), press the Enter key, and move to the lower half. Select the line with Thomas Mead's name, and give the Copy command.

Now move to the top window, move the insertion point to the line beneath "From:", and then use the Paste command to place the line under "From:". Add another line after the name by pressing Enter.

Lesson 31: Using the Clipboard with Two Files

In Chapter 3, you saw how to view two files at once (SAMPLE1 and REPORT1). As you are viewing two files, you can also copy or move information between them. (Be sure both SAMPLE1 and REPORT1 are open.) It is likely that you will want to move text from one file to another if you

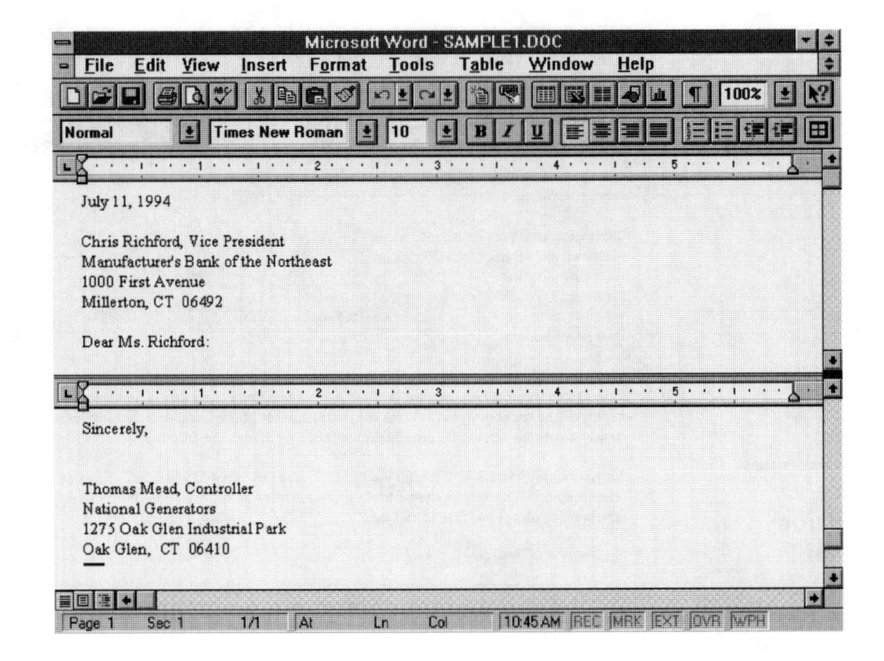

Window split for moving
Figure 4-3.

have documents that are made up of many files. Copying text is also common when you have multiple documents since you may want to repeat part of one document in another.

As you are editing SAMPLE1, you may need some of the information in REPORT1—for example, if you want to include the table of numbers. You can see those numbers by scrolling through REPORT1, and you can even copy the whole table to SAMPLE1 with the Copy and Paste commands.

To do this, add a line of text between the paragraphs of SAMPLE1, as shown here:

I am pleased to send you the latest update on the results of our expanded product line. In the next year we expect to continue increasing our profitable inroads into this new area. The enclosed summary documents our increased profit margin (7%) for the fourth quarter of our fiscal year (ending June 30), which is largely due to the successful introduction of our new model, the DC50.

Our current figures are:

As you can see, we are well within the projections we outlined to you when you helped us obtain short-term financing. Thank you again for all your assistance. If you have any questions regarding this information, please feel free to call me.

Now move to the REPORT1 window and select the numbers, as in Figure 4-4. Use the Copy command to copy these to the Clipboard, switch to the SAMPLE1 window, and use the Paste command to copy the text from the Clipboard after the new text, as in Figure 4-5.

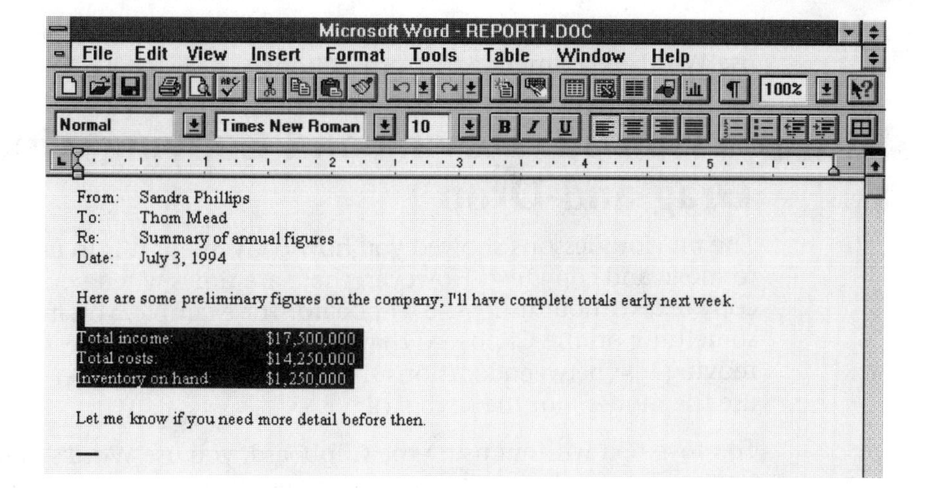

Figures selected
Figure 4-4.

You can also use a similar procedure if you are copying text from one file to another. The Clipboard retains its contents regardless of the source of the material.

When using two windows to copy or move information, some people prefer to leave the windows at full size (as shown in the preceding example), while others prefer to make the windows half size so they can see both windows. People with high-resolution monitors often shrink their windows to half-size

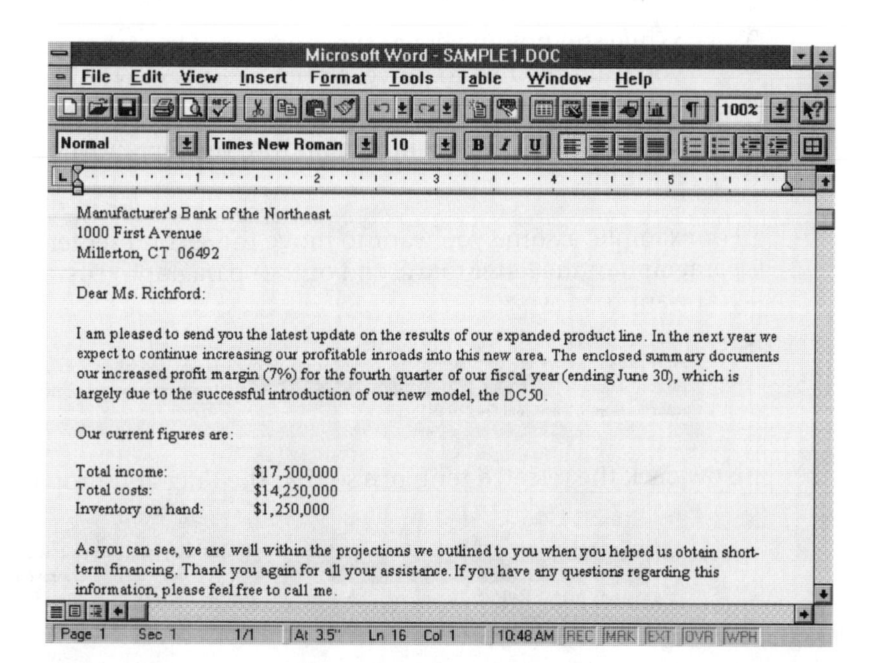

Figures pasted into SAMPLE1
Figure 4-5.

because they can still see a great deal of information in each window. As you use Word, experiment with both options.

Lesson 32: Moving and Copying with Drag-and-Drop

The previous lessons showed you how convenient it is to use the Clipboard to move and copy text. However, there are times when you want to move or copy text without using the Clipboard. For example, you may have something on the Clipboard that you do not want to lose. Or you may be moving text between locations that are close to each other and want to just use the mouse, not the keyboard.

To move text without using the Clipboard, you use Word's drag-and-drop feature. *Drag-and-drop* allows you to select text and drag it to a new location without cutting and pasting.

To move text with drag-and-drop:

1. Select the text.
2. Point in the selected text and hold down the mouse button. The pointer changes shape to include a gray box at the bottom of the arrow:

3. While still holding down the mouse button, drag to the position where you want the text to move. Notice there is now a dotted insertion point that moves with the pointer.
4. When you release the mouse button, the text moves to the new location.

For example, assume you want to move the second sentence of the last paragraph of the letter to the end of that paragraph. First, select the sentence you want to move:

As you can see, we are well within the projections we outlined to you when you helped us obtain short-term financing. Thank you again for all your assistance. If you have any questions regarding this information, please feel free to call me.

Now click the selected sentence so that the drag-and-drop pointer appears:

As you can see, we are well within the projections we outlined to you when you helped us obtain short-term financing. Thank you again for all your assistance. If you have any questions regarding this information, please feel free to call me.

Drag the insertion point to just after the period in the third sentence:

As you can see, we are well within the projections we outlined to you when you helped us obtain short-term financing. Thank you again for all your assistance. If you have any questions regarding this information, please feel free to call me.

Release the mouse button, and the sentence moves:

As you can see, we are well within the projections we outlined to you when you helped us obtain short-term financing. If you have any questions regarding this information, please feel free to call me. Thank you again for all your assistance.

You can even drag-and-drop across panes in a split window or across two windows into two different documents. If you do not like the drag-and-drop feature, you can turn it off by using the Edit options in the Options command from the Tools menu, as described in Chapter 11.

If you are using the keyboard, there is a feature similar to drag-and-drop that is not as direct. After selecting the text to move, press F2. Word prompts "Move to where?" at the bottom of the window. Use the arrow keys to move the dotted insertion point to the desired location and press Enter.

Lesson 33: Using the Spike to Collect and Move Text

Earlier in the chapter you saw how to move text one selection at a time using the Clipboard. Word has a feature called the *spike* that lets you delete many selections and, when you are finished collecting them, move them in a single step to a new location. This lets you collect many disconnected pieces of text and combine them in one place.

To use the spike, select the first item and press Ctrl-F3. The text disappears from its current location. Select the next item, press Ctrl-F3 again, and so on, until you have selected all the items. Put the insertion point where you want the collected items and press Ctrl-Shift-F3. (There is no mouse shortcut for using the spike.)

For example, assume that you want to move the first and third sentences of the first paragraph of the SAMPLE1 file to another document. The paragraph starts out:

I am pleased to send you the latest update on the results of our expanded product line. In the next year we expect to continue increasing our profitable inroads into this new area. The enclosed summary documents our increased profit margin (7%) for the fourth quarter of our fiscal year (ending June 30), which is largely due to the successful introduction of our new model, the DC50.

Select the first sentence and press Ctrl-F3.

> In the next year we expect to continue increasing our profitable inroads into this new area. The enclosed summary documents our increased profit margin (7%) for the fourth quarter of our fiscal year (ending June 30), which is largely due to the successful introduction of our new model, the DC50.

Select the third sentence (which is now the second sentence that is left) and press Ctrl-F3 again:

> In the next year we expect to continue increasing our profitable inroads into this new area.

Now open a new document and press Ctrl-Shift-F3:

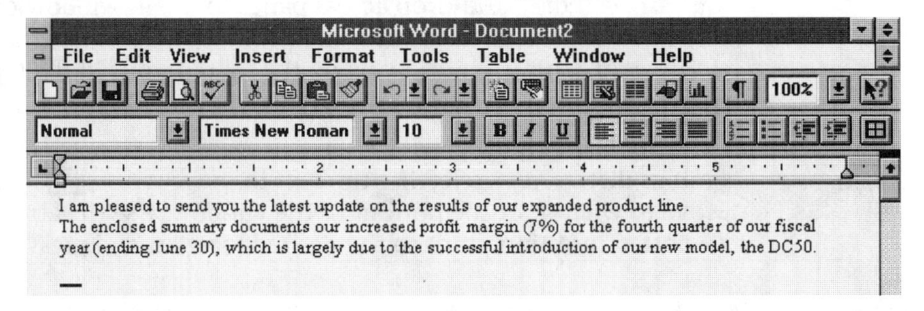

Review

Open the MAGAZINE and SAMPLE1 files at the same time. Copy the second sentence of the SAMPLE1 file (which starts "The enclosed...") to the beginning of the second paragraph in the MAGAZINE file using the Clipboard. Next, copy a sentence from the MAGAZINE file to the SAMPLE1 file using drag-and-drop editing.

Word For Windows
Word For Windows

CHAPTER

5

SEARCHING AND REPLACING

As you have seen, you can easily move a selection around the screen and change the selection. If you know where you want to go—for example, about 20 lines down or to the end of the file—you can scroll through your text quickly. However, you often want to go to a specific word or phrase in a long document. Instead of searching visually for the phrase, you can move to its exact position with the Find command. The Find command searches for the word or phrase you specify.

Searching with the Find command has many uses other than simply moving to a certain word or phrase. For instance, you can find the first occurrence of a particular word by moving to the beginning of a document and then searching for the word. You can review your text to see whether you defined new terms when they first appeared. Since you can also search for groups of words, you can easily check for phrases that you may have overused.

Replacing text with the Replace command is not as common as searching for text, but it is still a very valuable feature. For example, you can use the Replace command to look for each occurrence of an overused phrase and replace it with another phrase on a case-by-case basis. You can also use Replace to quickly change every occurrence of something, such as a changed or misspelled name.

Lesson 34: Searching for Text

The Find command quickly moves to the next instance of a word or phrase and selects it. The movement is always relative to your current position in a file; for example, if the insertion point is in the middle of a file and you search for the word "invoice", Word finds the next occurrence of "invoice" that appears in the text.

Move to the beginning of the SAMPLE1 file and give the Find command from the Edit menu. Word brings up the Find dialog box:

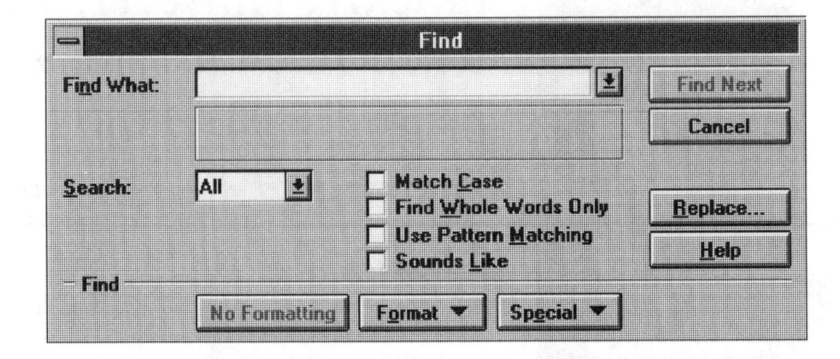

The blinking insertion point in the Find What box indicates that you should fill in the word or phrase you want to search for.

Type **please** and select the Find Next button (or press Enter). You can enter up to 255 characters in this field. The first instance of the word "please" in the letter, which in this case is in the word "pleased", becomes selected:

I am pleased to send you the latest update on the results of our expanded product line. The enclosed summary documents our increased profit margin (7%) for the fourth quarter of our fiscal year (ending June 30), which is largely due to the successful introduction of our new model, the DC50. In the next year we expect to continue increasing our profitable inroads into this new area.

If you want to search for the same word or phrase again, you do not need to retype it; the dialog box stays open. Simply select the Find Next button or press Enter, and Word searches again. When you are finished searching, select the Cancel button. If you close the Find dialog box and want to repeat the search, pressing Shift-F4 repeats the Find command without opening the dialog box.

The other options for the Find command are as follows:

- So far, you have used the Find command only to search forward in your document. The Search drop-down list lets you choose among Down (that is, forward) and Up (backward) in your text. The default choice, All, causes Word to look in the main text, annotations, footnotes, endnotes, headers, and footers.
- For Match Case, you must decide if Word should pay attention to whether the letters in the text are upper- or lowercase. If you do not choose this option, Word ignores case, meaning that Word does not differentiate between upper- and lowercase letters as it searches the text. Checking this box makes the search more restrictive: the text must be an exact match of the word or phrase you are searching for, including capital letters. Thus, if you check the box to match the case and you are searching for "the", Word does not stop when it finds "The".
- Choosing Find Whole Words Only indicates that you want Word to restrict your search to whole words and ignore words in which your selection is merely a part. If you choose this option, and the text you are searching for is "please", for example, Word does not stop if it finds "pleased". If you don't check the box, Word stops, even if the text you are searching for is part of another word, as you saw in the preceding example.
- If you aren't exactly sure how the text you are looking for is spelled, make a good phonetic guess and select the Sounds Like option. For instance, if the name "Jaymes" is in your document, you can enter "James" for the text to search for and select the Sounds Like option.
- The Special and Use Pattern Matching options are described later in this chapter.

You can also search for specific text formatting, such as letters in italics. These options, under the Format button at the bottom of the dialog box, are covered in Chapter 6.

Word remembers the text in the Find What choice and the setting for each of the choices whenever you use the Find command. For example, if you change the setting of the case choice to check for case, that setting is still selected the next time you give the Find command.

To see how to use the choices, move the insertion point to the beginning of the first full paragraph of the SAMPLE1 file and give the Find command. Type **As** (with a capital "A") and check the Match Case option:

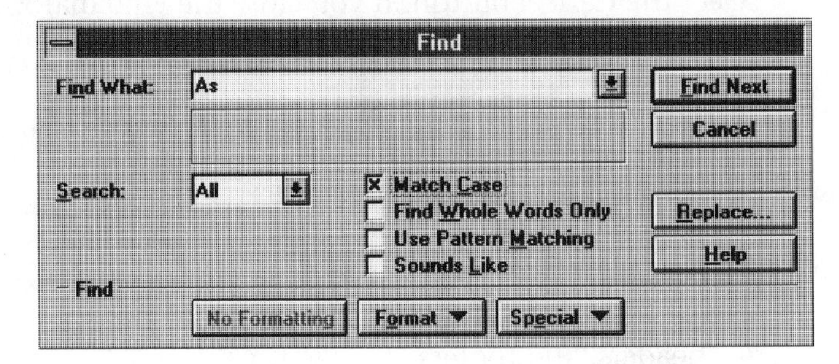

When you execute the command, the word "As" at the beginning of the second paragraph is selected. If you had not chosen to search for the matching case, the lowercase "as" in the word "pleased" in the first paragraph would have been found first. Select the Cancel button to close the dialog box.

To see the effect of the Find Whole Words Only option, move the insertion point to the beginning of the file and give the Find command again. Change Find What to **as**, check the Find Whole Words Only option, and choose the Match Case option to deselect it. Now, even though the search is not restricted to an uppercase "A", it is restricted to "as" only when it is a separate word. Thus, Word skips over the "as" in "Northeast" (and in "pleased", "increased", and "increasing"), going directly to the "As" in the second paragraph.

The text you search for can have as many as 255 characters. (You cannot see this much in the Find dialog box, but you can scroll left and right by selecting at the left and right ends of the text entry box.) If Word finds the text, the entire word or phrase is selected. If the text does not appear in the file, Word displays an alert box and does not move the selection or insertion point.

Lesson 35: Replacing Text

It is useful to be able to replace every instance of a particular word or phrase in a document with some other word or phrase. For example, you may want to change "pleased" to "happy" throughout a letter, or you may need to change many, but not all, instances of a person's name to another name. You may also want to replace a wordy or misused phrase with a more concise one throughout a document.

When you choose the Replace command from the Edit menu, you automatically change all instances of one word or phrase to another. You can also have Word show you each instance of the phrase you want to change so you can choose whether or not to change it based on its context. You can undo changes with the Undo command.

The choices in the Replace dialog box are similar to those of the Find command. For example, go back to the top of the file, give the Replace command, and enter **pleased** for Find What and **happy** for Replace With, as shown in Figure 5-1. Note that the Replace command started with the Find What text from the previous Find command.

The dialog box has buttons labeled Find Next, Cancel, Replace, Replace All, and Help. If you select the Replace All button, Word simply replaces each occurrence of the specified word or phrase throughout your document without asking for confirmation. If you select the Find Next button, Word stops at the first word to be replaced. Selecting the Replace button indicates that you want to make the replacement for the current selection, while selecting the Find Next button indicates that you do not. If you are finished replacing words, close the window or select Cancel.

As you might guess, the Replace command can ease the job of changing many items in a long file. For example, if one person is mentioned repeatedly throughout a long memo, and that person changes jobs within the company and is replaced by someone else, you may have to change many instances of the person's name and title. The Replace command allows you to do this with just one command. If the person's name needs to be changed in many, but not all, instances, choosing to confirm each replacement lets you look through the file easily.

If you do not choose to match the case when replacing text, Word intelligently chooses how to replace the letters. For instance, if you choose to change "airplane" to "boat" with no case requirement and Word finds "Airplane", it replaces it with "Boat", because this is most likely what you would want. The rule is that words with initial- or all-capital letters

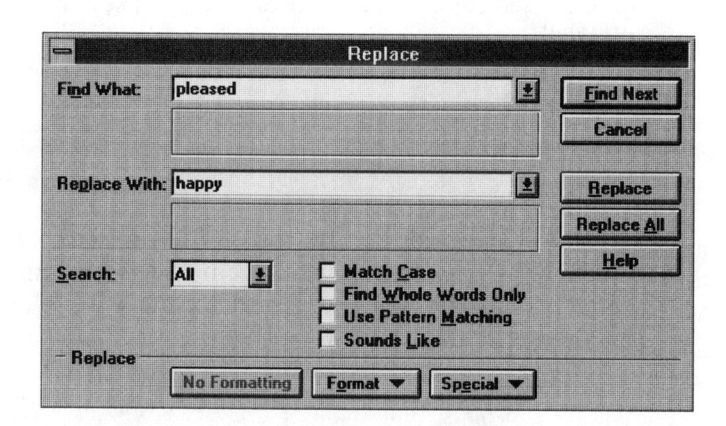

Replace dialog box
Figure 5-1.

("Airplane" or "AIRPLANE") are replaced with corresponding capital letters ("Boat" or "BOAT").

In the Replace command, the Find Whole Words Only option acts like it does in the Find command. When Word searches for the text in the Find What field, it stops only when it finds that text as whole words.

Lesson 36: Using Special Characters in Find and Replace

Word searches for the exact text you specify in the Find and Replace commands. However, there are times when you want Word to search for less specifically defined words.

Finding Unknown Characters

The Use Pattern Matching option in the Find and Replace commands allow you to look for characters that you are not sure about and for special characters, such as the Enter character. To look for a group of characters where you do not know one or more of the characters in the group, include a question mark "wildcard" in order to broaden your search. With Use Pattern Matching turned on, if Word sees a question mark in the text you tell it to search for, it assumes that any character can match it. (If you are familiar with using wildcard characters in searching for filenames in MS-DOS, this is identical to the question mark used there.)

For example, if you search for "f?r", Word stops when it finds "far", "for", "fur", and so on. The question mark indicates that any character at all (even numbers and punctuation marks) can be in the position you indicate.

Move to the beginning of the first paragraph and give the Find command. Enter **e?s** for the Find What text, be sure that the Use Pattern Matching option is selected, and then press the Enter key. Word selects the "eas" in "pleased":

I am pleased to send you the latest update on the results of our expanded product line. The enclosed summary documents our increased profit margin (7%) for the fourth quarter of our fiscal year (ending June 30), which is largely due to the successful introduction of our new model, the DC50. In the next year we expect to continue increasing our profitable inroads into this new area.

Now select the Find Next button, and Word selects the "eas" in "increased". Selecting the Find Next button again selects "ess" in "successful", and so on. Notice each of the sequences found begins with "e", ends with "s", and has exactly one character between them.

The Use Pattern Matching option has other patterns it can look for. For instance, the asterisk can be used to look for any group of characters. There are other options, but they are fairly advanced and rarely used.

Finding Special Characters

You may also want to search for characters that are special to Word but that you cannot normally enter in the Find or Replace command. For instance, you may want to find the word "The" preceded by a tab character. Since you can't normally enter a tab character as text to search for (Word moves to the next choice for the Find command), you need a way to indicate that you want to search for the tab character. You represent many codes with caret characters.

The Special button at the bottom of the Find and Replace dialog boxes lists the types of special characters you can find. These *caret characters* are special characters that you precede with a caret mark (^); however, if you choose the desired character from the list, Word fills in the Find What option for you. The caret characters are shown in Table 5-1. Note that you use two characters, the caret and the character indicated. A caret character is not a control character.

For example, the dialog box to search for "me.", followed by a paragraph mark and the word "Now" looks like this:

In the Replace command, you can enter any of the special characters from Table 5-1 for the Find What option. In addition, you can use the same characters in the Replace With field.

You can also indicate that you want the contents of the Clipboard inserted in place of the text found. To do this, use **^c** in the Replace With field. For example, assume that you have copied the name of your company with formatting to the Clipboard. Figure 5-2 shows how you would replace the words "our company" with the contents of the Clipboard by using the Replace command.

Character	Meaning
^a	Annotation mark
^b	Section break
^c	Contents of the Clipboard (only used in Replace)
^d	Field
^e	Endnote mark
^f	Footnote mark
^g	Graphic
^l	Newline character
^m	Page break
^n	Column break
^p	Paragraph mark
^s	Nonbreaking space
^t	Tab character
^w	White space (this is any number of spaces, tabs, paragraph marks, newline characters, division markers, and page break characters)
+=	En dash
^#	Any digit
^$	Any letter
^&	Contents of the Find What field (only used in Replace)
^+	Em dash
^-	Optional hyphen
^?	Any character
^ ^	Caret character (^)
^~	Nonbreaking hyphen
^*number*	Any character, where *number* is its ASCII value starting with a 0 (such as 0231)

Caret Characters
Table 5-1.

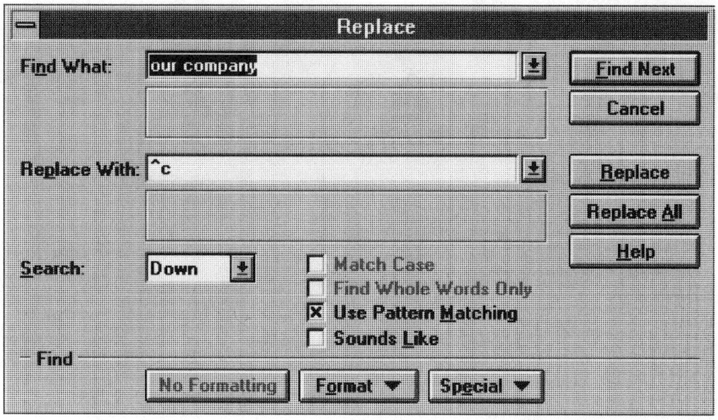

Replacing text with the contents of the Clipboard

Figure 5-2.

Review

Use the MAGAZINE file to experiment with the Find and Replace commands and their options. Search for the paragraph marks by using a caret character.

CHAPTER

6

BASIC FORMATTING WITH WORD

As part of the editing process, you will probably want to alter the way your text looks in order to present the information in an interesting form and to help your reader understand your meaning. Word's formatting capabilities let you choose exactly how your text looks when it is printed out.

Adding a formatting characteristic to text is called direct formatting. Direct formatting is actually what you normally do when typing or editing text. For example, when you make changes on a first draft, you might decide to underline a phrase or change the size of the text. In doing this, you are adding characteristics directly to text.

Although you may be tempted to always use direct formatting, you will see in Chapter 15 that there is a better way: using styles. *Styles* make formatting easier because you can add the same formatting to different parts of your document quickly. Even better, if you decide to change your formatting, changing styles is incredibly easier than changing direct formatting. Since the concepts in styles are based on the concepts in direct formatting, they are not presented until later.

Lesson 37: Introducing Formatting

The basic concept behind formatting with Word is that all text has certain characteristics associated with it. After you have specified the characteristics (such as underlining or indentation), Word automatically displays the text with those attributes. If you move the text to some other place in your document, the characteristics move with it.

You can enter an entire document without worrying about the formatting and then go back over it to add formatting, or if you wish, you can format text as you enter it. Each time you add a characteristic, you see it instantly on the screen. Both formatting methods work equally well. You can experiment with different formats, seeing which one best fits the meaning of the text. Word gives you three units to apply formatting to:

- Characters
- Paragraphs
- Sections

At the level of the smallest unit (character), Word lets you change the format of each character or groups of letters (such as words or phrases). For example, you can underline, boldface, or italicize characters, as well as change type font and size, with different formatting commands. Character formatting is most often used to make certain words stand out in your text. Word also calls this *font formatting*.

You have already learned to use the Enter key to make paragraphs in Word. Paragraphs are the second formatting unit. The paragraph is important to Word because Word stores formatting information for each paragraph when you press Enter. In fact, all of the characteristics of a paragraph are stored in a bit of white space that is placed at the end of the paragraph. (This white space is actually a paragraph mark.)

For instance, many people like to indent the first line of every paragraph five spaces. Some word processing programs require you to press the Tab key at the beginning of each paragraph. Word, however, remembers this format once you have specified it, and inserts the spaces for you in succeeding paragraphs unless you tell it otherwise. Other paragraph formats you can specify include the indentation of the entire paragraph, line spacing, borders, and alignment with the margin.

You may want to set different formatting characteristics for a particular paragraph. For example, when you include a long quotation in text, you usually indent the whole quotation a few spaces from the margin.

Since Word stores paragraph formatting characteristics in the paragraph mark, you can use the Copy and Paste commands to copy the formatting characteristics of one paragraph to another paragraph in a different location in your document. You do not need to do this as you type since Word uses the paragraph formatting of the previous paragraph when you start a new paragraph. Copy the paragraph mark you want to transfer to the Clipboard. Then select the paragraph mark you want to replace and give the Paste command. All of the formatting characteristics are then applied to the new paragraph.

Word lets you set up different characteristics for each *section,* which is the third formatting unit. These are characteristics such as page headings and margin size that do not change from paragraph to paragraph. You might have many sections in a document if you have many chapters or if you have many different page layouts within one document, such as in a brochure. To split a document into two or more sections, you add a section break where you want the section formatting to change with the Break command from the Insert menu. You can see the section formatting by using different views of your Word document.

It is important to remember that each element of text, whether it is a character, paragraph, or section, has a set of formatting instructions attached to it. The result is that formatting documents is easy with Word since you can copy the specifications from one formatting unit to another.

You may be wondering what all of these characteristics are. They are discussed in the next three chapters. For now, think of a direct formatting characteristic as a description of how the text looks or its position on the page.

Lesson 38: Giving Formatting Commands

You can give formatting commands in Word in three ways:

- Give commands from the Format menu

- Press special key combinations
- Click buttons in the Formatting toolbar

The formatting commands are much like the editing commands you have already learned. You apply formatting commands to selected text. If you give a formatting command when the insertion point is in a document (no text selected), the text you type at the insertion point has that formatting applied to it.

You do not need to use the menus to enter every formatting command. There are some character and paragraph formatting commands that can be entered by pressing the Ctrl key and a letter, such as Ctrl-B for boldface characters. These key sequences are described in the next two chapters.

You can give character and paragraph formatting commands by clicking buttons in the Formatting toolbar. These actions are described in the next two chapters.

Many of Word's dialog boxes for formatting include a preview area that shows how the changes you are making will look. As you change settings in the dialog box, the preview box changes so you can see the results before selecting OK. This helps if you are not sure how some formatting will look.

The most common type of formatting you use is character formatting. For instance, book and magazine publishers commonly use italics for emphasis, foreign words, and book titles. They use underlining and boldface in different kinds of headings. Chapter 7 discusses character formatting, Chapter 8 discusses paragraph formatting, and Chapter 14 discusses section formatting.

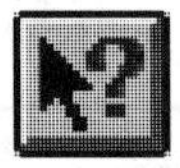

You can see what type of formatting is already applied to text with the Help button in the Standard toolbar. Click on this button, then click on the desired text. Figure 6-1 shows you the dialog box that appears.

Word has a handy feature that makes adding formatting to an unformatted document faster. The F4 key repeats the last editing or formatting action you gave (you saw this in Chapter 2 as the Redo command). Thus, if you change the formatting on a selection of text, you do not need to give the same command for the next selection; just press F4 (or give the Redo command from the Edit menu).

Lesson 39: Copying Formatting in Your Document

After you have applied formatting to part of your document, it is likely that you will apply that same formatting to other parts. Instead of having to give

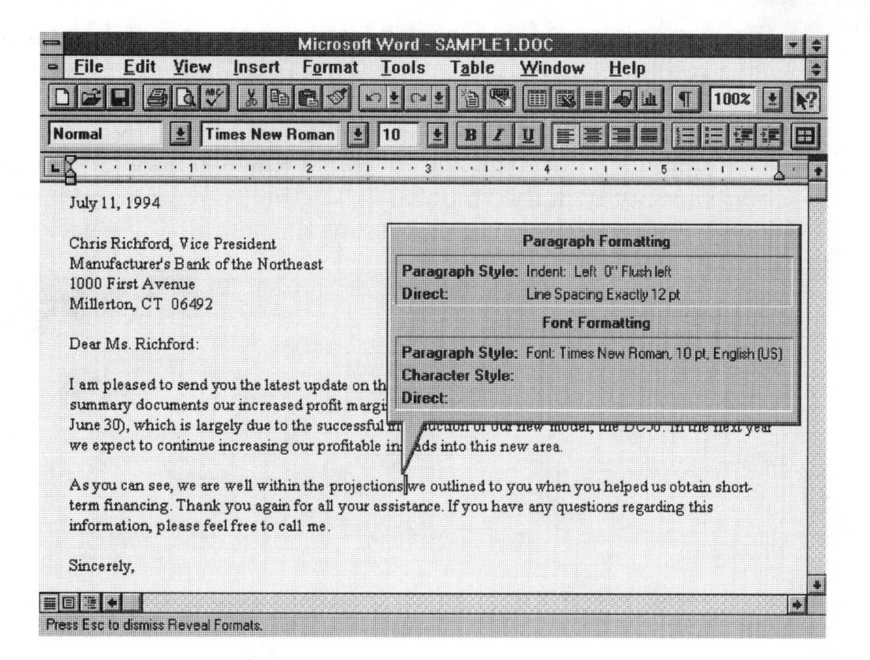

Formatting help dialog box
Figure 6-1.

the same formatting commands over and over, you can format one part the way you want it and then quickly copy that formatting to other parts that you want to look the same.

For example, assume that you typed in a research paper that has many quotations in it. You decide that each quotation paragraph should be indented from both the left and right margins by one inch. Instead of having to give the same command for each quotation paragraph, you would format the first quotation paragraph and copy that formatting to each other quotation paragraph.

Copying formatting is easy. Simply select the text that has the formatting you want to copy, click the Format Painter button in the Standard toolbar, and select the text you want to copy the format to.

To copy a character format, you select the characters with the desired character format, then click the Format Painter button in the Standard toolbar. To copy a paragraph format, you select the paragraph mark with the desired paragraph format, then click the Format Painter button in the Standard toolbar. For paragraph formats, you can select more than just the paragraph mark, but if you do, only the paragraph formats will be copied. You will see examples of copying formatting in the next two chapters.

Lesson 40: Searching for and Replacing Formatting

In Chapter 5, you saw how the Find command looks for text. The Find command normally ignores formatting when looking for text. However, you can specify in the Find dialog box that the command look only for text that has particular formatting by using the buttons at the bottom of the dialog box:

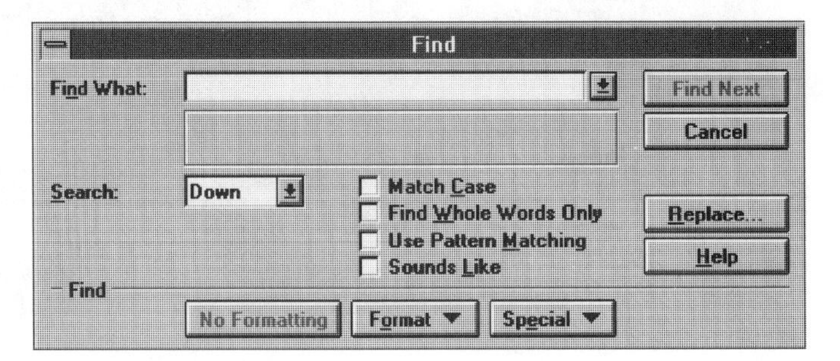

The No Formatting button clears any formatting specifications you may have already made; it is only available if you have specified formatting. The Format button is a drop-down list of the types of formatting you can search for (font, paragraph, language, and style). Each of these choices brings up dialog boxes similar to those you will learn about in the following chapters. In those dialog boxes, you choose the type of formatting you want to search for.

If you use the choices, you can either search for all text with the specified formatting or only for specific text that has that formatting. To search for the next text that has particular formatting, leave the Find What choice blank, select one of the commands from the Format button's drop-down list, and choose the desired format from the dialog box. You can choose many types of simultaneous formatting, such as bold and italic text.

When you select formatting from the dialog boxes, the choices are shown below the Find What box:

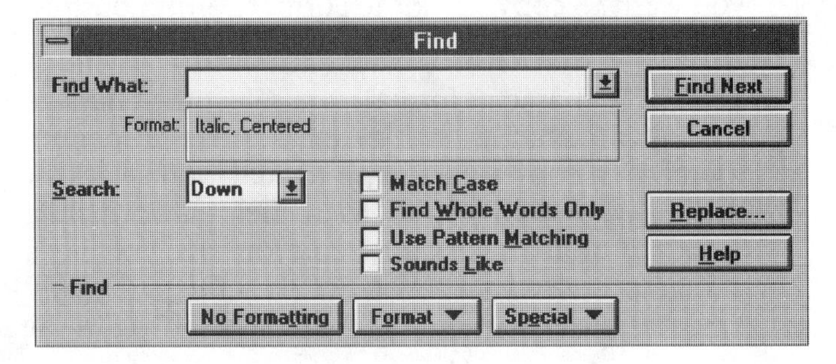

When you select the Find Next button after specifying the formatting, the next text that has that formatting is selected, regardless of the specific text.

To select specific text with specific formatting, enter that text in the Find What choice. Thus, to find the words "timely fashion" in italics, the dialog box would look like this:

Find
Find What: timely fashion
Format: Italic
Search: Down
Match Case
Find Whole Words Only
Use Pattern Matching
Sounds Like
Find Next
Cancel
Replace...
Help
Find
No Formatting
Format
Special

The Replace command works in a similar fashion to the Find command. In addition to finding text with particular formatting, you can specify the formatting of the replaced text. Normally, Word replaces text with the same formatting as that on the first character that was found. With buttons in the Replace command, you can specify the same text with different formatting without having to put the text in the Replace With choice. For example, the following illustrates how you can quickly replace all instances of "Annual Report" in italics with the same words not in italics:

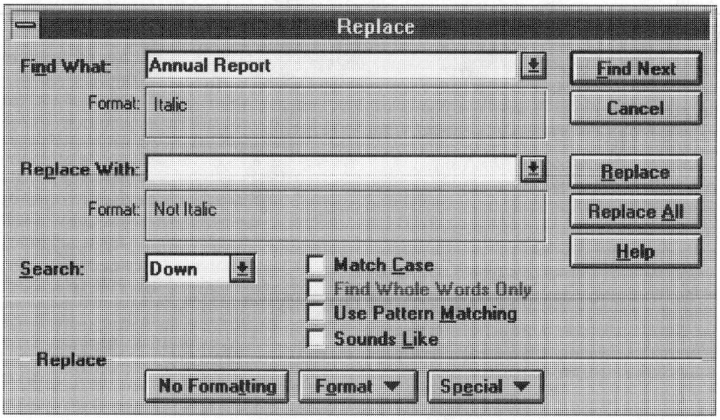

Replace
Find What: Annual Report
Format: Italic
Replace With:
Format: Not Italic
Search: Down
Match Case
Find Whole Words Only
Use Pattern Matching
Sounds Like
Find Next
Cancel
Replace
Replace All
Help
Replace
No Formatting
Format
Special

Review

Look in books and magazines you normally read and pay attention to how they use character and paragraph formatting. Note how much formatting there is on title pages of books and in magazine articles. Think about how you would implement that type of formatting in your work.

C H A P T E R

7 FORMATTING CHARACTERS

The purpose of character formatting is to make the reader notice a group of characters or words.

This is often useful for emphasis, but common publishing practices also require it; for instance, book titles should generally be shown in italics. Examples of some character formats are shown here:

bold characters
underlined characters
italicized characters
combinations
characters *with* different fonts

Lesson 41: Common Character Formatting

Type the text shown here, which you will use to experiment with character formatting:

Books and magazines often contain a variety of character styles which you can now incorporate into your reports and memos. For example, it is common to italicize foreign words such as deja vu, or to use italics to indicate emphasis. Bold characters are often used in headings to make them stand out on a page, sometimes in conjunction with underlining.

Word gives you even more character styles to work with, however. You may also choose to put a phrase in small caps to indicate that it stands by itself. If you want, you can use double underline for greater emphasis. If your printer supports other fonts, subscripts, superscripts, or strikethrough, Word lets you use those, too.

Save this on disk with the name CHARACT.

To change the formatting of a group of characters, first select the group, and then give the Font command from the Format menu. The Font dialog box, shown in Figure 7-1, appears.

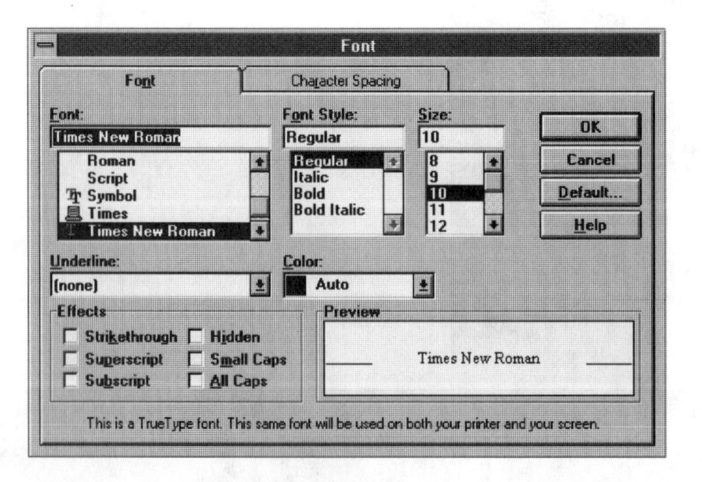

Font dialog box
Figure 7-1.

Some standard character formatting, such as for boldface, is either on or off. This type of formatting is called a *toggle* because it acts like a toggle switch. Choose it once and it's on; choose it again and it's off. In fact, you can choose more than one type of formatting for your text. For example, you might want a title on a report to be both underlined and bold.

You may have noticed the Preview box in the Font command. This shows an example of the results of your formatting before you select OK. As you add or remove formatting options, the characters in the Preview box change to reflect the new formatting.

You can also select character formatting from the Formatting toolbar, shown here:

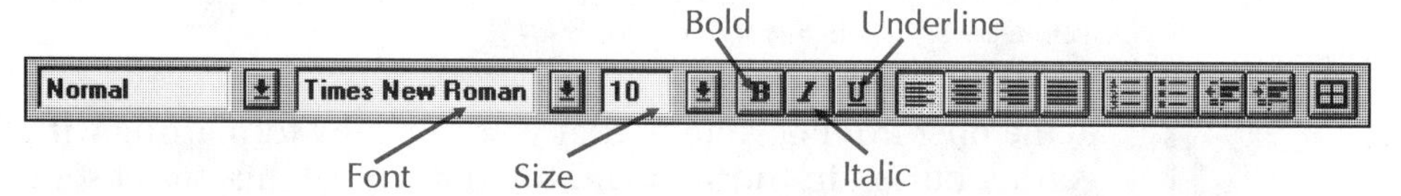

The buttons near the middle of the Formatting toolbar, marked **B**, *I*, and U, are used to make text bold, italic, or underlined. Just select the desired text and click the button. When a toggle is set on, the button looks like it is pressed in. For instance, if the selected text is in italics, the button looks like this:

The formats that most people use in their writing are plain (no emphasis), italics, bold, and underlining. Now, as an experiment, select the words "deja vu" in the text and give the Font command from the Format menu. Select the Italic option and then the OK button. When the dialog box disappears, the words "deja vu" become italic:

Books and magazines often contain a variety of character styles which you can now incorporate into your reports and memos. For example, it is common to italicize foreign words such as *deja vu*, or to use italics to indicate emphasis. Bold characters are often used in headings to make them stand out on a page, sometimes in conjunction with underlining.

Click once in the text or press the → key to remove the selection so you can see the italics more clearly.

Choosing bold and underline formatting is similar to choosing italics. Select the words "stand out" and then make them bold by clicking the **B** button in the Formatting toolbar, or press Ctrl-B. Select the word "underlining" and click the U button, or press Ctrl-U. (If you wish, you can also underline the period after the word.) The results look like this:

Books and magazines often contain a variety of character styles which you can now incorporate into your reports and memos. For example, it is common to italicize foreign words such as *deja vu*, or to use italics to indicate emphasis. Bold characters are often used in headings to make them **stand out** on a page, sometimes in conjunction with underlining.

As mentioned before, you can apply more than one format to a section of text. To practice this, select "in conjunction" and give the Font command. Now select Bold Italic from the Font Style option and select the OK button. The text looks like this:

Books and magazines often contain a variety of character styles which you can now incorporate into your reports and memos. For example, it is common to italicize foreign words such as *deja vu*, or to use italics to indicate emphasis. Bold characters are often used in headings to make them **stand out** on a page, sometimes ***in conjunction*** with underlining.

Remember from Chapter 6 that you can copy formatting with the Format Painter button in the Standard toolbar. To see this, select some of the characters from the word "conjunction" (be careful not to select the space after the word), click the Format Painter button, then select the word "contain" in the first sentence. That word becomes bold and italic.

Lesson 42: Other Character Formats

Word also lets you specify other types of formatting in the Font dialog box. In the area labeled Effects, the other choices are Strikethrough, Superscript, Subscript, Hidden, Small Caps, and All Caps.

(Don't worry about Hidden; hidden text is a leftover from earlier versions of Word that is of almost no value now. If you format characters as hidden, they will disappear from your screen unless you have Hidden selected in the View tab of the Options command.)

You can experiment with these to see what they look like. Your document might end up with:

Books and magazines often contain a variety of character styles which you can now incorporate into your reports and memos. For example, it is common to italicize foreign words such as *deja vu*, or to use italics to indicate emphasis. Bold characters are often used in headings to make them **stand out** on a page, sometimes ***in conjunction*** with underlining.

Word gives you even more character styles to work with, however. You may also choose to put a phrase in SMALL CAPS to indicate that it stands by itself. If you want, you can use double underline for greater emphasis. If your printer supports other fonts, subscripts, superscripts, or ~~strikethrough~~, Word lets you use those, too.

As you can see, it is easy to overuse character formatting. Most book and magazine publishers avoid using too many formats to prevent the text from looking like an old-time circus poster.

In the Underline drop-down list in the Font dialog box, you can choose from several types of underlining: single (regular), words only, double, and dotted. Here are examples of each:

single underline
words only underline
double underline
dotted underline

Subscripts and superscripts are often useful in scientific or technical papers. When you select Subscript or Superscript, Word changes the font to a smaller size and lowers or raises the letters with respect to the rest of the line.

To experiment with superscripts and subscripts, select the word "superscripts" in the CHARACT file, give the Font command, and select Superscript. Subscripts work the same way as superscripts. Note that Word may not show characters that are superscripted or subscripted past the top or bottom of the line.

If you have a color monitor or color printer, you can take advantage of Word's color formatting for characters. Choose a color from the drop-down list. The colors you can choose are black, blue, cyan, green, magenta, red, yellow, and white. The Auto choice uses the color you assigned for window text in the Control Panel program for Windows; this is usually black.

You can assign colors even if you do not have a color monitor or printer. Simply add the formatting to any text in your document. Word remembers the formatting, even if it cannot show it on the screen or printer. This way, if you later have access to a color device, your document will display and print in color. This is especially useful because color printers are expensive, so you can preview your text on a black-and-white printer but do the final printing on a color printer.

Lesson 43: Introduction to Fonts

Windows has many different alphabet sets you can use in your writing. Each different alphabet set is called a *font*; in other words, each font is a consistent text design. There are many ways to draw the standard alphabet. For instance, you may have very curly letters, very blocky ones, or letters with many intricate details. Actually, a font contains more than just the letters of the alphabet: it contains all the numerals, punctuation marks, and special symbols as well.

If you have not experimented with fonts before, you will find that using different fonts creates different moods for your letters and reports. This section covers the basics of type and fonts; if you are already familiar with fonts, feel free to skim through it.

Some fonts are designed for particular types of printers, but most are designed for all printers. There are two major varieties of fonts: PostScript fonts and TrueType fonts. TrueType is built into Windows, and the fonts that come with Windows are TrueType fonts. In order to use PostScript fonts, you need a PostScript-compatible printer. Most users can ignore the difference between the two and only use TrueType fonts.

Each font can have variations within it. The two major types of variations are characteristics and size. You have already seen the different formatting characteristics that Word can produce, such as underline, italics, and bold. You may have noticed that when you applied a format with the Font command from the Format menu, the letters still appeared on the screen in much the way they were before. That is because using characteristics allows the letters to retain the basic feeling of a font (such as the character widths).

The *size* of a font is defined as the amount of vertical space the letters take on a line. This amount includes the distance the letter goes above and below the *baseline,* which is where the bottoms of most letters line up, as well as the *leading,* which is the space between the very bottom of a letter and the very top of the letter on the next line. Here is an example that shows the elements that make up the size of a font:

Font size is measured in *points*; one point is 1/72 of an inch. For instance, the characters in a 12-point font are 12/72 or 1/6 of an inch high (including the leading that Windows automatically uses).

Each font has many different design characteristics that help define it. For instance, some fonts have *serifs,* which are little decorative lines used to finish off the stroke of a letter. Fonts without serifs are called *sans serif.* Here you can see the difference between serif and sans serif:

Serif

Sans Serif

A font can also have proportional spacing or monospacing. In a *proportional font,* the letters have different widths; for example, the "m" is much wider than the "i". In a *monospace font,* the letters and punctuation are all given the same amount of horizontal space, regardless of width. It is easy\to see the difference:

This is a monospaced font.

This is a proportional font.

Other design characteristics include whether the type has wide or thin lines, whether the characters are chubby or narrow, what kinds of embellishments are used in the letters, and whether the letters can connect (as in a *cursive,* or script, font).

Each font has a name. The following illustration shows some of the fonts available for Windows:

Courier
Helvetica
AvantGarde
Bookman
Times New Roman
NewCenturySchlbk
Palatino
ZapfChancery
Σψμβολ (Symbol)
Ζαπφ∆ιvγβατσ (ZapfDingbats)

You may not have all of these installed, or you may have more, depending on your version of Windows and whether you have installed other Windows programs. There are thousands of fonts available for Windows from many sources. See your Windows documentation for information on installing additional fonts.

Lesson 44: Changing Fonts

You can easily change the font of selected text with the Font command. The Font dialog box has two choices that relate to fonts: one for the font name and the other for the font size. The font names are in alphabetical order. For each font, Word lists only the sizes that are installed with the font, but you can enter any size you want between 4 and 1638 points (although you must enter whole numbers).

You can also change the font from the Formatting toolbar. This prevents you from having to choose the Font command just to change the font or size. The font list on the Formatting toolbar has a very handy feature: instead of just having the alphabetical list of fonts, it also puts the most recently used fonts at the top of the list. Thus, if you change some text from Arial to Helvetica, then select some more text to change, Helvetica appears at the top of the list.

Some fonts come with additional styles other than bold and italic. If the currently selected font has additional styles built into it, those styles are listed in the Font dialog box in the Font Style list. For instance, some fonts have a SemiBold style that appears halfway between regular and boldface in weight.

You can also change the font and size in the Formatting toolbar. The drop-down lists in the Formatting toolbar act the same as those in the Font dialog box.

For practice, select the first sentence of the text in the CHARACT file and give the Font command. Select the AvantGarde font and a size of 9 points. The selected paragraph now looks like this:

Books and magazines often contain a variety of character styles which you can now incorporate into your reports and memos. For example, it is common to italicize foreign words such as *deja vu*, or to use italics to indicate emphasis. Bold characters are often used in headings to make them **stand out** on a page, sometimes ***in conjunction*** with underlining.

You can enter a font size that is not listed by typing a number for your size choice in the Size option of the Font command or in the Formatting toolbar.

Once you have experimented with all of the available character formatting and some of the fonts, print out the file on your printer to see how it looks. You saw briefly how to print in Chapter 2.

Lesson 45: Changing Character Spacing

The second tab in the Font dialog box allows you to change the intercharacter spacing and the vertical position of characters on the line. Figure 7-2 shows the dialog box after you have selected the Character Spacing tab.

The Spacing option lets you specify how much space there is between the selected characters. The choices in the drop-down list are Normal, Expanded, and Condensed; the By option tells Word how much to expand or condense (you can use fractional points in the By option). If you choose Expanded or Condensed, you can specify how many points you want to expand or condense the spacing.

For instance, assume you want to make the letters in "You may" at the beginning of the second sentence of the second paragraph appear slightly farther apart. Select the words, choose the Font command, the Character

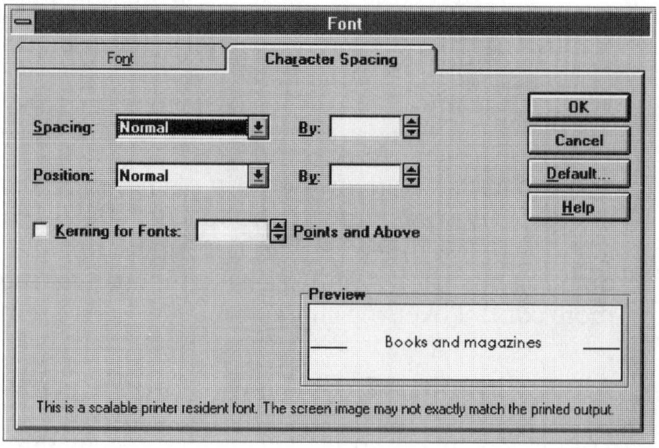

Font
Font | Character Spacing
Spacing: Normal By:
Position: Normal By:
Kerning for Fonts: Points and Above
OK
Cancel
Default...
Help
Preview
Books and magazines
This is a scalable printer resident font. The screen image may not exactly match the printed output.

Font dialog box with Character Spacing tab
Figure 7-2.

Spacing tab, and Expanded. Then enter **2.5** points for the By option. The result is:

Word gives you even more character styles to work with, however. Y o u m a y also choose to put a phrase in SMALL CAPS to indicate that it stands by itself. If you want, you can use double underline for greater emphasis. If your printer supports other fonts, subscripts, superscripts, or strikethrough, Word lets you use those, too.

To see the characters condensed, select Condensed and enter **1.5** points for the By option:

Word gives you even more character styles to work with, however. Youmay also choose to put a phrase in SMALL CAPS to indicate that it stands by itself. If you want, you can use double underline for greater emphasis. If your printer supports other fonts, subscripts, superscripts, or strikethrough, Word lets you use those, too.

Kerning is another method of changing the character spacing. Kerning only happens on particular pairs of letters, and is really only useful on fonts larger than 10 points. Kerning moves two compatibly shaped letters closer. For example, look at the following two paragraphs. The top paragraph has the Kerning for Fonts choice selected, while the second paragraph has it deselected. Notice the difference in the spacing:

We Tell You
We Tell You

Notice how the capital "W", "T", and "Y" in the first line are closed up around the following letters, whereas in the second line they are not as close.

Word automatically kerns for characters at or above the size you specify in the Kerning for Fonts option in the Character Spacing tab.

You can also change the position of characters on a line with the Position choice. This works just like the Spacing choice, but moves the characters up and down. It is different than the Superscript and Subscript choices in that it does not change the font size when it changes the position. This gives you more control over the characters.

Lesson 46: Symbols and Special Characters

Your PC has many special characters that are directly accessible through the keypad at the right of the keyboard. For example, many European languages use umlauts on some vowels, as in "ö". To type this character, press the Num Lock key so that your keyboard indicates it is in Num Lock mode (a small light near the top right of the keyboard will show). Hold down the Alt key, press 0 on the keypad and, while still holding down the Alt key, type the number associated with the letter. In the case of "ö", that number is 246.

It is often difficult to remember all of the key combinations, since each font can have up to 255 characters. To make inserting these characters easier in Word, Microsoft includes the Symbol command from the Insert menu. This command shows you a table of all the characters in the current font, such as those in Figure 7-3. The table is in the order that the characters appear internally in the font.

To insert a particular character in your text, put the insertion point where you want the character, give the Symbol command, choose the font you want from the top of the dialog box, click the desired character, and click

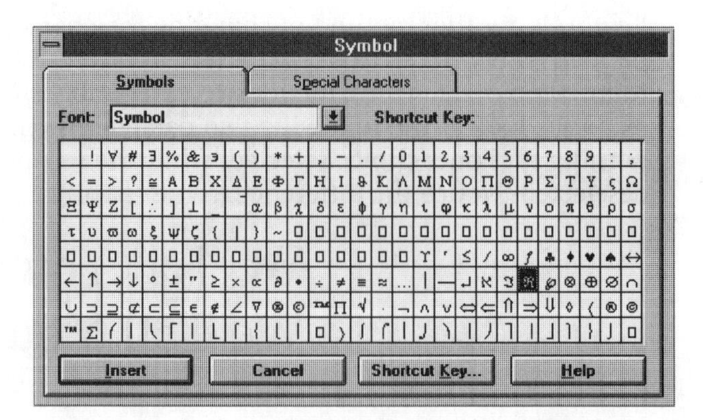

Symbol dialog box
Figure 7-3.

the Insert button. You can insert as many characters as you want this way, since the Symbol window stays open until you close it by choosing the Cancel button.

The Symbol command is particularly useful with the fonts that have symbols in them. As you can see, the Symbol font that is initially shown is made up of symbols that you might want to use in scientific or technical documents. Choosing the symbols with the Symbol command is much easier than looking them up in a table and pressing the corresponding keys.

Although the international characters can also be entered directly by using the Alt key and the keypad, the Symbol command is much more efficient and requires less memorization.

The Special Characters tab of the Symbol dialog box lets you insert other special characters into your document. That dialog box is shown in Figure 7-4. For example, if you want to enter a copyright symbol into your document, select that line in the list and select the Insert button.

Lesson 47: Selecting Character Formatting with the Keyboard

Using the Font command or the Formatting toolbar to change character formatting, fonts, and font sizes can be tedious and slow if you need to give the command over and over. Word allows you to select character formatting and fonts with key combinations to make formatting faster.

Table 7-1 shows the key combinations used to select character formatting, fonts, and font sizes. As before, select the text you want to change, and then use the appropriate key combination.

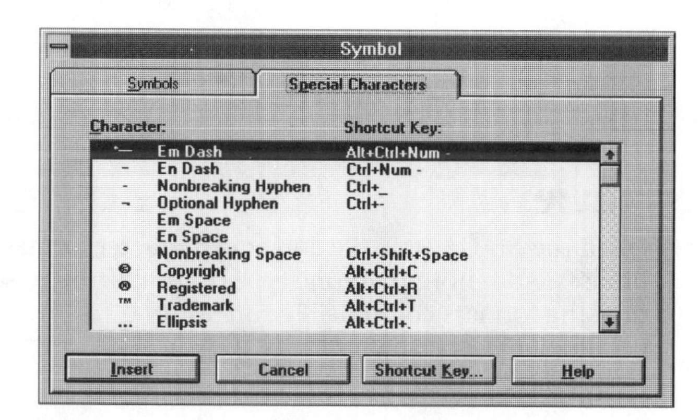

Symbol dialog box with Special Characters tab
Figure 7-4.

Format	Key Combination
Normal for style	Ctrl-Spacebar
Italic	Ctrl-I
Bold	Ctrl-B
Underline	Ctrl-U
Word underline	Ctrl-Shift-W
Double underline	Ctrl-Shift-D
Small caps	Ctrl-Shift-K
All caps	Ctrl-Shift-A
Subscript	Ctrl-=
Superscript	Ctrl-Shift-=
Change font	Ctrl-Shift-F
Change font size	Ctrl-Shift-P
Increase font size	Ctrl-Shift->
Decrease font size	Ctrl-Shift-<

Character Formatting with Ctrl-Key Combinations
Table 7-1.

For example, select the words "Books and magazines" in the CHARACT file; then press Ctrl-I to put the words in italics. To add underlining, press Ctrl-U. The result looks like this:

Books and magazines often contain a variety of character styles which you can now incorporate into your reports and memos. For example, it is common to italicize foreign words such as *deja vu*, or to use italics to indicate emphasis. Bold characters are often used in headings to make them **stand out** on a page, sometimes ***in conjunction*** with underlining.

To make the words normal again, press Ctrl-Spacebar. This key combination removes all formatting that is different from the standard for the current paragraph style (described in Chapter 13).

Review

Open the MAGAZINE file and add character formatting to various words and phrases. Add more than one type of formatting to some words and notice how the formats combine. Be sure to try different fonts and sizes to see how they look when printed.

Word For Windows

C H A P T E R

8 FORMATTING PARAGRAPHS

One of the best ways to make letters and reports look professional is to use consistent formatting throughout the document. For example, if you indent your paragraphs, all paragraphs should probably be indented the same amount.

All headings should also be formatted consistently so the reader can quickly determine what you are saying. In a report, it is often important to see section headings and topics quickly. If your document is organized around an outline, consistently formatting each level of information helps the reader to understand the meaning of the whole document.

Formatting paragraphs in Word is quite easy because Word associates a format with each paragraph. You can specify paragraph formatting when you enter the paragraph, and you can change the formatting later if you change your mind (just as you can with character formatting, described in Chapter 7). Word automatically uses the same format for each paragraph until you tell it otherwise. As a result, all of your text paragraphs will look the same until you give different formatting commands.

Tab stops are a format characteristic that you can set for a paragraph. Word's tab stops work just like those on a typewriter, but with one additional feature: if your writing includes figures and columns, you can use one set of tab stops for one set of columns and a different set for another set of columns.

There are many other interesting paragraph formatting features. For example, you can tell Word that you want a border (such as a solid line) around a paragraph to make headings stand out. Paragraphs can be formatted by using buttons in the ruler and Formatting toolbar, commands from the menus, and Ctrl-key combinations. This chapter includes instructions for all of these methods.

Lesson 48: Basic Formatting for Paragraphs

Word stores a paragraph's format in the mark at the end of the paragraph. You may have noticed that an extra blank character is inserted at the end of each paragraph after the period; this is the paragraph mark that is inserted when you press the Enter key. You can see the paragraph mark by clicking the Show/Hide Paragraph button on the Standard toolbar. This also shows other characters, as described in Chapter 11.

You can choose from a variety of paragraph formatting options. To see a list from which you can make your choices, select any text in the paragraph, or place the insertion point anywhere in the paragraph and give the Paragraph command from the Format menu. For example, load the SAMPLE1 file into Word and put the insertion point in the first text paragraph. Now give the Paragraph command.

The Paragraph dialog box has two tabs. The first tab is for Indents and Spacing, and is shown in Figure 8-1. The second tab is for Text Flow (such as how lines are kept together), and is shown later in this chapter.

In the Paragraph dialog box, as in other Word dialog boxes, you simply choose the characteristics that you want the selected text to have. Since paragraph formatting applies to whole paragraphs, if you have selected only

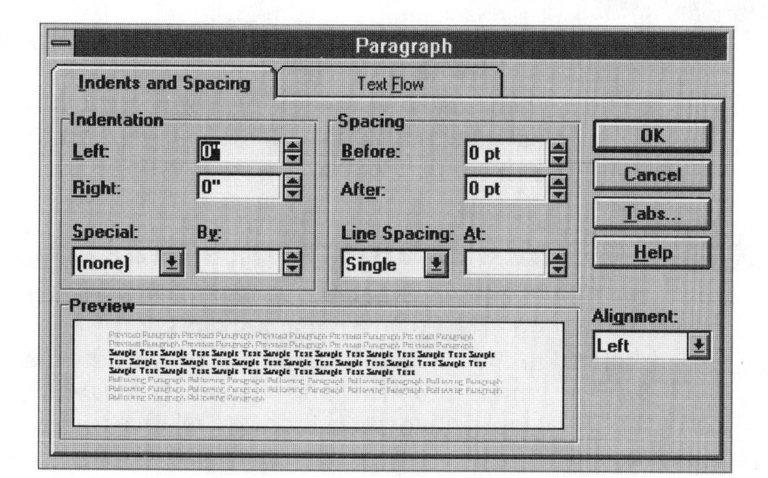

Paragraph dialog box (Indents and Spacing tab)
Figure 8-1.

part of a paragraph or the insertion point is placed in it, Word applies the formatting to that entire paragraph.

Many of the paragraph formatting commands can also be executed with Ctrl-key sequences, like those used in character formatting, as described later in this chapter.

You can set many types of paragraph formatting from the Formatting toolbar. The buttons to the right of the character formatting buttons let you change the alignment and tab stops. These are both described in lessons later in this chapter. The Formatting toolbar looks like this:

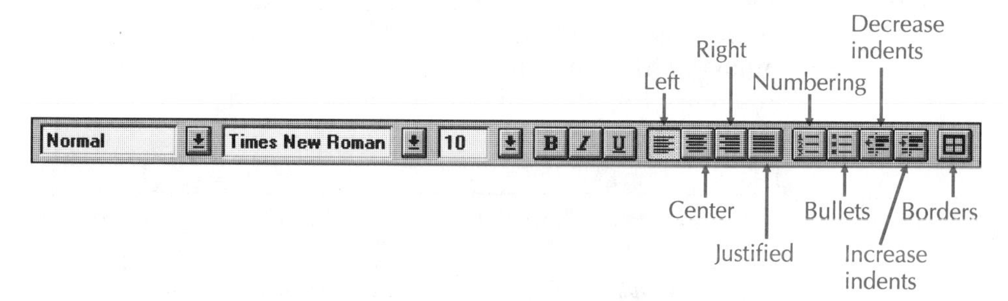

Another way of setting many paragraph formats is directly on the ruler. You can show the ruler with the Ruler command from the View menu:

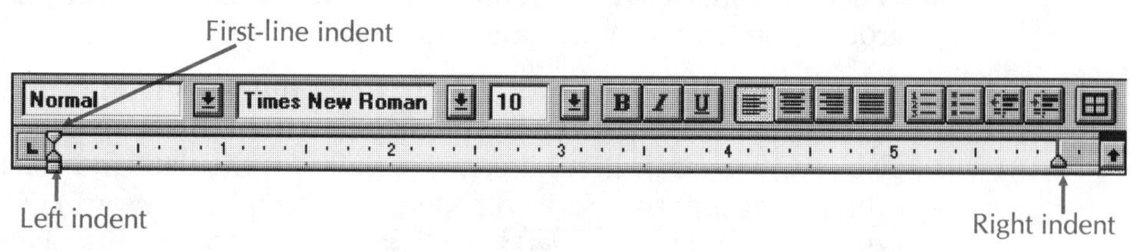

The ruler sets your paragraph indentations and shows where each tab stop is in the selected paragraph. The numbers on the ruler are incremented by inches. When you enter the settings for paragraph indentations, you normally give the position in inches, but you can change this with the Options command described in Chapter 11.

Lesson 49: Indenting Paragraphs

The most common changes that you make to paragraph formats are to the indentation of the whole paragraph and of the first line. These can be changed in the Paragraph dialog box or with the markers for the left indent, first line, and right indent on the ruler. Throughout this section, remember that paragraph indentation is always relative to the margins for the document. Setting the page margins is covered in Chapter 14. You can experiment with paragraph formatting using the SAMPLE1 file.

There are three measurements for indentation: left, right, and first line. The left indentation is applied to all lines, as is the right indentation; these are specified in the Left and Right options in the Paragraph dialog box. The first line indentation is specified in the Special drop-down list. The three choices for the Special option are (none), First Line, and Hanging. Choosing (none) means that you want the first line to line up with the other lines in the paragraph. First Line moves the first line to the right, while Hanging moves the first line to the left.

In common business letters and memos, the first line of each paragraph is indented from the margin by 1/2 inch. To do this, put the insertion point in the first full text paragraph, or select any part of it, choose the Paragraph command from the Format menu, select First Line from the Special drop-down list, and enter **.5**" in the By option:

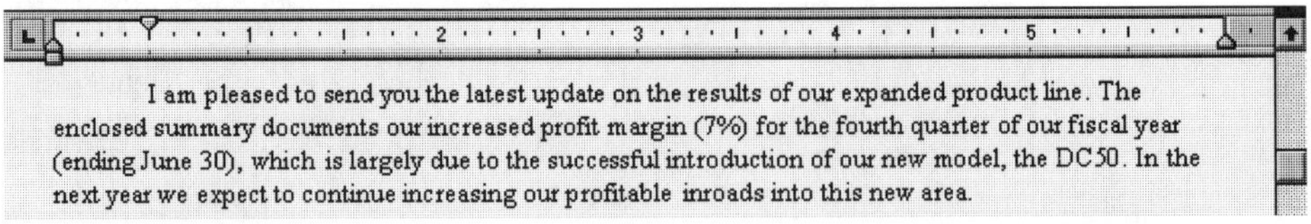

I am pleased to send you the latest update on the results of our expanded product line. The enclosed summary documents our increased profit margin (7%) for the fourth quarter of our fiscal year (ending June 30), which is largely due to the successful introduction of our new model, the DC50. In the next year we expect to continue increasing our profitable inroads into this new area.

When you change the indentation, the text is automatically wrapped around, just as it is when you enter text by typing.

Sometimes you may want to indent an entire paragraph from the left and right margins. This is common for direct quotations in reports. Indenting is also used a great deal in letters, especially for the date and closing. (Remember that these are considered paragraphs in Word.) On a normal typewriter, you use the Tab key or Spacebar to move to the place you want. In

Word, you indicate the indentation from the left margin, and every new line (unless you've selected a different first-line indent) starts there.

To see how this is done, select the date at the beginning of the SAMPLE1 letter, give the Paragraph command, and set the Left option to 3 inches. Figure 8-2 shows the new position of the date. If you move the date, you will probably also want to indent the closing and the name and address.

The measurement indicated by the Special option is relative to the measurement in the left indent indicator. For example, if you want to indent the entire first paragraph 1 inch from the page margin, and indent the first line 1/2 inch beyond that, put the insertion point in the paragraph, set the Left option to 1 inch, choose First Line in the Special option, and set the By option to .5 inch.

> Dear Ms. Richford:
>
> I am pleased to send you the latest update on the results of our expanded product line. The enclosed summary documents our increased profit margin (7%) for the fourth quarter of our fiscal year (ending June 30), which is largely due to the successful introduction of our new model, the DC50. In the next year we expect to continue increasing our profitable inroads into this new area.

If you do not want to indent the first line but want to move the entire paragraph 1 inch from the margin, you set the Special option to (none).

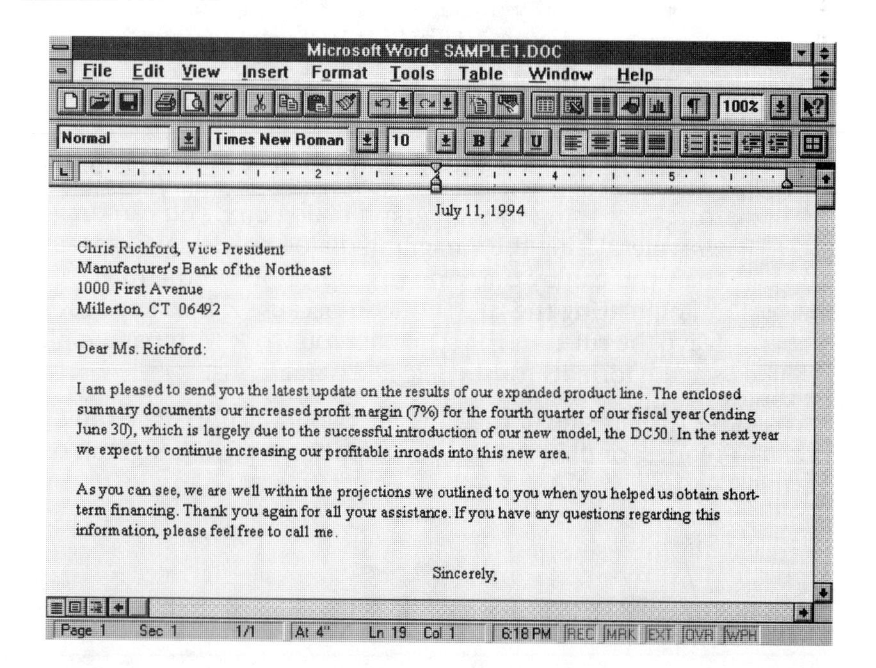

July 11, 1994

Chris Richford, Vice President
Manufacturer's Bank of the Northeast
1000 First Avenue
Millerton, CT 06492

Dear Ms. Richford:

I am pleased to send you the latest update on the results of our expanded product line. The enclosed summary documents our increased profit margin (7%) for the fourth quarter of our fiscal year (ending June 30), which is largely due to the successful introduction of our new model, the DC50. In the next year we expect to continue increasing our profitable inroads into this new area.

As you can see, we are well within the projections we outlined to you when you helped us obtain short-term financing. Thank you again for all your assistance. If you have any questions regarding this information, please feel free to call me.

Sincerely,

Date in SAMPLE1 indented 3 inches
Figure 8-2.

This brings up an interesting situation. What if you want the first line to start to the left of the rest of the paragraph? This format is called a *hanging indent* or an *outdent*. To see how this is formatted, select any part of the first full paragraph, give the Paragraph command, set the Left option to 1 inch, the Special option to Hanging, and By to .5 inch. The result is shown here:

Dear Ms. Richford:

I am pleased to send you the latest update on the results of our expanded product line. The enclosed summary documents our increased profit margin (7%) for the fourth quarter of our fiscal year (ending June 30), which is largely due to the successful introduction of our new model, the DC50. In the next year we expect to continue increasing our profitable inroads into this new area.

It is unlikely that you will change a paragraph's right indentation unless you are also changing the left margin. Experiment by changing the right indent on the first full paragraph to 1 inch:

Dear Ms. Richford:

I am pleased to send you the latest update on the results of our expanded product line. The enclosed summary documents our increased profit margin (7%) for the fourth quarter of our fiscal year (ending June 30), which is largely due to the successful introduction of our new model, the DC50. In the next year we expect to continue increasing our profitable inroads into this new area.

As always, the Undo command removes the effects of the last changes.

Instead of using the Paragraph dialog box, you can drag the indicators on the ruler. Using the Paragraph dialog box lets you specify more exact values than you can by dragging the indicators on the ruler. Also, many users find manipulating the ruler difficult because it is so small. It is, however, useful to leave the ruler on the screen as you work with paragraph formats so you can see the formats for the selected paragraphs.

At the left side of the ruler are two indicators. The top one is for the first line (corresponding to the Special option in the Paragraph command), and the bottom one is for the other lines (the Left option). As you drag either one, Word draws a vertical dotted line to help you see where the indentation will appear.

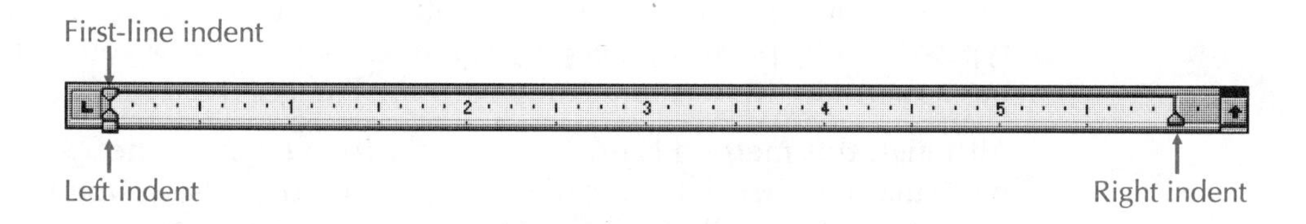

Dragging the small square under the left indent marker drags both markers at the same time.

These indentation choices illustrate the reason that you want to treat related text (like an address) as one paragraph by using newline instead of Enter. Remember that you use newline (Shift-Enter) to go to a new line without starting a new paragraph. When you change the margin with the Paragraph command, all the lines are formatted together since they are in one paragraph.

For example, assume you want to move the lines with Thomas Mead's name, company, and address 3 inches from the left margin. If each line ends in a newline character, you can give just one command for the set of four lines, instead of having to format each line. To see how this works, change the paragraph's breaks to newline characters (if you did not use newline originally) by selecting the blank character at the end of each line:

Replace the paragraph mark with the newline character (Shift-Enter). Notice that the screen looks the same. Do this for all lines in the address except the last. Then select or leave the insertion point in any part of this paragraph, give the Paragraph command, and set the left indent to 3 inches. All of the lines move.

Lesson 50: Line Spacing for Paragraphs

In Word you can modify the number of lines above, below, and inside a paragraph. In the examples you have typed up to this point, you have inserted blank lines between paragraphs as if you were doing so on a typewriter—by pressing the Enter key an extra time. Now you will see how to have Word do this automatically with the Paragraph command.

Although this method is not much easier than pressing the Enter key a particular number of times after each paragraph, it allows you to enter text more consistently. Remember that one of the goals of using Word's formatting features is to make your documents look as consistent as possible. Instead of your having to remember how many lines you want after each paragraph and pressing the Enter key that many times, Word remembers to do this for you in the paragraph format.

To see the utility of using automatic spacing in your document, first eliminate all of the extra blank lines. You can do this by selecting the paragraph mark at the end of each blank line and deleting it. An easier method, however, is to move the insertion point to the beginning of the document, give the Replace command from the Edit menu, enter **^p^p** in the Find What option (to indicate two consecutive paragraph marks), and enter **^p** in the Replace With option (to indicate a single paragraph mark). This is shown in Figure 8-3. Select the Replace All button to change all the instances of the double paragraph mark. Note that you had more than a single paragraph mark after the closing ("Sincerely") so there will still be an extra line. Your document now looks like the one in Figure 8-4.

If you want to insert blank lines between paragraphs, it is usually better to specify them as space after the paragraph, not before. This prevents blank

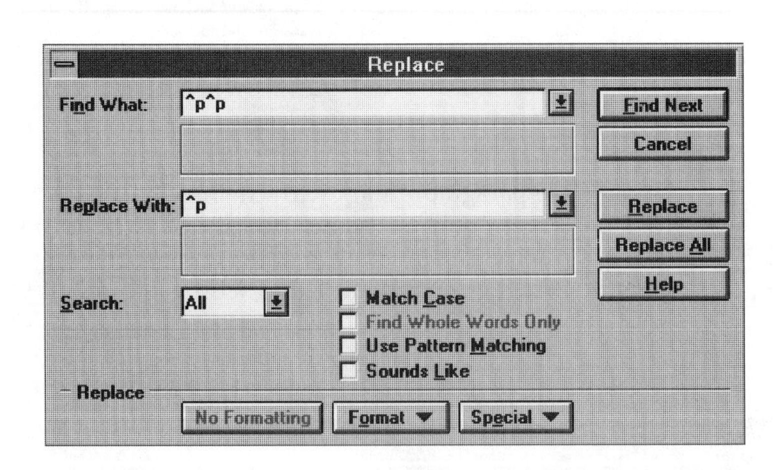

Replacing double paragraph marks with single ones to eliminate blank lines
Figure 8-3.

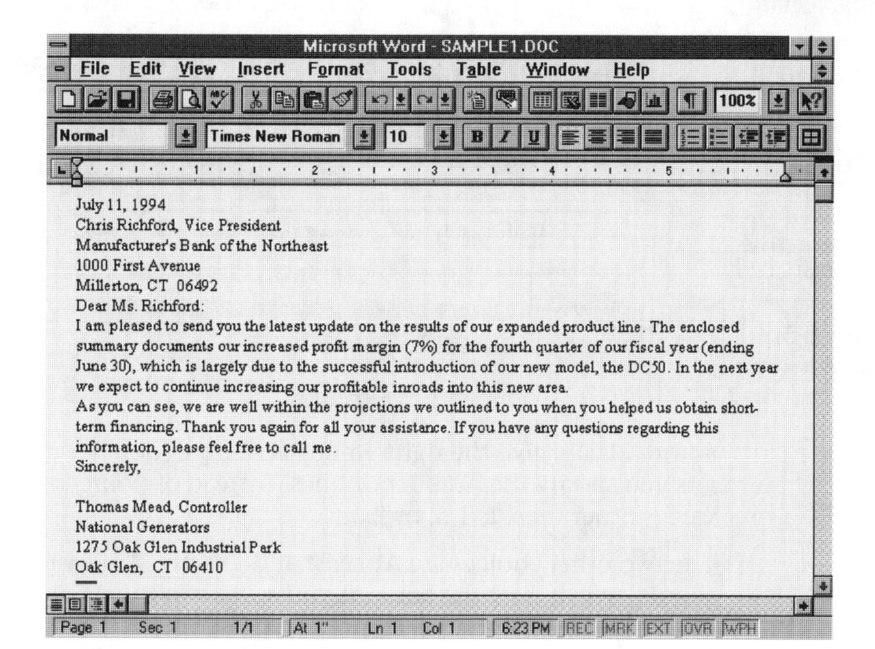

Blank lines removed from SAMPLE1
Figure 8-4.

space from appearing at the top of pages if a paragraph starts there, and it makes general formatting easier. Thus, you should set the After option in the Paragraph dialog box to "12 pt" for the first text paragraph in SAMPLE1.

You can enter the Before or After measurements in many ways. The simplest is to enter the number of lines, since you usually want the space to be related to the size of the characters in the paragraph. You can see the result in the Preview box after pressing the Tab key.

Reformat each paragraph in the letter by selecting the entire document, giving the Paragraph command, and specifying 12 pt. The result looks just like the letter with the extra blank paragraphs. However, the lines between the closing and Thomas Mead's name should be specified as two lines before the name.

The Line Spacing option in the Paragraph command allows you to specify that a particular paragraph be double or triple spaced. To double-space a paragraph, select any part of it and select Double from the Line Spacing drop-down list. The result is shown in Figure 8-5.

Word normally starts with the Line Spacing choice set to Single. This setting lets Word adjust the line height for you if you change font sizes, and gives your text a generally open look. The drop-down list under the Line Spacing option lets you change this. The settings, 1.5 Lines and Double, also

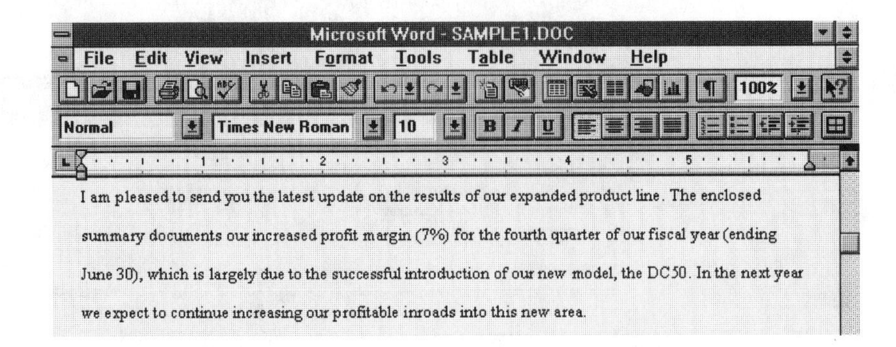

Double-spaced paragraph
Figure 8-5.

automatically give the right amount of space for taller characters. Multiple lets you specify the number of lines (instead of points) in the At option for values other than 1, 1.5, or 2.

The two other choices are At Least and Exactly. At Least indicates that Word should give at least the amount you specify in the At option if the font sizes change or you have superscripts and subscripts within the paragraph. Exactly means that the amount you specify in the At option is used regardless of font size and placement. Be sure to type in the amount in the At choice next to the Line Spacing option.

In Chapter 6, you learned how to copy formatting with the Format Painter button in the Standard toolbar. Note that you must select the paragraph mark for the paragraph you are copying the formats from before you choose the Format Painter button.

To see how to copy paragraph formatting, select the end of a paragraph in which you have changed the line spacing, click the Format Painter button, then select any part of another paragraph. The latter paragraph takes on all of the copied paragraph formats.

Lesson 51: Aligning Paragraphs and Using Keeps

All of the paragraphs you have typed so far have been *left-aligned.* This means that each line begins all the way at the left margin (unless you have indented the paragraph) and is formatted with wordwrap. The right margin is *ragged,* which means that if a word falls a little short of the right margin, it stays there. Books and magazines often use *justified* margins, which means that, in addition to beginning at the left margin, the lines are filled with spaces so that each one ends on the right margin. (For example, this book uses left-justified margins.) Justified text is not only easy to read, it gives a professional look to your reports.

Almost all of your writing will be either left-aligned or justified; however, Word also lets you center each line of text in a paragraph, which is often useful for headings or for text that needs to stand out on a page, such as warnings. For a trendy look, you can even format right-aligned text, which makes the left margin ragged and aligns the right margin. The four types of paragraphs (left-aligned, justified, centered, and right-aligned) are illustrated in Figure 8-6.

Clear the SAMPLE1 file from your screen and enter the text for each example paragraph in Figure 8-6. Then set the alignment by selecting part of the paragraph and either clicking the desired alignment button in the Formatting toolbar or choosing from the Alignment choice in the Paragraph dialog box. For example, to center-align a paragraph with the Formatting toolbar, you would click the second button:

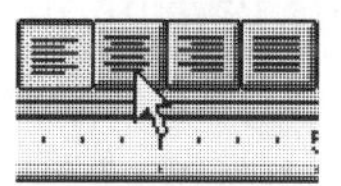

Note that regardless of how you change the alignment, the Formatting toolbar will show the alignment by making the appropriate button look

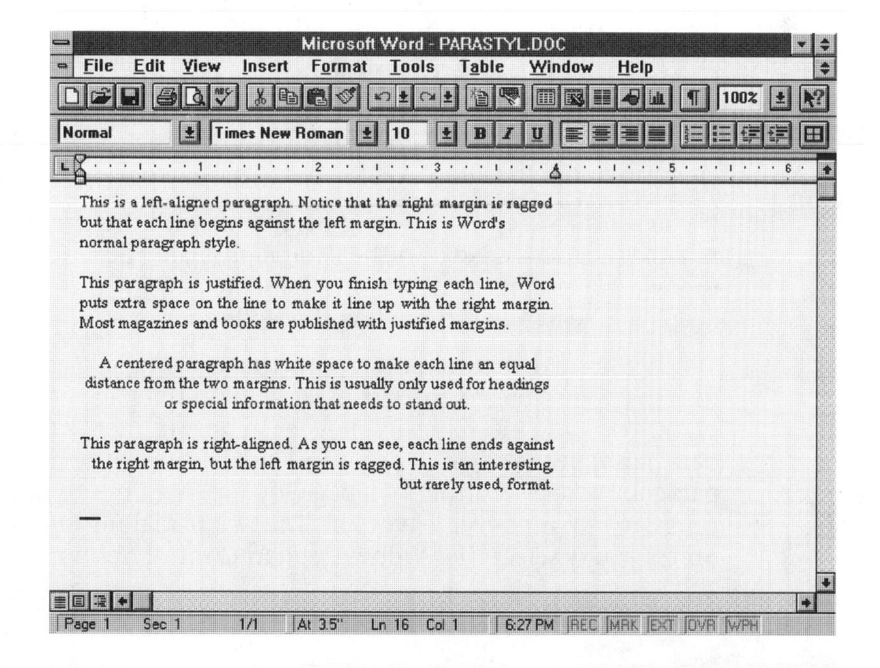

Examples of paragraph alignment
Figure 8-6.

pressed down. Experiment by adding text to the centered and right-aligned paragraphs to see how Word shuffles the characters as you type them.

Remember that you can use the newline character to start a new line without starting a new paragraph. You can use newline together with the centered format to make text stand out on a page. For example, enter the following text as a single paragraph with newline characters:

WARNING!
Do not use this product
without first consulting your physician.

Now center the paragraph from the Formatting toolbar or by choosing Centered from the Paragraph dialog box. The result should look like this:

WARNING!
Do not use this product
without first consulting your physician.

There are times when you want to keep a whole paragraph together—in tables or figures, for instance, where blank space at the bottom of a page is preferable to splitting up the information. To keep a paragraph together, select the paragraph and choose the Keep Lines Together option in the Text Flow tab of the Paragraph dialog box. That dialog box is shown in Figure 8-7.

If you want to keep the selected paragraph with the paragraph that follows it, select Keep with Next in the Paragraph dialog box. This tells Word that the two paragraphs must stay on the same page, which can be useful for keeping a heading with the text that follows it or a caption under a table.

When you write memos and reports that are longer than one page, you may find that Word breaks the last paragraph on the page in an inappropriate place. You can automatically prevent *widows* (only the last line of a paragraph on the top of a page) and *orphans* (only the first line of a paragraph on the bottom of a page) by moving lines to or from a page as necessary. Word never leaves one line of a paragraph stranded on a page unless you deselect the Widow/Orphan Control option.

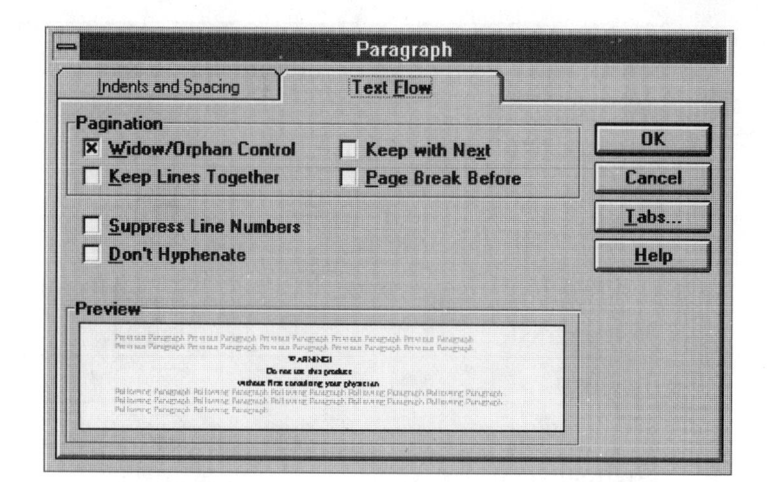

Paragraph dialog box (Text Flow tab)

Figure 8-7.

The Page Break Before option is not used very often. It causes Word to force a page break before the paragraph without your having to put in a page break character. This is described in more detail in Chapter 14.

Lesson 52: Selecting Paragraph Formatting with the Ctrl Key

With direct formatting, you can choose many of the paragraph formats with Ctrl-key combinations, just as you did in Chapter 7 with character formatting. Table 8-1 shows the formats available.

As you can see, some of these key combinations, such as Ctrl-M and Ctrl-Shift-M, do not set an absolute format. Instead, they change the current settings of the paragraph by a small relative amount. You can use these key combinations repeatedly to move the margins.

Lesson 53: Using Tabs

Setting up aligned columns in your text is often one of the hardest chores in word processing. Even if the tabs are set just right, your data often does not fit on the page. Adding a column of text can be nearly impossible. However, if you set the tabs correctly with Word, you will find that making columnar text is very easy. You can set your tab positions either before or after you enter your tabbed text.

There are two methods for creating tables in Word. You can set up tables with tab stops, similar to the way you might on a typewriter, or you can use the table feature. For a short columnar table, using tab stops is quick and

Format	Key Combination
Normal	Ctrl-Shift-N
Increase left indent 1/2 inch	Ctrl-M
Decrease left indent 1/2 inch	Ctrl-Shift-M
1/2-inch hanging indent	Ctrl-T
1 line before	Ctrl-0 (zero)
Left-aligned	Ctrl-L
Justified	Ctrl-J
Centered	Ctrl-E
Right-aligned	Ctrl-R
Single-spaced	Ctrl-1
1 1/2-spaced	Ctrl-5
Double-spaced	Ctrl-2
Remove direct formatting	Ctrl-Q

Paragraph Formatting with Ctrl-Key Combinations
Table 8-1.

easy. However, there are disadvantages to tabs that the table feature overcomes. For example, if you use tab stops, only the far-right column can have text automatically wrap in the column. Also, changing the width of a column is more difficult with tab stops. This chapter shows you how to use tab stops to align columns since they are easier to learn than the table feature. Tables are covered in Chapter 13.

You set and move tab positions with the ruler or the Tabs dialog box. In your text, you skip to the tab stop the same way you do on a typewriter—by pressing the Tab key.

Word comes with a set of tabs defined as the default. These are set to every 1/2 inch. This is useful when you are typing letters and memos that don't require any special tab stops. You can change the setting for the default tab distance in the Tabs command from the Format menu. When you enter a new tab stop, Word automatically erases all the default tabs to the left of that new tab.

Word has four different types of tabs: *left, center, right,* and *decimal.* The type of tab indicates where the text lines up against it. A left tab is like a tab stop on a typewriter: the text begins at the tab stop and continues to the right. A right tab is the opposite of a left tab: the text starts to the left of the tab stop and ends at the tab stop.

The following example should clear up any confusion between these two types of tabs:

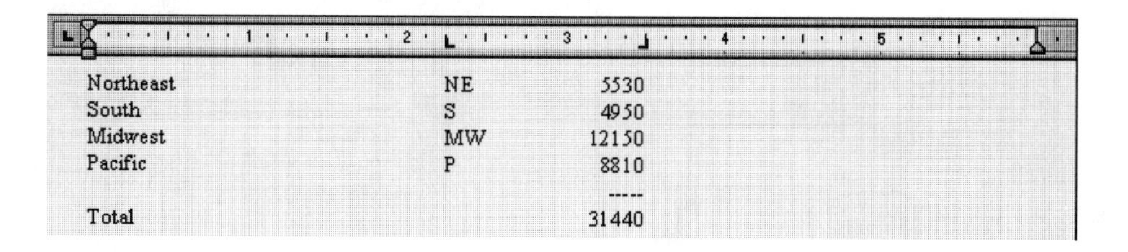

Northeast	NE	5530
South	S	4950
Midwest	MW	12150
Pacific	P	8810

Total		31440

The first tab (at 2 1/4 inches) is a left (normal) tab stop, and the second (at 3 1/2 inches) is a right tab stop. Notice that the numbers in the third column (that is, after the second Tab character) all end at the tab. In general, left tabs are used for text and right tabs are used for numbers. Right tabs are especially useful if you include a sum for the group of numbers because numbers of different lengths then line up correctly.

A center tab causes the text to be centered around the tab stop, much like a centered paragraph. This tab is useful for headings of columns. A decimal tab causes numbers with decimal points to line up with the decimal point on the tab. These two types of tabs are shown here:

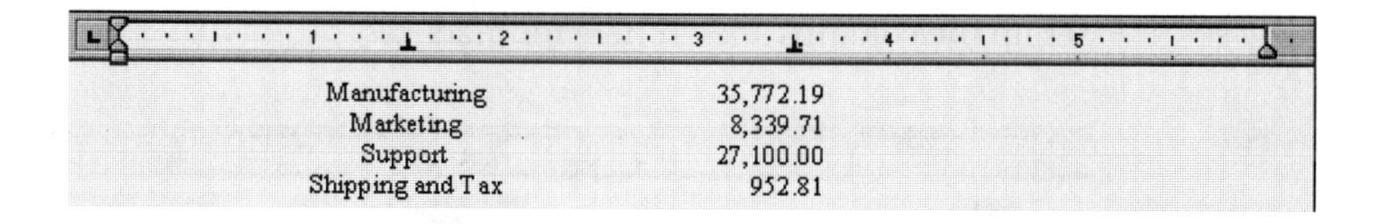

Manufacturing	35,772.19
Marketing	8,339.71
Support	27,100.00
Shipping and Tax	952.81

The tab stop at 1 1/2 inches is a center tab and the tab stop at 3 1/2 inches is a decimal tab.

Lesson 54: Setting Tabs

Setting tabs on the ruler is fairly easy. You can select the type of tab you want by clicking on the tab alignment button at the left of the ruler:

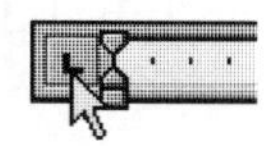

Click to change the tab type, then place the pointer in the lower part of the ruler and click where you want the tab to be set. You can repeat this for as many tabs as you want. The four types of tabs are

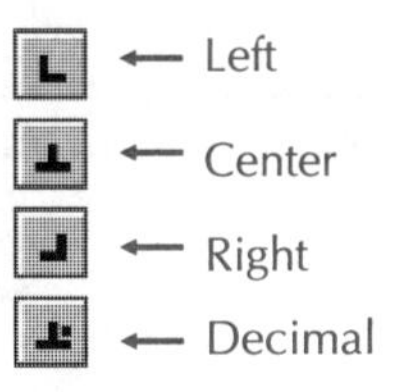

For example, to set a right tab at 2 1/4 inches, click the tab alignment button on the left side of the ruler until it shows the right tab stop and then point to the space between 2 and 2 1/2 inches in the ruler and click:

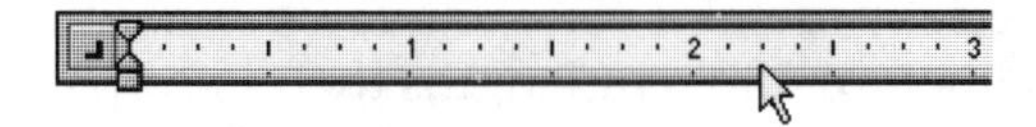

You can move a tab setting on the ruler line by dragging it around. For example, drag the tab you just set to 2 1/2 inches. To delete a tab stop, drag it down off the ruler.

Set up the columns shown here for practice:

Terrence	88	Regular	88.00
Connors	150	Senior	125.00
Long	130	Regular	130.00
Yee	50	New	67.50

The second column is right-aligned, the third column is left-aligned, and the fourth column is decimal-aligned. (If you need help setting this up, the three tab stops are a right-aligned tab at 2 1/4 inches, a left-aligned tab at 3 inches, and a decimal-aligned tab at 4 1/2 inches.)

You can also specify a tab by giving the Tabs command from the Format menu or selecting the Tabs button in the Paragraph dialog box.

Double-clicking a tab stop in the ruler also brings up this dialog box. The Tabs dialog box looks like this:

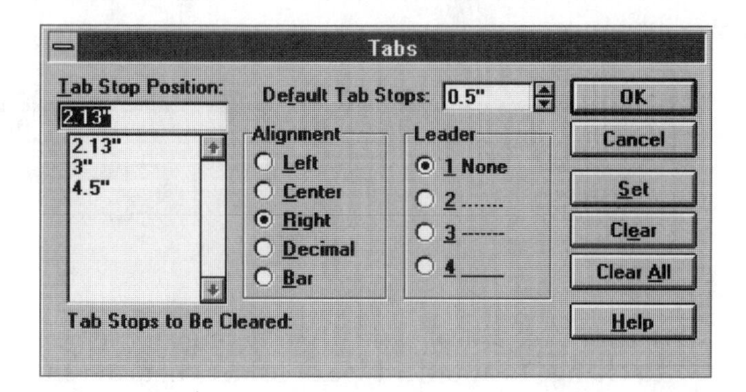

In the Tabs dialog box, select a type of tab, and then enter the desired location in the Tab Stop Position choice. You can use this choice to fine-tune the position of a tab. For example, if you have a tab set at 1 inch and you want it at 1 1/8 inches, select the tab stop on the ruler and type **1.125** in the Tab Stop Position choice.

To change the type of a tab, select the tab from the list at the left of the Tabs dialog box and select a different button in the Alignment choices. If you wish, you can clear all the tabs you have set for this paragraph by opening the Tabs dialog box and selecting the Clear All button. Be sure to select all the paragraphs you want to work on before changing the tabs.

You may have noticed that there is a fifth type of tab in the Tabs dialog box called "Bar". This is not, in fact, a tab stop, but a method for drawing a vertical bar at a particular position. This is a bit confusing because it does not interact with the tab character. However, it is useful for drawing a vertical line in a table that is created with the Tab key.

Lesson 55: Using Leader Characters

The Leader choice in the Tabs dialog box is one of Word's advanced features that is incredibly easy to use. Many columnar lists, such as financial summaries and tables of contents, often use characters to connect the columns of information across the page. These characters, usually dots, are called *leader characters* because they lead to the text at the next tab stop. Unless you specify otherwise, Word does not use a leader character.

For practice, change the first tab stop in the previous example to include a dot leader character. With the Tabs dialog box open, click the tab stop on the ruler, and then choose "2...." from the Leader section. The columns look like this:

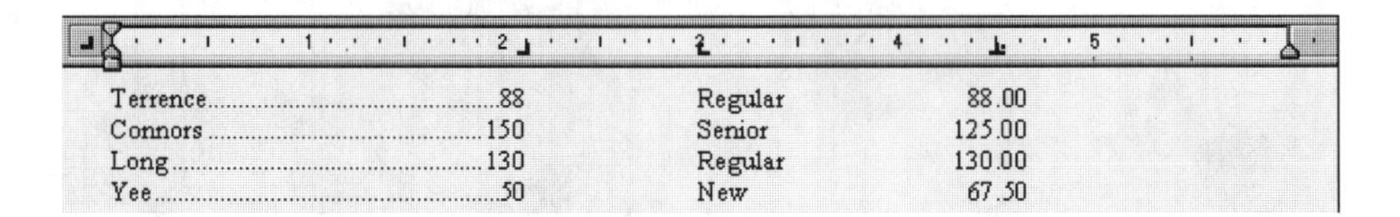

Terrence..	88	Regular	88.00
Connors..	150	Senior	125.00
Long..	130	Regular	130.00
Yee..	50	New	67.50

This is a great deal easier than typing all the periods yourself. It is also easy to change to another type of leader character in a column since you don't have to erase the old characters and type the new characters for each entry. For example, try changing the leader character to dashes or underscores.

Lesson 56: Working with Columns of Tabs

If you are editing a columnar list, you may want to move or delete a column of information. For example, you may want to switch two columns or remove a column in the middle of your list. To make such a move you need a way of selecting a single column.

There may be other times when you want to add a column in the middle of some other columns. In this case, you need to add a new column of tab characters.

The procedure for selecting a column of text with the mouse is as follows:

1. Put the insertion point at one corner of the column. Usually, you should select a character in the upper-left corner:

Terrence	88	Regular	88.00
Connors	150	Senior	125.00
Long	130	Regular	130.00
Yee	50	New	67.50

2. Hold down the Alt key.
3. Extend your selection by holding down the Alt key and dragging to the lower-right corner of the column:

Terrence	88	Regular	88.00
Connors	150	Senior	125.00
Long	130	Regular	130.00
Yee	50	New	67.50

If you are editing a column made with tabs, be sure to include the tab characters that are before or after the column in your selection.

You can select more than one column at a time with this method. Word simply treats everything you select as a single column. (Note that you can select any text, not just text that is arranged in columns, in this method.)

Once you have selected a column of text, you can treat it as you would any other text. You can cut it, copy it to the Clipboard, delete it, add character formatting to it, and so on.

To select a column with the keyboard, put the insertion point at one corner of the desired selection, press Ctrl-Shift-F8, and use the keys that move the insertion point to extend the selection.

For example, to switch the positions of two columns, use the steps you would to move columns. First select the desired column, give the Cut command, move the insertion point to the first character of the column you want to paste in front of, and give the Paste command. If you want to move one column of several over to the far right, you must first make sure that in each line, the right column has a Tab pressed before the Enter or newline. If you are showing formatting characters, the tab character looks like a small right arrow. Then (having already cut the column you want to move) move the insertion point in front of the top paragraph or newline mark and give the Paste command.

Lesson 57: Highlighting Paragraphs with Borders and Shading

Word lets you emphasize a paragraph by surrounding it with a border or by placing a bar above it, below it, or next to it. You have a wide selection of borders and bars. To add a border to a paragraph, select any part of the paragraph and give the Borders and Shading command from the Format menu. Word displays the dialog box shown in Figure 8-8, which lets you place lines and select the distance from the text, the line type, and shading. The second tab in the dialog box lets you specify shading, as described later in this lesson.

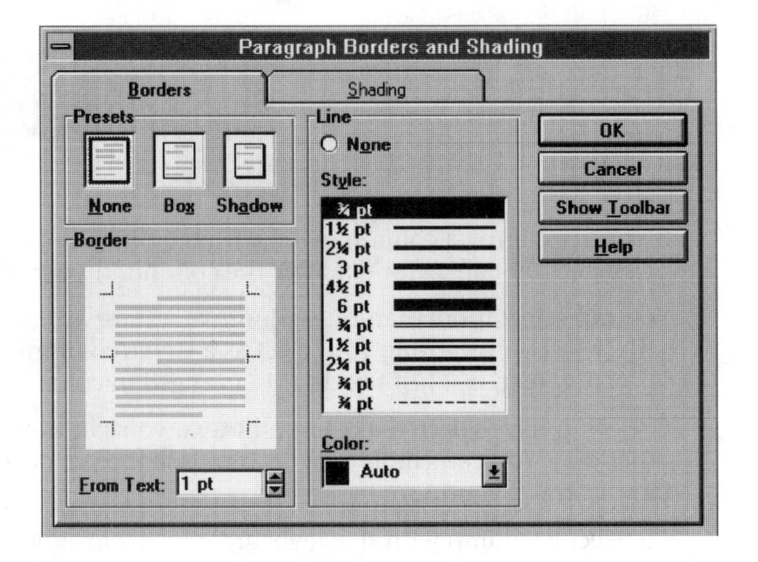

Borders tab in the Paragraph Borders and Shading dialog box
Figure 8-8.

You can add lines to the top, bottom, left, and right of a paragraph; if you select all four, you put the paragraph in a box. To select a line to add, click between the appropriate guides in the Border box. To deselect all the lines, click None in the Presets section. You can also choose from the three preset border types (no border, a simple box, or a shadowed box).

For example, to add a border to the left side of the paragraph, you would click at the left side of the box:

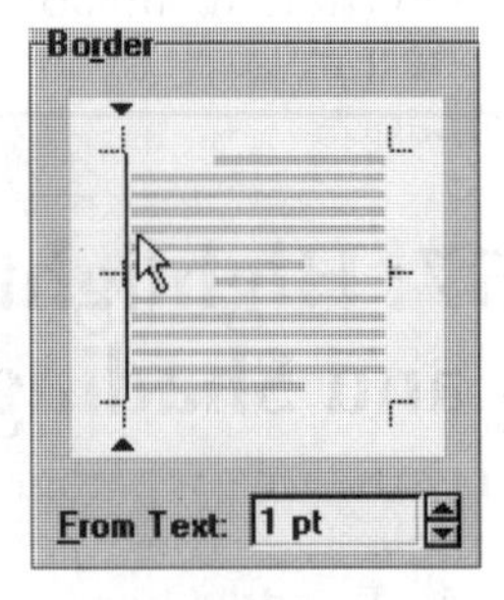

You can also add lines between paragraphs. If you select two paragraphs and double-click outside the guides, Word puts both paragraphs in a single box. However, if you want a line between the boxes, click between the center guides:

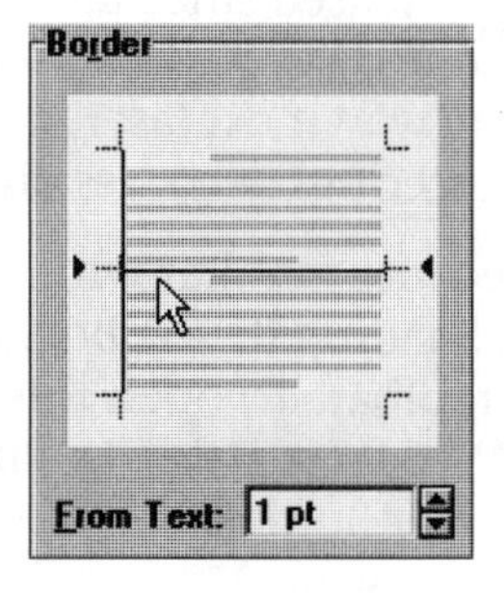

Each line can have a line style that consists of the thickness of the line, whether it is single or double, and whether it is dotted. These are selected from the choices in the Line options. You can also specify a color for the lines from the Color choices.

The Shading tab changes the dialog box and lets you select an amount of shading to put behind the paragraph. The Shading dialog box is shown in Figure 8-9.

To specify a shading, select a pattern from the scrolling list. The list is quite extensive. The first choices are simply gray patterns at various densities, while patterns farther down have stripes and grids. You can also specify the foreground and background colors for the shading.

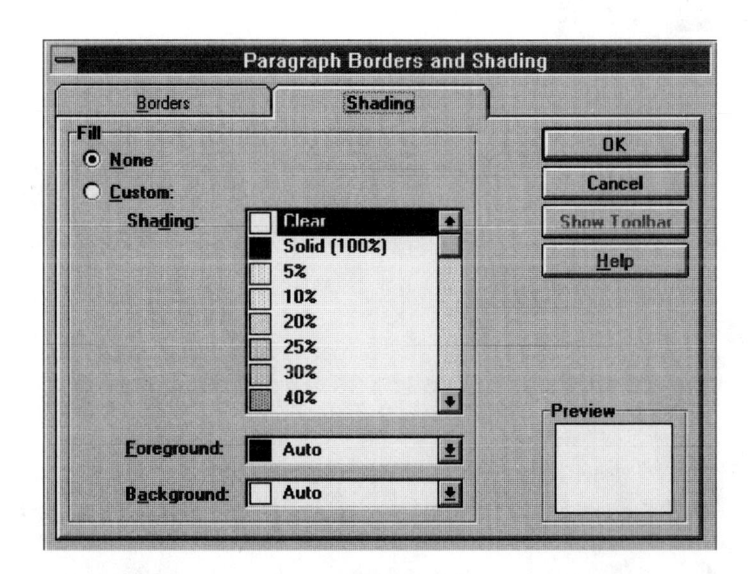

Shading tab in the Paragraph Borders and Shading dialog box

Figure 8-9.

Shading is rarely used since almost any level of shading makes it hard to read the text when it is printed, particularly on dot matrix or inkjet printers. Because of the way most laser printers are designed, any choice other than 10 or 12.5 percent gray comes out much too dark.

Once you become familiar with adding borders, you may not need to use the Borders and Shading dialog box. Instead, you can quickly add borders using the Borders toolbar. To open this toolbar, click the Borders button at the right side of the Formatting toolbar or use the Toolbars command in the View menu. The Borders toolbar looks like this:

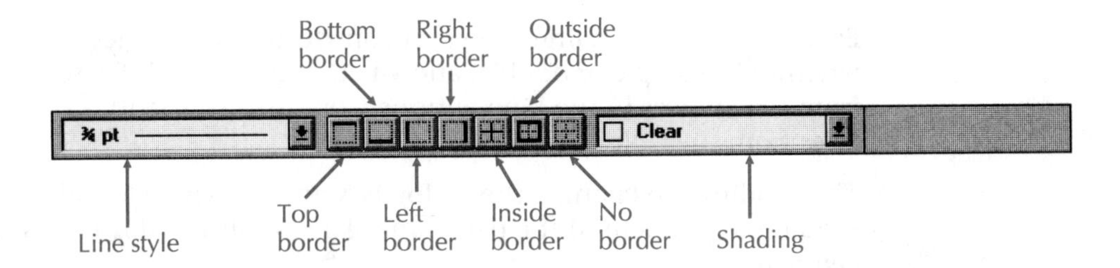

The first four buttons add the specified outside border. The fifth button adds an inside border and the sixth adds an outside border (this is the same as the four buttons combined). The last button clears any buttons that are set.

Review

Add paragraph formatting to your MAGAZINE file. Experiment with combinations of first-line and left indentations.

Add a table to your MAGAZINE file (if you already typed in a table, make sure it has a single tab character between each column). Select the table and change the tab settings to find a result that makes the information in the table clear. Finally, add borders to the table.

Word For Windows
Word For Windows
Word For Windows

CHAPTER

PROOFING YOUR DOCUMENTS

Much of the time you spend writing is taken up by editing and formatting your document. Good writers know that you also need additional help in making your document look just right. Word includes many tools that let you improve your writing and make it look as good as possible on the page.

Because most people are not perfect spellers, Word has included an easy-to-use spelling checker that works closely with the other parts of Word.

The thesaurus that comes with Word allows you to find synonyms for words and to look at the many meanings a word can have.

Word also has a grammar checker that can find common mistakes in your writing. It looks for things such as overused phrases and incorrect tense.

Word also includes a hyphenation program to help your text look better when printed. Justified text looks significantly better if the long words in the text are hyphenated to reduce the amount of white space between words. Of course, inserting hyphens yourself is tedious. The hyphenation feature frees you from the task of putting hyphens in the words that need them, and it uses the same dictionary that the spelling checker uses.

Word's proofing tools work in many languages. The default is English (US) for copies of Word sold in the United States. If you have text that is in other languages and want to check its spelling, you must buy additional dictionaries.

To specify what language you want to proof in, you select the text, give the Language command from the Tools menu, and specify the language. The Language dialog box looks like this:

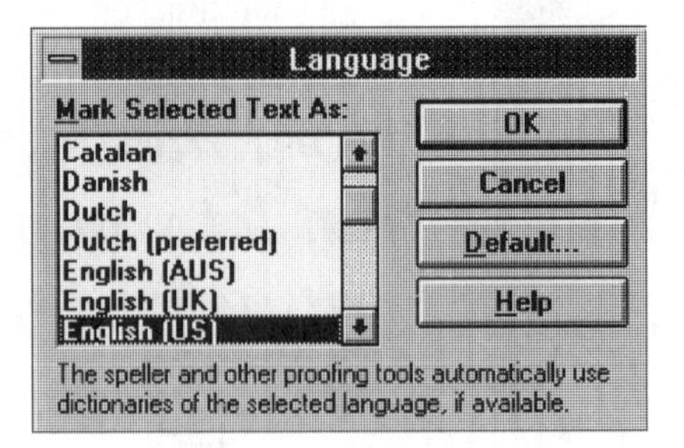

You can also change the default language in this command by selecting the language and then selecting the Default button.

If you want to prevent some text from being looked at by any of the proofing tools, select it and choose "(no proofing)" from the top of the list in the Language dialog box. This is useful if you have text that you know will never be found in any dictionary, such as purposely misspelled words or technical terms that you don't want proofed.

Lesson 58: Introduction to Spelling Checking

The second most useful program for most writers is a spelling checker. (The first, of course, is the word processor.) Even if your spelling is nearly flawless, it is likely that your proofreading is not, and a single spelling mistake in a report or memo can have a very negative effect.

The idea behind spelling checkers is fairly simple. When you run a spelling checker, it reads your document and compares the words in it against a list of all the words it knows. It then tells you the words that it does not recognize. You can correct the words or, if they are proper words that the spelling checker does not know, add the words to the dictionary so the spelling checker recognizes them the next time.

Of course, even a good spelling checker is not perfect; you will probably use words that it does not know, and it will indicate that you have misspelled them. Most dictionaries that come with spelling programs do not include proper names, so a program may think you misspelled something if, for example, it sees the name "Mendez" in your text. Also, spelling checkers cannot spot proper words that are used incorrectly in context, as in "I son the race."

The dictionary in Word's spelling checker is quite comprehensive. This makes it unlikely that it will not recognize a correctly spelled word. It is easy to "teach" the spelling checker new words, such as proper names or obscure words.

If Word thinks you have misspelled a word in your document, it can offer help by checking through its dictionary and making a few suggestions for what you intended. For example, if you have the misspelled word "postion" in your document, Word guesses "position" and "positron."

The spelling checker uses two types of dictionaries when it checks a document. It searches these dictionaries invisibly, so you need not keep track of the names.

The *main* dictionary contains many common words. It comes with the Word for Windows. You cannot add words to this dictionary or change it in any way.

Custom dictionaries are for words that do not appear in the main dictionary but are still valid. You can tell the speller to check one or more custom dictionaries. You create custom dictionaries with the Options button in the Spelling dialog box. Most people have just one custom dictionary that contains all their additional words, although you might want to keep more than one if you have different types of specialized words for different types of writing.

As it checks your document, Word lists the unrecognized words (those not found in the dictionaries) one at a time. For each word, you have the following choices:

- Add the word to one of the custom dictionaries.
- Correct the word in your document by typing the correct spelling or by selecting one of the guesses.
- Ignore the word, indicating that you know it is not recognized but don't care to add it to the custom dictionary.

The spelling checker is easy to use. If you are creating a large document, you may want to check the spelling after you enter, but before you edit, all the text, and again just before you print the text.

Lesson 59: Using the Spelling Checker

Before you give the Spelling command, you should set up the spelling checker. Give the Options command from the Tools menu, and select the Spelling tab. Other tabs in the Options command are described in more detail in Chapter 11. You see the dialog box shown in Figure 9-1. This is the same as the Options button in the Spelling dialog box.

The Always Suggest option tells Word you want it to always make suggestions when it finds a word that it does not recognize. This is handy, but it also slows down the process of spelling checking, particularly on slower PCs, PCs with slower hard disks, or PCs on networks where the dictionaries are kept on central servers. If you find that most of the words that are not recognized are words you are adding to a custom dictionary, you should probably not select this option.

The From Main Dictionary Only option tells Word to only look in the main dictionary for suggested words. This is faster than looking in custom dictionaries, but it limits the suggested words to those that Word already knows. If your custom dictionary has many entries for specialized words or

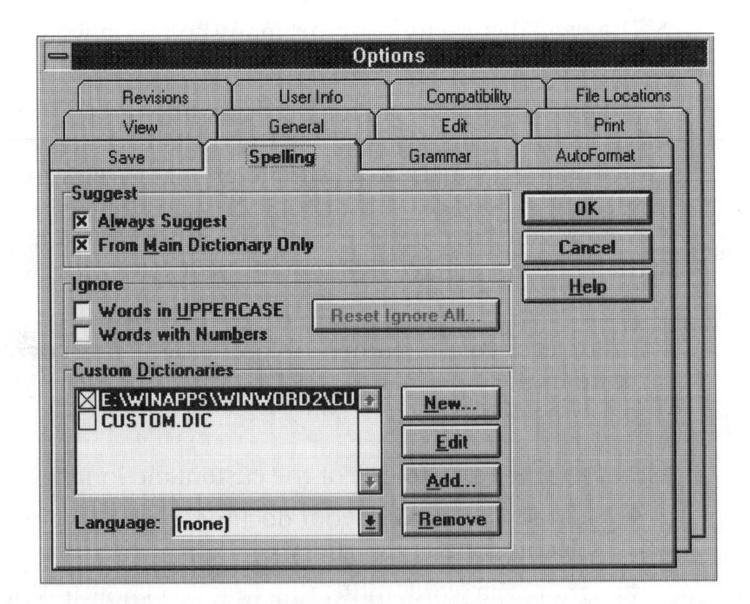

Spelling options
Figure 9-1.

for proper nouns that are not found in the main dictionary, you will probably want to deselect this option.

The Ignore choices tell Word to ignore certain types of words when it is checking. If you have many acronyms in all uppercase letters, you may want Word to ignore them (although it is safer to add them to a custom dictionary instead). If you have many words that include numbers, such as in technical literature, you may want to select Words with Numbers for those words to be ignored. The advantage of leaving Words with Numbers deselected is that you may have accidentally forgotten to put a space between a word and the following number, such as "with4" instead of "with 4".

The Custom Dictionaries option lets you choose which custom dictionaries you want to use. To create a new custom dictionary, select the New button and give a filename. To use a custom dictionary that has already been created (such as a companywide custom dictionary on a network), select the Add button and specify its location. To choose a custom dictionary to be used, select it in the list. You can have more than one custom dictionary selected.

When you are ready to check the spelling of a document, open the document (in this case, SAMPLE1), and give the Spelling command from the Tools menu or click the Spelling button in the Standard toolbar. Word displays the dialog box shown in Figure 9-2.

Word automatically starts checking your document and shows the first word it does not recognize. If the Always Suggest choice in the Options dialog box is on, you also see a list of suggestions.

You now have many choices:

- If you want to change the word in your document to something else, type the new word in the Change To option. Word puts the first suggestion in the list in the Change To option by default, but you can type over that if you want. You can also select another suggestion from the list, and Word automatically puts that in the Change To option.
- Ignore ignores this word one time. Use this if the word is correct in its context but you do not want to add it to a custom dictionary.
- Ignore All causes the Spelling command to ignore this word throughout the document. This differs from the Ignore button in that Word won't stop if it sees the word again.
- The Change choice changes the word in your document to the one in the Change To option one time.
- Change All causes the Spelling command to change the word to the one in the Change To option automatically if it comes to the misspelled word again.

- ✦ The Add choice adds the word to the custom dictionary shown in the Add Words To option. You select the custom dictionary you want to add to in that drop-down list.
- ✦ The Suggest button is active only if the Always Suggest choice is turned off. If you don't have automatic suggesting, use the Suggest button each time you want Word to guess the misspelled word.
- ✦ The AutoCorrect button adds the misspelling and the correction to Word's AutoCorrect list. The AutoCorrect feature, described in Chapter 19, helps prevent spelling mistakes as you type.
- ✦ The Options button brings up the Options dialog box with the spelling settings showing.
- ✦ Undo Last reverses the last change you made. This is useful if you clicked Change instead of Ignore or Add for the previous word and realized that the word was valid or that the word that was suggested wasn't right.
- ✦ Cancel stops the spelling checker.

After you take care of the first word that was not in the dictionary, the spelling checker quickly jumps to the next one. This keeps happening until you reach the end of the document or you select the Cancel button.

The first few times you run the spelling checker, you will probably find yourself adding a slew of words to the custom dictionary. You will probably add dozens of proper names (including street and city names) as well as jargon from your industry. Within a week or so, you will add fewer words to the custom dictionary and will mostly be finding actual spelling mistakes.

You can edit a custom dictionary by choosing the Edit button in the Options dialog box. Custom dictionaries are just Word documents, so you can use the standard editing actions on them.

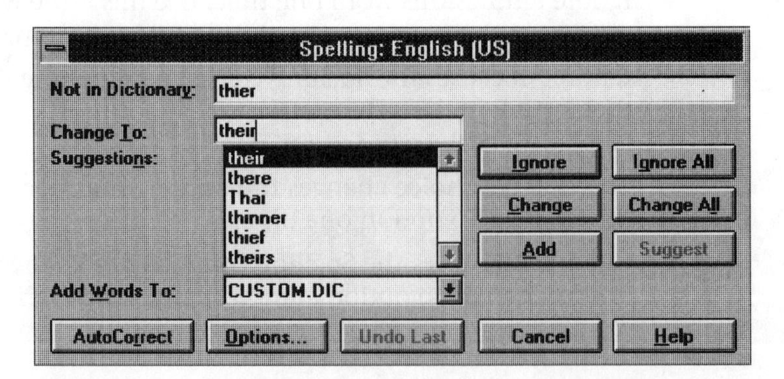

Spelling dialog box
Figure 9-2.

Lesson 60: Using the Thesaurus

As you are writing, you may get stuck trying to come up with just the right word for a particular thought. The thesaurus can be helpful in this case.

If you want to find a synonym for a particular word in your document, select the word and give the Thesaurus command from the Tools menu. The dialog box shows the synonyms for that word. If you select the word "pleased", you see this dialog box:

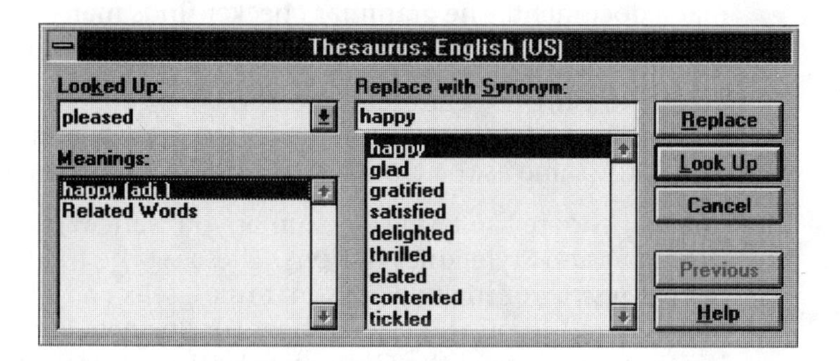

To replace the word in your document with one of the choices in the Replace with Synonym list on the right, select the new word and select the Replace button. For example, select the word "delighted" in the window and select Replace. Word puts that word in your document in place of "pleased".

If you see a word in the list at the right that seems close but not exact, select it and select the Look Up button. This brings up a list of synonyms that may be closer to what you want. For example, select "elated" and select the Look Up button; you see the choices shown here:

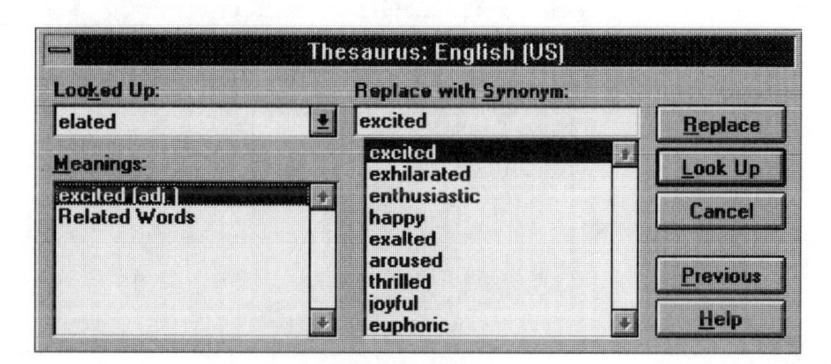

Some words have many meanings. If the word you have selected has more than one meaning, the meanings are listed in the Meanings list on the left. At the bottom of this list might also appear "Related Words" and/or "Antonyms". If you select either of these, the synonyms list on the right is replaced by a list of words with similar meanings (related words) or words meaning the opposite (antonyms).

Lesson 61: Grammar Checking

Spelling errors are often the easiest to pick out in writing. However, grammar errors such as the wrong verb tense ("I will ran the race") and poor writing style ("I hope you don't find nothing wrong with the new tool") can also mar a document. The grammar checker finds many writing mistakes in your document and even suggests how to change them to sound better.

Before running the grammar checker, it's a good idea to check the grammar settings in the Options command in the Tools menu, shown in Figure 9-3. This is the same as the Options button in the Grammar dialog box.

You can choose the level of grammar you want Word to check in the Use Grammar and Style Rules options. These set the rules that are chosen. To further restrict or include grammar rules, select a type of style rules from the list. Generally, you will either select For Business Writing or For Casual Writing. Next, select the Customize Settings button. You see the dialog box shown in Figure 9-4.

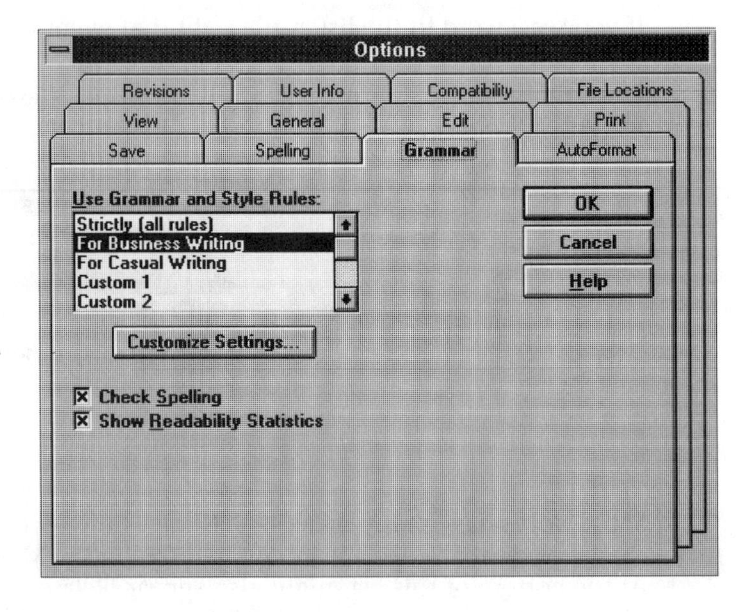

Grammar options
Figure 9-3.

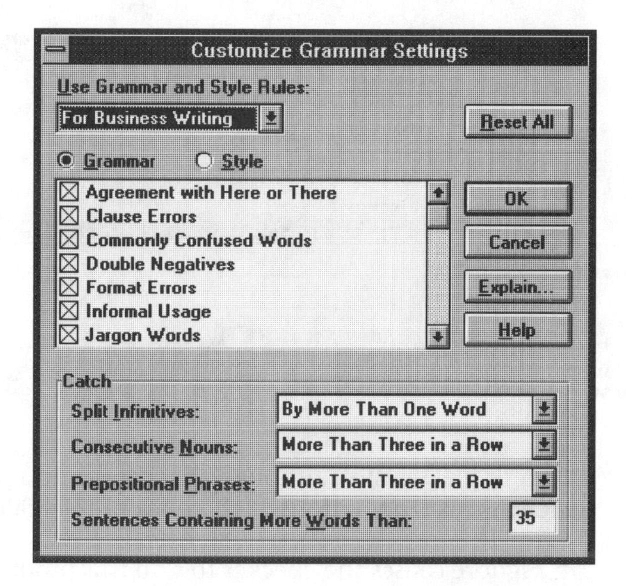

Custom grammar settings
Figure 9-4.

There are two "rule groups" at the top of the dialog box. The first rule group is for grammatical mistakes. The second rule group is for style—that is, words and phrases that are technically correct but can be improved. You can turn off any of the rules by deselecting them in the list. You would want to turn off a rule only if you find that the grammar checker stops at too many instances of that rule in your document and you generally ignore the checker's advice.

The Catch options specify how far the grammar checker should look to catch split infinitives, consecutive nouns, and multiple prepositional phrases. The default settings are usually fine. When you have specified all the grammar settings in this dialog box, select OK.

The Show Readability Statistics choice lets you see a summary of your document after you check the grammar. Some people find this information interesting, but it is generally of little value in improving your writing.

To start checking a document, put the insertion point at the place where you want to start, such as before the first text paragraph of a letter, and give the Grammar command from the Tools menu. Word checks the spelling as it checks the grammar so it can look for usage mistakes. When the checker finds a possible mistake, you see a dialog box like the one shown in Figure 9-5.

In this example, the grammar checker questions whether you want to use the passive voice in "I am pleased". It is often better to use the active voice,

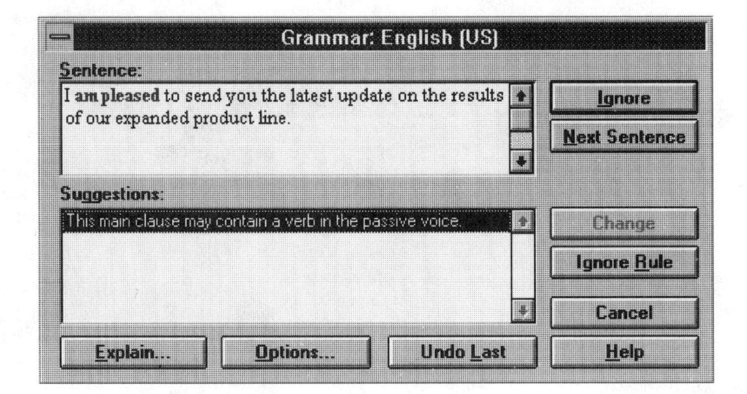

Grammar dialog box
Figure 9-5.

as in "It pleases me", although that sounds too personal in a business letter such as this. The buttons at the right of the dialog box show your choices:

- ✦ Ignore causes the checker to skip this problem in this one instance.
- ✦ Next Sentence indicates that you know there are problems with the sentence that you will correct later, so the checker should ignore the entire sentence.
- ✦ Change corrects the phrase in question to the suggested phrase, if there is one. In this case, there is no suggestion, so the button is not available.
- ✦ Ignore Rule causes the checker to skip this type of error throughout the document.
- ✦ Cancel stops the grammar checking process.
- ✦ The Explain button brings up a dialog box that tells a bit more about the suggestion. In this case, the dialog box shows the following:

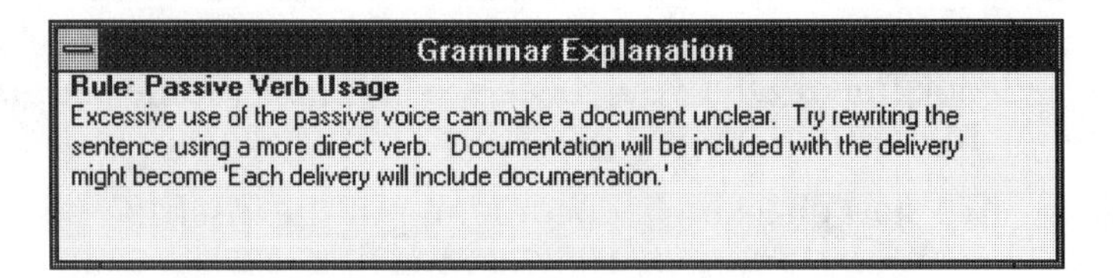

- ✦ The Options button brings up the Options dialog box with the grammar settings showing.

✦ Undo Last reverses the last change you made. This is useful if you clicked Change instead of Ignore for the previous sentence and realized that you don't like the change.

When you have finished checking the document, the grammar checker displays the dialog box shown in Figure 9-6 if you have chosen the Show Readability Statistics choice.

Although the grammar checker can help find problems in your writing, you should certainly not rely on it. The rules in it are general and are not a replacement for your spending time editing your writing or finding an editor to help you. Using Word's grammar checker may make your writing sound stilted or overly formal. For documents where writing is not critical, you will find the grammar checker to be a good quick guide to finding problems.

Lesson 62: Hyphenation

You may think that there is only one kind of hyphen, but Word has three: normal, nonbreaking, and optional hyphens. Each time you hyphenate a word, you can indicate the kind of hyphen you want so that wordwrap produces the effect you want.

A *normal* hyphen is one that is always printed. For example, the phrase "self-reliant" contains a normal hyphen since you always want the hyphen to appear in the printed text.

Readability Statistics

Counts:	
Words	145
Characters	725
Paragraphs	7
Sentences	6
Averages:	
Sentences per Paragraph	0.9
Words per Sentence	24.2
Characters per Word	4.7
Readability:	
Passive Sentences	16%
Flesch Reading Ease	65.0
Flesch-Kincaid Grade Level	8.7
Coleman-Liau Grade Level	20.6
Bormuth Grade Level	11.5

OK   Help

Grammar statistics dialog box
Figure 9-6.

A *nonbreaking* hyphen is like a normal hyphen, except that Word never breaks the hyphenated word if it occurs at the end of a line. For instance, if you use a normal hyphen, you may end up with a paragraph that looks like this:

> There are many different spreadsheets that perform "what-
> if" calculations.

Since there is a normal hyphen between "what" and "if", Word breaks the line there. In many cases, this is all right, but in this case it looks a bit clumsy. If you want to prevent Word from breaking a word at its hyphen, use a nonbreaking hyphen, which you enter by pressing Ctrl-Shift--. The result of using a nonbreaking hyphen is the following:

> There are many different spreadsheets that perform
> "what-if" calculations.

If a paragraph contains many long words, wordwrap causes the paragraph to look very uneven. For instance:

> His telecommunications discussion was
> significantly sidetracked as he started
> expostulating about interplanetary associations of
> antediluvian civilizations.

To make the lines more even, you need to hyphenate some of the words. If you want Word to hyphenate a word, you can enter an *optional* hyphen. You usually do this only when you notice that a particular set of lines is broken unevenly. You can also let Word help you hyphenate your entire document.

An optional hyphen is not used until it is needed. You can include optional hyphens anywhere in a word. To enter an optional hyphen, use Ctrl--. You do not see these hyphens unless they are necessary for proper wordwrap. If you use optional hyphens in the previous example, the result is as follows:

> His telecommunications discussion was significant-
> ly sidetracked as he started expostulating about
> interplanetary associations of antediluvian civili-
> zations.

Deciding which words to hyphenate and adding the optional hyphens can be very tedious and time-consuming. Word can help you hyphenate by automatically putting optional hyphens in every word that is at the end of a line and might be split. The Hyphenate command from the Tools menu lets you decide where the hyphen goes in each word at the end of a line or gives you the option of hyphenating without confirmation.

The Hyphenation command from the Tools menu adds hyphens from the location of the insertion point to the end of the document. If you want to hyphenate only part of the document, select that part before giving the command. The Hyphenation dialog box looks like this:

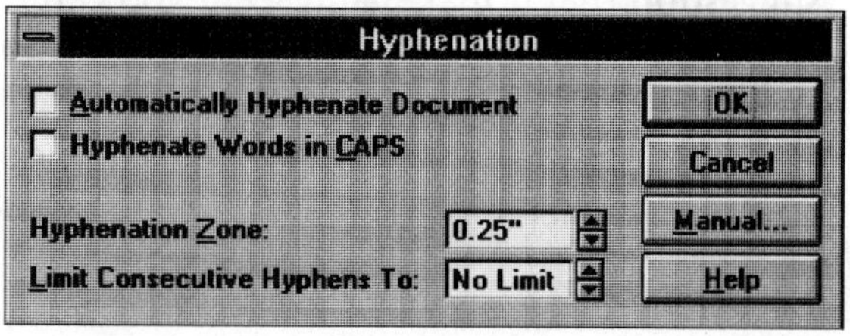

The Automatically Hyphenate Document option tells Word to add optional hyphens as you type. This is rarely necessary and it can be a bit disconcerting to see words near the ends of lines broken as you type them. The Hyphenate Words in CAPS option tells Word whether or not to skip words in all capital letters when it hyphenates.

Choose the Manual button. For each word, the program shows you where it thinks the hyphen should go and asks you to enter a response, as shown here:

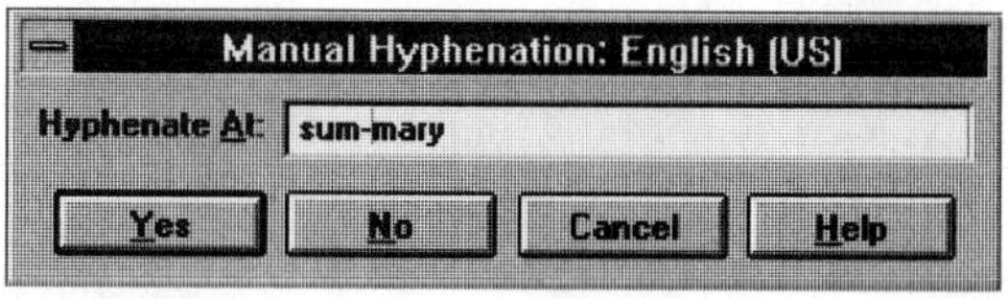

Choose the Yes button to confirm the choice or No to move to the next word.

The Hyphenation Zone option tells Word how close to the right margin the word should be to cause hyphenation. The larger the measurement, the fewer the words that will be hyphenated. You can also limit how many consecutive lines might end in hyphens. Having too many adjacent lines with hyphens can make your document difficult to read, and you should probably set this option to 2 or 3.

Review

Run the spelling checker on letters you have typed in Word. What type of words does it not recognize?

Type the word **running** into a document, select it, and give the Thesaurus command. Investigate the synonyms and note the differences in meaning of each.

Run the grammar checker on your MAGAZINE document. Consider each suggestion that it makes and see if you can rewrite the article to incorporate the suggestions. Also, see whether or not you think the suggestions make the writing any better.

Type a few paragraphs of your choice and format them to be very narrow. Give the Hyphenation command and note how different the paragraphs look.

Word For Windows
Word For Windows

CHAPTER

10 PRINTING YOUR DOCUMENTS

Word and Microsoft Windows have many advanced features that make printing easy. When you edit and format text, for example, you do not need to know what type of printer your text will be printed on. Instead, when you are ready to print, you just give the Print command from the File menu, and it determines what it needs to do in order to use as many of the formats you specify as it can.

This is important because there is no standard method for instructing different printers how to perform certain tasks, such as printing superscripts or choosing different fonts. Most of the instructions are complex and involve strange character codes. Word does not require you to remember these codes. Instead, it stores the text formatting with your file, and when you print, it interacts with a special Windows file called a *printer driver* to determine how to use your printer's special features so they correspond to the format.

Different printers, of course, produce output of different quality. They also print at different speeds, have different special features, and range in cost from around $150 to over $10,000.

Although you learned a bit about printing in Chapter 2, this chapter gives you the rest of the information on how to tell Word what type of printer you have and how to use the options of the Print command.

Lesson 63: Giving the Print Command

When you first give the Print command, you should tell Word about your printer with the Printer button in the Print dialog box. This lets you set up your printer in the same way that you can from the Control Panel in Windows (in fact, it is a better idea to do this from Windows before you even run Word). The Print Setup dialog box is shown in Figure 10-1. See your Windows manual for more detailed information on choosing and setting up your printer.

Select the printer you want to set up and select the Options button. The next dialog box you see depends on the type of printer you have. For example, Figure 10-2 shows the setup dialog box that is specific for the Apple LaserWriter II NT.

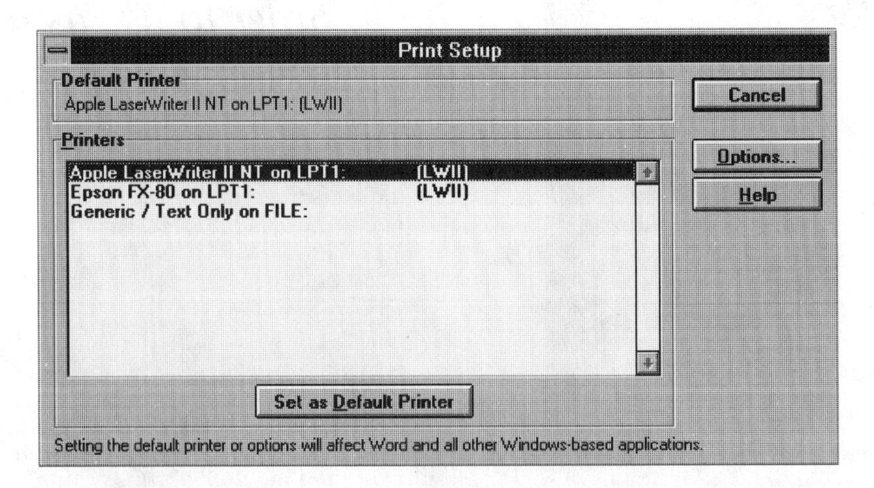

Print Setup dialog box
Figure 10-1.

Setup dialog box for Apple LaserWriter II NT
Figure 10-2.

After you have set up your printer, choose the Print command from the File menu. Figure 10-3 shows a typical Print dialog box.

You can specify what to print in the Print What drop-down list. The choices are shown here:

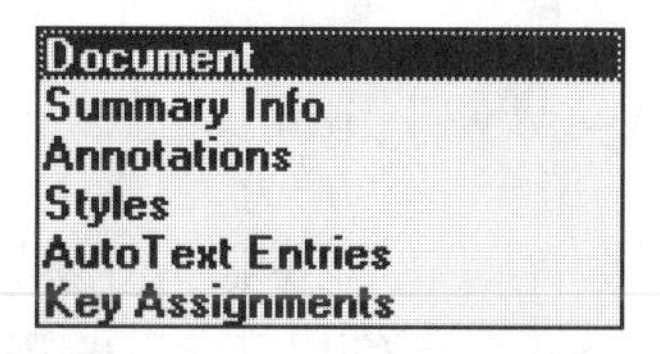

Choosing Document, which you will use most often, causes Word to print the document. The other choices are discussed in chapters that cover the related topic: Summary Info is described in Chapter 22, Annotations in Chapter 17, Styles in Chapter 15, AutoText in Chapter 19, and Key Assignments in Chapter 24.

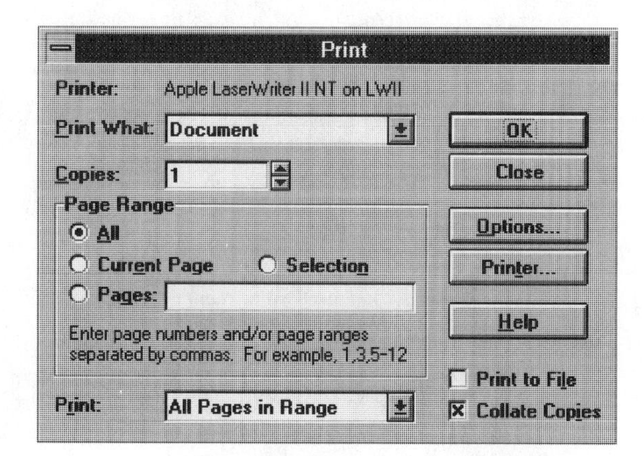

Print dialog box
Figure 10-3.

If you want to print more than one copy of a file, use the Copies option. This is a convenient way to print many copies of a letter or memo without having to give the Print command over and over. If you set the Copies option to 2 or greater, you may also want to select the Collate Copies option. If this is not selected, Word prints the specified number of copies of the first page, then that number of copies of the second page, and so on. With Collate Copies selected, a whole copy of the document is printed, then the next copy, and so on. Leaving Collate Copies deselected usually causes Word to print faster, but you then have to collate the printed pages by hand.

You can choose to print only certain pages from your document by using the Page Range options. You can instruct Word to print:

- The entire document (this is the default choice)
- Just the selection
- The current page
- Particular pages you specify

To specify pages, enter a range with commas or hyphens. For instance, if you enter **2,4**, Word will print pages 2 and 4; if you enter **2-4**, Word will print pages 2, 3, and 4.

You can tell Word to only print the odd or even pages in your document. This is handy if you want to print on both sides of the paper. You can print all the odd pages first, turn the paper over, then print all the even pages.

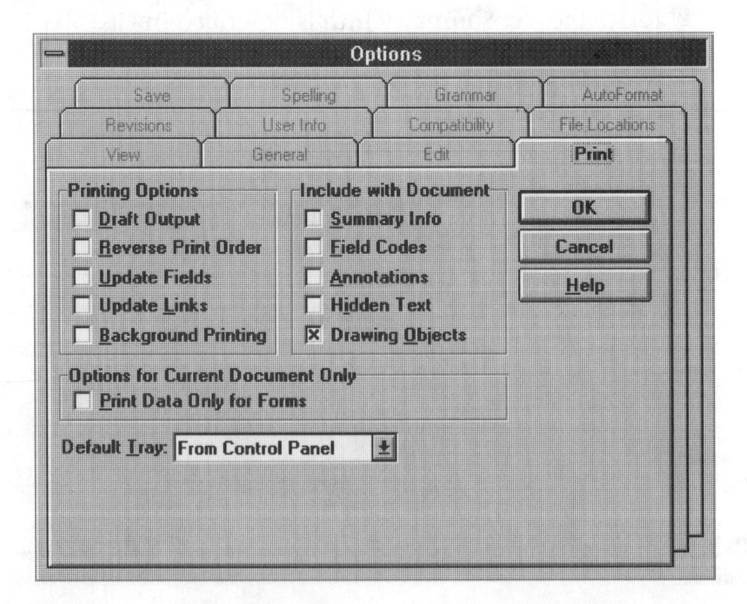

Print options dialog box
Figure 10-4.

If your printer is not available, you can print to a file and then send that file to the printer later. This file will contain all the special control sequences specific to your printer. Depending on the type of printer you have, this file can become huge, so this option is rarely used.

Lesson 64: Setting Print Options

The Options button in the Print dialog box brings up the Options dialog box for printers, as shown in Figure 10-4. This is the same as the Print tab of the Options command from the Tools menu.

The options allow you to change the way that Word prints your document. The choices are listed in the following table.

Option	Description
Draft Output	Uses the printer's draft mode, if it has one. This is usually faster but produces lower quality than normal printing.
Reverse Print Order	Prints the document in reverse order, last page first.
Update Fields	Updates all fields (described in Chapter 26) before starting to print.
Update Links	Updates all linked information (described in Chapter 21) before starting to print.
Background Printing	Causes the printing to be spooled if you are using Windows' Print Manager.
Summary Info	Prints a separate page with the summary information (described in Chapter 22).
Field Codes	Prints the field codes in the text (described in Chapter 26).
Annotations	Prints the annotations (described in Chapter 17) at the end of the text on a separate page.
Hidden Text	Includes the hidden text in the printed output.
Drawing Objects	Prints the drawings (you can deselect this to speed up printing).

Option	Description
Print Data Only for Forms	Only prints a form's data (as described in Chapter 20).
Default Tray	Specifies which printer tray you will use for this document.

Review

Experiment with the choices in the Print dialog box by selecting them and printing the MAGAZINE document. If you have more than one type of printer available, try different choices on each type of printer.

Word For Windows

CHAPTER

11

WORD SETTINGS

Word has commands that allow you to set various options for the way you use Word. For example, you can adjust the way Word's screen looks and the amount of information that Word gives you.

Lesson 65: Overview of Word's Many Options

The settings described in this chapter are remembered when you quit from Word and are automatically used when you start Word again. You can also save different sets of settings and use them at different times—for example, if two people use the same PC and want to use different settings.

The Options command from the Tools menu lets you specify many different types of settings. You have already seen some of these in earlier chapters because the settings affect a wide range of Word's commands. You can also access the Options command through other commands. For example, you saw how to access the spelling options from the Spelling command in Chapter 9.

This chapter covers many of the tabs in the Options command. They are described in approximate order of most to least used. Some of the tabs are covered in other chapters because they directly relate to other lessons. The tabs that are covered in other parts of this book are

- Spelling options, in Chapter 9
- Grammar options, in Chapter 9
- Print options, in Chapter 10
- AutoFormat options, in Chapter 15
- Revisions options, in Chapter 26

To start this chapter, choose the Options command from the Tools menu, then choose the tab described in each lesson. You do not need to close the Options dialog box between lessons; simply choose the appropriate tab.

Lesson 66: General Options

The settings described here affect your general use of Word. They are shown in Figure 11-1.

Background Repagination turns on automatic repagination. This is described in Chapter 14.

Help for WordPerfect Users lets you use the WordPerfect keyboard command equivalents and, as you use them, tells you the corresponding Word commands. This is very convenient if you are starting to use Word after having used WordPerfect version 5.0 or version 5.1. Navigation Keys for

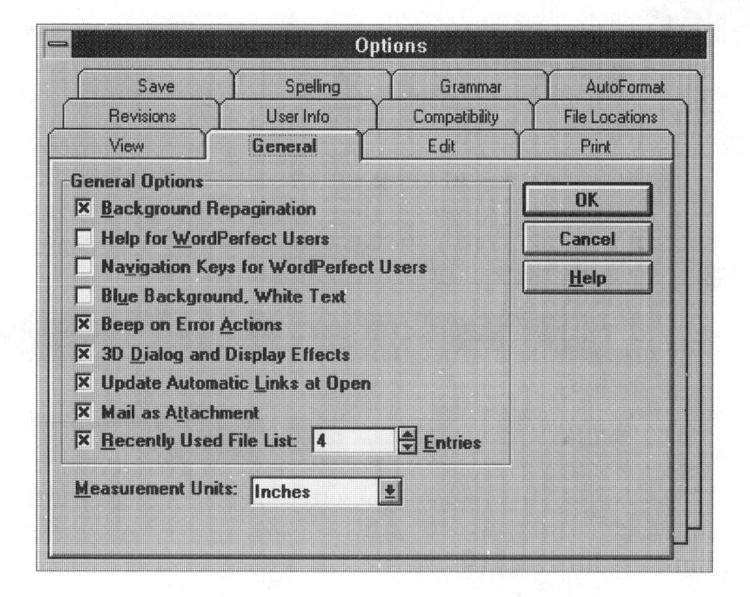

General tab of the Options dialog box
Figure 11-1.

WordPerfect Users is similar, but it uses the WordPerfect cursor control key equivalents for such keys as Pg Up and Pg Dn.

If you prefer the look of character-based programs like WordPerfect, you can select Blue Background, White Text to change the look of the screen. However, many people find this harder on their eyes than the standard black characters on a white background.

Deselecting Beep on Error Actions mutes Word. This is sometimes useful if there are many PCs in the same office and you do not want to disturb your coworkers.

The 3D Dialog and Display Effects option changes Word's display of dialog boxes and buttons. If you are running Word on a monochrome screen, you probably want to deselect this option to make the dialog boxes easier to read.

Update Automatic Links At Open causes all links to be checked each time you open a document. With this option selected, you will immediately know that all of the linked documents are still available. Links are described in Chapter 21.

If you have an electronic mail package that Word recognizes, the Mail As Attachment option allows you to attach documents to mail messages from within Word.

The Recently Used File List is the list of files that appears at the bottom of the File menu. You can specify how many of the recently used files you want to see. If you are using a SuperVGA or other high-resolution video adapter, you can increase this number to 8 and still see all the files on your screen.

The Measurement Units option lets you set the units that Word uses when it prompts you for linear measurement, such as in the Paragraph command and on the ruler. You select the choice you want to use when you give measurements. The choices are shown here:

Choice	Meaning
Inches	Inches (1 in. = 2.5 cm.)
Centimeters	Centimeters (1 cm. = 0.4 in.)
Points	1 point = 1/72 in. (Points are used for measurement by typesetters and are described in Chapter 7.)
Picas	6 picas = 1 in.

Lesson 67: View Options

Figure 11-2 shows the View settings that determine how things look, what you see, and what you don't see. Note that a few of the options in this dialog box change depending on the view you are using when you give the Options command (the one pictured is for normal view).

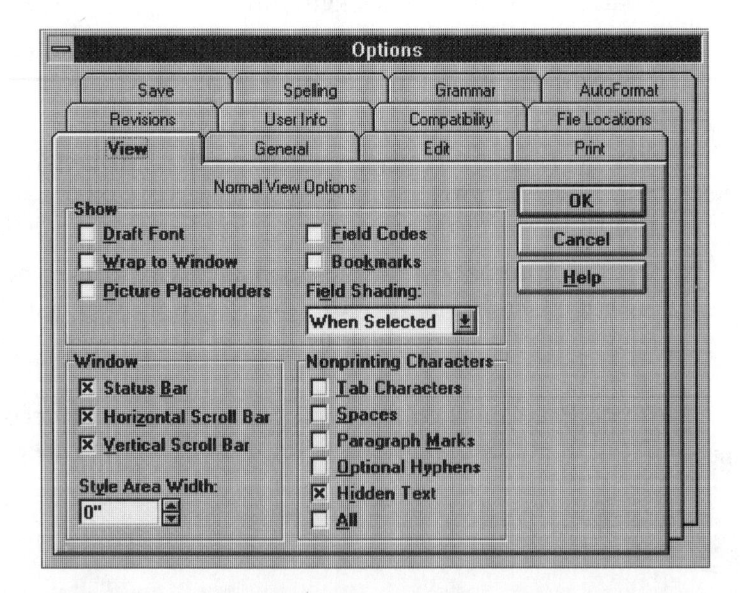

View tab of the Options dialog box
Figure 11-2.

The Show choices tell Word to display document items on the screen so you can determine better what you have entered in a document. The Window choices tell Word what parts of the screen you want to see. The Nonprinting Characters choices cause Word to display special characters in place of those you normally can't see.

Show Options

The Draft Font option reduces all formatting display to underline and bold and shows graphics as empty boxes. If you have a slow PC, this speeds up the display, but not much faster than Picture Placeholders (described below). In page layout view, you can also select the Drawings option that speeds up the display by only showing boxes for each object.

If your text is wider than the window and you are in normal view, selecting Wrap to Window causes the text to wrap at the window borders. This is handy if you are editing a wide document.

Turning on the Picture Placeholders option makes scrolling faster because Word does not show the actual graphic in your documents, only a gray rectangle. This can be especially useful on slower PCs or when you have very complex pictures because of the time Word spends in redrawing each view of the picture. Also, you may want to use this if your graphics are stored on a network and therefore take a long time to access.

Selecting Field Codes tells Word to show the field codes themselves instead of the results of field calculations. Fields are described in Chapter 26. The Field Shading option allows you to put shading around the results of a field so you can identify the fields easily. Similarly, choosing Bookmarks shows the bookmarks in your document (these are also described in Chapter 26).

Three additional choices are available in page layout view. Drawings specifies whether or not to show drawings. Like Picture Placeholders, deselecting this option can speed up viewing your document. The Object Anchors option shows you which text each object is associated with in page layout view. Text Boundaries is useful when you have positioned paragraphs and tables in a document; selecting this option causes each text box to be surrounded by a dotted border.

Window Options

If you want to have more room in your windows, you can choose not to show the horizontal and vertical scroll bars. The horizontal scroll bar, which is rarely used, can be turned off to give you an extra line of text on the screen. If you rarely read the messages in the status bar at the bottom of Word's window, you may want to turn off the status bar as well.

The style area is an area to the left of the selection bar. If you have enough horizontal width for your documents and want to see the styles listed next to each paragraph, set the Style Area Width option to a small amount so you can see the listing.

Nonprinting Characters

The Nonprinting Characters choices display characters that you would not normally see. The characters that appear when you select the choices are shown in the following table.

Choice	Display Character
Tab Characters	Tab character (→)
Spaces	Spacebar character (shows as dots)
Paragraph Marks	Paragraph (¶) Newline (↵) Cell end (¤)
Optional Hyphens	Optional hyphen (¬) Nonbreaking hyphen as regular hyphen
Hidden Text	Hidden character formatting as dotted underline
All	All of the above

Lesson 68: Edit Options

Figure 11-3 shows the editing options. These change the way Word acts when you give certain editing commands.

Typing Replaces Selection causes Word to delete any selected characters when you start typing. This is the standard for almost every Windows program but may feel strange to you if you have used non-Windows word processors.

Drag-and-drop Text Editing controls whether that feature is active. Drag-and-drop editing is described in Chapter 4.

The Automatic Word Selection option causes Word to select the word following any space that is selected. Also, once you have selected a word, Word automatically selects additional whole words at a time. Thus, if this is selected, as you are selecting characters, after you select a space, Word changes to selecting whole words at a time.

The Use the INS Key for Paste setting allows you to use Ins as a shortcut for the Paste command from the Edit menu.

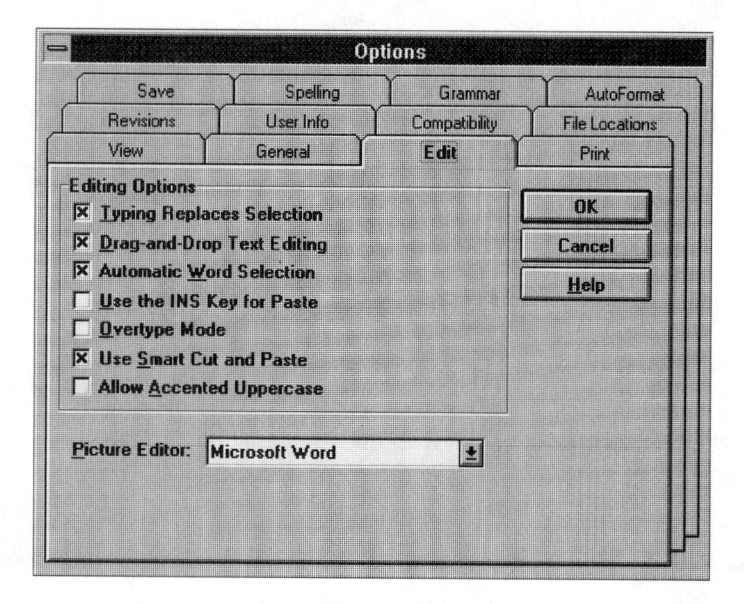

Edit tab of the Options dialog box
Figure 11-3.

The Overtype Mode setting is a rarely used feature that causes Word to delete characters to the right as you type, effectively typing over them.

Selecting Use Smart Cut and Paste causes Word to remove spaces after words that are deleted so that the following word does not have two spaces before it. Also, if you paste a word from the Clipboard, Word automatically puts a space before it.

The Allow Accented Uppercase option affects languages that have accents or other marks above capital letters (such as French). This option causes proofing tools to suggest accents over capital letters.

When you edit pictures in Word (as described in Chapter 12), Word automatically starts the specified program in the Picture Editor drop-down box.

Lesson 69: Save Options

The Save settings change the way the Save and Save As commands work. The options are shown in Figure 11-4.

Save Options

Always Create Backup Copy causes Word to create a backup copy of a file when you give the Save or Save As command. The backup has the document name and a .BAK extension. You can also change this option in the Save As dialog box.

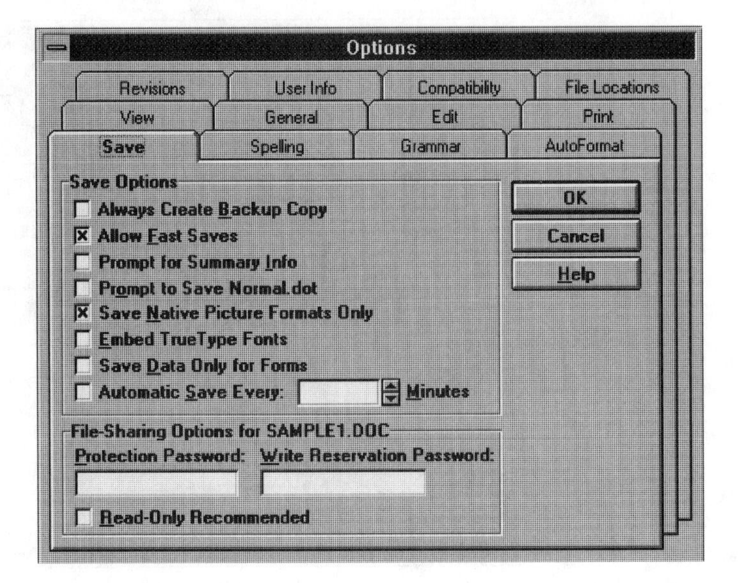

Save tab of the Options dialog box
Figure 11-4.

The Allow Fast Saves option lets Word save files in a faster manner. This is generally good (especially if you are editing long files), but some programs that can read Word files can only read those that have been saved in the slower method. Also, files saved with the fast save method often are larger than files saved with the slower method. After a few fast saves, Word normally reverts to a slow save to reduce the size and complexity of a file.

The Prompt for Summary Info option tells Word whether or not to display the Summary Info dialog box you see the first time you save a file. It is described in detail in Chapter 22.

Word will normally save the default template automatically when you quit from Word (templates are described later in this chapter). Select the Prompt to Save Normal.dot option if you want to be prompted before the save is made, such as if you made changes that you don't want saved.

The Save Native Picture Formats Only option causes your saved files to be smaller when you import graphics from other computers such as the Macintosh. If this is not selected, pictures are stored in both formats in the file; when it is selected, only the Windows version is stored.

You will probably never select the Embed TrueType Fonts option since it causes your files to grow significantly. It is only useful if you are giving a file to someone else who does not have the same TrueType fonts as you. Note that giving such fonts to other users may not be legal, depending on the types of fonts you use.

If you use forms (described in Chapter 20), you can cause the saved file to have only the data from the form, not the form itself.

The Automatic Save Every:_ Minutes option saves your work at regular intervals. This is useful if you often work for long stretches, forgetting to save your work. However, be sure not to select this option if you are making experimental changes to a file that you don't intend to save, because the changes may get saved anyway.

File-Sharing Options for Current Document

When you choose the Save tab in the Options command while a document is open, the options at the bottom of the tab are for that specific document. Changing these settings does not affect any other documents.

The two passwords in this area prevent others from seeing or changing the document. Before opening the document, Word prompts for the password. Each password can be up to 15 letters long and can include letters, numbers, spaces, and most punctuation. The letters in the password are case-sensitive, meaning that if you specify uppercase letters in the password, the user must also type uppercase letters. For example, if you set the password to "Golden Road" but type "golden road", you will be denied access.

The types of access are

- Protection Password specifies a password that must be given before the document can be viewed. If you give the wrong password, you cannot see the document.
- Write Reservation Password is less restrictive. If you give the wrong password when opening the document, you can see it but cannot save any changes to it.
- Read-Only Recommended is even less restrictive. Word does not prompt for a password. However, when you open the file, Word suggests that you open it for reading only.

If your company has a security policy for documents, you should be sure to follow that policy using these options.

Lesson 70: User Info Options

The User Info settings let you enter information used by Word. Your name and initials are used by the Summary Info dialog box (described in Chapter 21) and in annotations (described in Chapter 17). Your mailing address is used by Word's automatic envelope printing as the return address. The choices are shown in Figure 11-5.

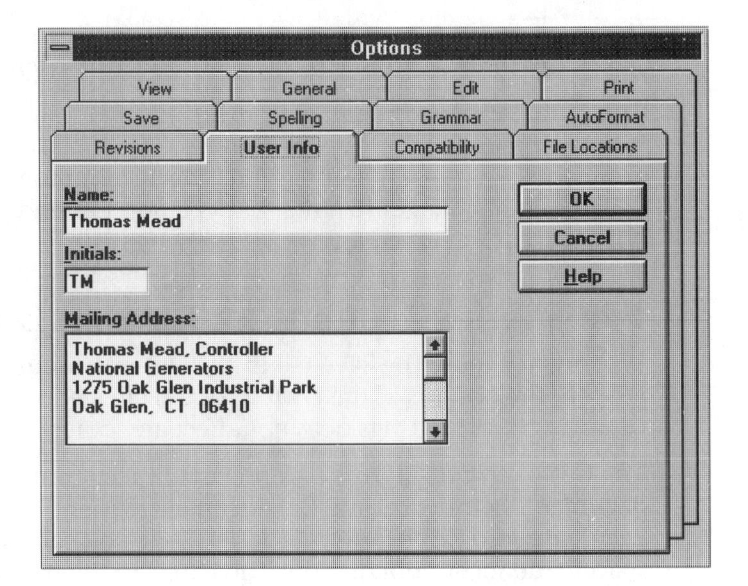

User Info tab of the Options dialog box
Figure 11-5.

Lesson 71: Compatibility Options

As you will see in Chapter 21, Word can open files that were created in other word processors. The options shown in Figure 11-6 control how it opens and

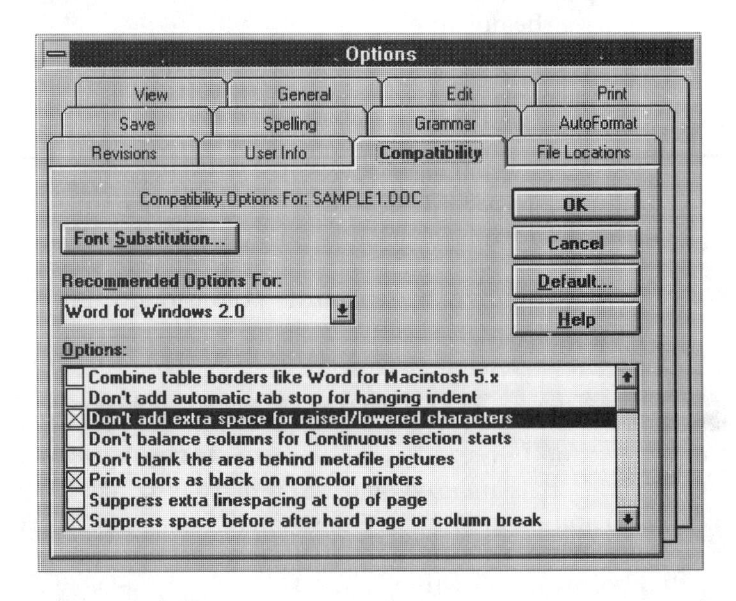

Compatibility tab of the Options dialog box
Figure 11-6.

displays these files. They compensate for peculiarities in other word processors or features that do not exist in Word.

If the current document uses fonts that are not available to Word, the Font Substitution button lets you specify which fonts to use. This is particularly useful when transferring files from the Macintosh and from Unix systems.

You may want to change the settings on the options in the scrolling list at the bottom of the dialog box depending on the program from which you are converting. The list under the Recommended Options For option shows Word's suggested settings for a particular word processor. Be sure to make selections for all the word processors you intend to import from. You will generally not change these defaults.

Lesson 72: File Locations Options

You can tell Word where to look for particular files in the File Locations tab, shown in Figure 11-7. For instance, when you give the Open command the first time you start Word, Word has to choose a directory to display. Also, Word needs to know where particular files are stored when it starts. You can specify the directories in this dialog box. The locations you specify and what they represent are listed in the following table.

Location	Description
Documents	First directory used by the Open command
Clipart Pictures	First directory used by the Picture command
User Templates	Location of your templates
Workgroup Templates	Location of shared templates
User Options	Location of options files
AutoSave Files	Location in which Word stores temporary files
Dictionaries	Location of your dictionaries
Tutorial	Location of the tutorial files
Startup	Location of special startup items

To change a location, choose the Modify button and select the desired directory from that dialog box. Generally, the only ones you will want to change are Documents and Clipart Pictures because these specify where your own documents are; the other options specify where Word looks for its standard files, and are thus not usually changed.

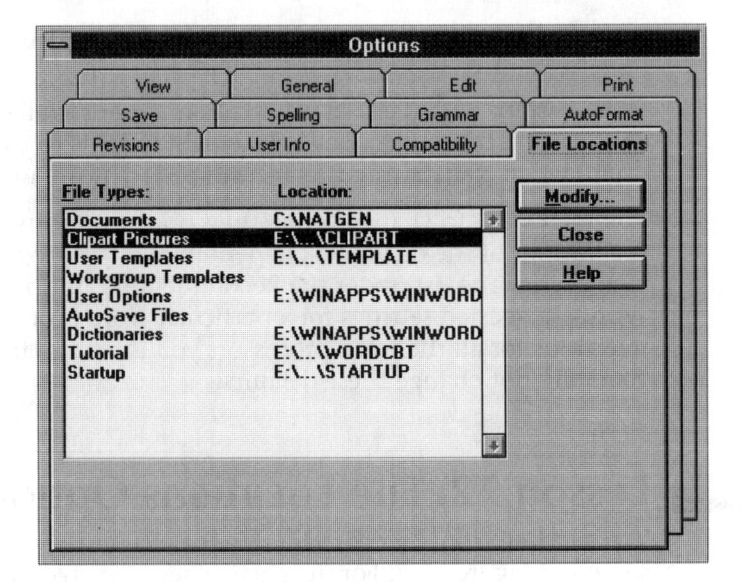

File Locations tab of the Options dialog box
Figure 11-7.

Lesson 73: Using Document Templates

Most business letters have the same general format. The letterhead in business stationery is always in approximately the same place. The date is usually in the same place and, although the position of these elements changes from letter to letter, the closing name and address are the same. It would be nice to have a way of placing all that information in every new letter you start and a way to create similar base documents for memos, reports, and so on.

Word's document templates fulfill those needs and more. A document template is a standardized document you can create that contains the following elements:

- Text you want the document to start and end with (such as the date, your name and address, and the closing text for letters)
- Styles
- AutoText entries
- Macros
- Keyboard equivalents
- Menu assignments
- Toolbar customization

Starting a new document based on a document template is like copying a document and using that as the base for your new document. However, using templates is easier because you don't have to do any copying.

When you create a new document, you choose the template you want for that document in the Use Template section of the New command. Up to now, you have been choosing the normal template (saved as NORMAL.DOT on disk), which is the default template. However, you can choose any template you want. After you create a standard template for letters, for example, you will choose that template in the New dialog box whenever you begin a new letter.

To create a template, you use the Save As command. Choose Document Template from the Save File as Type drop-down list. Whatever you have in the document window will be saved as the common text for the template. Your current styles, AutoText entries, macros, keyboard equivalents, menu assignments, and toolbar changes are saved as well. Templates have a .DOT extension.

You can also create a template by modifying an existing one. Give the Open command, select Document Templates in the List Files of Type drop-down list. You now see a list of only the templates. Choose one, open it, modify it as you wish, give the File Save As command, and enter a new name for the template.

Templates have many uses. For example, Figure 11-8 shows a template for the minutes of a regular meeting. The template also has a style sheet with formats for items commonly included in the minutes, such as action items

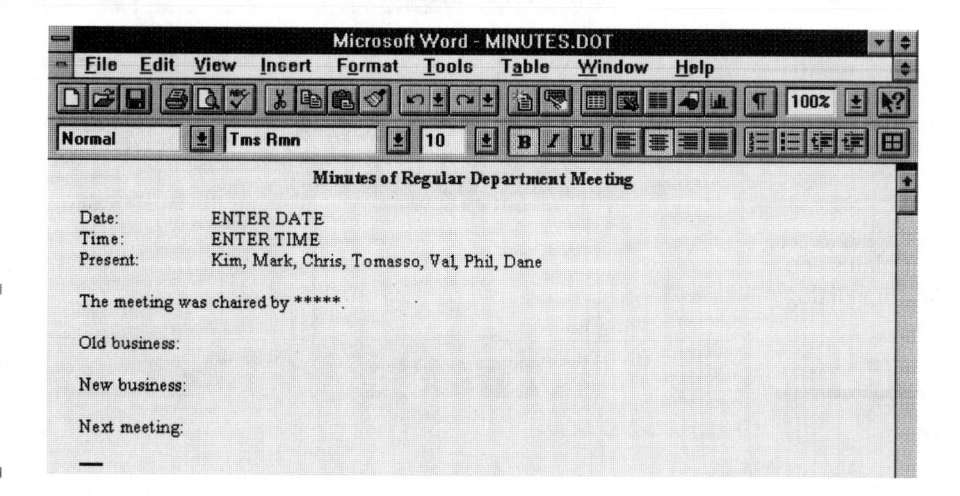

Example template for minutes of a meeting
Figure 11-8.

and open questions. Since the same people come to the meeting each week, their names are kept in the template's AutoText entries as well.

There is a second type of templates, called *global templates,* that lets you access all of the features of a template except its text. When you open a global template, its features are merged with the document's template (the global template's settings take precedence when there is a conflict). The normal template is, in fact, a global template, meaning that the features in the normal template are available to all documents.

To add the features of another template to the global template, use the Templates command from the File menu. The Templates and Add-ins dialog box appears, as shown in Figure 11-9. If the desired template is in the list, simply choose its name so that the check box to the left of it is selected, then choose OK. If the template you want isn't in the list, choose Add to find the template.

You can copy parts of templates to other templates using the template organizer. Choose the Organizer button from the Templates and Add-ins dialog box, which brings up the Organizer dialog box, shown in Figure 11-10. For each of the four tabs (Styles, AutoText, Toolbars, and Macros), first select the source file in the Styles Available In list on the left and the destination file in the Styles Available In list on the right. In the source list box at the top of the dialog box, select the styles you want to copy from the source to the destination file, and then select the Copy button. This is an easy way to copy some of the attributes of a template without copying all of them.

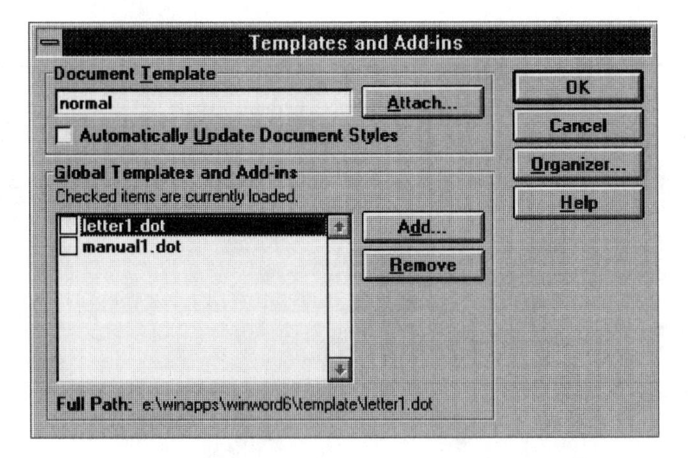

Templates and Add-ins dialog box
Figure 11-9.

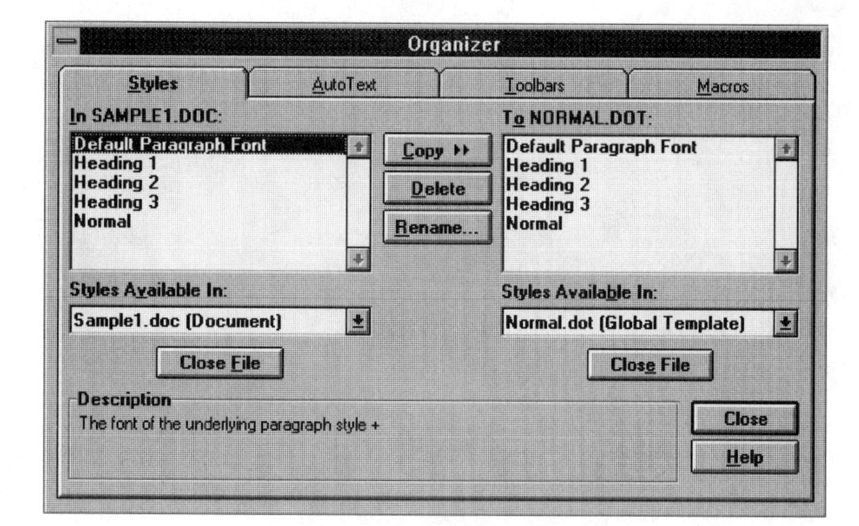

Organizer dialog box
Figure 11-10.

Review

Experiment with different view options of your MAGAZINE file. Which of the options do you generally want on all the time, which do you want occasionally, and which will you probably never use?

Think about how templates can save time in your daily work. What text would you include in a template?

Word For Windows
Word For Windows
Word For Windows

PART 2

ENHANCING YOUR DOCUMENTS

CHAPTER

12

PICTURES IN YOUR DOCUMENTS

There will probably be times when you want to include art and graphics in your text. Word allows you to use drawings from graphics programs such as CorelDraw in your text by pasting them from the Clipboard with the Paste command. You can also create graphics from within Word or open graphics files that you have stored on disk.

Word includes additional advanced tools that also create pictures. These allow you to create graphs from tables of numbers, to create equations for scientific writing, and to embellish your text.

Lesson 74: Using Art in Your Text

There are two main purposes for including art in your text: to illustrate something that is being written about and to provide decoration. Informational images are useful if you are talking about a product, process, or a location where there are some salient features best described with a picture. Decorative art often makes an otherwise boring report more interesting to read.

The most common method for including art in your text is to create the art in another program, copy it to the Clipboard in that program, switch to Word, and paste the image into your document by using the Paste command. As you will see throughout this chapter, you can also create images directly in Word and use them in a similar fashion.

For example, suppose you want to include a product illustration in the SAMPLE1 file from the Windows Paintbrush program you already use. First draw the product illustration in Paintbrush and copy it to the Clipboard with the program's Copy command. Switch from Paintbrush to Word.

Open the SAMPLE1 file, put the insertion point at the end of the first paragraph, and add a new sentence: **Here is a picture of the DC50.** Now press Enter a few times and give the Paste command. Word puts the picture in the letter, as shown in Figure 12-1.

It is likely that you will want to put your graphics in *frames* that allow you to place the graphics precisely where you want them on the page. Frames are described in Chapter 20.

(If, when you paste the picture in from the other program, you can only see a tiny part of the bottom of the picture, it means the paragraph in which it was pasted has an absolute height, such as "exactly 12 pt", instead of a relative height, such as "Single". If this happens, choose a relative height for that paragraph from the Paragraph command in the Format menu.)

Lesson 75: Opening Graphics Files

Although transferring pictures through the Clipboard from a graphics program is easy, it is not always convenient. For example, if you want to transfer 10 pictures into a particular document, you have to switch back and forth between the graphics program and Word. You may find it faster to open that program's graphics files directly in Word. You can also use this

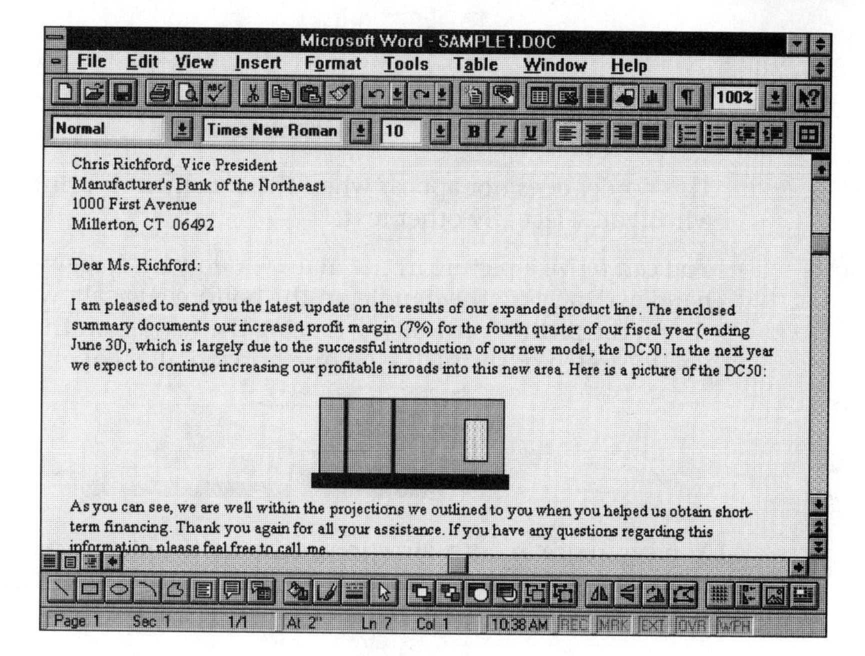

Picture inserted in document
Figure 12-1.

method if someone else has created the graphics files for you and you do not have the graphics program on your PC.

To open a picture document, give the Picture command from the Insert menu. In the List Files of Type drop-down list, select the type of file you want to import. This causes Word to list only those graphics files that match the type you indicate.

Word can open many types of Windows and MS-DOS graphics files, but not all, depending on the types of *filters* you installed with Word. The types of files it can open are covered in depth in Chapter 21.

After you insert a picture, you will probably want to put it in a frame (described in Chapter 20) so you can position it more accurately. You may also want to link to the graphics file instead of importing it into your document; this is described in Chapter 21.

Lesson 76: Resizing and Cropping Graphics

Word treats a picture as if it were a character. When you select a picture, Word surrounds it in a border with eight boxes (called *handles*) on the corners and edges of the border.

This border does not appear when the document is printed and disappears when you select any other text.

You can resize a picture in the main window by dragging on one of the handles. Dragging the handle on the bottom edge allows you to stretch or shrink the picture vertically. Dragging the handle on the right edge allows you to stretch or shrink the picture horizontally. For example:

You can resize in both directions, keeping the picture proportionally sized, by dragging the handle in the lower-right corner. This is a good way to keep the vertical and horizontal dimensions the same.

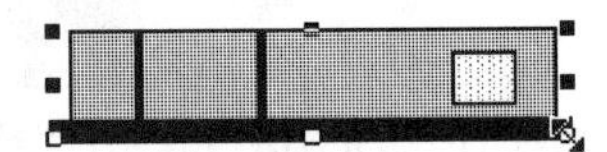

As you resize a picture, the bottom line of the Word window shows the percent of change if you drag the corner. This is useful if you want to resize by a specific amount, such as 50 percent.

If you hold down the Shift key while in the main window, Word crops the picture instead of resizing it. *Cropping* cuts the right side or bottom off the picture if you move the handles inward. If you move the handles outward, Word puts a blank border around the graphic. It is unlikely that you will use Word to crop pictures; resizing them is much more common.

Lesson 77: Adding Graphics to Word Documents

Word comes with a simple drawing program so you can design graphics for use in Word without using another program. The drawing program, called Microsoft Draw, can create good-looking drawings, but you may need a more advanced drawing program if you need to create more complicated pictures.

To create your own graphic in Word, select the Drawing button on the Standard toolbar. This displays the Drawing toolbar at the bottom of the screen. The Drawing toolbar buttons are shown here:

	Line		Send to Back
	Rectangle		Bring in Front of Text
	Ellipse		Send Behind Text
	Arc		Group
	Freeform		Ungroup
	Text Box		Flip Horizontal
	Callout		Flip Vertical
	Format Callout		Rotate Right
	Fill Color		Reshape
	Line Color		Snap to Grid
	Line Style		Align
	Select		Create Picture
	Bring to Front		Insert Frame

If you are familiar with other painting or drawing programs, you will probably be able to create pictures immediately. If not, you may need a bit of practice in order to get good graphics from Word's drawing tools.

When you use a drawing tool to draw in your document, Word anchors the item you draw to a paragraph. Initially, the item is anchored to the paragraph to which it is closest. If you move the item, Word reanchors the item to the nearest paragraph at the new location. Knowing the paragraph to which an item is anchored is important because the item will move with the paragraph.

For example, if you draw a square to the right of a paragraph, and then add text above the paragraph, the square will move down with the paragraph. If you select the paragraph and cut it to the Clipboard, the square will also be cut, and will reappear with the paragraph when you later paste it.

You can see which paragraph an item is anchored to by choosing the Object Anchors option in the View tab of the Options command. With that option turned on, selecting an object will display an anchor at the left of the window:

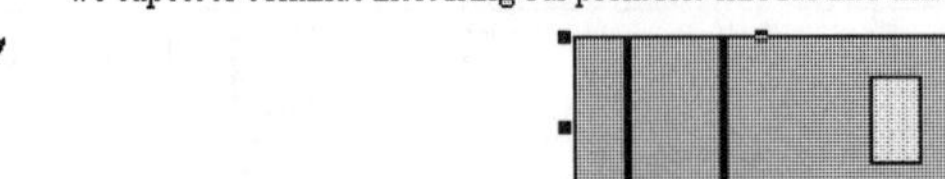

You can also see the anchors by selecting the Show Paragraph button from the Standard toolbar.

You use the line, freeform, rectangle, rounded rectangle, oval, and arc tools to draw items. With these tools, you click in one corner of the desired item and drag to the diagonally opposite corner. For example, to draw an oval, click the oval tool, click in the drawing area at the upper-left corner of the desired oval, drag to the opposite corner, and release the mouse button. The item is automatically selected:

With these drawing tools, holding down the Shift key while you drag restricts the motion of the tool. Restricting the oval tool causes you to draw perfect circles, restricting the rectangle tool causes you to draw perfect squares, and so on. Experiment with the drawing tools, with and without the Shift key.

The freeform tool lets you draw a polygon with multiple segments. Select the tool, click once at one of the corners, then continue to click for each line segment. If you click and drag, Word makes many corners that allow you to make the object look curved. If you make a mistake on one or more of the corners, the reshape tool lets you drag any individual corner.

Once you have drawn one or more items, you may want to modify them. You must select an item before you can modify it. If it is not already selected, you can select it with the selection tool. Click the selection tool, and then click the item you want to select. You must click directly on a line in the item to select it.

To move an item, select it and drag its outline to another position. To resize an item, select it and drag any of the handles. Drag a corner handle of an item to change its width and height.

If you want to rotate or flip an item vertically or horizontally, select the item and choose the Flip Horizontal, Flip Vertical, or Rotate Right buttons. You can use these in combination to get various effects.

All drawing items have lines, fills, and patterns. The *line* is the border of an item, and the *fill* and the pattern are in the interior. You can also modify a selected item with the Fill Color, Line Color, and Line Style buttons. Each of these buttons brings up a menu of available colors or line styles. For example, the Line Style button shows this menu:

You can also change all of the formatting for an item by double-clicking on the item or selecting it and choosing Drawing Object from the Format menu. The dialog box has three tabs: Fill, Line, and Size and Position. Figure 12-2 shows the Fill tab. You can choose the background color, pattern, and pattern color from the dialog box. The Line tab is similar. The Size and Position tab lets you give precise measurements for the item.

If you draw more than one item, you can tell Word you want to always treat them as a group. Simply select all the items and select the Group button. You can undo this with the Ungroup button. It is handy to group items that will always move together.

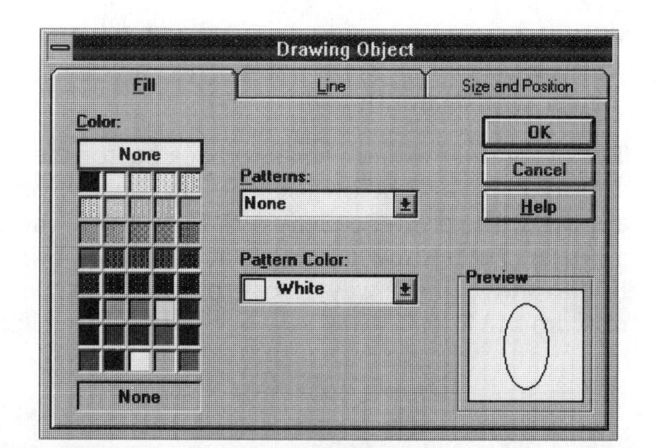

Fill tab of the Drawing Object dialog box
Figure 12-2.

You may want to align some objects with each other. For example, if you draw a circle and a square, you may want to be sure their tops are perfectly even:

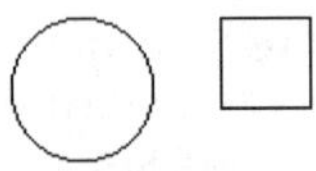

Select the items and choose the Align button. You see this dialog box:

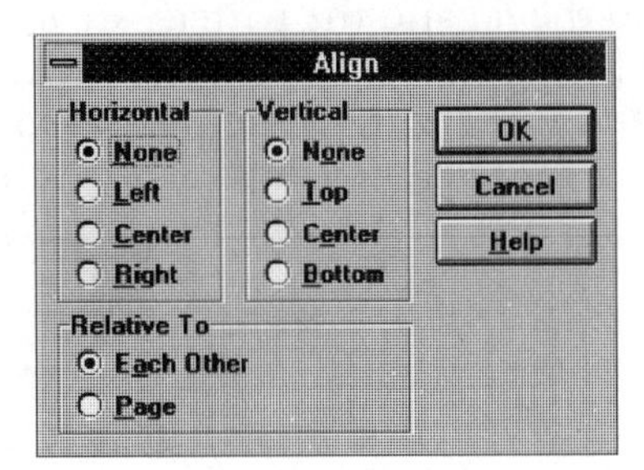

In this case, you would specify Top and Each Other to align the tops to each other, then select OK.

The Snap to Grid button makes it easier to align objects as you draw them. In its dialog box, you can specify what kind of grid you want:

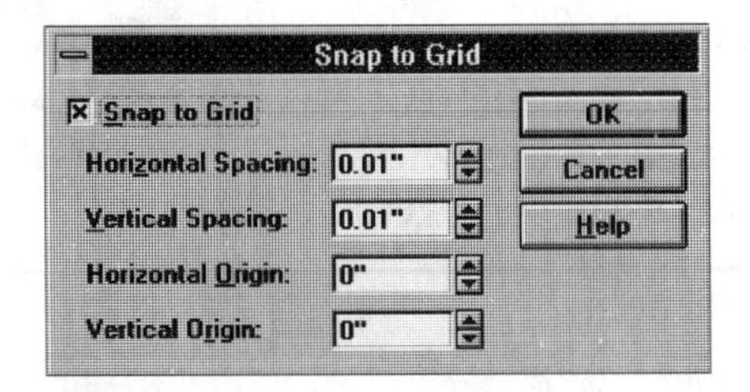

With the Snap to Grid option selected, when you create or move an item, it will always start at a grid point. This can be useful for quickly aligning objects with each other.

The Bring to Front and Send to Back buttons let you control how items appear above and below each other. This lets you layer your items so they appear in the proper order even if you move them. For example, if you draw a line and then draw a circle that is on top of the line, you may want the line to show all the way across the circle, or you may want the circle to obscure the line:

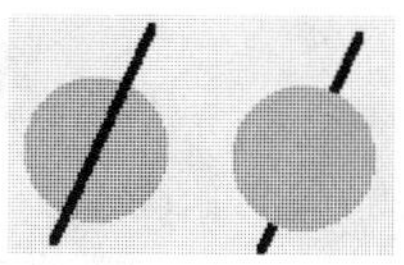

To switch the position of two items, select one of them and then select either the Bring to Front or Send to Back button.

The Bring in Front of Text and Send Behind Text buttons move objects with respect to the text in your document. Thus, you can have an object that blocks out part of the text or shows up behind it:

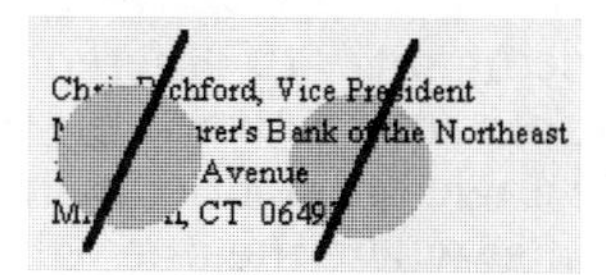

The text box tool allows you to type text into your drawing. The name "text box" is a bit misleading because you can also paste graphics or import pictures in a text box, as you learned earlier in this chapter. To create a text box, select the text box tool, click in one corner where you want the box, and drag to the diagonally opposite corner. You can then put the insertion point in the box, type, and format the text. You can resize the text box by selecting it and dragging its handles.

Text boxes by themselves are not used often. However, the Callout button, a very handy feature, uses text boxes. You may have noticed that some of the drawings in this book have additional text added to them, and the text is tied to part of the drawing by an arrow; this is called a *callout*. Word's callout feature makes it incredibly easy to add a callout to a drawing.

To make a callout, choose the Callout button, then click in the drawing where you want the arrow to appear. Drag to outside the drawing where you want the callout text to appear. Word draws the lines and creates a text box for the callout, as shown here:

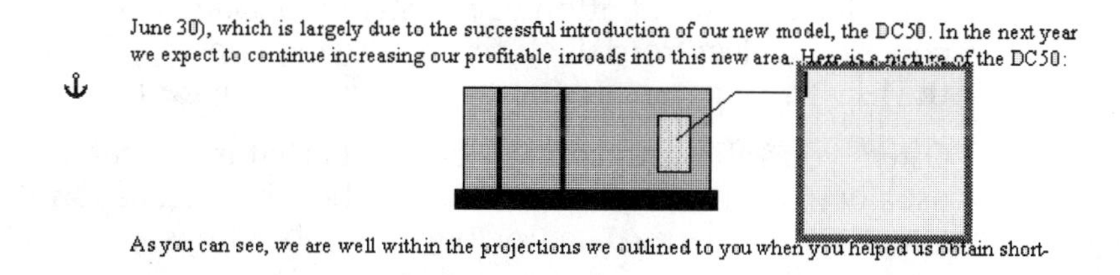

Type the text you want in the text box, then resize it as desired.

You can change the type of callout line easily. Select the callout and choose the Format Callout button. You see the dialog box shown in Figure 12-3.

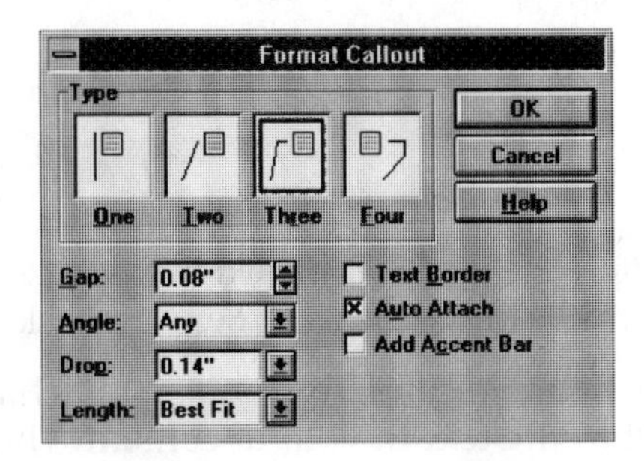

Format Callout dialog box
Figure 12-3.

You can experiment with different types of callout lines. The Gap option changes the distance between the text and the line, the Angle option changes the angle of the line that attaches to the callout, and the Drop option specifies where the line will attach to the callout text. You can even add a border to the callout with the Text Border choice.

As you can see, Word's drawing features give you a great deal of flexibility. Although art is not often used in business documents, it is common to see lines and other shapes used for accents. Feel free to add drawing items to your documents to see if they enhance them.

Lesson 78: Creating Graphs

Word includes a separate program, called Microsoft Graph, for creating charts that you can include in your Word documents. This program is useful if you do not have another program that can create charts and graphs. (However, it does not have the sophisticated capabilities of programs such as Excel, Lotus 1-2-3, or Quattro Pro.) Microsoft Graph is a simple program that lets you enter numbers into a table and create many types of charts from it. It is covered here briefly, to get you started. For more detailed instructions, see the manual that comes with Word.

To start Microsoft Graph, put the insertion point where you want the chart and click the Chart button in the Standard toolbar. You can also start it by choosing Object from the Insert menu and choosing Microsoft Graph from the list. The program's window is shown in Figure 12-4.

Often, you will want to chart some data that is in your Word document, usually in a table. In that case, select the table before you start Microsoft Graph and copy the data (including any headings) to the Clipboard.

The program has two windows: the datasheet and the chart window. The datasheet is a table with the data that will be graphed. It looks like this:

Document3 - Datasheet

	1st Qtr	2nd Qtr	3rd Qtr	4th Qtr
East	20.4	27.4	90	20.4
West	30.6	38.6	34.6	31.6
North	45.9	46.9	45	43.9

The chart window shows how the graph will look when pasted into your document. You can modify the graph by selecting items in the chart window and choosing commands from the Format menu. The chart window looks like this:

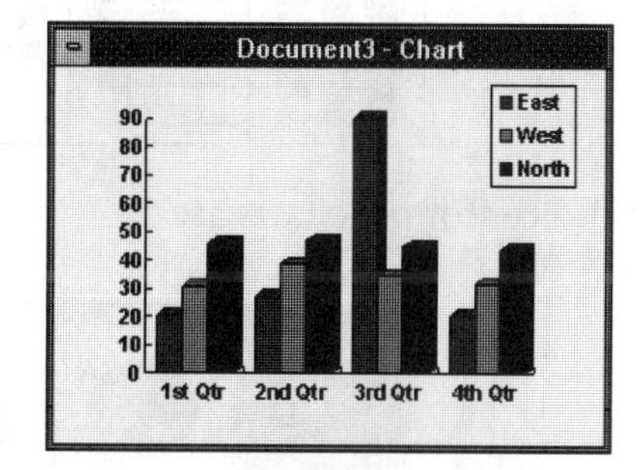

To change the format of items in the chart window, you select them and choose from the menus. For example, to change the font used in some text, select the text and choose Font from the Format menu. As another example, you can change the pattern used in a series of bars by selecting the series of bars and choosing Patterns from the Format menu.

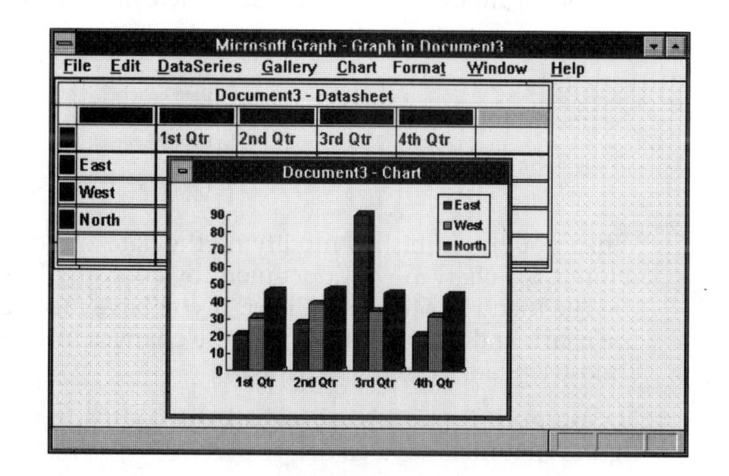

Program window for Microsoft Graph
Figure 12-4.

The DataSeries, Gallery, and Chart menus allow you to make changes to the whole chart. The Gallery menu lists the many kinds of charts you can display, such as pie charts, area charts, and so on. For example, if you want to insert a column chart in your Word document, the gallery choices for the column charts are

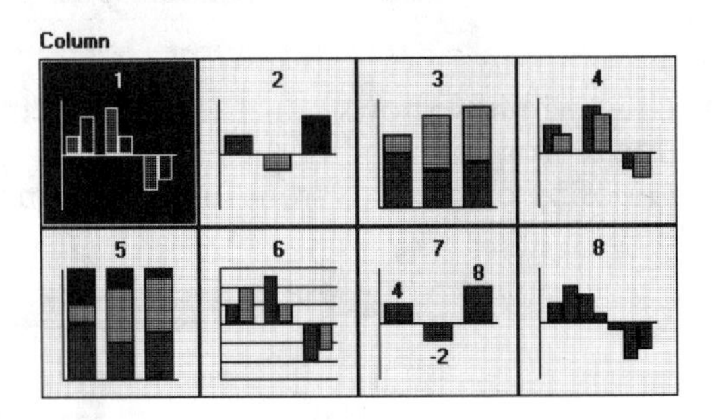

Gallery choices for pie charts are

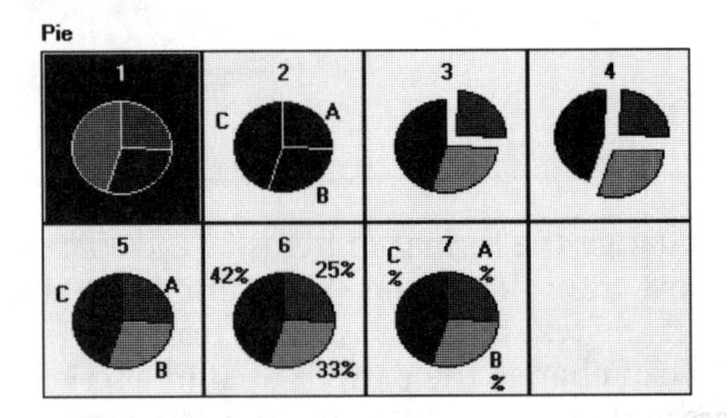

Use the Chart menu to change things like how the axes are displayed and whether or not the chart has grid lines. You can resize the chart by making the chart window larger or smaller. The Chart menu looks like this:

When you have finished modifying the data and chart windows, you reinsert the chart in your document by choosing Exit and Return To from the File menu in Microsoft Chart. If you have made changes to the data or the chart, and simply want to see the changes in your Word document, choose Update from the File menu.

For example, Figure 12-5 shows a letter comparing two years' financial figures that includes a chart.

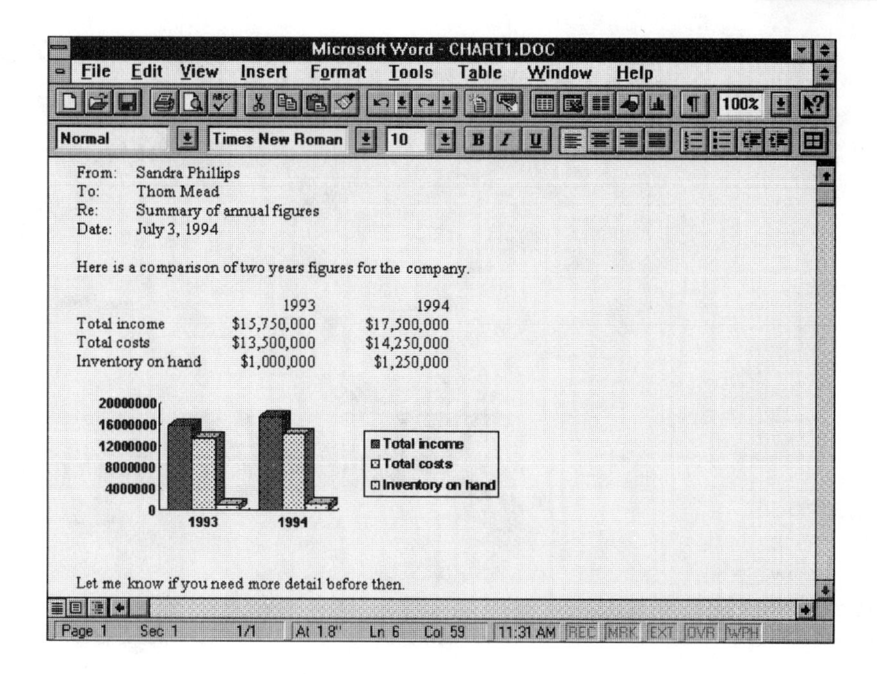

Document with chart added

Figure 12-5.

If you later want to update the chart, simply double-click on the chart. Microsoft Graph starts up automatically with the correct data.

Lesson 79: Creating Equations

Some people need to include mathematical equations in their writing. The Microsoft Equation Editor, which comes with Word, allows you to create a picture that is a description of the equation you want. You can edit this picture in the editor and place it in your document as you would other pictures.

The Microsoft Equation Editor is described in detail in the Word manual. Because few people need to use mathematical equations in their writing, it is only described briefly here.

To insert an equation in your document, put the insertion point where you want the equation to appear, choose the Object command from the Insert menu, and choose Microsoft Equation 2.0 from the list. Word inserts a frame (described in Chapter 20) and changes the window to resemble Figure 12-6.

The editor has many templates for common equations; you simply enter the desired variables and constants in the template. The editor knows about common math formatting. For example, if you put parentheses around an

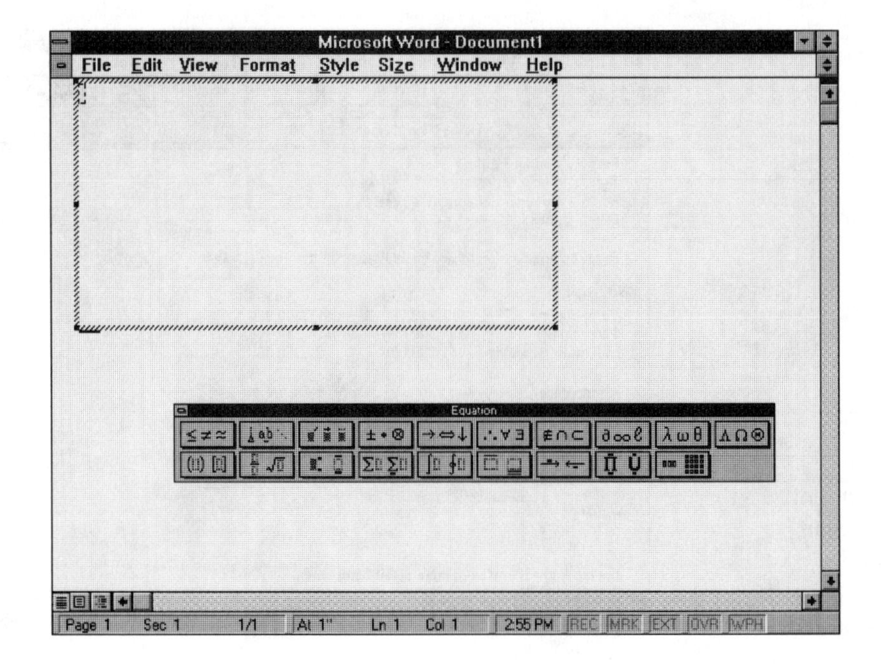

Create mathematical equations in this window
Figure 12-6.

expression, and that expression gets taller (such as by inserting a fraction), the parentheses automatically grow.

The first row of rectangular buttons at the top of the window are drop-down palettes of symbols grouped by mathematical function. The second row are palettes of equation templates. The variable part of the template is represented by a dotted rectangle (called a *slot*). You enter items in your equation by choosing them from the palettes or by typing them from the keyboard.

For example, assume you want to represent the square root of the fraction "x divided by x prime". You would first choose the square root template from the second template palette:

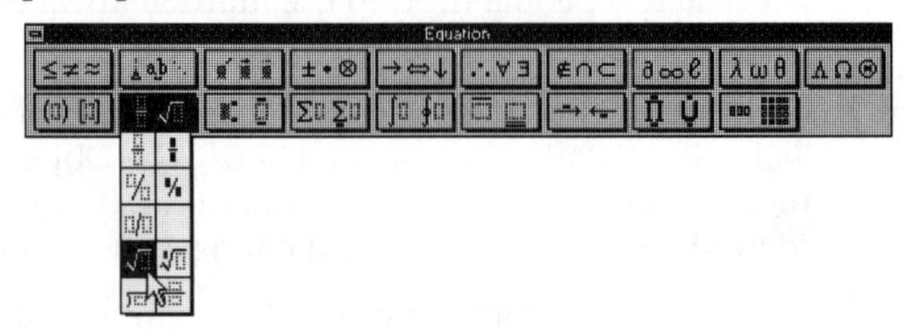

The window now shows the square root symbol and its slot:

Next, choose the fraction template from the second template palette. The result is:

Note that the square root symbol automatically grew to the height of the fraction. The insertion point is in the slot for the top half of the fraction, so type in the letter "x". Press the Tab key to move the insertion point to the lower slot. Type an "x" again.

$$\sqrt{\frac{x}{x}}$$

Click on the third symbol palette:

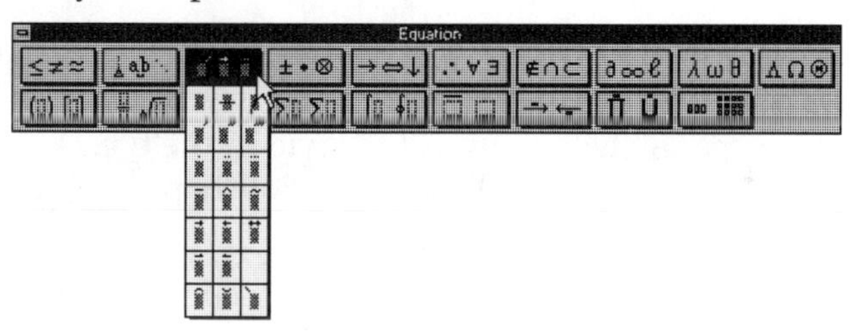

Choose the single prime character, which is the first choice in the second row. Your equation now looks like this:

$$\sqrt{\frac{x}{x'}}$$

When you are finished building your equation, click outside the frame. This closes the Equation window and you can resume normal editing.

You can also format parts or all of an equation with the editor. The Style menu contains descriptions of types of text, which correspond to fonts that you can define. The Sizes menu lets you specify the size of the selected item based on its definition, such as subscript. You can also specify the spacing and alignment of the templates.

Lesson 80: Enhancing Your Text with WordArt

Word's character formatting, described in Chapter 7, gives you many options for adding formatting such as boldfacing and italics. As you can see in magazines, there are many other exciting changes you can make to text that can enliven a document. The WordArt program that comes with Word lets you add special shapes and designs to text.

Note that the result of using WordArt is a picture, not formatted text. WordArt adds the styling you specify, then inserts the result as a picture in your document. To edit the result, you have to double-click on the WordArt picture to start WordArt again.

To insert a WordArt picture in your document, put the insertion point where you want the text to appear, choose the Object command from the Insert menu, and choose Microsoft WordArt from the list. WordArt adds its own toolbar and opens a dialog box in which you enter the text you want to style:

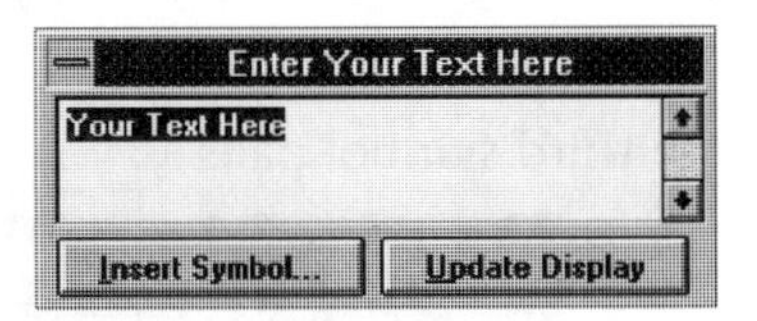

Type the text you want to style in the box. You can also put text in the box by pressing Ctrl-V if you previously put the desired text in the Clipboard.

After you have modified your text, you insert it as a picture in your document by clicking in your document where you want to work next. The WordArt toolbar disappears. To start WordArt again, double-click on a WordArt drawing.

The WordArt toolbar has many options:

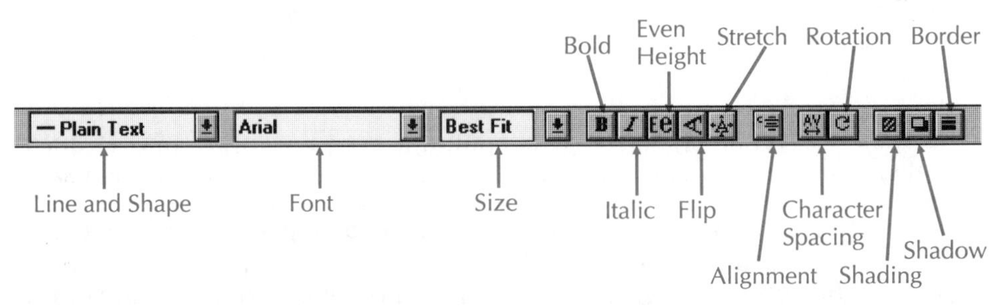

The Line and Shape button brings up the following choices for the orientation of your text:

For instance, the curve at the beginning of the second row causes the text to be shaped along an arch. The filled-in shapes at the bottom of the choices change both the slant and the height of the letters.

WordArt comes with many decorative fonts built in. These fonts are fancier than many standard fonts. You can specify the font size or choose Best Fit to make the text fit the display rectangle.

The Bold and Italic buttons do what you would expect. The Even Height button makes all the letters the same height, even if they would normally be different due to capitalization. The Flip button rotates each letter in the text. The Stretch button causes all the letters to stretch to fill the text box if you have changed the height or width of the box.

You can specify how the text is aligned in the frame if you did not choose Best Fit for the size. The Alignment button has six choices: center, left, right, stretch justify, letter justify, and word justify. The three justification choices let you specify how Word will space the letters.

The Character Spacing button brings up the following dialog box:

You choose the type of spacing you want for all the text at once.

The Rotation button lets you rotate the whole text along the shape you have chosen. The Shading button specifies a type of shading for the inside of the text (such as stripes or dots). The Shadow button has many types of shadows you can add from many lighting positions. You can also add a border to the text with the Border button.

There are so many choices for the buttons and dialog boxes that you should give yourself a few hours to play with WordArt. The combinations of some of the effects (particularly shadows and rotation) can lead to surprising results.

After you have inserted the picture in your document, you can change the frame size as you would with any picture. This is useful for changing the arc of arched text or the height of stretched text.

You can use WordArt for designing logos. For instance, here is one possible logo for National Generators:

Here is a more whimsical one:

To make a letterhead, you can simply put the picture in a centered paragraph above the other text in the letterhead, such as the address and phone number. You can store letterhead in templates, as described in Chapter 11.

Lesson 81: Adding Captions to Pictures

In long documents (such as this book), it is common to have captions under some or all of the art. A *caption* can just describe the art, or it can include a label such as "Illustration 12-3" and some descriptive text. Of course, the next caption for a similar type of art would be "Illustration 12-4", and so on.

Word makes adding either type of caption easy. It also makes renumbering your captions easy. For instance, if you later add an illustration in the middle of your document, it would be tiresome to have to renumber all of the captions that came after the new one. Word's caption feature makes such renumbering automatic.

To add a caption to an item, select the item and choose the Caption command from the Insert menu. The dialog box looks like this:

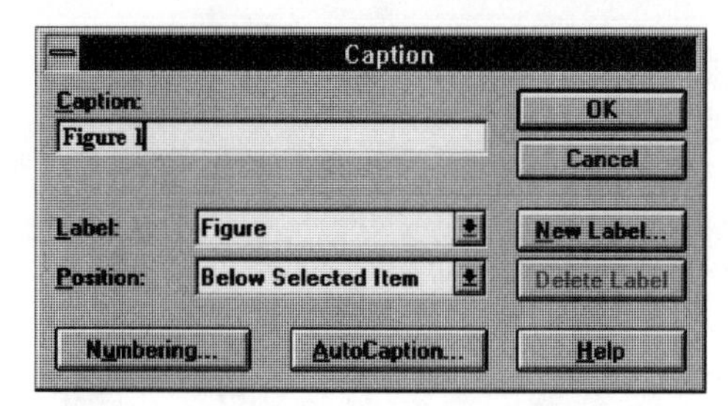

Before typing in the descriptive text, choose the type of label you want from the Label drop-down menu. If you want a different type of label, choose the New Label button and add your own.

Type in your descriptive text in the Caption option at the top of the dialog box. You can also specify the position of the caption, although you are likely to leave the default choice, Below Selected Item. When you select OK, the caption is added to your document.

Word automatically renumbers captions using fields, an advanced feature described in Chapter 26. If you use Word's captions, you should select the Update Fields option in the Print command's options so that your caption numbers are updated before you print your document.

Review

Open the MAGAZINE file and choose a spot to insert a graphic. Create that graphic by using Word's graphics capabilities. (Remember, this does not need to be a work of art.) Insert the graphic into the text. Select the graphic and make it twice as large.

Think about what kind of chart you might add to the MAGAZINE file that relates to the text you typed in. Is there an equation that might be appropriate?

Look at a flyer you have received recently. What parts could be livened up using WordArt?

CHAPTER

13 WORKING WITH TABLES AND LISTS

Many Word documents include tabular material such as financial tables. Almost all documents also include lists such as procedure lists. This chapter covers both topics.

Lesson 82: Creating Lists

Describing a group of items as a list is very common. Lists appear in almost every kind of document you might write. The way that you present a list to the reader has a big impact on how the reader understands the information. Word gives you many ways to present lists in your Word documents.

Before you create a list, you should think about the most appropriate way to show it. For instance, compare the look of the following three lists:

book cases, desks, tables, desk chairs, and side chairs

- book cases
- desks
- tables
- desk chairs
- side chairs

1. book cases
2. desks
3. tables
4. desk chairs
5. side chairs

The first list appears as it would in a paragraph (this is sometimes called an *in-line list*). It is a more conversational way of presenting a list. Of course, you already know how to enter in-line lists: you simply type them as you would any other text.

The second method is a *bulleted list.* In a bulleted list, each item has the same conceptual weight. The third list is a *numbered list.* Numbered lists are best used for steps or processes, not lists in which the order does not matter.

Many people get confused about what types of lists to use for what purposes. The general rule is that a list of equivalent items should be a bulleted list, and a list of steps or a process should be a numbered list. If you put numbers on a list of equivalent items, it implies that there is a hierarchy of the items when, in fact, they are all equally important. Conversely, if you put bullets on a list of steps, it will not be clear to the reader that the steps must be followed in order.

Note that bulleted and numbered lists have only two elements: the bullet or number, and the text. If your list has more than two elements (such as more than one column of text), you want to use Word's table feature, described later in this chapter.

In a list, each item is a separate paragraph. Making bulleted or numbered lists is easy. Simply type in the paragraphs (without the bullets or numbers), select all the paragraphs in the list, and click on the appropriate button from the Standard toolbar. If you do not have the Standard toolbar showing, choose the Bullets and Numbering command from the Format menu, select the type of list from the top of the dialog box, and click OK.

When you use Word's list-making commands, the bullet or number is added to the beginning of each paragraph followed by a tab character. By default, the paragraphs are formatted with a hanging indent of .25 inch. This allows the bullets or numbers to align to the left of the paragraph text.

You can specify exactly how you want the list to look using the Bullets and Numbering command from the Format menu. Use this command for either bulleted or numbered lists. Choose the type of list from the tabs at the top of the dialog box. (The Multilevel tab lets you create more complex lists, described later in this lesson.)

Bulleted Lists

Figure 13-1 shows the Bullets and Numbering dialog box for bulleted lists. You can choose the bullet character and size you want to use (this also becomes the default for the Standard toolbar button) by choosing one of the six choices. You can choose whether or not to reformat the paragraphs with a hanging indent by choosing the Hanging Indent choice.

To remove the bullets from a bulleted list, select the paragraphs and click the Bullets button in the Standard toolbar so that it is not depressed. Alternately, you can give the Bullets and Numbering command again and choose the Remove button.

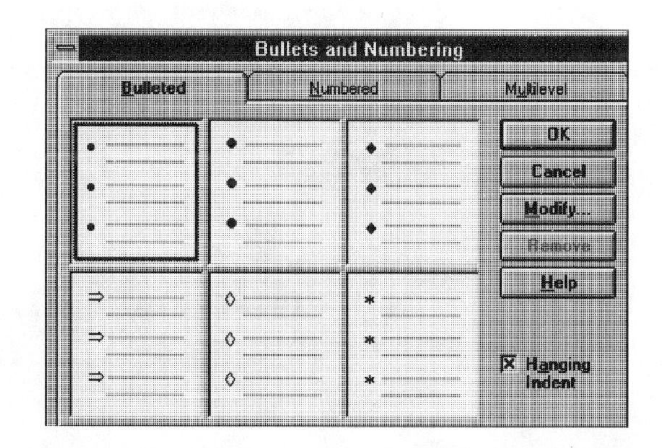

Bullets and Numbering dialog box, Bulleted tab
Figure 13-1.

The Modify button in the Bullets and Numbering dialog box brings up the Modify Bulleted List dialog box, shown in Figure 13-2. You can also modify the position of the bullets here. If you select the Bullet button, another dialog box appears that allows you to choose a bullet character from a complete list of letters and symbols in any font.

Numbered Lists

Figure 13-3 shows the Bullets and Numbering dialog box for numbered lists. Choose one of the numbering styles for your list and select OK.

In this dialog box the Modify button brings up the Modify Numbered List dialog box, shown in Figure 13-4, with choices for changing the numbering style, the text that goes before and after the numbers, and the starting number. To choose the type of number you want, select one of the styles from the Number list box, shown here:

Choice	Description
1, 2, 3, 4	Standard numerals
I, II, III, IV	Uppercase Roman numerals
i, ii, iii, iv	Lowercase Roman numerals
A, B, C, D	Uppercase letters
a, b, c, d	Lowercase letters

To choose the text that goes before and after the numbers, type the before and after text in the Text Before and Text After boxes, respectively. For example, if you want the numbers in parentheses, you would put a (in the

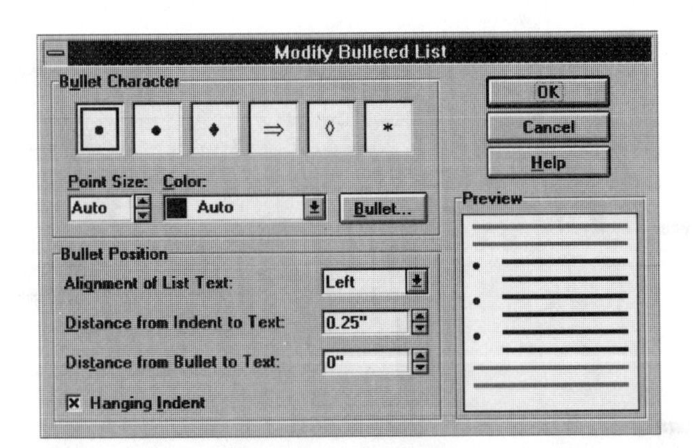

Changing the bullet style
Figure 13-2.

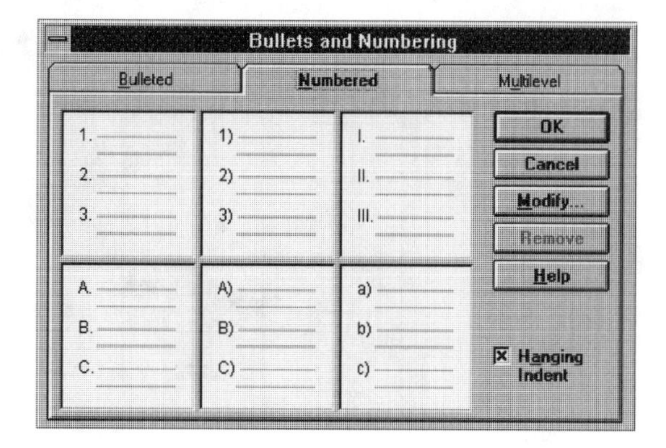

Bullets and Numbering dialog box, Numbered tab
Figure 13-3.

Text Before box and a **)** in the Text After box. To choose the number you want the list to start at, select a number from the Start At list box.

Multilevel Lists

You can also create multilevel lists. A multilevel list is one that contains lists within lists, such as in a structured outline. Multilevel lists can have more than one level of numbering, or can have sublevels containing bullets rather than numbers. Figure 13-5 shows the Bullets and Numbering dialog box for multilevel lists. Note that some of the multilevel lists are numbered, while others have a combination of both numbers and bullets.

Lesson 83: Introduction to Tables

Word's table feature produces tables that are better looking and easier to manipulate than tables that just use tabs. With the table feature, the lengths of the lines of text in your tables shrink and grow naturally as you delete and

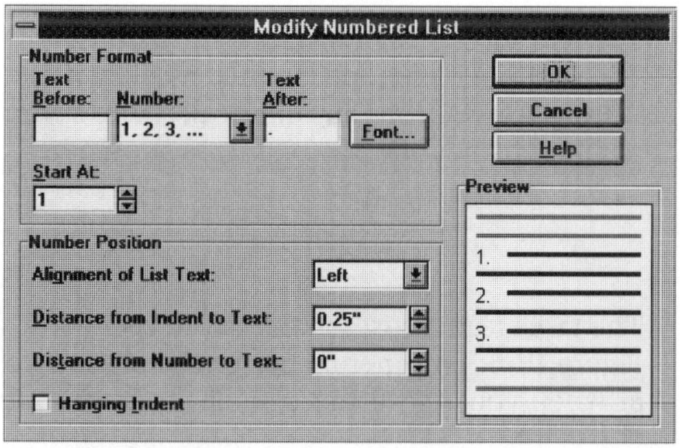

Changing the numbering style
Figure 13-4.

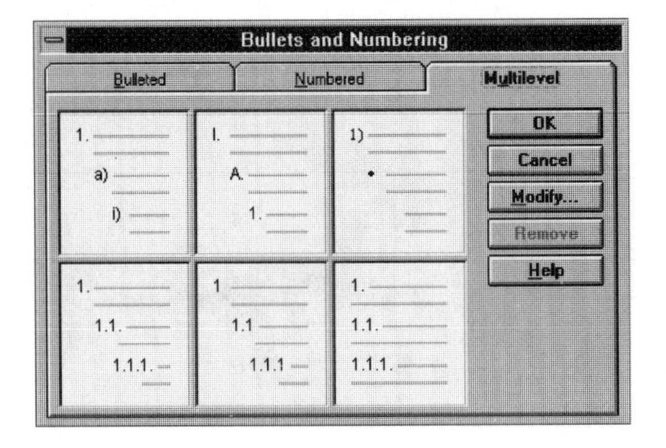

Bullets and Numbering dialog box, Multilevel tab
Figure 13-5.

add text to items, and the formatting within a column or row can be controlled more carefully. Since most business writing includes many types of tables, you should learn to use the table feature so you can create more attractive and informative tables.

A table is made up of cells. A *cell* is a block in the table. A horizontal line of cells is a *row*; a vertical line of cells is a *column*. For example, the table here has six cells: three in the first row and three in the second row.

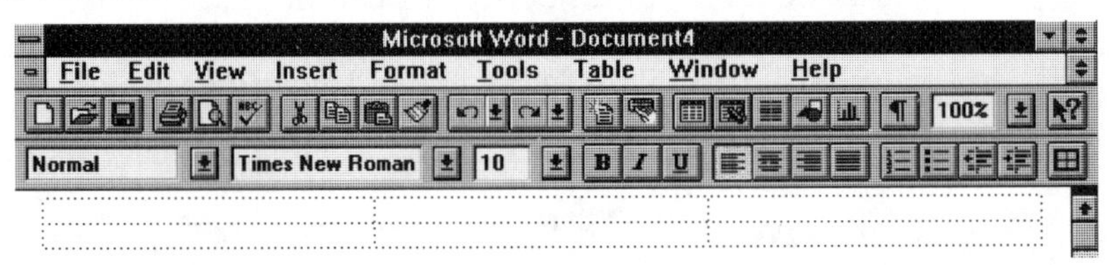

Usually, the information in a row pertains to a single item. All the cells in a column usually deal with one type of data (such as dates, amounts of money, descriptions, and so on). You can manipulate tables by individual cells, rows, and columns. As you will see, all the rows in a table do not have to be identical or have the same number of columns.

You can specify the format of the information within a cell the same way you can in a paragraph. In fact, a cell can contain more than one paragraph. Within a cell, Word automatically wraps words just as it does in the paragraphs in your document, as shown here:

The table feature uses many Word commands in the Table menu, shown in Figure 13-6. This menu changes when you do not have a cell selected, such as when you are starting a table. To start a table, give the Insert Table

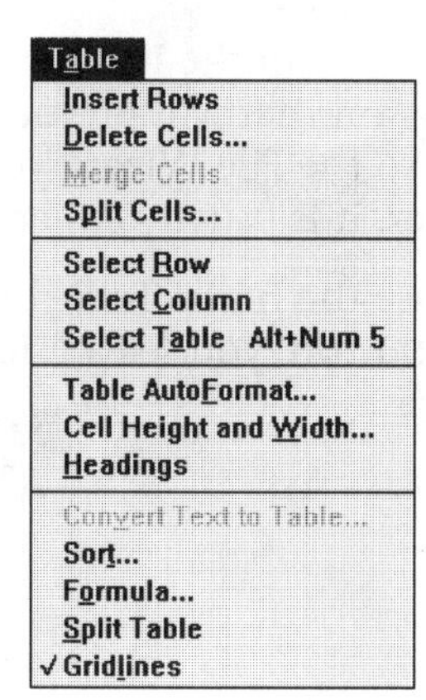

Table menu
Figure 13-6.

command from the Table menu. To change the height and width of cells or of rows and columns of cells, use the Cell Height and Width command. As you will see later in this chapter, you use the Insert Rows, Insert Columns, Delete Rows, and Delete Columns commands to add or remove cells. You can also convert text that is in tabular format (text separated by tab characters) to a table by using the Convert Text to Table command.

When you work with tables, it is often useful to see the boundaries on cells. The default is for you to see a grid for all the tables in your text. (Note, however, that the grid will not print.) You can turn this default off with the Gridlines command, but you should have table grid lines visible as you experiment with the tables in these lessons.

Lesson 84: Creating Tables

In a new document, give the Insert Table command to start a new table. You will see the following dialog box:

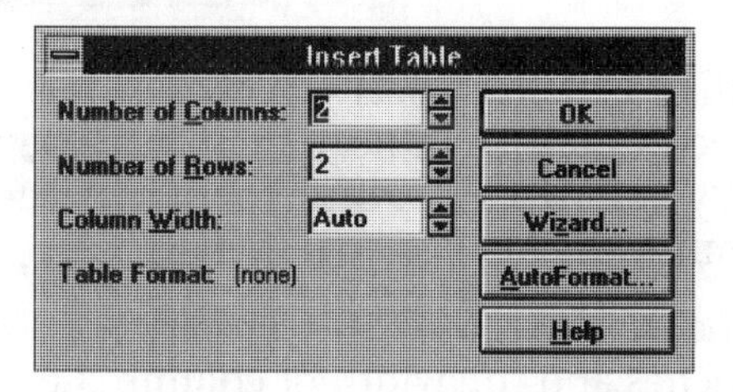

Change the value for Number of Columns to 3 and Number of Rows to 1, and select the OK button. Word displays the table with one row:

(The Wizard button in the Insert Table dialog box brings up Word's Table Wizard, a program that will prompt you for the values when creating a table. This is similar to the File Wizard you saw in the New command in the File menu. However, it is usually easier to create tables without the Table Wizard.)

You can also use the Insert Table button from the Standard toolbar. When you click this button, you see a grid:

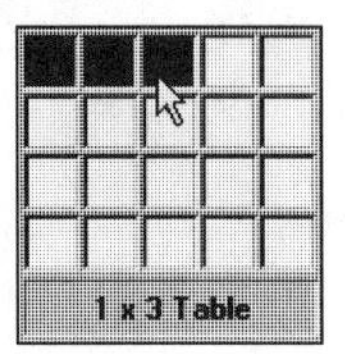

Drag to the size that you want the table to be, in this case, one row and three columns. If the table you want to make is bigger than four rows by five columns, drag past the right or bottom edge of the grid to make it expand. Then the grid will display more rows and columns for you to select.

For this example, you want to make two narrow columns and one wide one. You can put the insertion point in a cell by clicking in it or using the direction keys. In this case, the insertion point is already in the first cell, as you want. Give the Cell Height and Width command from the Table menu and choose the Column tab; you see the dialog box shown here:

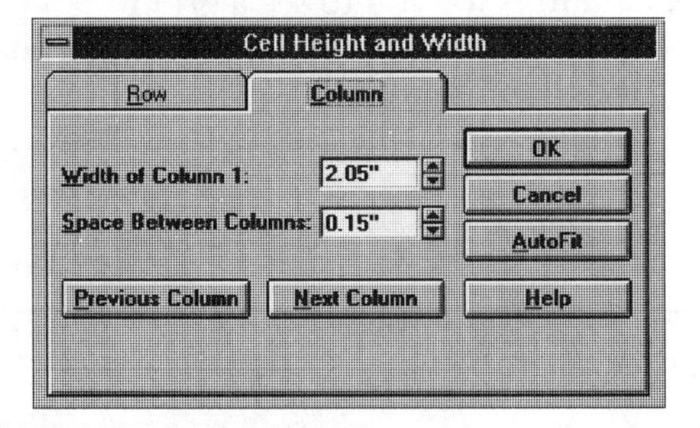

Width of Column 1 lets you change the width of the selected column. Space Between Columns indicates the space between columns in the row. It is usually best to leave a little room between the columns so the text of the columns does not run together.

For the example, use this command to set the width of columns 1 and 2 to 1.5 inches and the width of column 3 to 3 inches. To do this, change the column width for column 1 to 1.5 inches, select Next Column, change it to 1.5 inches, select Next Column, change it to 3 inches, and choose OK. The table grid looks like this:

The Row tab of this command lets you make settings that apply to the entire row:

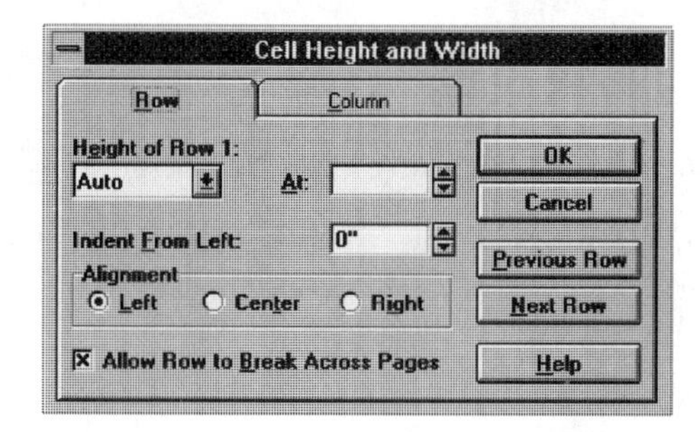

The options are as follows:

- Height is the height of the row. Usually you leave this set to Auto, indicating that Word should adjust the height based on the contents of the cells. You can also choose Exact or At Least and enter an exact amount such as 1 inch in the At option.
- Indent From Left sets the indentation for the first cell in the row from the left margin.
- Alignment tells Word how to align the row between the margins (Left, Center, or Right).
- Allow Row to Break Across Pages specifies that the row might be broken if it appears at the bottom of the page.

Note that the Row Height choices apply to the entire row, not just the cell you selected. All cells in the row change if you change one of these settings.

You can now see how to enter text in a table. Put the insertion point in the first cell and type **Task**. Press the Tab key to move to the next cell, type **Who**, press Tab, and type **Comments**. The table should now look like this:

Be sure the insertion point is at the end of the third column and press Tab to create the next row. Note that you do not press Enter in the third column because a cell can have more than one paragraph in it. When you press Tab (from the far-right cell), Word creates another row:

Task	Who	Comments

13

In the first cell in the second row, type **Select new blade supplier**. Note how Word automatically wraps the text within the column. Fill out the rest of the column, as shown in the following illustration, and then add the next two rows.

Task	Who	Comments
Select new blade supplier	Roger	Get newest catalogs first
Check fuel lines	Jane	Talk to Robert about current federal and state codes
Make new invoice forms	Roger	Enter information from Excel

Remember to add new rows by pressing Tab at the ends of the rows.

You can also set the column widths on the ruler without the Column Width command. Display the ruler by choosing the Ruler command from the View menu, as shown here:

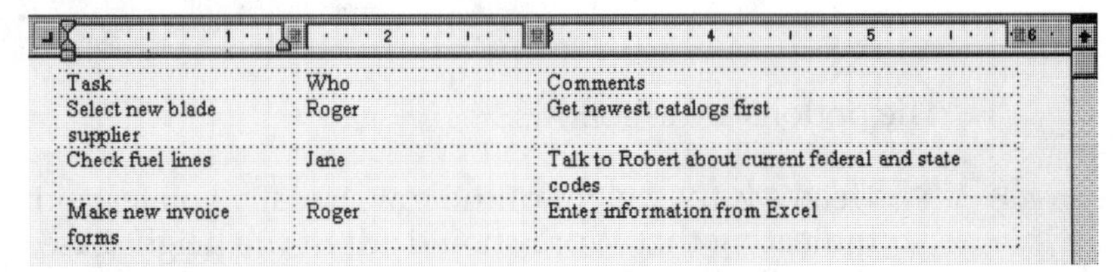

Task	Who	Comments
Select new blade supplier	Roger	Get newest catalogs first
Check fuel lines	Jane	Talk to Robert about current federal and state codes
Make new invoice forms	Roger	Enter information from Excel

You can then drag the column marks (the gray boxes) to change the width. Because cells in a column can have different widths, whenever you want an entire column to have the same width, select the column and use these marks to change the table. Instead of using the ruler, you can also simply put the mouse pointer between two columns and drag.

When you drag in the ruler or in the table to change a column width, you are only changing the width of the one column, not the entire table. Thus, all the columns to the right of the one you are resizing change their widths at the same time. If you only want to change the width of the two columns whose boundary you are moving, hold down the Shift key while you move on the ruler or between the columns.

Since each cell has a paragraph in it, you can change the character and paragraph formatting easily. To select a column, move the pointer near the top of the cell in the first row or give the Select Column command. The pointer becomes a downward-pointing arrow. Click this pointer to select the column, as shown here:

Task	Who	Comments
Select new blade supplier	Roger	Get newest catalogs first
Check fuel lines	Jane	Talk to Robert about current federal and state codes
Make new invoice forms	Roger	Enter information from Excel

For example, assume that you want to center the text in all of the cells in the second column. Select the column and select the Centered button from the Standard toolbar. The paragraphs in those cells become centered:

Task	Who	Comments
Select new blade supplier	Roger	Get newest catalogs first
Check fuel lines	Jane	Talk to Robert about current federal and state codes
Make new invoice forms	Roger	Enter information from Excel

There are many other formatting choices you might want to make for whole rows or columns of cells. For example, you might want to make the whole first row bold. To select the row, click in the row's selection bar at the left of the window or give the Select Row command. Then choose the Bold button from the Formatting toolbar. You might also want to right align or decimal align numbers in some columns.

If you have experimented with selecting and moving in your table, you may have noticed that the actions are somewhat different than in regular paragraphs. To select a cell, you click within the cell's selection bar (the thin area to the left of the text of the cell). To select a row, you click in the selection bar of the row. You saw that to select a column, you select from the top of the column when the pointer turns to a downward-pointing arrow.

There is a second way to create a table. You may already have text with tab characters in it that you want to convert to tables. The Convert Text to Table command from the Table menu makes it easy to convert old-style tables into new tables. To convert these types of text into a table, select the text to be converted and give the Convert Text to Table command. Word can usually determine how you want to convert, changing tab-delimited columns into table columns.

For instance, you might have formatted a list of names and participants in some seminars as follows:

Keller, Stanley, Anderson, Thatcher   Customer service seminar for all C.S. staff. Receptionists are invited to this seminar.
Nolan, Timmer, Fellston   Group dynamics seminar for engineering staff and affiliated technicians.

Note that each paragraph has one Tab character. To turn this list into a table, simply select the paragraphs and give the Convert Text to Table command. Word forms the table:

Keller, Stanley, Anderson, Thatcher	Customer service seminar for all C.S. staff. Receptionists are invited to this seminar.
Nolan, Timmer, Fellston	Group dynamics seminar for engineering staff and affiliated technicians.

Lesson 85: Modifying Table Structures

To add rows or columns to your table, use the Insert Rows or Insert Columns command. To insert a row(s), select the row(s) where you want the new blank row(s) to be; then give the command and the selected row(s) will move down. To insert a column(s), select the column(s) to the right of where you want the new column(s), then give the command and the selected column(s) will move to the right. You can use the Insert Table button in the Standard toolbar for either of these actions.

For instance, assume that you want to add a row between the first and second rows in the table. Select the second row, and give the Insert Rows command from the Table menu:

Task	Who	Comments
Select new blade supplier	Roger	Get newest catalogs first
Check fuel lines	Jane	Talk to Robert about current federal and state codes
Make new invoice forms	Roger	Enter information from Excel

Deleting cells is equally easy. To delete one or more rows or columns, select them and choose the Delete Cells command from the Table menu.

If you have selected a group of cells that are not an entire row or column, you can delete them by specifying which way the rest of the table should be shifted. For example, if you want to delete a single cell from the new second row, first select it or put the insertion point in it, as shown here:

Task	Who	Comments
Select new blade supplier	Roger	Get newest catalogs first
Check fuel lines	Jane	Talk to Robert about current federal and state codes
Make new invoice forms	Roger	Enter information from Excel

Give the Delete Cells command and indicate that you want to shift the cells to the left (to move the cells that are to the right of the deleted cell to the left when it is deleted), and select OK. Your screen will look like this:

Task	Who	Comments
Select new blade supplier	Roger	Get newest catalogs first
Check fuel lines	Jane	Talk to Robert about current federal and state codes
Make new invoice forms	Roger	Enter information from Excel

Notice that the second row now has only two cells instead of three. Word's tables do not require you to have the same number of cells in each row.

If you have selected a group of cells that are not a row or column and you are inserting cells, you can specify whether the added cells should shift the other cells horizontally or vertically in the Insert Cells command. For example, if you want to add a cell to a row, select the cell that will be positioned before the one you want to add, give the Insert Cells command, select Shift Cells Right, and select OK.

You can move rows and columns with the Cut and Paste commands from the Edit menu. For instance, if you select a column and choose the Cut command, the column and its contents are removed. You can then select another column and choose the Paste command: the column in the Clipboard is inserted to the left of the selected column. You can also use drag-and-drop editing with rows and columns. Both of these actions are the same as those described in Chapter 4.

You may have a table that you want to split into two tables with a text paragraph in between. For instance, you may have made a large table of results by department and you realize that there should be an explanation in the middle of the table for the bottom half. To split a table, put the insertion point in the row that you want to be the first row of the second table and choose the Split Table command from the Table menu.

Lesson 86: Borders for Cells

Remember that the grid lines you see around tables on the screen do not print. You can, however, add borders to tables just as you can to paragraphs (as you saw in Chapter 8). You can add borders to just some cells or to the entire table, depending on what you select. You add borders by giving the Borders and Shading command from the Format menu. The Table Borders and Shading dialog box, shown in Figure 13-7, shows the choices. They are the same here as they were for paragraphs.

You can put borders to the left, right, above, or below a cell. You can also add borders between cells vertically or horizontally. For example, if you

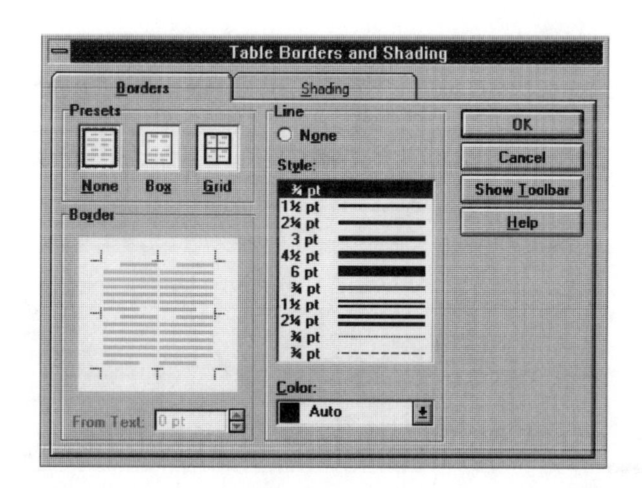

Table Borders and Shading dialog box
Figure 13-7.

select a row of cells, give the Borders command, and select the vertical line between the middle guides, Word draws vertical and horizontal lines between the cells in that row.

The Borders toolbar is particularly handy if you are adding different kinds of borders to the tables in your document.

Lesson 87: Advanced Table Handling

As you have seen, tables are easy to create, modify, and format. This lesson shows you some of the other features that set Word's table handling apart from other word processors.

Formatting tables can be tedious if you have to repeat the character, paragraph, and border formatting commands each time in a table. Word's Table AutoFormat command from the Table menu (not the Format menu) makes formatting as easy as picking a format from a list. Figure 13-8 shows the dialog box for the Table AutoFormat command.

The list of formats at the left gives the predefined table styles that you can choose from. The two sections at the bottom of the dialog box tell Word where to apply the formats; generally, you will leave those selections alone. For example, the Simple 2 format looks like this:

Task	Who	Comments
Select new blade supplier	Roger	Get newest catalogs first
Check fuel lines	Jane	Talk to Robert about current federal and state codes
Make new invoice forms	Roger	Enter information from Excel

Many tables have headings that describe the contents of each column in the table. For example, the first row of the table you saw earlier in this chapter would be a heading, as shown in the illustration at the top of the next page.

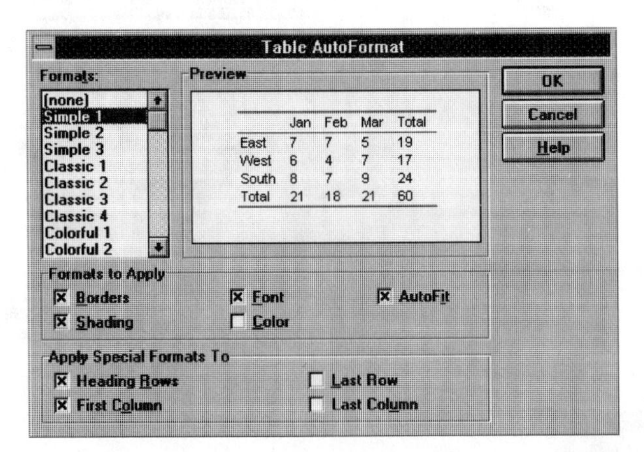

Table AutoFormat dialog box
Figure 13-8.

Task	Who	Comments
Select new blade supplier	Roger	Get newest catalogs first
Check fuel lines	Jane	Talk to Robert about current federal and state codes
Make new invoice forms	Roger	Enter information from Excel

If your table is long enough to appear on more than one page, you probably want the heading to appear at the top of the second page. Instead of manually putting in a new row at the top of that page, you can simply select the first row of your table and choose the Headings command from the Table menu. This causes that row to appear at the top of the page when a table is broken across pages.

As you get better with tables, you may want to get a bit fancy with your design. For instance, you may want to make a table with a heading that has a single cell that is over two columns, such as:

Jobs	**Participants**	
Layout	Robert	Jane
Pre-plan	Jane	Chris
Timing	Jane	Robert
Implement	Chris	Sam

You could create this effect by making a table, deleting one of the cells in the first row, and carefully lining up the new column widths. Word makes this task much easier. Instead of deleting cells, simply select the two cells that are above the two columns and choose the Merge Cells command from the Table menu.

If you have a single cell or column of cells that you want to split into two cells or two columns of cells, the process is similar. Simply select the cell or column and choose the Split Cells command from the Table menu.

Lesson 88: Calculations in Tables

If you use tables for numbers, you may want to perform calculations on the values in the table. For instance, if the rows in the table are sales figures, you may want the last row to be the sum of the values in the rows above it. Of course, you could use a spreadsheet program (or a calculator) to perform these calculations, but Word lets you do your calculations from within the table itself with the Formula command from the Table menu.

The Formula command uses fields, an advanced Word feature described in Chapter 26. Because of this, you need to know a fair amount about fields in order to use this feature well, and it is only covered briefly here.

To create a formula, you put the insertion point in the table cell in which you want the calculation made. For example, assume that you had the following table and wanted the last row to have the sums of the rows above it for each column:

Region	January	February	March
New York	33,473	27,118	30,210
Philadelphia	18,420	19,911	19,287
Atlanta	26,430	30,487	32,187
Totals:			

Put the insertion point in the first cell of the last row and choose the Formula command from the Table menu. You see

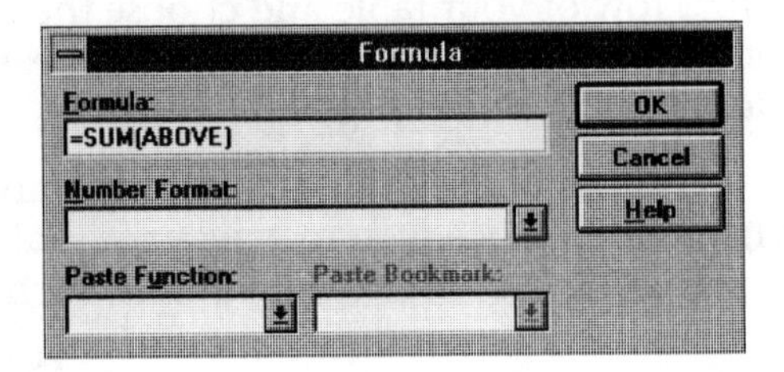

The default formula is the one you want (namely, the sum of all the cells above this one). You can also choose a number format for the result. When you choose OK, Word puts the result of the formula in the cell:

Region	January	February	March
New York	33,473	27,118	30,210
Philadelphia	18,420	19,911	19,287
Atlanta	26,430	30,487	32,187
Totals:	78,323		

The formula you enter has two parts: the function and the cells on which it works. The more useful functions are AVERAGE, MIN, MAX, PRODUCT, and SUM; Word also has logical functions such as IF, AND, and OR. The cells on which it works can be specified as ABOVE, BELOW, LEFT, and RIGHT to indicate all the other numeric cells in the same column or row. You can also specify the exact cells on which the function should work.

If you change the numbers in the table, the results of the formula should change as well. Because these are fields, Word can update the results easily. Simply select the cells with the formulas and press F9 (this is explained in more detail in Chapter 26).

Review

Find a table in a magazine article and add it to your MAGAZINE file. Be sure to use the same character and paragraph formatting that is in the original table.

Add a border with a double line to just the cells in the heading of the table. Then add a border to the other cells with a single line.

Word For Windows
Word For Windows

C H A P T E R

14

PAGE LAYOUT AND SECTION FORMATTING

This chapter describes the third level of formatting: section formatting. A section can be thought of as one chapter in a larger document, but it can also refer to the entire document. Section formatting lets you specify such things as page margins, headers and footers, page numbers, and so on.

Lesson 89: Introduction to Sections

In Chapters 7 and 8, you learned how to format characters and paragraphs to improve their appearance. The third unit of formatting is the section, which allows you to specify the page formatting of your text when it is printed out. Page formatting, often called *page layout,* generally consists of setting the page margins and the position of the *headers* and *footers* (the text at the top and bottom of each page, such as the chapter name and the page number).

Most often you will use the same page layout throughout a section or document. Sometimes, however, you may use a few different page layouts. For example, the preface of a report may have different page number formatting than the main text. Word lets you change the page layout for each section.

If you want your document to be one long section, you do not need to do anything special. To split a document into two sections, put the insertion point where you want the section break and give the Break command from the Insert menu:

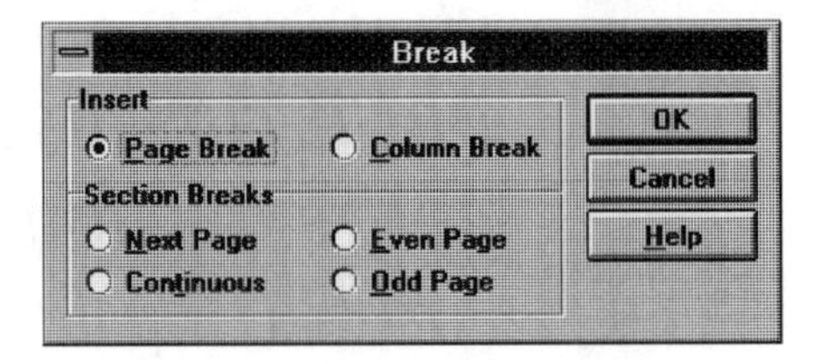

The four section break options, which specify where to start the section, let you choose whether you want the section to continue on the same page as the previous section or to start on a different page. These choices are:

Choice	Result
Next Page	Starts section on the next page
Continuous	Continues from previous section without break
Even Page	Starts section on the next even page
Odd Page	Starts section on the next odd page

If you are in normal view (but not if you're in page layout view), Word displays a double dotted line:

::::::::::::::::::::::::::::::::End of Section::::::::::::::::::::::::::::::::

You can delete the section mark by selecting it and pressing the Backspace key or choosing the Cut command.

Many commands in Word change the format for a section. The formatting characteristics of each section are kept in the section mark at the end of the section, just as paragraph characteristics are stored in the mark at the end of a paragraph. You can bring up the Page Setup command by double-clicking the section mark. A section mark holds the section formatting for the section preceding the mark (just like a paragraph mark holds the formatting for the paragraph just before the mark).

There are four commands that affect section formatting:

- Page Setup from the File menu sets the margins and the description of the paper you are using. It also tells where a section starts and how pages are aligned with the top and bottom margins.
- Header and Footer in the View menu lets you enter headers and footers for the pages in the section.
- Page Numbers in the Insert menu enters a page number on the pages in the section.
- Columns from the Format menu specifies the number of columns of text in the section.

These commands are described throughout this chapter.

Figure 14-1 shows the beginning of a summary for a funding proposal. It is used to illustrate formatting throughout this chapter and the next one. You

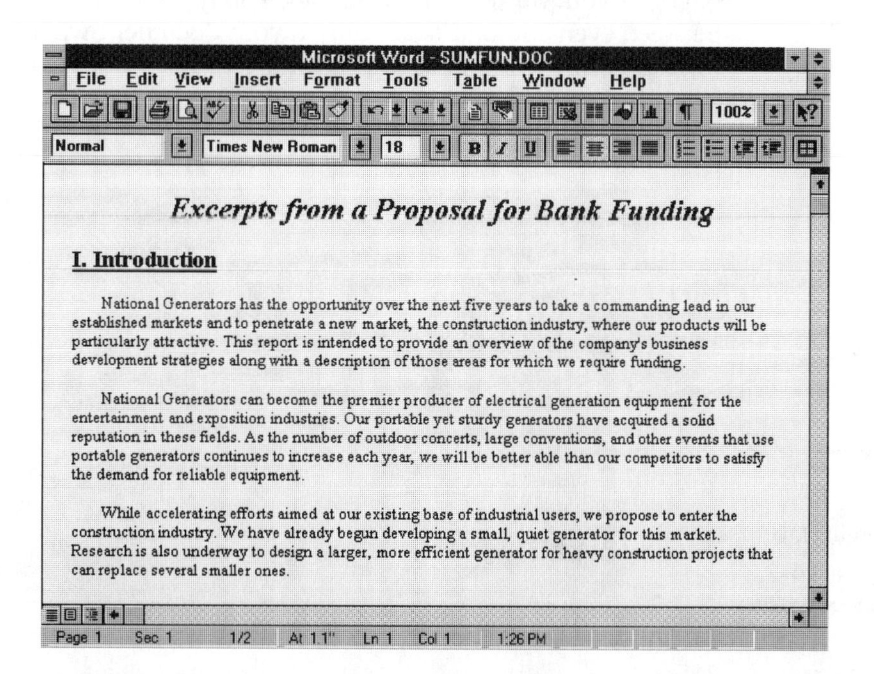

Funding proposal summary
Figure 14-1.

do not need to type the report into Word; however, you may want to type sections when trying out the examples.

Lesson 90: Setting Margins and Paper Size

Use the Page Setup command from the File menu to specify the page margins and other options that affect the look of your sections. Figure 14-2 shows the Margins tab of the Page Setup dialog box.

Some users get confused between margins and indents. Page margins are measured from the edge of the paper; paragraph indents are measured from the left and right page margins. Page margins are set in the Page Setup command for the entire document, while paragraph indents are set by the Paragraph command for each paragraph. Figure 14-3 may help clear up the difference.

The concept of odd and even pages is basic to many choices in section and document formatting, particularly in headers and footers. If you examine books and magazines, you find that they always begin on the right page. (For example, look at the beginning of this book.) This means that all right-hand pages have odd numbers (1, 3, 5, and so on) and all left-hand pages have even numbers (2, 4, 6, and so on). If you want to differentiate between left and right pages, select the Mirror Margins option in the Page Setup command.

Knowing whether a page is odd or even often helps in formatting your pages, as you will see in this chapter. You need to specify a difference between even and odd pages only if your document will eventually be printed *back-to-back*, or *double-sided,* meaning on both sides of a piece of

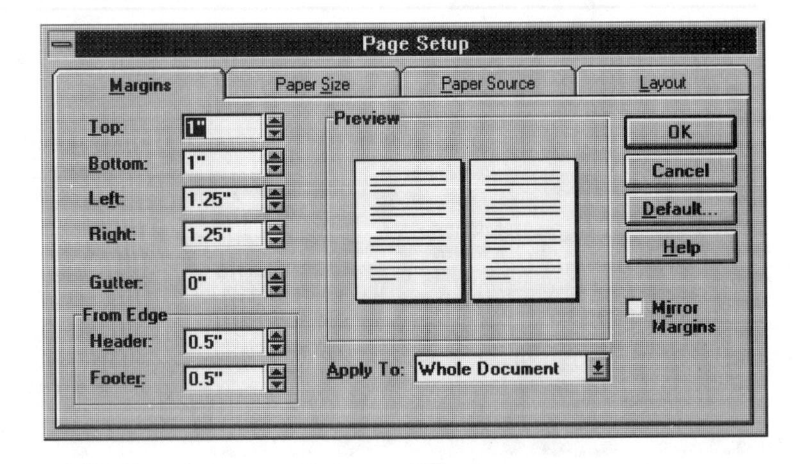

Page Setup dialog box, Margins tab
Figure 14-2.

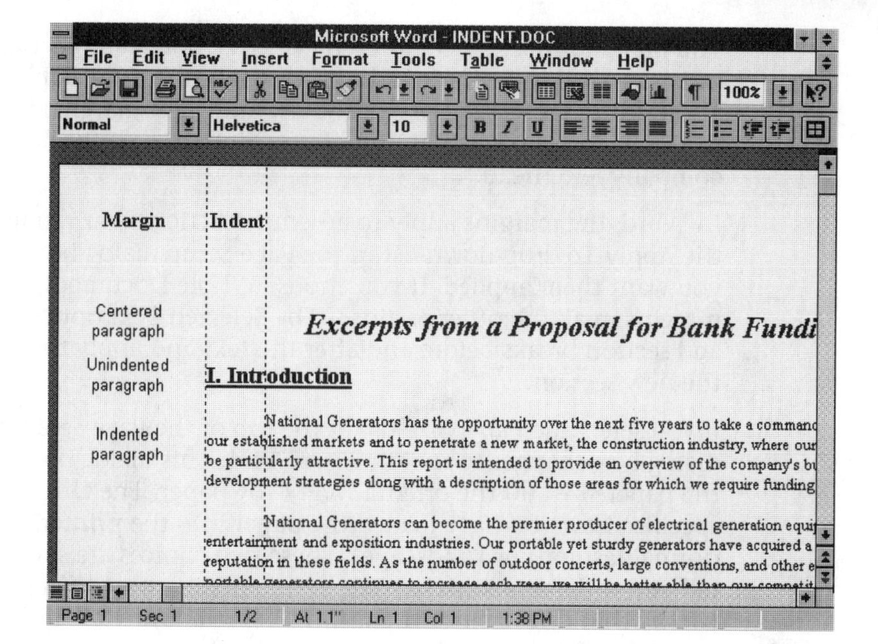

Difference between margins and indents
Figure 14-3.

paper. If your document will be on only one side of the paper, you can ignore the difference between even and odd pages.

If you are going to bind your document, you may want to set a gutter width. The *gutter* is the center space between two pages of a book that is not used in printing; in this case, it is the amount of space that is used in binding the document. Since binding a document or punching holes takes up a certain amount of space from the left side of odd-numbered pages and the right side of even-numbered pages, Word allows you to stretch the margins, alternating between left and right pages. Set the gutter width to the amount that would be lost in binding. When your pages are printed and bound, the text will not run into the gutter and will thus be easier to read. Note that the margins in this book are wider on the inside of each page, since the binding steals a bit of paper width.

Word determines the line length of a page in this way:

line length = page width – (left margin + right margin + gutter)

The top and bottom margins are set by default to 1 inch, and the left and right (or inside and outside) margins are set to 1.25 inches. These four values are the ones you are most likely to reset. Word gives you wide margins so that your headers and footers do not appear too near the edge of the page.

You may, however, need different settings. For example, many publishers insist on a 1.5-inch border around text submitted for publication. You may also want to reduce the size of the left and right margins for business letters to 1 inch so the page doesn't look so empty or so it fits better on your company letterhead.

In Word, the margins apply to an entire section. You can use the choices in the Apply To drop-down list in the Page Setup dialog box to specify where you want them applied. If you choose Whole Document, Word changes the margins in all the other sections. The Selected Text option causes Word to add section breaks before and after the text and apply those margins just in the new section.

If you select the Paper Size tab at the top of the Page Setup dialog box, the dialog box changes to that in Figure 14-4. This dialog box lets you change the paper size and the orientation of the paper. The Orientation choice specifies how you have loaded the paper into the printer: Portrait (the normal fashion) or Landscape. (These two choices are sometimes known as tall and wide, respectively.) You can remember the difference between these two by thinking of fine art paintings: portraits are tall and narrow and your eyes move from top to bottom, while landscapes are short and wide and your eyes move from left to right.

If your printer has more than one way of putting paper in it, you can choose where the paper comes from in the Paper Source tab. For instance, some laser printers have two input trays. You can specify one tray for the first piece of paper and the second tray for the others. This is handy if you are printing letters on letterhead stationery: you put the letterhead in the top tray and the second sheets in the bottom.

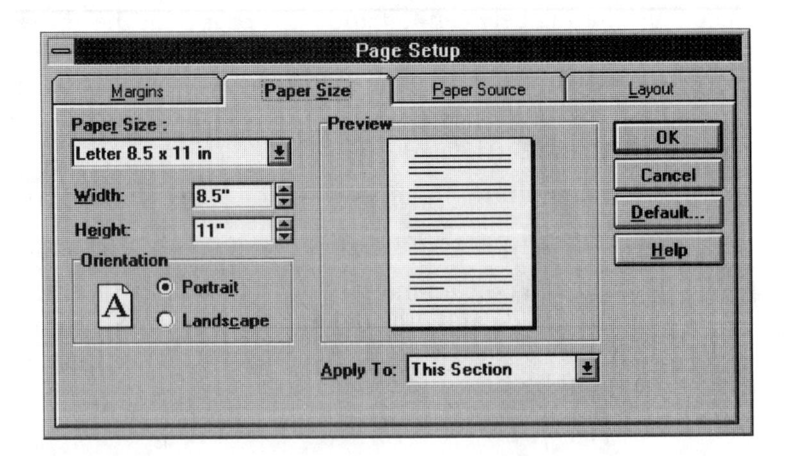

Page Setup dialog box, Paper Size tab
Figure 14-4.

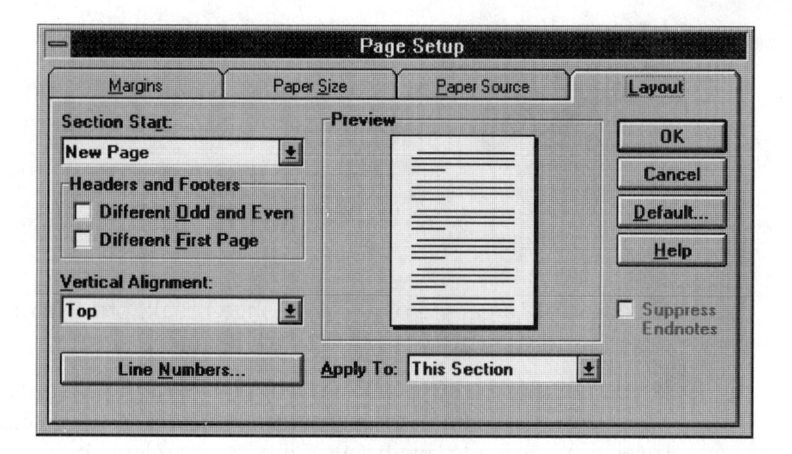

Page Setup dialog box, Layout tab
Figure 14-5.

The Layout tab, shown in Figure 14-5, specifies a few other section formatting features.

- ✦ The Section Start option lets you change where the section begins (you specified this when you entered the section mark).
- ✦ The Vertical Alignment choice tells Word how to align the text on the page vertically. Normally, you will want to keep the first line lined up with the top margin, but you can also choose to center the text vertically or to increase the interline space so that the text is aligned with both the top and bottom margins. These are only useful on a page that is not full.
- ✦ The Header and Footer options are described later in this chapter.

Lesson 91: Repaginating and Page Breaks

Word keeps track of each page break in your document in normal view by default. This makes the program run a little more slowly than if it didn't do this, but it is usually not noticeable. To turn off background repagination, use the Options command in the Tools menu, choosing the General choices. In page layout view and print preview, Word always repaginates your document as you edit.

Word puts a line of dots across the page at the places where page breaks occur:

We will need to add one senior mechanical engineer and two technicians in R and D. We will also need a technical services manager, two product managers, and a merchandising manager in marketing. The advertising budget will include campaigns in trade magazines and attendance at national trade shows.

....

National Generators has shown a profit each year since its founding in 1974. Pretax profits were $3.25MM on sales of $17.5MM (20%). This year sales are expected to reach $19MM and a pretax profit of $4.2MM (22%). Five year projections call for $50MM in sales and pretax profit of $12MM (25%).

To force Word to start a new page, set the insertion point at the desired location and give the Page Break command from the Insert menu, or press Ctrl-Enter. If you are in normal view, Word prints a line of dots with the words "Page Break" across the screen to indicate the forced page break:

Page Break

If you want to get rid of a forced page break, put the insertion point right after it and use the Backspace key to delete it.

If you want to be sure that a particular paragraph appears at the top of a page, you can format the paragraph to cause a page break instead of inserting a forced page break. To do this, select the paragraph, give the Paragraph command, choose the Text Flow tab, and select Page Break Before.

When you start using Word to edit long documents, using the scroll bar or the Pg Up and Pg Dn keys to move through the document can be inconvenient. To move from page to page, you can use the Go To command from the Edit menu. You can also open the Go To dialog box by double-clicking the page number in the lower-left corner of the document window. The Go To dialog box looks like this:

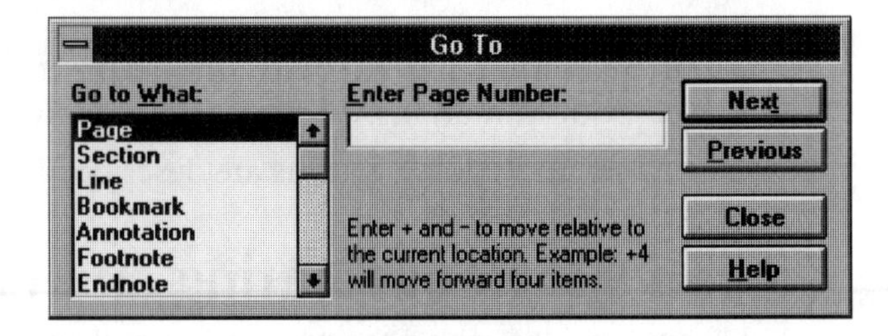

Be sure Page is chosen in the Go To dialog box, and enter a page number. Word moves the insertion point to the beginning of that page. If your document has more than one section, you can also use the Go To command to go to a particular page in a particular section. For example, to go to page 7 of the third section, type **7S3** in the Enter Page Number text box. You can also go to the beginning of sections with the Section choice in the dialog box.

Lesson 92: Using Headers and Footers

Word allows you to put headers and footers at both the top and bottom of each page and to change their text as often as you want. Your headers and footers can be more than one paragraph, or they can be just a page number on the page.

In the Layout tab of the Page Setup dialog box, you can choose to have different headers and footers appear on odd or even pages. You can also specify that the first page of a section has a unique header and footer.

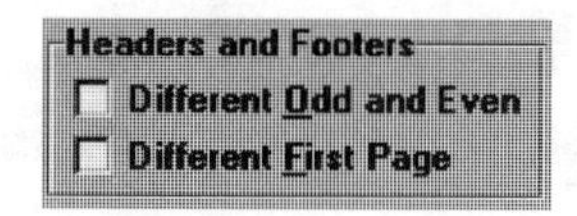

Depending on your requirements, you can have up to six different headers and footers in a document. Often, however, you will have similar or identical text at the top or bottom of even or odd pages or no text at all.

Before you start, decide if you want to have different headers and footers on even and odd pages if you are going to print on two sides of the paper. Also, decide whether you want headers and footers on the first page of the section. You usually do not want a header on the first page of a chapter since a header distracts the reader from the chapter title. Notice how there are no page numbers on the first page of chapters in this book for example.

Creating headers and footers is fairly easy. First, decide what information you want to present; then decide which part of that information should be at the top and which part at the bottom of the page. If all you want is a page number, see the next lesson.

To edit the header or footer, put the insertion point in the section with the header or footer you want to change, and choose the Header and Footer command in the View menu. This puts you in page layout view and displays the Header and Footer toolbar:

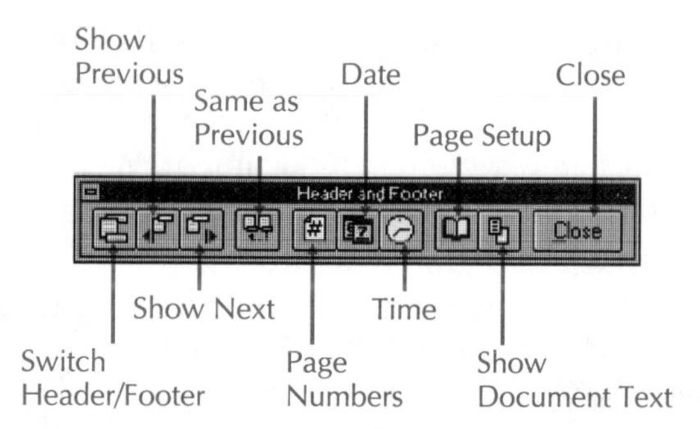

After you choose the Header and Footer command in page layout view, the areas for the headers and footers are marked:

Header

If you chose Different Odd and Even in the Page Layout command, Word identifies the type of header or footer you are editing:

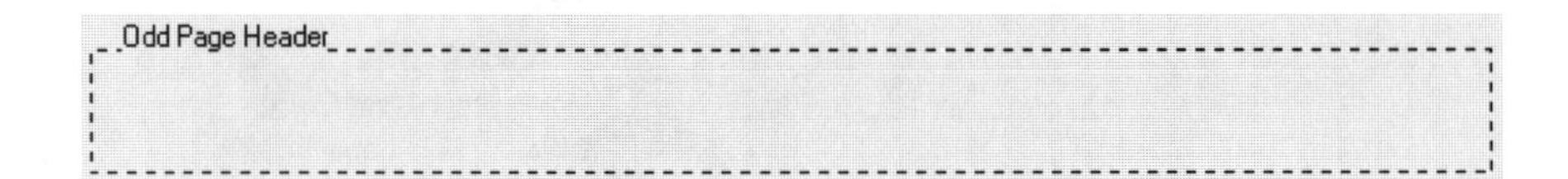

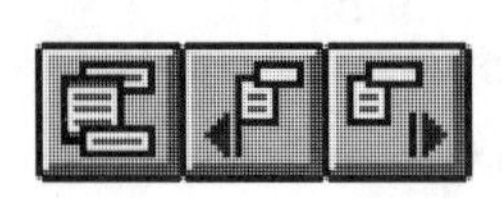

You can move between the different headers and footers with the buttons in the Header and Footer toolbar. The Switch Header/Footer button moves you between the header and footer on the same page, while the Show Previous and Show Next buttons take you to the preceding and following pages.

Simply type the desired text in the header or footer area. Within the paragraphs that are headers and footers, you can use any character or paragraph formatting you want. For instance, you might have a chapter name in bold and the page number in italics. You can use paragraph formatting to line up the parts of the header or footer with the margins or to center them between the margins. Tab stops, described in Chapter 8, are especially helpful here (Word supplies default tabs for the header and footer).

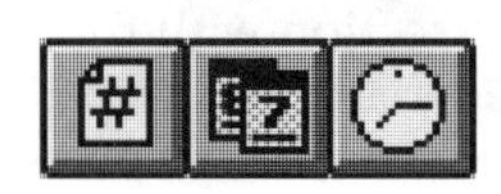

The three buttons in the middle of the Header and Footer toolbar let you enter the page number, date of printing, and time of printing, respectively, in your header or footer. For instance, to have a footer that says "Page" and the page number, type **Page**, press the Spacebar, and click the Page Numbers button.

The Header and Footer toolbar also includes a Same as Previous button. You use the Same as Previous button if you want to change the header or footer you are editing to be the same as the one in the previous section. When you create a new section in a document, Word automatically copies all the headers and footers to that new section, so this button does not normally need to be used.

You can specify the header and footer positions in the Margins tab of the Page Setup command, or you can modify them using the vertical ruler in page layout view or print preview. In the Page Setup command, enter values in the From Edge options to place the header and footer:

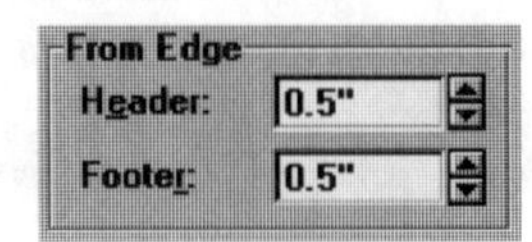

In page layout view, you change the header and footer positions by dragging the header and footer margins in the vertical ruler. The white margin is shown at the left of the header or footer:

Note that the text starts immediately after the bottom of the header area.

Now you can actually create the header. Here are the steps for creating the header "Funding Proposal, page " and the page number on the right side of the page (for odd pages):

1. Choose the Layout tab of the Page Setup command and specify Different Odd and Even, but be sure that Different First Page is not selected:

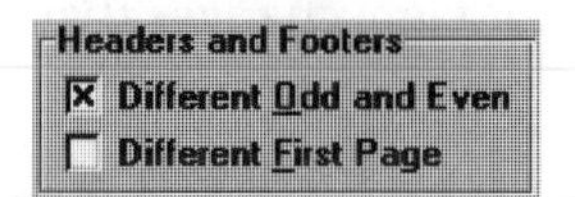

2. Give the Header and Footer command from the View menu.
3. Select the Odd Header. Note that the title at the top of the entry area tells you which header or footer you are editing. If the Even Header is the first one selected, choose the Show Next button from the Header and Footer toolbar.

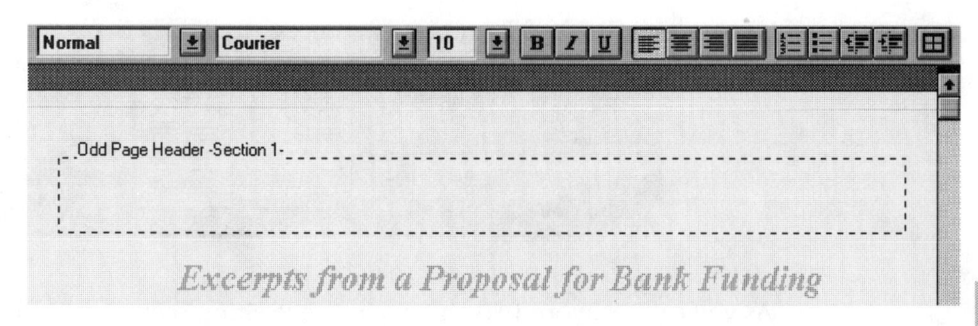

4. Press Tab twice so that you are at the right margin. Type the text **Funding Proposal, page** followed by a space.

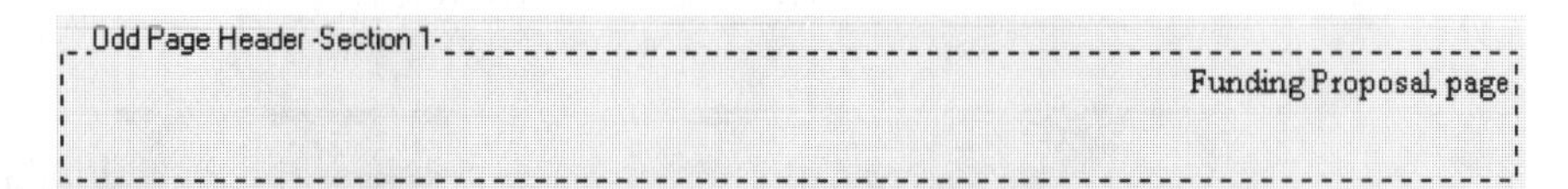

5. Select the Page Numbers button. Word inserts the page number in the heading. Don't worry that it shows an actual page number; the real page number will appear when you print.

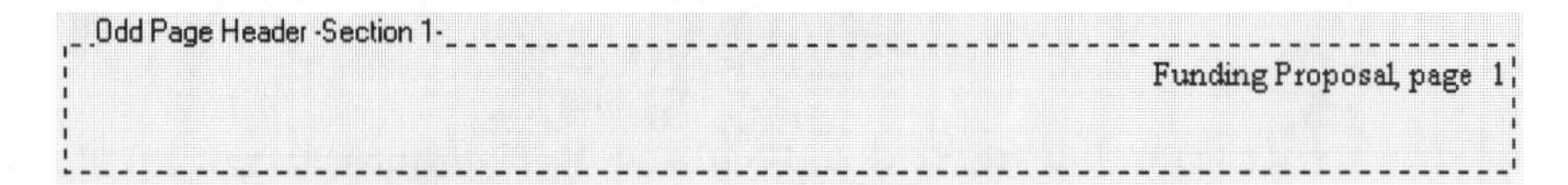

6. Select the Close button.

Enter other headers and footers in the same way.

You can change the text of the headers and footers in page layout view simply by editing the text. Remember that headers and footers are the same throughout a section, so changing the text of a header or footer on one page in page layout view changes that text for the entire section as well.

Lesson 93: Page Numbering

If all you want in the header or footer of a section is a page number, you can give the Page Numbers command from the Insert menu. This creates a header or footer containing just the page number. If you followed the directions in the previous lesson, you do not need to use this command.

The Page Numbers dialog box looks like this:

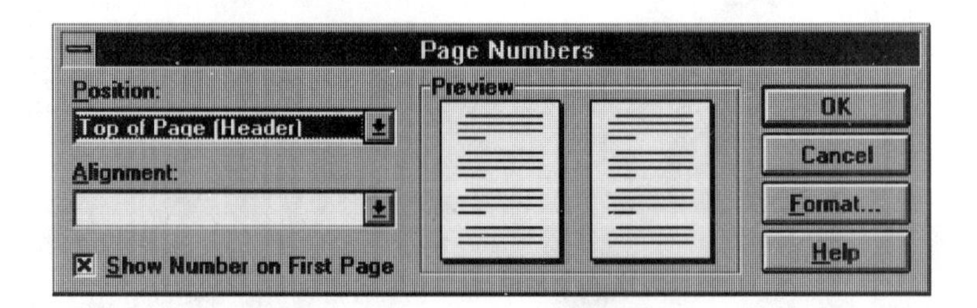

As you can see, your two choices in the Position section will create a header or a footer. The choices in the Alignment section tell Word what type of paragraph formatting to use when it creates the header or footer.

Whether you used the Header and Footer command or the Page Numbers command, you can modify the way page numbers appear in your document. Give the Page Numbers command and select the Format button in that dialog box. You see the following:

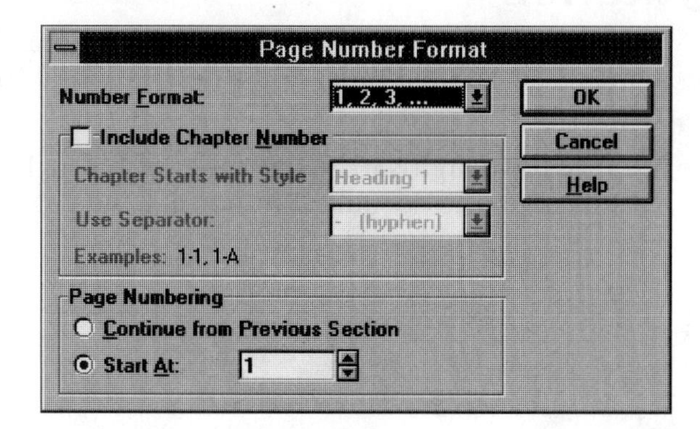

You can choose a format for page numbers. This is extremely useful when you submit articles and reports for publication because many publishers have guidelines about the format of page numbers. The formats for the page numbers that are available are as follows:

Format	Choice
Numeric	1 2 3
Roman numeral (upper)	I II III
Roman numeral (lower)	i ii iii
Alphabetic (upper)	A B C
Alphabetic (lower)	a b c

You can also choose to include the chapter number with the page number. This is handy with documents in which you want both to show. For instance, page 3 in Chapter 8 would have its header or footer as "8-3". In order to use this option, you must be using styles, as described in Chapter 15.

Page numbering can start at 1 in each section or at the number after the last page of the previous section. If you choose the Continue from Previous Section option, Word continues numbering from the previous section in the file; if this is the first section, it starts at 1. If you choose Start At and fill in a number, it will start there.

You can use this option to restart the page numbering to 1 in a book with two numbering sequences. For example, this book has front matter numbered with lowercase Roman numerals. The first page of the first chapter starts again at 1. If this were a Word document, the front matter would be a different section from Chapter 1.

Review

Add a header and footer to the MAGAZINE file. Put the page number in the right corner of the header and a description of the article in the right corner of the footer.

Change the margins to be narrower by 1/2 inch in each direction. Note how that changes the document in normal and page layout views.

Word For Windows
Word For Windows
Word For Windows

C H A P T E R

15

USING STYLES TO SIMPLIFY FORMATTING

Up to this point you have had to specify the formatting characteristics for the characters and paragraphs in your text. Microsoft Word also allows you to define a set of styles for your documents that is automatically used when you format. When you use styles instead of direct formatting, you specify the style for each type of paragraph (such as a normal paragraph or a section heading), and Word formats the paragraph by finding the corresponding style in the document's set of styles. You can also use styles on some types of text, such as for product names or book titles.

Lesson 94: Introduction to Styles

Styles can be thought of as formatting guides. Each style is a type of paragraph or character and the formats associated with them. For example, to format a normal paragraph in your text, your instructions might be "justified text, indent the first line 1/2 inch, and skip a line before the paragraph." Instead of having to format each paragraph this way when you enter or edit the text, you simply tell Word that you are entering a normal paragraph. Word looks up the formatting for your normal paragraph in the style sheet and applies it to the paragraph. If you use boldface Helvetica each time you give a product name in a document, you might make a character style called "Product Name" that makes the characters boldface and changes the font to Helvetica.

Using styles in Word consists of two steps. First, you must create the styles by defining the types of styles you want. To do this, you use the Style command from the Format menu. In addition to defining styles, you can use the many predefined styles that come with Word. After you design the styles, you format your document by labeling its elements with styles. As you will see, there are many ways to specify the styles used in your documents. Word also lets you copy styles from document to document easily.

Styles are kept in documents or templates (templates are described in Chapter 11). One of the excellent features of formatting with styles is that you can have many different sets of styles in different documents that use the same style elements, but you can format them differently. Thus, a normal paragraph in one template might be double spaced and ragged right, but in another it might be single spaced and justified. You might use the first template to print rough drafts so you can correct mistakes easily and then use the second template to print your final document.

Word lets you specify the types of styles you want and allows you to modify and add styles easily; you do not need to stick to predefined styles. You might have styles for normal paragraphs, long quotations, running heads, section headings, and so on.

Using styles does not prevent you from using direct formatting, but you will probably find that using styles almost exclusively makes writing and printing easier. You can, however, use some direct formatting when it is faster or when you are sure you will not want to change the format.

A big advantage of styles is that, if you have used only styles and want to change the format of one type of paragraph in all of your different documents, you do not need to change any of them individually with direct formatting: simply change your style sheets. Your new formatting is automatically used.

For example, you may have a style called Chapter Heading that corresponds to boldface, 24-point, centered text. If you later want all the chapter headings to be underlined and left aligned, you only need to change the style; you do not need to search through all of your files for the chapter headings. Similarly, if you want to change the product names from boldface Helvetica to italicized Palatino, you only need to change that character style.

If you want to begin using styles but do not yet want to create your own styles, use Word's predefined styles. These appear in the Style command along with your own styles. Of course, you can modify the attributes of these predefined styles if you wish.

If you want to convert a directly formatted document to styles, you should first unformat the entire document. To unformat a document, select the entire document with the Select All command from the Edit menu, press Ctrl-Shift-N to make all paragraphs normal, and then press Ctrl-Spacebar to remove all character formatting.

Lesson 95: Defining Your Styles

Now that you understand the concept behind styles, the next step is to create a style with which you can experiment. In addition, you will modify some of the predefined styles.

The rest of this chapter uses the report shown in Chapter 14 for its examples. You may want to enter the first section heading and the first few paragraphs of the report so you can try out examples as they are presented. When you enter the text, be sure not to use any direct formatting commands. The top of the text is shown in Figure 15-1.

To start making styles, give the Style command from the Format menu. You see the dialog box shown in Figure 15-2. The list of styles is usually the styles you are using in your document. You can also list all styles or just the styles you have defined by selecting from the List drop-down list. The buttons at the right of the Style dialog box take you to different dialog boxes.

To see how to define a style, choose the New button in the Style dialog box. In the New Style dialog box, shown in Figure 15-3, you can see all of the types of formatting you can specify in a style.

You will create a style for the report title. You will also modify two other styles: the Heading 1 style used for the section headings and the Normal style used for all regular text paragraphs.

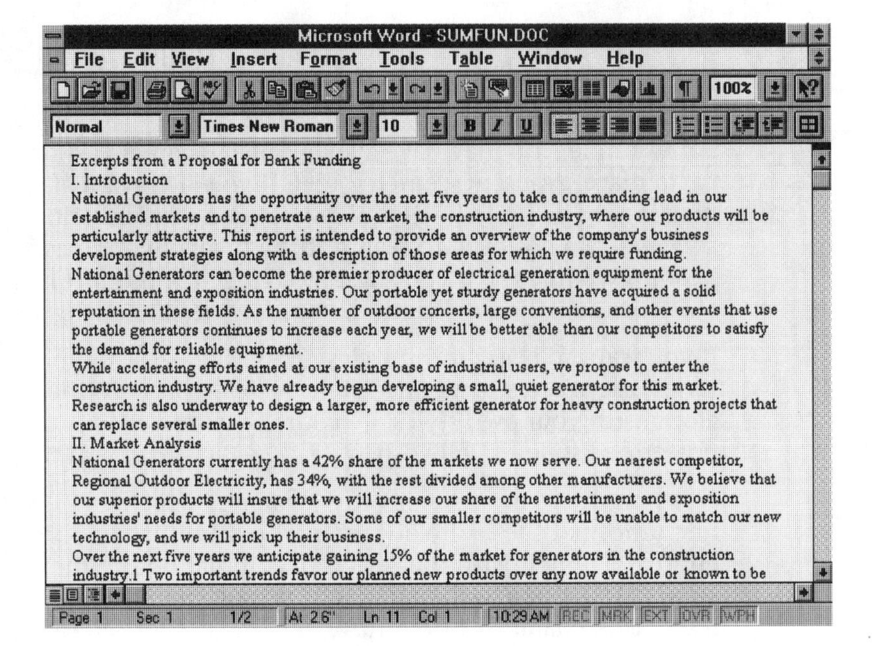

Top of report with formats removed
Figure 15-1.

When you create a new style, Word starts with the formatting that is in the currently selected paragraph. Thus, if you know what kind of formatting you want to use in that new style, give the appropriate formatting commands on a sample paragraph before giving the Style command.

To begin, close the Style dialog box and select the title paragraph. This is currently in Normal style (as is everything in a file before you start giving style commands).

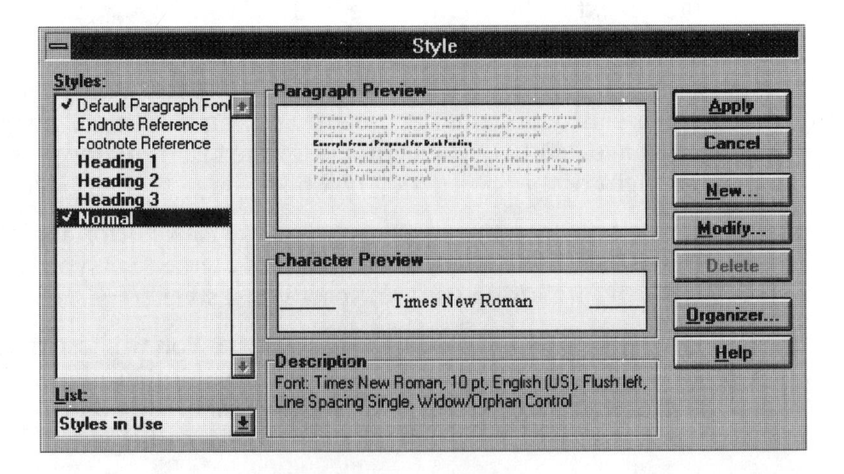

Style dialog box
Figure 15-2.

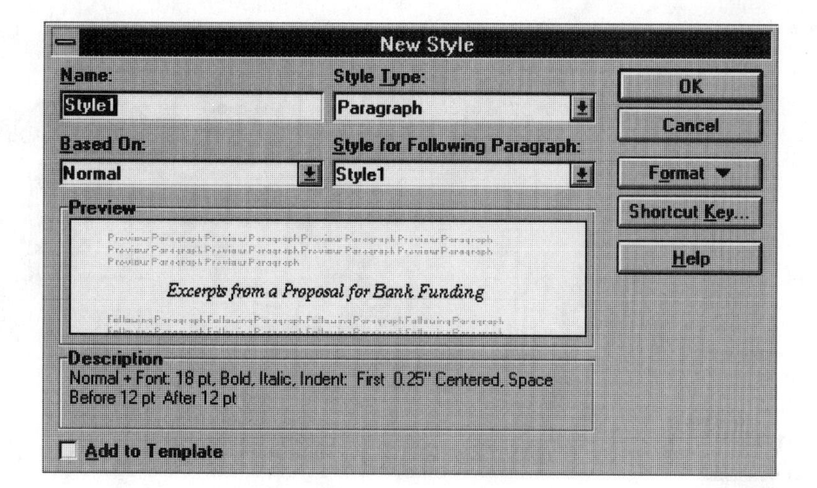

Modify Style dialog box
Figure 15-3.

The Formatting toolbar shows what style is used on any paragraph:

Add some direct formatting to this paragraph so you can see how Word learns formatting from text. Make the characters 18 point, bold, italic, and centered, with one line after. The top of your document now looks like this:

Be sure the insertion point is in the title paragraph and give the Style command. Select the New button. The New Style dialog box for entering new styles is shown in Figure 15-4. Enter the new style's name in the Name option. For this example, type **Doc Title**. Note that the character and paragraph formatting for this paragraph are shown in the Description (by example) box:

Description
Normal + Font: 18 pt, Bold, Italic, Indent: First 0.25" Centered, Space Before 12 pt After 12 pt

Select the OK button, and the new style is defined.

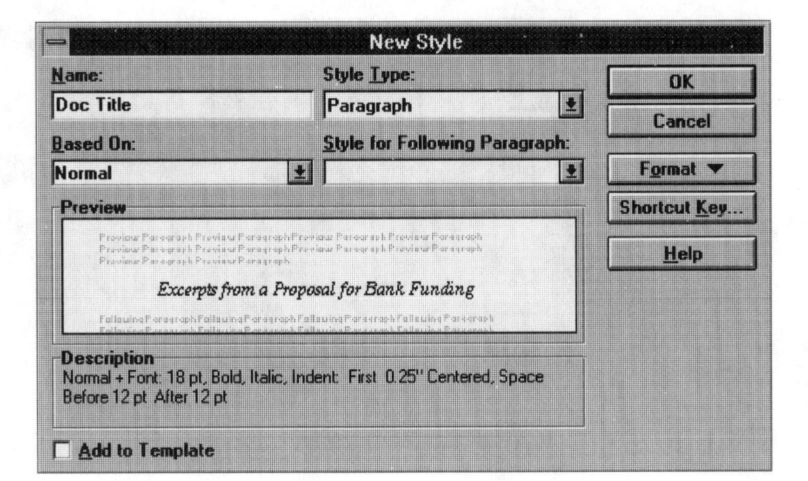

New Style dialog box
Figure 15-4.

Next, you want to modify the predefined style called Heading 1 so you can use it on the headings in the report. Select the Heading 1 name in the Styles list at the left of the Style dialog box.

In the case of the headings, you want them to be in Times New Roman font, bold, underlined, 14 point, and kept with the next paragraph. Note that this predefined style already comes with some formatting, such as "Bold", and "Space Before 12 pt".

To change the formatting to what you want, choose the Modify button. The Modify Style dialog box looks almost exactly like the New Style dialog box. Choose the Format button, then use the Font and Paragraph choices in that list, just as if you were using direct formatting. These choices bring up dialog boxes that look identical to the ones for the commands from the Format menu. When you are finished changing the formats for this style, select the OK button.

Next, change the style for normal paragraphs. Select Normal from the list of styles, select Modify, select Paragraph from the list in the Formats button, and specify 12 points before and justified. Again, select the OK button.

You have now added a new style and changed the formatting in two predefined styles. Select Close to close the Style dialog box. Clicking Apply would apply the style in the Style list to the current selection, which is not what you want to do right now.

15

Lesson 96: Using Styles in Your Documents

Now that you have defined some styles, you can start applying them to your documents. You can give text a style by selecting the text and selecting the style from the drop-down list in the Formatting toolbar. You can also select the list by pressing Ctrl-S. This list is a drop-down list of all the styles created for your document. The list looks like this:

Default Paragraph Font
Doc Title
Endnote Reference
Footnote Reference
Heading 1
Heading 2
Heading 3
Normal

You can also see the names of your styles in the *style area,* an area to the left of the selection bar. By default, the style area is not shown. To show it, choose the View tab of the Options command in the Tools menu, and give a measurement other than 0 for the Style Area Width choice (.6 inches is probably sufficient). You will then see

Normal

National Generators has the opportunity over the next five years to take a commanding lead established markets and to penetrate a new market, the construction industry, where our products particularly attractive. This report is intended to provide an overview of the company's bu development strategies along with a description of those areas for which we require funding.

Normal

National Generators can become the premier producer of electrical generation equipment f entertainment and exposition industries. Our portable yet sturdy generators have acquired a reputation in these fields. As the number of outdoor concerts, large conventions, and other events th portable generators continues to increase each year, we will be better able than our competitors to the demand for reliable equipment.

For example, select any part of the first section heading, "I. Introduction". Select Heading 1 from the Styles list to indicate that this is a heading. The style is applied:

Notice that the paragraph is now formatted properly and that "Heading 1" appears in the style drop-down list. Now select any part of the document title, drop down the style list, and choose the Title style. You can continue adding styles to the rest of the document.

To see the power of style sheets, suppose you decide to have the normal paragraphs left aligned instead of justified. Give the Style command, choose the Normal style from the list, select the Modify button, select Paragraph from the Format button, change the formatting to left aligned, select OK in the Modify Style dialog box, and select Close in the Style dialog box. As soon as you return to editing, all your normal paragraphs are changed to the new style, as shown in Figure 15-5.

Lesson 97: Working with Styles

As you have seen so far, there are many things you can do with styles. This lesson shows you more details about using styles and shows how styles interact with many other Word features.

Character Styles

The styles you added and modified so far in this chapter have all been paragraph styles. Character styles are not used as often as paragraph styles, but are just as easy to work with. In the New Style or Modify Style dialog boxes, simply choose Character from the Style Type drop-down lists.

For example, assume you want to create a character style called "Product Name". In the Style dialog box, choose New, type **Product Name** in the Name option, choose Character from the Style Type list, choose Font from the list in the

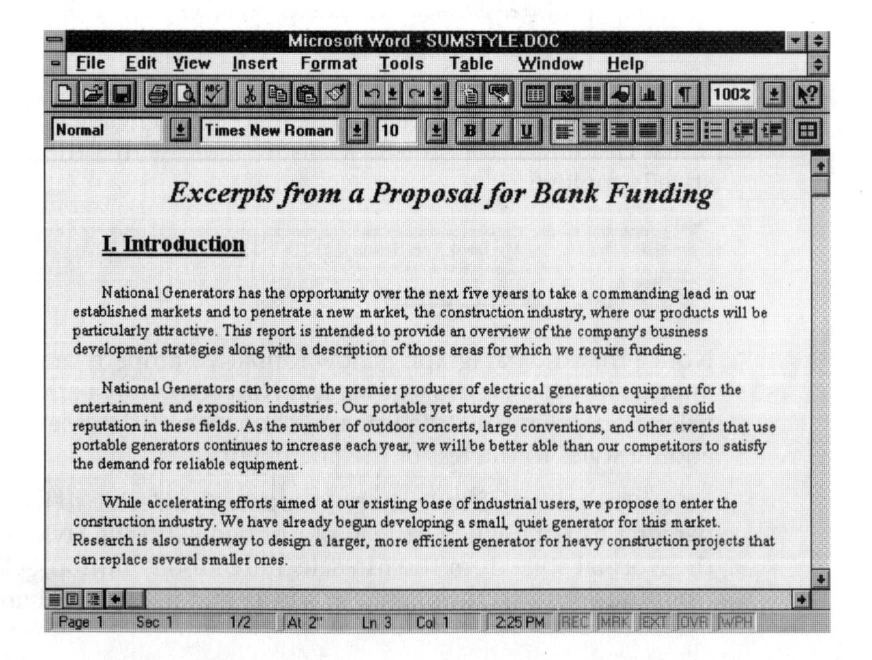

Excerpts from a Proposal for Bank Funding

I. Introduction

National Generators has the opportunity over the next five years to take a commanding lead in our established markets and to penetrate a new market, the construction industry, where our products will be particularly attractive. This report is intended to provide an overview of the company's business development strategies along with a description of those areas for which we require funding.

National Generators can become the premier producer of electrical generation equipment for the entertainment and exposition industries. Our portable yet sturdy generators have acquired a solid reputation in these fields. As the number of outdoor concerts, large conventions, and other events that use portable generators continues to increase each year, we will be better able than our competitors to satisfy the demand for reliable equipment.

While accelerating efforts aimed at our existing base of industrial users, we propose to enter the construction industry. We have already begun developing a small, quiet generator for this market. Research is also underway to design a larger, more efficient generator for heavy construction projects that can replace several smaller ones.

New style applied to normal paragraphs

Figure 15-5.

Format button, and select Bold. Select OK in the New Style dialog box, and the character format appears in the list in the Style dialog box:

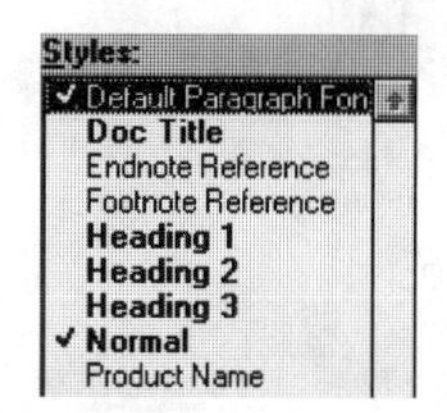

Note that character styles are shown in regular weight characters in the list while paragraph styles are shown in boldface.

Merging Styles

Styles are saved as part of a document or a template. You might have different styles stored in different documents, or you might borrow documents or templates from other people. If there are styles in one file that you want to use in another file, you *merge* the styles.

The process of merging styles is fairly easy using the template organizer you saw in Chapter 11. Be sure neither of the files is open. Give the Style command and choose Organizer; this brings up the Organizer dialog box with the Styles tab selected, as shown in Figure 15-6. If there are other files open in these lists, choose the Close File button, then choose the Open File button to open the desired document or template.

To merge one or more styles from the file on the left to the one on the right, select the styles you want to copy and choose the Copy button. If some of the styles you are copying have the same name as those in the destination file, Word prompts you with:

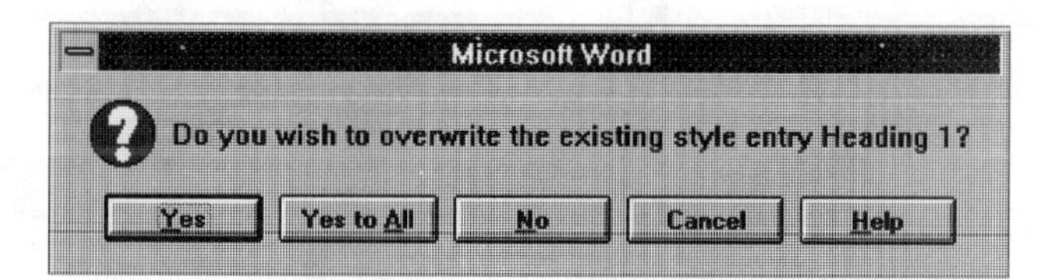

If you are sure you want to replace all the style definitions with the new one, select Yes to All. When the copying is complete, close each file, indicating that you want to save the changes in the target file.

Remember that Word comes with many templates that you can choose from. Most of these templates have distinctive formatting for the predefined styles like Normal and the heading style. Word makes it easy to preview the

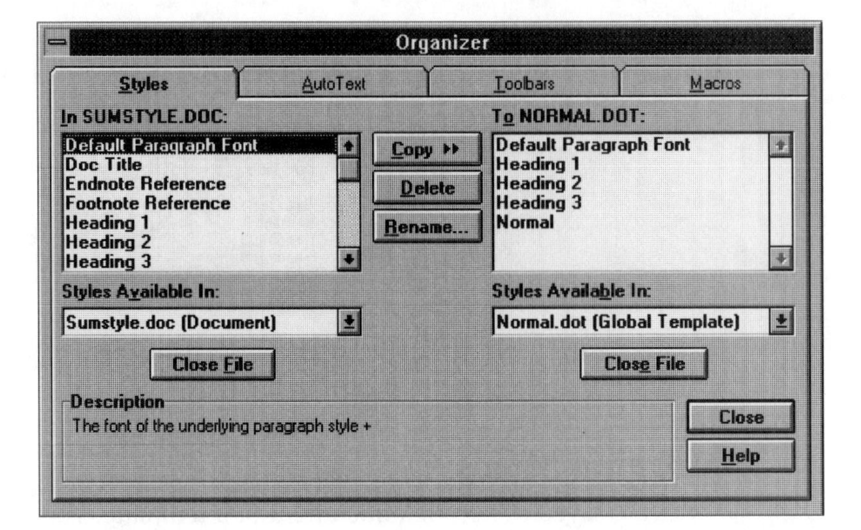

Organizer dialog box, Styles tab
Figure 15-6.

results of merging those templates with your current document using the Style Gallery command from the Format menu. The dialog box for that command is shown in Figure 15-7. Simply choose one of the templates from the list at the left of the dialog box, and Word shows how your document will look in the Preview area.

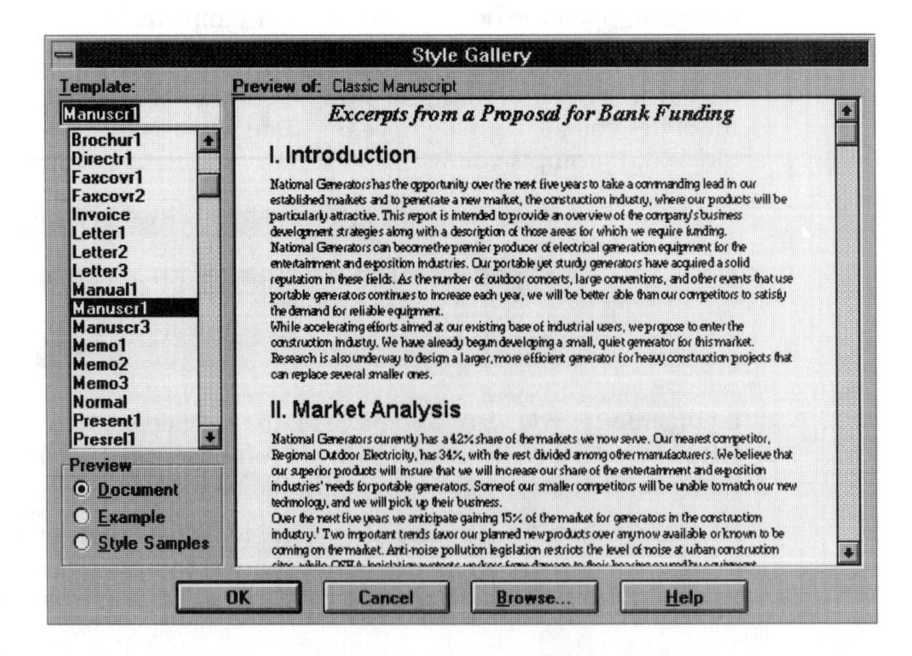

Style Gallery dialog box
Figure 15-7.

This method for storing style sheets shows excellent reasons for using styles. For example, it is usually most convenient to edit text on the screen when it is single spaced (so that more lines fit on the screen) but more convenient to edit it on paper when it is double spaced (so you can write additions or corrections between the lines). You can keep a document that has its Normal paragraph style formatted for double spacing. When you merge this master file's style sheet into a single-spaced document, it causes all the Normal paragraphs to be double spaced. You can then print the document and close it without saving the changes (in this case, the double spacing).

Basing Styles on Other Styles

You may have noticed that the Description box in the various style dialog boxes starts out with "Normal +" for each predefined style (other than Normal itself). This, plus the Based On choice in the New Style and Modify Style dialog boxes, are part of an advanced style feature that lets one style be affected by another. By default, all predefined styles are based on the Normal style.

To understand styles that are based on other styles, assume that a style called A is based on a style called B. The description of the formatting for A is "B + Bold", and the formatting for B is "Normal + Centered". This means that A is like Normal, but it is both bold (from its own definition) and centered (from B's definition).

Style	Based on	Format
B	Normal	Normal + Centered
A	B	B + Bold = Normal + Centered + Bold

If you now change the formatting for B to be "Normal + Justified", A automatically changes to justified alignment as well. This is because A is still "B + Bold", so A changes to whatever B is, and then adds bold.

Style	Based on	Format
B	Normal	Normal + Justified
A	B	B + Bold = Normal + Justified + Bold

The power of this feature is that since all default styles are based on Normal, you can change one formatting feature of the Normal style and have that change be reflected in all other styles as well. For instance, assume that you use the Times New Roman font throughout a document and you decide you want to use Helvetica instead. You need only change the font for the Normal style to Helvetica, and all styles that are based on Normal also change to Helvetica.

A formatting characteristic in a style based on another style does not change if the changed style has the same characteristic. For example, if your headings are based on Normal but they use the Courier font, and you change the font for the Normal style to Helvetica, the fonts in the heading styles stay in Courier. This means that you can safely change the formatting of your "base" styles without having to respecify all the formatting for styles based on them.

To specify which style you want to base another style on, first select the style you are changing, select the Modify button, and then choose the style it is based on in the Based On drop-down box. The formatting shown changes to reflect the differences between the style and the style it is based on.

Description
Heading 1 + Font: 18 pt, Not Bold, Italic, Centered

Of course, you don't have to base your styles on Normal. In fact, you don't have to base a style on any other style; in this case, you would select "(no style)" from the top of the Based On list. You might not want to base a style on any other style if you thought you might change a base style but wanted the other style to remain unchanged.

Deleting and Renaming Styles

After you add styles to a document or template, you may find that you no longer want some of them. For instance, you may have added both a book title and a magazine title character style, then later decided to just have a single title style. Deleting styles is simple: in the Style dialog box, choose the style from the list, then choose the Delete button.

You may also want to rename some of your styles. This is particularly true if you work with other people who also use Word. You may have developed a set of styles with names you like, and they have styles with similar purposes but with different names. To rename a style, select it in the Style dialog box and choose the Modify button. In the Modify Style dialog box, type the new name for the style and select OK.

Using Styles for Headings

As you will see in other parts of this book, some of Word's predefined styles have special applications. For example, there are styles that affect how footnotes appear in your document (footnotes are described in Chapter 17). The most important of the predefined styles are the heading styles (that is, "Heading 1", "Heading 2", and so on). These are used in many parts of Word.

When you create documents with levels of headings, you should always use the predefined styles. This will allow you to interact with other Word features that you will see later in the book. Of course, Word's choices for the default formatting of these styles may not suit you, and you can change the formatting as you have seen earlier in this chapter. Regardless of how you change the formatting, you should use the Heading styles in your work.

One of the best reasons to use the Heading styles is for Word's outline feature, described in Chapter 23. If you use Heading 1, Heading 2, and so on, you can turn your entire document into an outline with a single command. This makes it easy to see the structure of your document and to move parts of your text around quickly.

Another reason to use the Heading styles is Word's automatic numbering of headings. You can number the headings in your entire document with a single step using the Heading Numbering command. The numbers are automatically updated if you move headings or add headings in the middle of your document.

Lesson 98: Getting the Most from Styles

Styles can make formatting all your documents, from letters to entire books, a much easier task. Even for large reports it is unlikely that you will use more than 15 styles, and only 5 or so will probably be used with any frequency.

You will find that using styles has many advantages over direct formatting, and in the few places where styles are not appropriate, you can still format directly. Once you start thinking in terms of style elements ("this is a heading," "this is a normal paragraph," and so on), you will find that your printed documents are much clearer because they are presented in a more organized manner.

Copying styles from one piece of text to another is identical to copying other paragraph formats. You can convert files that use direct formatting to style sheet formatting by applying a style to one paragraph and then copying that style to all other paragraphs to which it applies. You can also search for styles with the Find command, as you saw in Chapter 5.

You can use the Style box at the left side of the Formatting toolbar for more than just choosing styles. If you have selected a paragraph that already has formatting on it and select a style from the list, Word lets you redefine the formatting for that style to be the formatting in the paragraph.

For instance, assume that you want to change Normal paragraphs from left aligned to justified. Select any Normal paragraph and click the Justify button in the Formatting toolbar. Even though Normal is still shown in the styles list in the Formatting toolbar, select that list and choose Normal again. Word displays

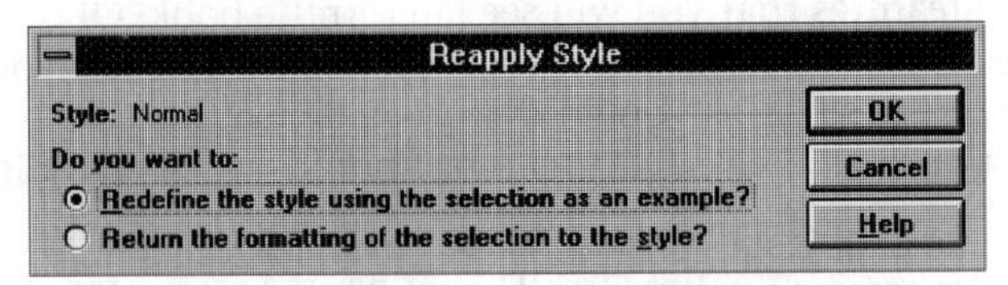

Choose the first option to redefine the Normal style. This is significantly faster than using the Style dialog boxes.

To print your style sheet, give the Print command and choose Styles from the Print What drop-down list in the dialog box. Word prints each style and its elements.

Lesson 99: Using AutoFormat Instead of Formatting

Once you start, using styles is quite easy. You may have already created documents in other word processing programs that don't have styles, and converting them to Word's styles means going through each paragraph and assigning it a style.

If you have many long documents for which you have not already used styles and you want to convert them, Word's AutoFormat command may be of interest. It takes a document with no styles and guesses the styles you would have used. For instance, if it sees a bold centered paragraph at the top of a new page, it assumes that this would be a Heading 1 paragraph and gives it that style. It also detects things like bulleted lists that were created with asterisks and spaces and coverts those to bullet styles.

Using the AutoFormat command to convert old documents works well, but is by no means perfect. Because you know more than Word does about the meaning of a paragraph, it is likely that you will make better choices about what kind of style to give to some paragraphs. Also, even though it may be a bit tedious, it really does not take that long to apply styles manually even to a long document. A 100-page report that took months to write can be manually converted to styles in a few hours.

The Word manual suggests that you can regularly write your documents with no styles, then run the AutoFormat command. This may be acceptable if you are not particular about formats and don't want to learn how to use styles. However, applying styles as you write takes only seconds and results in better-looking documents that have more consistent formatting.

To use AutoFormat, open the unformatted document and choose AutoFormat from the Format menu. In the first dialog box, choose the Options button so that you can review the settings from the Options menu. These are shown in Figure 15-8. You will probably want to leave all the options selected.

Word scans the document and chooses styles for you. It then lets you choose what to do:

You can choose to review the changes or simply accept them and later change the ones you don't like.

Review

Look in books and magazines and think about how they might use styles for the various types of paragraphs such as headings, subheads, and normal paragraphs. Also look for the types of character formatting that lend themselves to styles.

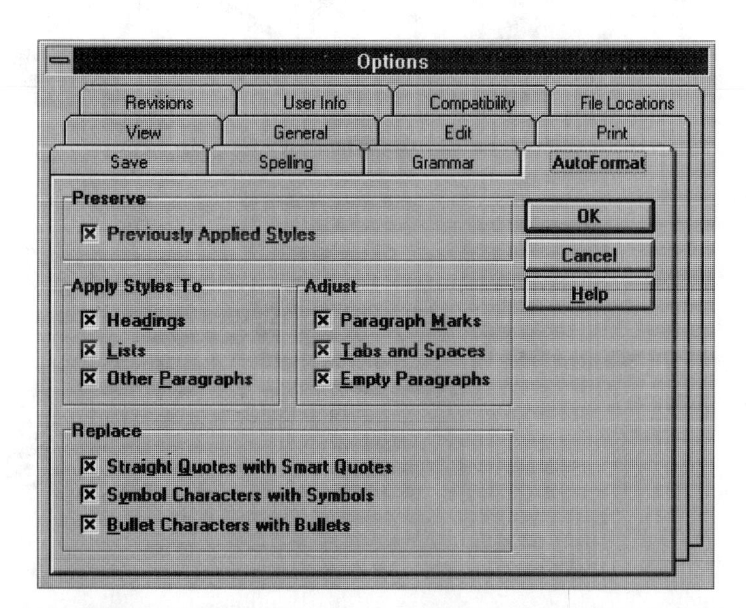

AutoFormat options
Figure 15-8.

C H A P T E R

16

TABLES OF CONTENTS AND INDEXES

Tables of contents and indexes are not only time-consuming and tedious to prepare manually, but they also must be updated whenever you modify your document. Some word processing packages automatically compile tables of contents or indexes, but those that do usually restrict you to a preset style of printout that may not meet your needs.

With Word, however, you can easily create entries for the

table of contents or index, and you have great flexibility in styling your printout. In addition, you can generate a new table of contents or index whenever you choose. These features make Word one of the most popular programs for business and academic use.

The methods used for creating a table of contents and an index are similar. You indicate what you want in your table of contents or index as you edit or format your document. When you have finished editing and formatting, you give a command that collects the entries and generates a table of contents or index based on the entries and their page numbers. Thus, the table of contents and index are not made automatically, but you can create them or update them at any time with a single command.

Word also lets you make tables of figures and tables of authorities. Tables of figures are becoming more common as more documents have art in them. Tables of authorities are generally only used by lawyers; the method for creating them is very similar to tables of contents and is not covered in this book.

Lesson 100: Planning a Table of Contents

Before you start using Word to generate tables of contents for your documents, you should consider the purpose and structure of a table of contents. A table of contents appears at or near the beginning of a document. It tells the reader what is presented in the document, in what order, and on what page. A document that is only one or two pages long generally does not need a table of contents.

A table of contents can be a simple list of where each section of the document begins, or it can be a detailed road map of the document. For example, the tables of contents of some books contain only the chapter names and beginning page numbers. This keeps the table of contents short (it usually fits on one page) and gives the reader a feel for the general categories and progression of subjects.

Some tables of contents are meant to show almost the entire contents of a document. These are much longer than simple tables of contents and are often hard to browse through. Of course, someone looking for a particular subject will be more likely to find it in a detailed table of contents. However, some authors prefer to create an index for detailed listings and keep the table of contents brief.

The format of a table of contents is also important. If you list two or more levels of headings in a table of contents, using styles makes the table of contents significantly easier to read. Compare the unformatted and formatted tables of contents shown in Figure 16-1.

Installation	1
Unpacking	2
Checking the crates	2
In case of damage	3
Removing the main unit	4
Other units	8
Connecting to equipment	10
Adding fuel	10
Testing	13
Starting for the first time	14

Installation	**1**
Unpacking	2
Checking the crates	2
In case of damage	3
Removing the main unit	4
Other units	8
Connecting to equipment	10
Adding fuel	10
Testing	**13**
Starting for the first time	14

Tables of contents without and with formatting
Figure 16-1.

Lesson 101: Indicating Table of Contents Entries

There are two methods for indicating to Word what you want in your table of contents:

- Use the predefined styles Heading 1, Heading 2, and so on, in your document. You can specify these styles yourself or you can use the outlining feature, which uses these styles automatically. Styles are covered in Chapter 15 and outlining is covered in Chapter 23.
- Mark the paragraphs you want to include in the table of contents with fields. Fields are introduced in Chapter 26.

The styles method is much easier than the fields method and is described here. Using styles makes sense, particularly if you also use outlining, since all your chapter titles have the same formatting, all your top-level headings have the same formatting, and so on. The fields method gives you a bit more flexibility, but at the high cost of your having to be very careful to mark every heading. If you don't notice that you skipped adding a field to a heading, it will not appear in the table of contents.

To indicate the paragraphs you want in the table of contents, use the predefined styles Heading 1, Heading 2, and so on, in your text. For example, in this book, the chapter names would be Heading 1 and the lesson names Heading 2.

You can check the organization of your table of contents by viewing your document in outline view, as described in Chapter 23. When you click one of the numbers in the outline bar, Word hides all of the headings and text at a level below that number.

Note that you have to use styles to mark entries this way. You cannot simply apply direct formatting to the headings. If you do not want to use styles, you must use the fields method for indicating entries. The fields method is not described in this book because it uses fairly advanced concepts that do not benefit most users.

Lesson 102: Creating the Table of Contents

Once you have marked all of the entries, you can create a table of contents with the Index and Tables command from the Insert menu. Briefly, this command performs the following steps:

1. Repaginates your document (if you do not have automatic repagination turned on)
2. Searches through your document from the beginning for Heading styles
3. Collects copies of those entries and their associated page numbers
4. Puts the entries at the insertion point

The Index and Tables command has many interesting features that are described in this lesson and later in the chapter. Even if you skip these descriptions, you can quickly generate a simple table of contents just by giving the Index and Tables command. With a bit more planning and work, however, you can create more complex tables of contents and figure lists.

You can update the table of contents at any time after placing the insertion point where you want the table of contents to appear. If you change your document by adding, deleting, or moving text, you should update the table of contents and the index before you print your document so that they reflect the most current revision.

The Table of Contents tab of the Index and Tables dialog box is shown in Figure 16-2. You can choose the format for the styles used in the table of contents. These formats replace the formats you currently have for the table of contents styles. If you want to keep the current formatting styles, choose Custom Style from the bottom of the list.

Use the options at the bottom of the dialog box to further refine your table of contents. You can choose whether or not to show the page numbers (you might not want to if the document is short and many headings appear on the same page). You can also specify how many levels of headings you want to appear in the table of contents. The Right Align Page Numbers and Tab Leader options let you specify how the page numbers appear on the page.

After you choose OK, Word puts the table of contents at the insertion point in your document. Word formats the table of contents with the predefined styles TOC 1, TOC 2, and so on.

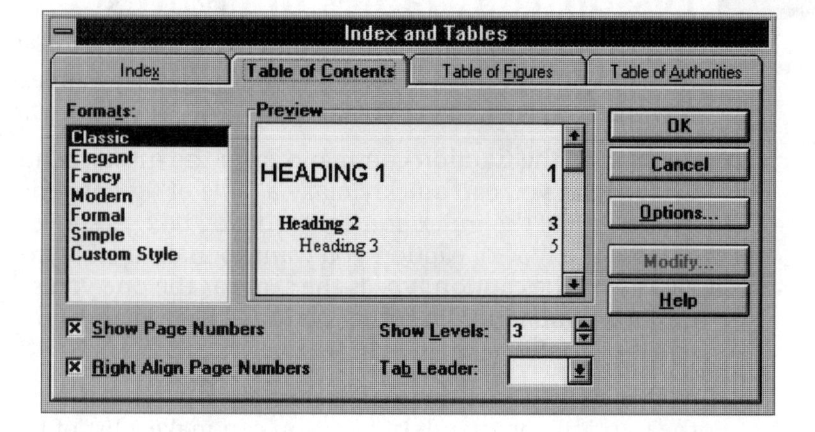

Index and Tables dialog box (Table of Contents tab)
Figure 16-2.

You may want to precede the text with a heading such as "Table of Contents" and possibly put it in its own section. This is common for tables of contents that are more than half a page long.

Once you have the table of contents in your document, you can format it any way you want. In general, you use the predefined styles. You can use normal character and paragraph formatting on the text, but it is much better to change the formatting on the styles instead. If you use direct formatting instead of style formatting and remake the table of contents, any direct formatting changes you made are lost.

Although it is most common to use the Heading styles to make the table of contents, you don't have to. In the Index and Tables dialog box, select the Options button. That dialog box is shown in Figure 16-3. You can select which table of contents level is associated with which style. If you choose to use the field codes instead of styles, select Table Entry Fields in this dialog box.

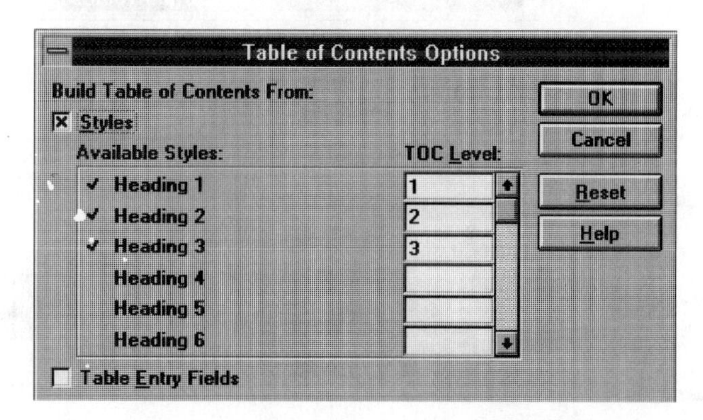

Table of contents options
Figure 16-3.

Lesson 103: Tables of Figures

Many reports have numerous figures and tables. It is useful to list these elements and let the reader know what pages they appear on. In the same way that you create tables of contents, you can also create other lists.

If you used the Caption command from the Insert menu as described in Chapter 12, you can quickly make a table of figures. Choose the Table of Figures tab of the Index and Tables dialog box, as shown in Figure 16-4. Choose the type of caption you want to make a table from in the Caption Label list. The caption type is the same as the one you specified in the Caption command. The other options in this dialog box are the same as for tables of contents.

As you can see, you can make tables for any type of caption that you used in the Caption command. In fact, you can make a list of figures from any kind of style that you used. Choose the Options button from the Table of Figures dialog box:

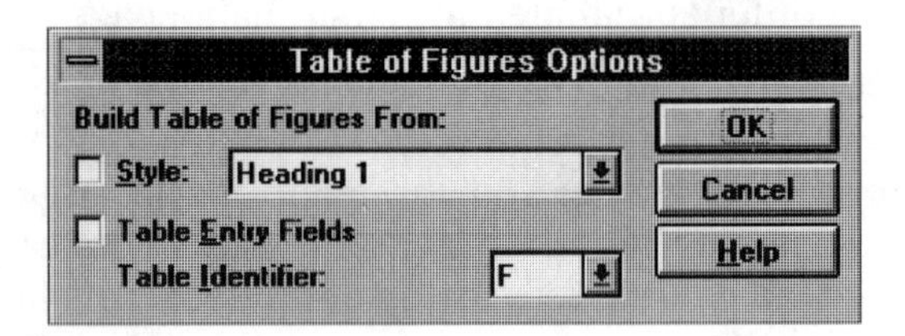

You can choose any style, or even use field codes.

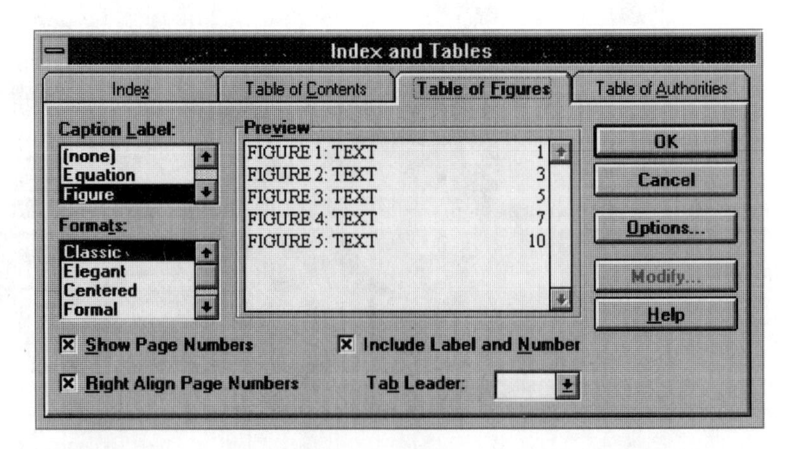

Index and Tables dialog box (Table of Figures tab)
Figure 16-4.

Lesson 104: Marking Index Entries

The steps used to make an index are almost identical to those used for a table of contents, and the results are also similar. However, you cannot mark index entries with styles; they must be marked with fields.

Indexes are very different from tables of contents. In a table of contents, you list the items in your document in the order in which they appear. In an index, you alphabetically list items that are in your text, but sometimes you also list words that do not appear in the text. This is to help your reader search for specific items under different names.

In a table of contents, the text is the same as the text in the headings in your document. The words that appear in an index, however, are not whole lines or phrases and thus must be marked in some other fashion. There are two steps to creating an index: selecting the entries that will make up the index, and then assembling the index itself.

Determining what to include in an index is something of an art. Important words always go into an index, but phrases can be more difficult to categorize. For example, assume a sentence in your text reads, "The 17th century was a period of rapid growth in religious thought." You would certainly index "religious thought," but would you index it under "religion," under "17th century," or both? If you already have many subentries under the word "religion" in your index, you wouldn't want to put the entry "thought" by itself under "religion"; you would want to add "17th century" to clarify it. You might even want to add an entry here for "theology" even though that word doesn't appear in the sentence.

To mark a word or phrase that appears in your text, select it and press Alt-Shift-X. Word displays the Mark Index Entry dialog box shown in Figure 16-5. In this case, the phrase "Fire equipment" was selected before pressing Alt-Shift-X. You will most often want to just select Mark.

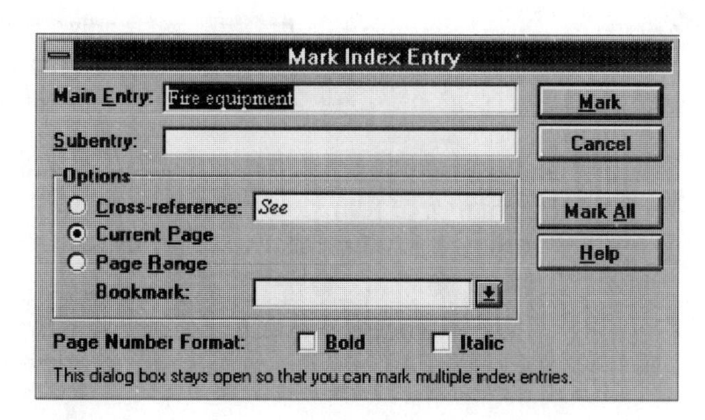

Mark Index Entry dialog box
Figure 16-5.

If you want the page number to appear in bold or italics when the index is created, choose one of those options. The Cross-reference field lets you enter text to use for the entry instead of the page number. The Page Range option lets you specify a bookmark (described in Chapter 26) to use for the page number instead of the actual page it appears on. You can ignore these options for now.

To mark a word or phrase that is not in your text, place the insertion point at the place you want the index to refer to and press Alt-Shift-X. The dialog box will look the same except that there will be nothing in the Main Entry box. Type the text you want and select Mark.

Most indexes are multilevel indexes, meaning that some entries are headings with subentries under them. For example, part of an index with subheadings might look like this:

Fans 23
Fire equipment 12
Generators
    Installation 5
    Purchasing 17
Half-height restrictions 21

"Fans" and "Fire equipment" are individual entries. "Generators" is a main entry, and "Installation" and "Purchasing" are subentries under "Generators". Word allows up to five levels of entries. However, indexes rarely have more than three levels, and most have only two.

Marking multilevel entries is easy. In the text box, you enter the first level in the Main Entry area and the subentry in the Subentry area. For instance, the options for "Installation" under "Generators" looks like this:

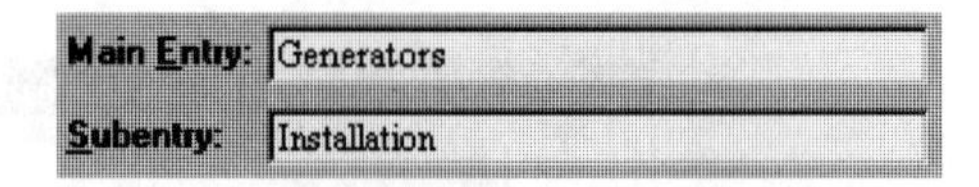

There is another method for marking entries in your document. You can create a *concordance* of terms that you always want indexed. You then tell Word to compare the concordance to your document and add any matching index entries.

Creating a concordance is easy. Simply start a new Word document and insert a two-column table. The entries in the first column of the table are the words you want to search for; the second column is for the associated index entries. Word searches your document for exact matches, so be sure that the entries in the concordance have exactly the capitalization you want.

To add index entries from your concordance to a document, open the document and choose the Index tab from the Index and Tables command. In that dialog box, choose the AutoMark button and specify the location of your concordance file.

Lesson 105: Creating an Index

After you have marked all your entries, creating the index is very easy. Simply put the insertion point at the place where you want the index (usually at the very end of the document) and give the Index and Tables command from the Insert menu. The Index tab for that dialog box is shown in Figure 16-6.

You will almost always want an indented index. A run-in index is one in which all entries are on the same line with subentries and separated by a semicolon; this is rarely used. The Formats choices are similar to those you saw earlier in this chapter.

When you execute the command, Word places the alphabetically sorted index entries at the insertion point. You can format the output any way you want, just as with the table of contents. Word uses the styles Index 1, Index 2, and so on, for the entries, so it is best to change those styles instead of using direct formatting. Note that the entries are identical to the ones that you marked, and Word does not capitalize them for you.

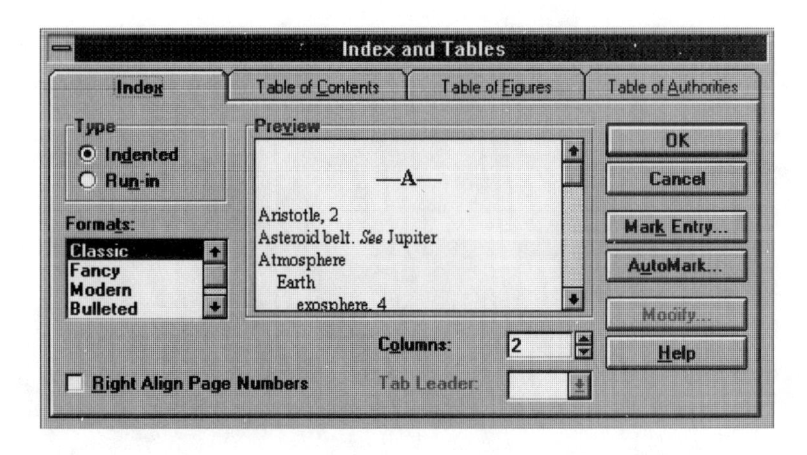

Index and Tables dialog box (Index tab)
Figure 16-6.

Review

Look in a few books and reports and note how the table of contents is formatted. Pay attention to whether all headings are included or just higher-level headings.

In the same books and reports, look at the indexes. How complete are they? Do they use second-level headings?

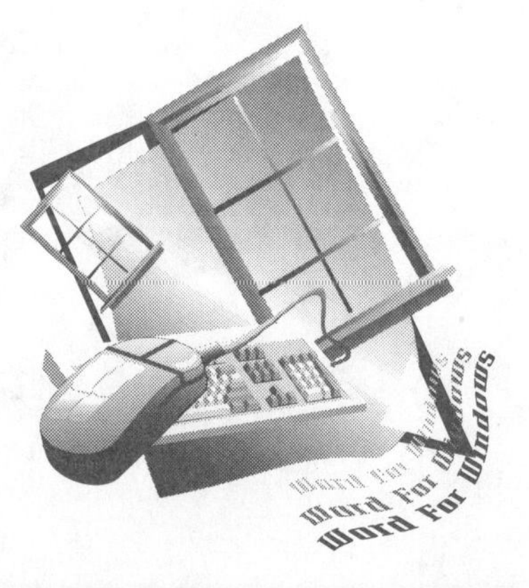
Word For Windows
Word For Windows

C H A P T E R

17 FOOTNOTES, ENDNOTES, AND ANNOTATIONS

Many writers find footnotes hard to incorporate correctly in text; however, Word lets you include footnotes easily. Endnotes are just like footnotes but they appear at the end of the section or the end of the document.

Lesson 106: Using Footnotes

In general, footnotes are used for two purposes: to give a reference for a quotation or an idea, or to give a supplementary note. They are commonly used in academic and scholarly papers but are becoming more common in financial reports.

Footnotes consist of the *reference mark* (usually an asterisk or a number) and the *footnote text*. To enter these, you choose Footnote from the Insert menu. Most people prefer to use sequentially numbered footnotes. Word keeps track of the current footnote number and even renumbers your footnotes if you take one out, add another, or rearrange them.

To insert a footnote, put the insertion point at the place where you want the reference mark and give the Footnote command from the Insert menu. The following dialog box appears:

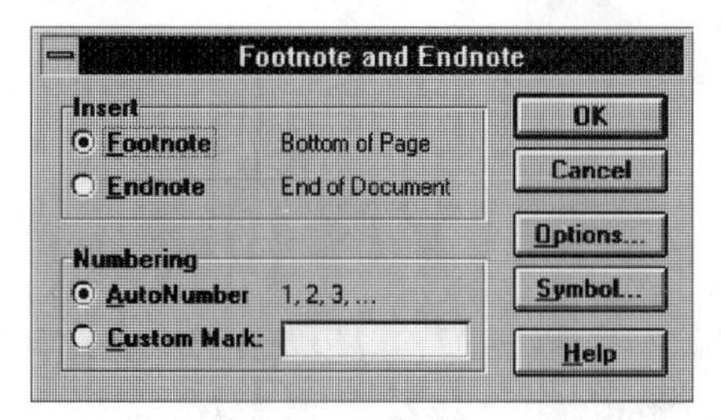

Select Footnote in the Insert box. If you enter a character (or up to ten characters) for the Custom Mark, Word uses that as the reference mark. If you leave the AutoNumber option selected, Word automatically numbers the footnotes in sequence.

When you select OK, Word splits the main text window, creating a *footnote pane* at the bottom. You can then enter and edit the footnote text in this pane. Figure 17-1 shows the split screen. To return to where you were before you entered the footnote, click in the top pane or press F6. To close the pane, choose the Close button.

If you want to open the Footnote pane without creating a footnote, choose the Footnote command from the View menu or press the Shift key when you drag down the split bar. You can also open the Footnote pane by double-clicking an existing reference mark. If you leave the footnote pane open as you scroll through your document, Word scrolls the footnote pane to the first footnote of the page you are on.

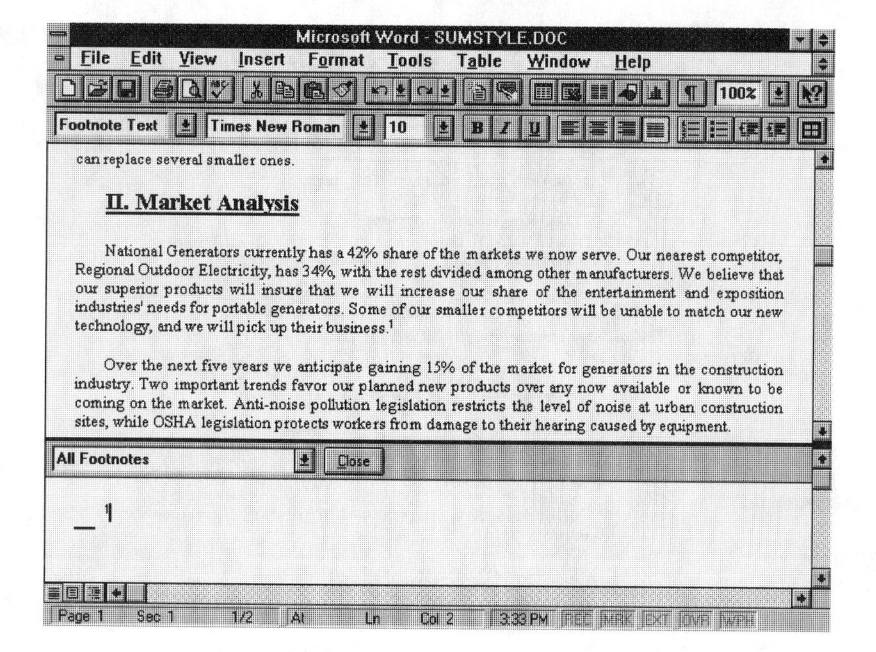

Footnote pane showing at the bottom of the screen

Figure 17-1.

The preceding discussion assumes that you are in normal view. If you are in page layout view or print preview, you do not need the footnote pane because Word simply moves to the bottom of the page. Thus, there is no footnote pane in these views.

To see how footnoting works, assume that you want to add another footnote to the report you saw earlier in Chapter 14. Remember, that report already had some footnotes in it. Move the insertion point to just after the period following the words "trade shows", just before the fourth heading. Give the Footnote command and select the OK button since the automatic numbering choice is already selected by default. Now enter the text for the additional footnote, as shown in Figure 17-2.

Notice that Word automatically renumbers the footnote that follows your new footnote. If you use automatic numbering, Word keeps track of footnotes that you insert or delete and correctly numbers them.

You can edit footnotes just like other text. To delete a footnote, simply delete its reference mark in the text. To move a footnote, select the reference mark and use the Cut command to move it to the Clipboard; you can then paste it wherever you want.

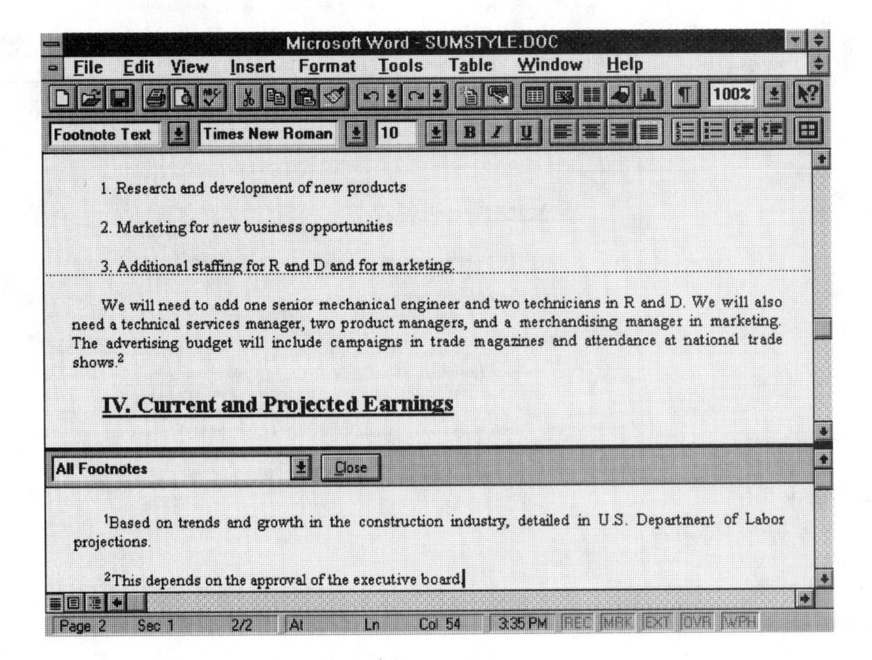

Footnote added
Figure 17-2.

Lesson 107: Formatting Footnotes

Word lets you change the appearance of the footnotes, the reference marks, and the separators between the text and the footnotes. This gives you flexibility in determining how your documents appear. Selecting the Options button in the Footnote command shows the following dialog box:

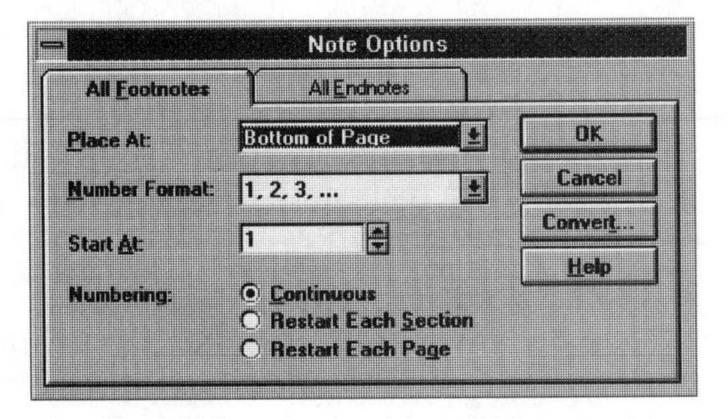

There are two choices in the Place At drop-down list for the place where footnotes appear in your printed document:

- ✦ Bottom of Page puts the footnotes at the bottom of each page, even if there is white space (such as the end of a section or if you have inserted page breaks).

- Beneath Text puts the footnotes directly under the text. If you have white space at the bottom of a page, Word puts the footnotes higher on the page.

You can also change the number format for the footnotes. The formats are listed in the following table:

Format	Choice
Numeric	1 2 3
Alphabetic (lower)	a b c
Alphabetic (upper)	A B C
Roman (lower)	i ii iii
Roman (upper)	I II III
Symbols	* † ‡ §

The Start At and Numbering choices let you choose how the footnotes are numbered. You would want to restart the numbers in each section if each section of your document represents a chapter and you want the numbers to start at 1 for each chapter.

You can change the formatting of the footnote text and reference marks with the style commands you learned about in Chapter 15. This makes it easier to change just the footnote formatting without changing other formatting.

You can also change the characters Word uses to separate the text and the footnotes at the bottom of the page, although it is unlikely that you will want to use these. Choose the separators from the list at the top of the footnote pane and edit them in the pane itself.

Lesson 108: Endnotes

Endnotes are almost identical to footnotes, except that they appear at the end of the section or document instead of at the bottom of each page. The commands you use are almost identical to those for footnotes.

To insert an endnote, choose the Footnote command, but select Endnote from the Insert box. The other options in this dialog box are the same as for footnotes.

If you choose the Options button, you will notice that the endnote options are slightly different.

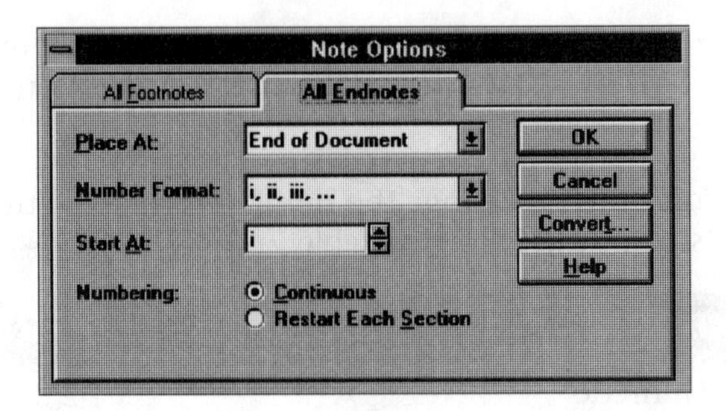

The two options for Place At are End of Section and End of Document. If each section in your document is a chapter, you can place endnotes at the end of each chapter. This is sometimes the preferred method, particularly if you have many endnotes.

You can convert footnotes to endnotes, and vice versa, in the footnote pane. In that pane, select All Footnotes or All Endnotes from the drop-down list at the top of the pane, then select the notes you want to convert. Point to the selected notes and hold down the right button on your mouse. From the list that pops up, choose either Convert to Footnote or Convert to Endnote.

Lesson 109: Creating Annotations

You can use annotations to leave yourself easy-to-find notes and markers in your text. Since annotations are stored just as footnotes are, you can add them, move them, and edit them in a fashion similar to the methods you learned earlier in this chapter.

When you are writing a long report, frequently you will not have all the information you need. You may want to continue writing the text around the unknown data instead of waiting until you receive the data to add the sentence or paragraph that goes with it. A convenient method for doing this is to write what you can and then select all the text that is uncertain. Give that text special formatting (such as double underlining) and add an annotation. If you find the missing data before the final draft of the report, simply select the text, unformat it, and add the new information. After you perform the task the annotation reminded you to do, you can easily remove it.

Word treats annotations similarly to footnotes; however, it identifies annotations with your initials and a number instead of with footnote numbers. If many people are marking a document, their annotations have their own initials. This makes it easy to determine who wrote what. Word uses the initials that you entered in the User Info tab of the Options command from the Tools menu for the reference mark.

To enter annotations, put the insertion point where you want the annotation to begin and give the Annotation command from the Insert menu. This command adds the mark and opens the annotations pane shown in Figure 17-3. You can add as much annotation text as you want and format it any way you like. Deleting and moving annotations is identical to footnotes.

You can edit your annotations by first opening the pane. Give the Annotation command from the View menu, or simply double-click on an annotation reference mark. You can also hold down the Ctrl key while splitting the screen to automatically select the annotations pane. The pane shows the annotations closest to your location in the document.

The drop-down list at the top of the annotations pane makes reviewing annotations easier. You can choose All Reviewers to see all the annotations, or select specific reviewers from the list.

If your computer is equipped for recording and playing back sound, you do not need to type in an annotation: you can record your voice instead. The Insert Sound Object button at the top of the annotations pane starts your sound recorder (depending on the software that came with your sound board).

To print just your annotations, give the Print command and select Annotations in the Print What drop-down list. To print both your text and

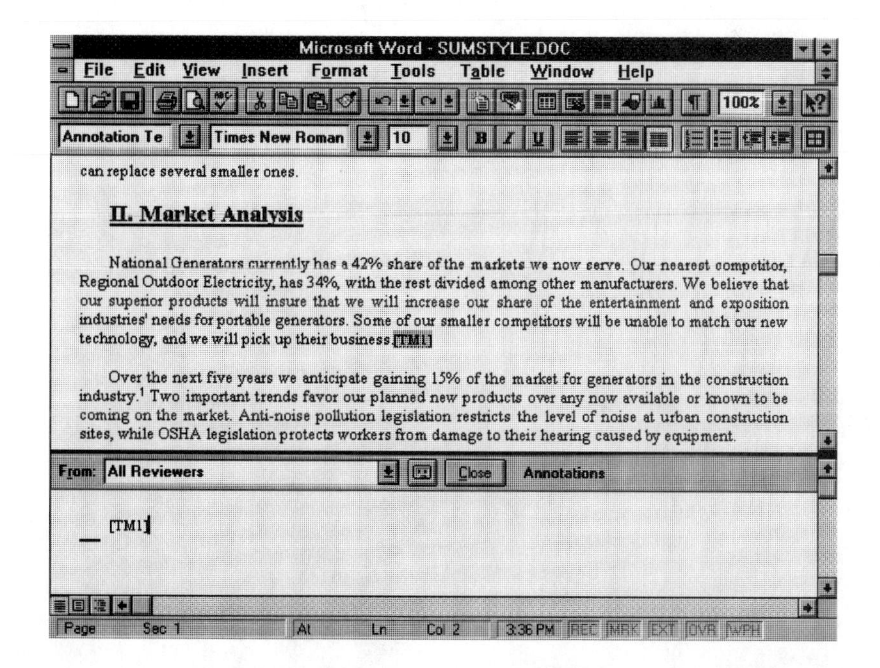

Annotations pane showing at the bottom of the screen

Figure 17-3.

annotations in the same output, give the Print command, select the Options button, and select Annotations in the Include with Document choices. Annotations appear at the bottom of pages, just like footnotes.

The Go To command from the Edit menu is useful when you are searching for annotations. In the dialog box, choose Annotations in the Go to What list and select a reviewer from the Enter Reviewer's Name list.

Review

Look in books that have footnotes and/or endnotes and notice how they are formatted. Think about whether the footnotes would be more useful as endnotes or vice versa.

Think about how you would use annotations on a project you are working on. When would you review them? Would using annotations make it easier to keep track of people's comments, or would it make the project harder to manage?

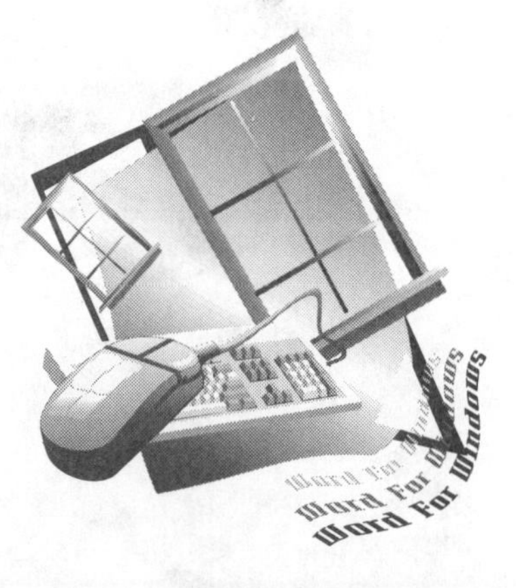
Word For Windows
Word For Windows

C H A P T E R

18 CREATING FORM LETTERS

When Word first appeared, only a few word processing programs included features that let you create form letters from a file of names and addresses. This feature is sometimes referred to as mail merge or print merge. Today, many programs give you this capability in a limited fashion. The merge feature in Word is more sophisticated than in other word processing programs and produces letters that look much more personalized.

The basic concept behind the merge feature is fairly simple. Your *main document* contains the letter you want to send to many people, with special placeholders (*fields*) for the parts that change from letter to letter (like the recipient's name and address). Your *data source* contains the names of the fields and the information that Word puts into the fields in the main document. The data sources you will learn about here are Word documents with a single table in them. All the information for each letter is in one row of cells (called a *record*) of the data source.

The main document contains the text that is the same in each letter, while the data source contains the text that is different from letter to letter. Both files are regular Word documents that you can edit and format by using the methods you have learned so far.

Instructions kept with your main document tell Word which file is to be the data source. You create the main document with Word. You can create the data source with Word, a database management system like Paradox or Access, or a spreadsheet program like Excel or Lotus 1-2-3. The format of the data source is very straightforward; it is not difficult at all to set up data sources to go with your main documents.

When you print your file with the Mail Merge command from the File menu, Word reads the first record from the data source, substitutes the field information for the field names in your main document, formats your letter, prints it, then reads the next record from the data source, and so on.

You can include fields in the middle of a paragraph, and Word formats the paragraph with the new information in it. Thus, if you have a field called "Amount" and that field in one record of your data source is equal to 1533, Word properly reformats a paragraph that contains the sentence "You still owe us $1533, which we would like you to send immediately."

You assign a name to each field consisting of up to 40 letters (no spaces, and no punctuation marks other than underscores), such as "Amount" or "LastPayment". Note that there is no space in the name "LastPayment"; all field names must be one word. You use the field name in both the main document and the data source, and the names must match. However, the order in which the field names are used in the main document does not need to match the order in which the field names appear in the data source. In fact, you can use the data assigned to a field many times in your main document.

Note that the data source can be many types of files from different programs. In this chapter, you will create a data source that is another Word document, but you can also use files like Excel spreadsheets, Microsoft Access databases, or 1-2-3 files as your data source.

Lesson 110: Creating the Main Document and Data Source

You type in the body of your main document just as you normally enter text in a Word document. For now, don't enter any field names; Word helps you with that after you create the data source. Instead, type **XX** where the fields would go.

Type the example in Figure 18-1, which is a main document that could be used to inform customers of balances due. Note the "XX" where the field names from the data document will be put later. For example, the first field will be the person's name, the second field their company, and so on. Save this file as BALANCE1.

You can create the data source manually, but it is much easier to use the *mail merge helper*. The Mail Merge command from the Tools menu creates a new file that has a table in the exact format needed for merging (tables were discussed in Chapter 13). Before giving the Mail Merge command, be sure that the BALANCE1 file is open.

For this example, you will use the following fields for the BALANCE1 letter:

Company
Name
Address
City
State
Zip
Amount
LastPayment

It doesn't matter whether you use upper- or lowercase letters, but remember you cannot use spaces in the name.

When you give the Mail Merge command from the Tools menu, you see the dialog box shown in Figure 18-2. The three steps shown there are the three steps you will use to create your merge documents.

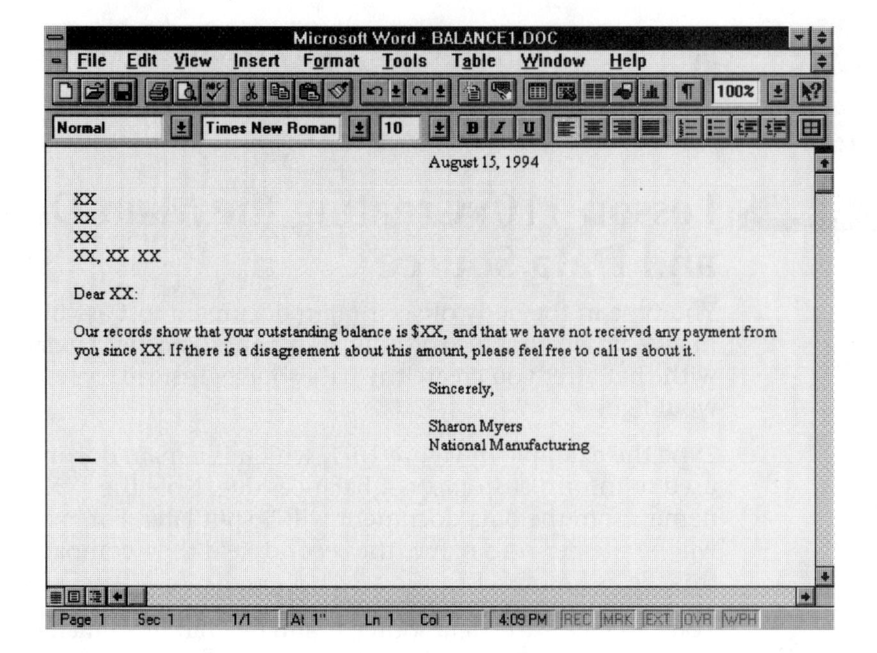

BALANCE1 text without field names
Figure 18-1.

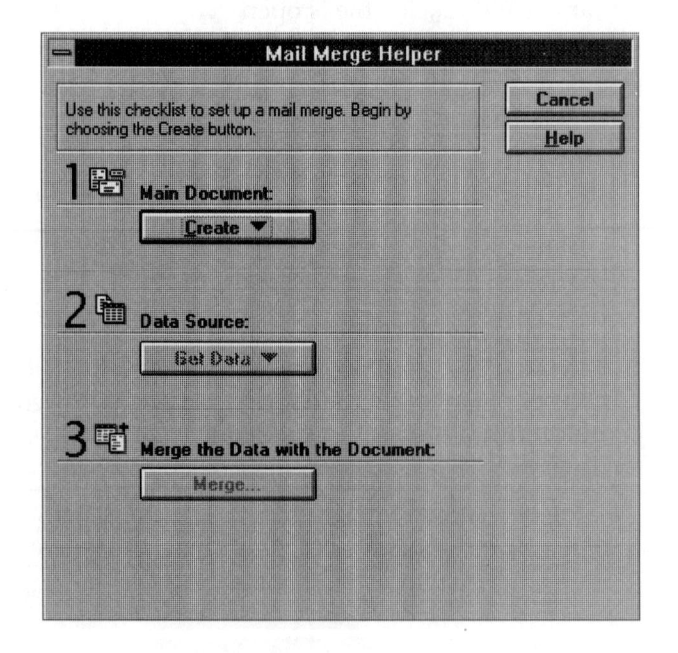

Mail Merge Helper dialog box
Figure 18-2.

Under step 1, Main Document, the Create button's drop-down list lets you choose the type of main document you want to work with. In this case, choose Form Letters. Word prompts:

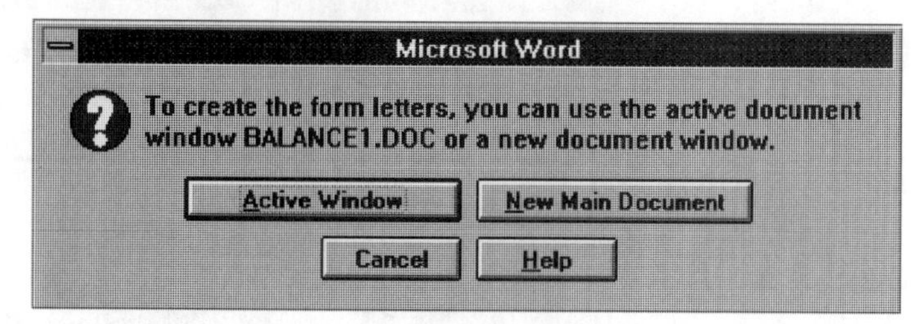

Choose Active Window because you have already typed in your main document there.

Step 2, Data Source, tells Word where the data source is. In the drop-down list for the Get Data button, select Create Data Source because you do not have a data source yet. You see the dialog box in Figure 18-3, which is where you will define the fields for your data source.

Word has some common field names in the list on the right, but you will enter your own names. To reduce confusion, you should delete the preassigned field names from the list before starting to enter your own. Choose the Remove Field Name button many times until all the entries are gone.

Enter the name of the first field in the Field Name box and select the Add Field Name button (or press Enter). Remember that the order of the fields in

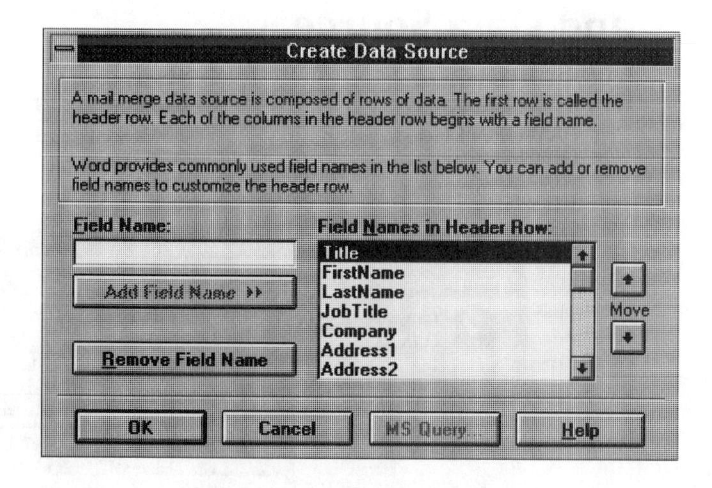

Create Data Source dialog box
Figure 18-3.

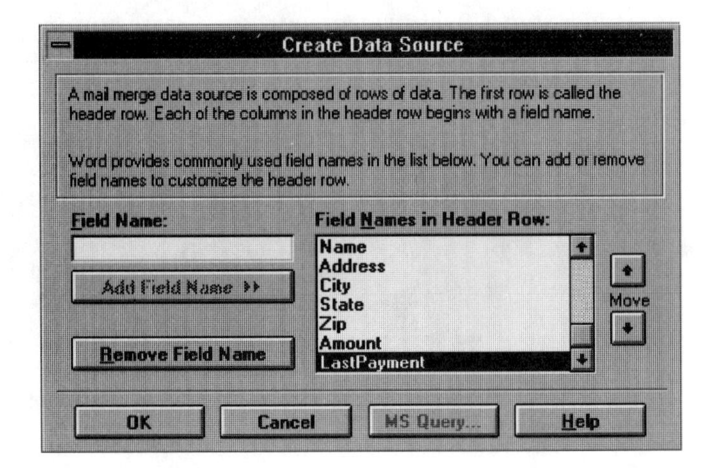

All field names entered
Figure 18-4.

the data source does not matter. In this case, type the name **Company** and select Add Field Name, type **Name** and select Add Field Name, and so on, for all the field names. When you have finished, the window looks like the one in Figure 18-4. Select OK to close the window.

Word now displays a standard Save As dialog box. This allows you to save the data source that you have just specified on disk. Enter **PAYMENT1.DOC** for the filename and select OK. Word now asks you what you want to do in the dialog box shown in Figure 18-5.

Lesson 111: Finishing the Main Document and Data Source

Choose the Edit Data Source button so that you can start entering your names and addresses. This brings up the data form shown in Figure 18-6. The PAYMENT1 data file is just a Word document with a table in it, and you

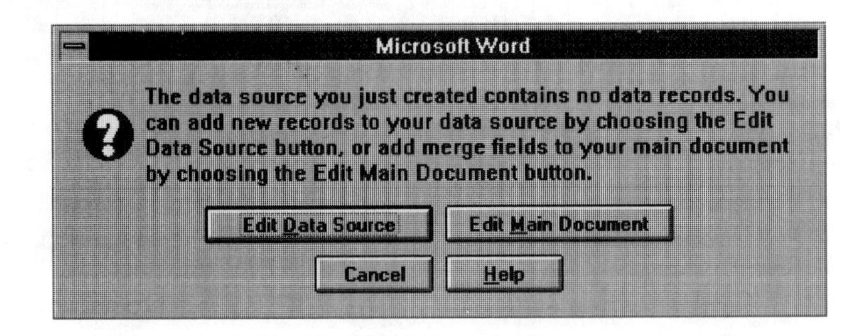

Choice for next action
Figure 18-5.

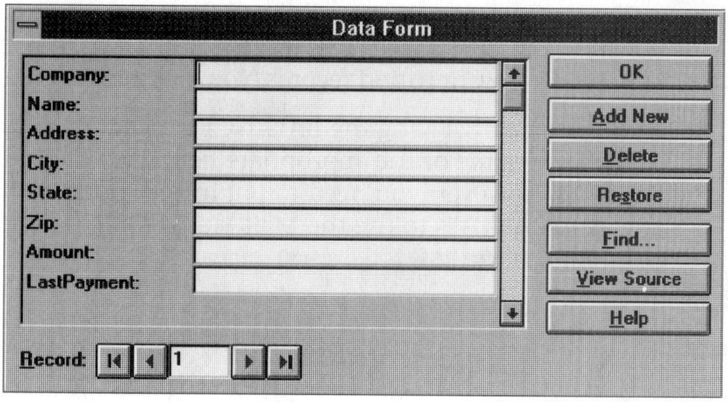

Empty data form
Figure 18-6.

could just edit it using the table techniques you learned in Chapter 13. However, Word makes it even easier to enter data using the data form.

The data form is like other dialog boxes in Word. You can type in any of the fields. In this case, all the fields fit on the screen; if there were more, the scroll bar would be active and you could scroll the fields. Click in the Company field and type **Industrial Mining Co.** Click in the Name field and type **Michael Townsend**, and so on, until the data form looks like Figure 18-7.

To enter this record in the database, choose the Add New button. This also brings up a new, blank record. Each time you enter a record, choose the Add

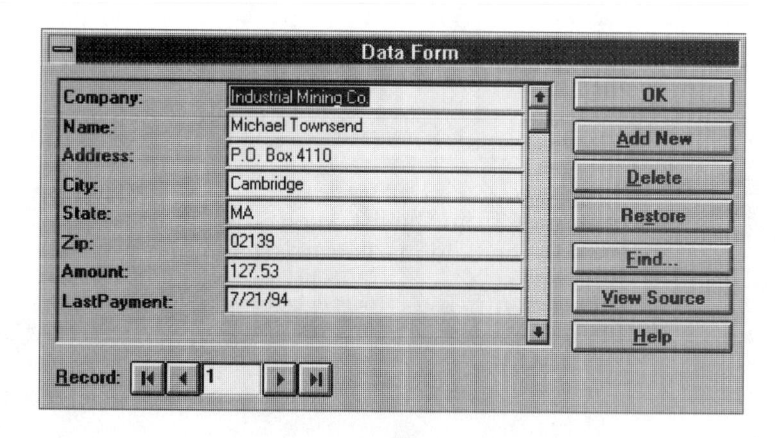

Data form filled in with first record
Figure 18-7.

New button. Add the record shown in Figure 18-8 and choose the OK button when you are finished. This leaves just the two records in your data source file. If you later want to add records, you will start by choosing the Add New button.

You are now viewing the BALANCE1 letter. You want to replace each "XX" with the name of the appropriate field. You cannot simply type in the field names, however; you need to put in the special merge characters. The easy way to do this is to use the Mail Merge toolbar that Word has opened at the top of the window:

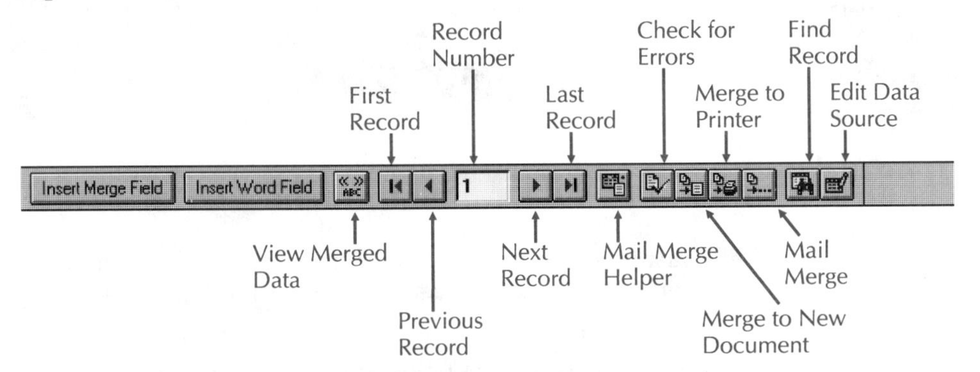

Select the first "XX", which will be the person's name (don't select the paragraph mark after the "XX"). You want to replace this with the field called "Name" so click the Insert Merge Field button in the Mail Merge toolbar. This drops down a list of the fields from your data source:

Select "Name" from the list. Word then replaces the "XX" with "Name" enclosed in the field markers, as shown here:

Data Form

Company:	City of Olsenburg
Name:	Tamara Fine
Address:	91 Oak Avenue, Suite 320
City:	Olsenburg
State:	IL
Zip:	60606
Amount:	118.18
LastPayment:	6/31/94

OK
Add New
Delete
Restore
Find...
View Source
Help

Record: 2

Data form filled in with second record
Figure 18-8.

Select the second "XX", which you want to be the company and choose "Company" from the list under the Insert Merge Field button. Keep doing this until your document looks like the one in Figure 18-9.

You can add formatting, such as italics, to the field names if you wish. This causes the information in the fields to be printed with that formatting. Note that you add formatting to the main document; formatting in the data source file is ignored.

Lesson 112: Viewing and Printing Form Letters

The Mail Merge toolbar gives you access to all the features you need for viewing and printing your form letters. Use the controls near the middle of

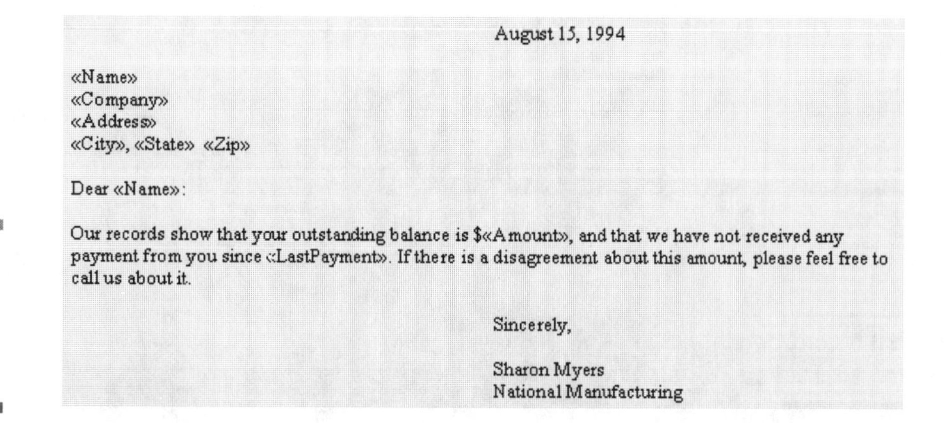

August 15, 1994

«Name»
«Company»
«Address»
«City», «State» «Zip»

Dear «Name»:

Our records show that your outstanding balance is $«Amount», and that we have not received any payment from you since «LastPayment». If there is a disagreement about this amount, please feel free to call us about it.

Sincerely,

Sharon Myers
National Manufacturing

Main document with field names filled in
Figure 18-9.

this toolbar to choose which letter you want to view or print:

Next, choose the View Merged Data button to show the results of merging, as shown in Figure 18-10.

It is unlikely that you had any errors merging the document following the steps so far. As you use Word's more advanced features for merging, however, you may have some errors. To see your errors, choose the Check for Errors button. That brings up the following dialog box:

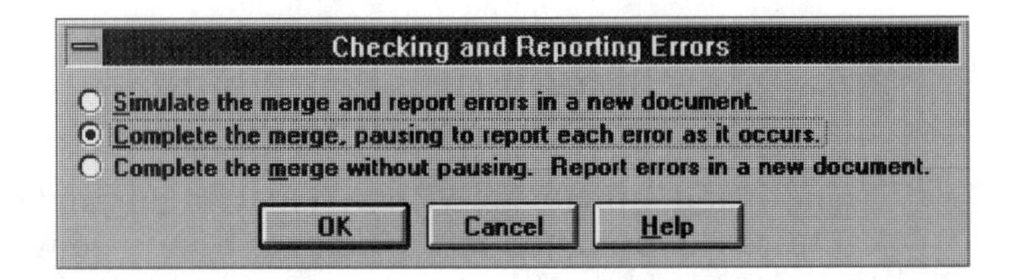

Select the first choice and choose OK.

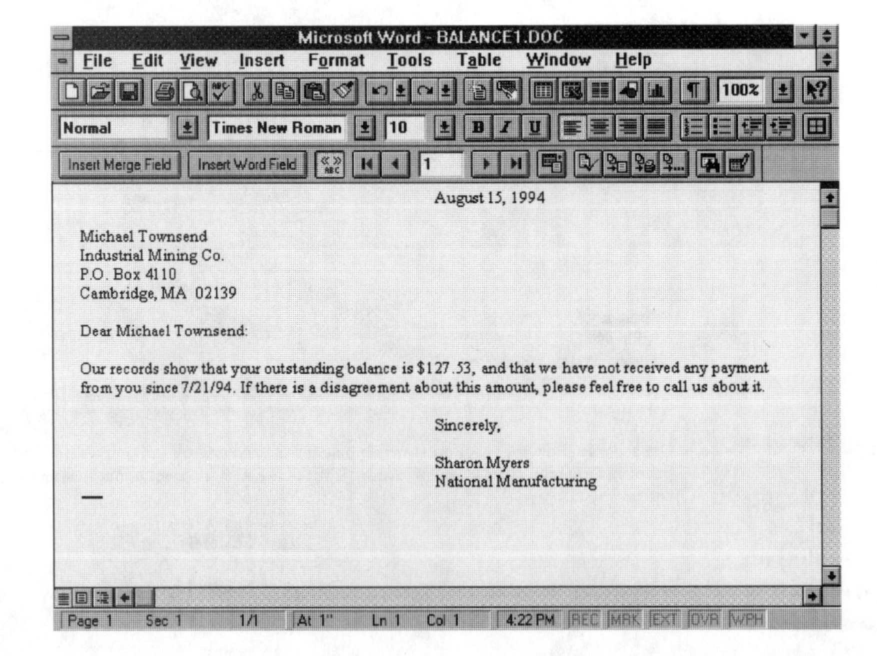

Figure 18-10. Main document with data merged from the first record

If you have many records in your data source, you may not know the record number you want to view or print. The Find Record button in the Mail Merge toolbar lets you choose records by their content. Its dialog box is:

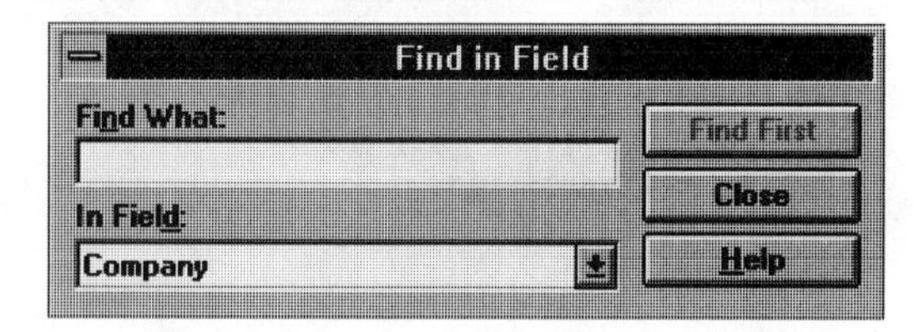

Type the text you want to search for in the Find What option and choose the field from the drop-down list.

There are two ways to print the merged documents:

- ✦ Print them directly
- ✦ Create a new document with the merged results, then print that document

The second method is better because it lets you view the documents before you print. To create a merged document with all the records, choose the Merge to New Document button. Word creates a new document, as seen in Figure 18-11. As you can see, Word filled in the fields in the body of the paragraph and correctly wrapped the text.

Notice that the new document has two sections. Word creates a new section for each record in your data source.

There are many times you will not want to merge all the records, or you may want to change some other merge parameters. You can control the merge process better with the Merge dialog box. Choose the Mail Merge button from the Mail Merge toolbar to see the Merge dialog box:

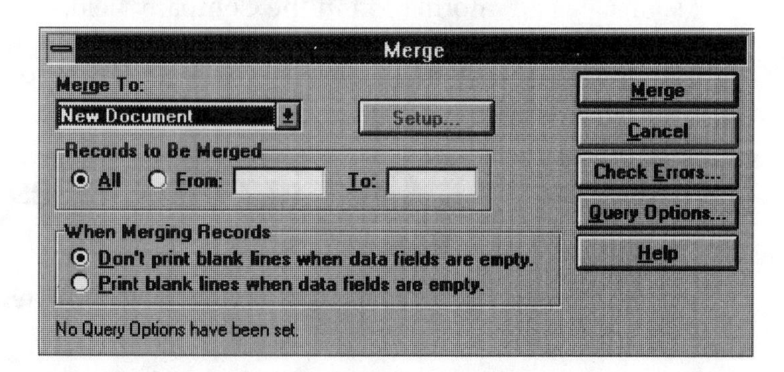

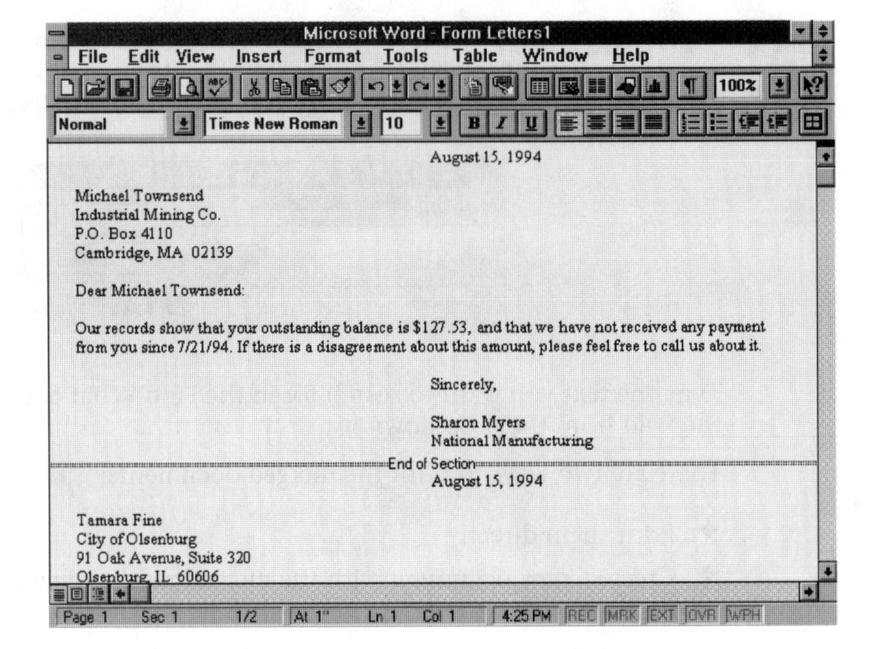

All records merged into a new document
Figure 18-11.

The two choices in the Merge To section define what happens when you select the Merge button. Printer causes the results to be sent to the printer, while New Document causes the results to be saved in a new file.

The Records to Be Merged choice lets you specify which records in your data source you want to use. You can enter record numbers in the From and To choices to restrict the records you print. For example, if you want to print from the first three records, enter **1** and **3** for these options. You will see other ways to choose records later in this chapter.

The last set of options tells Word what to do when you have blank lines caused by fields with no data. For example, if one of the records in your data source has no information in the Company field, you might not want to print the blank line that would result in the main document. However, if you were printing mailing labels, you would want to print that line so that the labels lined up properly.

Lesson 113: Creating Envelopes and Mailing Labels

Envelopes and mailing labels are similar to form letters. Each one has variable information that is stored in the data source. In fact, an envelope is just like a form letter except that it is on different sized paper. Mailing labels are different in that you print many labels per page.

Before creating envelopes, be sure that Word knows the address you want to use for the return address. In the User Info tab of the Options command from the Tools menu, fill in the Mailing Address field if you have not already done so. This is covered in Chapter 11.

To create an envelope, start a new document and choose the Mail Merge command from the Tools menu (you probably want to save your previous work first). In step 1 of the dialog box, choose the Create button and Envelopes. In the next dialog box, choose Active Window just like you did for form letters. For the data source, open the PAYMENT1 file that you created earlier in this chapter since these are the names and addresses you want to create envelopes for. Word asks you if you want to set up the main document, which you do.

You next see the Envelope Options dialog box shown in Figure 18-12. (This is the same as the Envelopes and Labels command from the Tools menu.) Choose the envelope size, the mailing options, and the format for the return and sender's addresses. The Font buttons let you specify the font for the addresses. It is best to leave the locations set to Auto until you have tested the printing, then move them later if Word's default positions aren't right for you. Choose the OK button when you have made the envelope options settings.

You next see the Envelope Address dialog box shown in Figure 18-13. Here is where you will enter the field names, just like you did in the main document

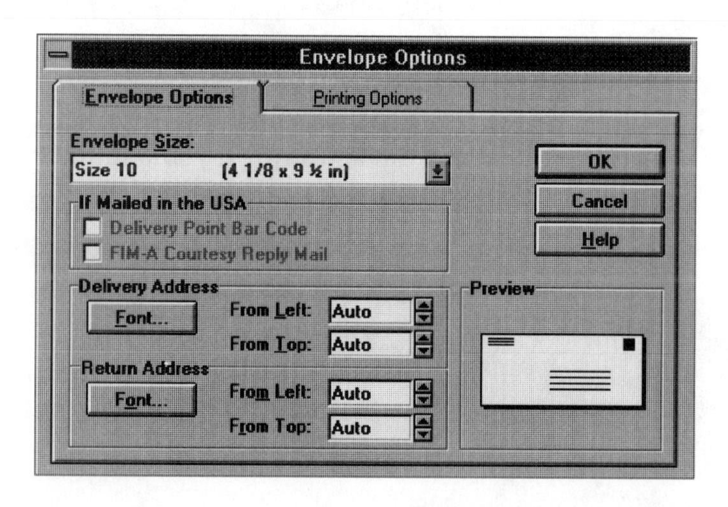

Envelope Options dialog box
Figure 18-12.

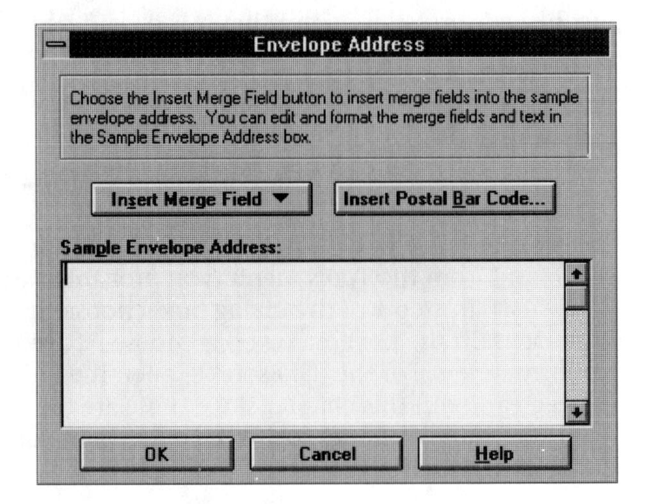

Envelope Address dialog box
Figure 18-13.

of the form letter. Choose each name from the Insert Merge Field button, pressing Enter to insert paragraph characters where needed. You can enter text as well, such as the comma and spaces for the city and so on. To enter tab characters, press Ctrl-Tab. You will probably want to use tab characters to place the postal code.

Your address should look like this:

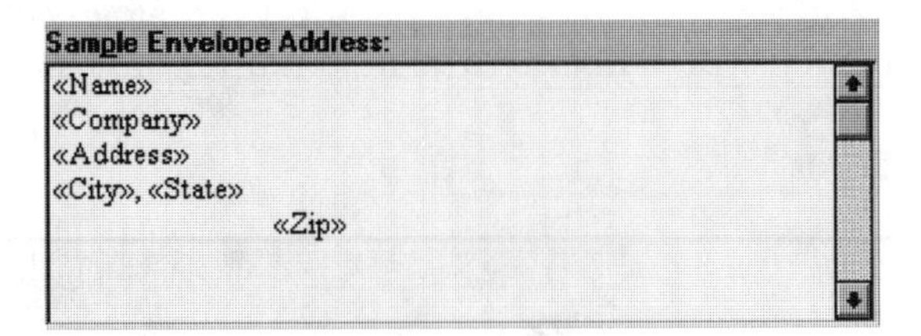

Remember that you can add any text you want to the envelope. For instance, you might want to add something like this:

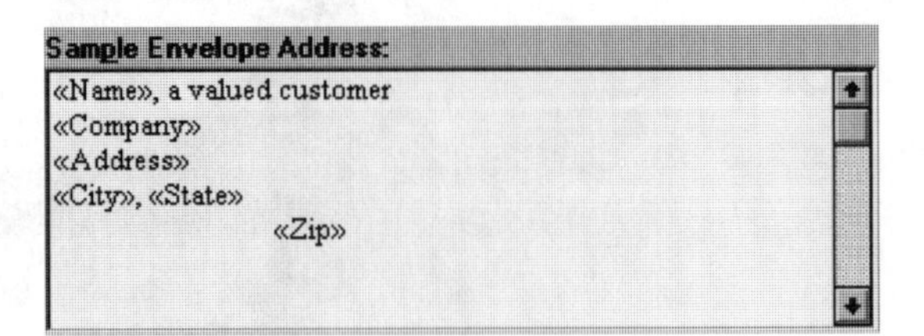

You may also want to add bar codes to the address for letters sent in the United States. This speeds delivery and can sometimes save you postage. To insert a POSTNET mark, create a line above the name and address and choose the Insert Postal Bar Code button:

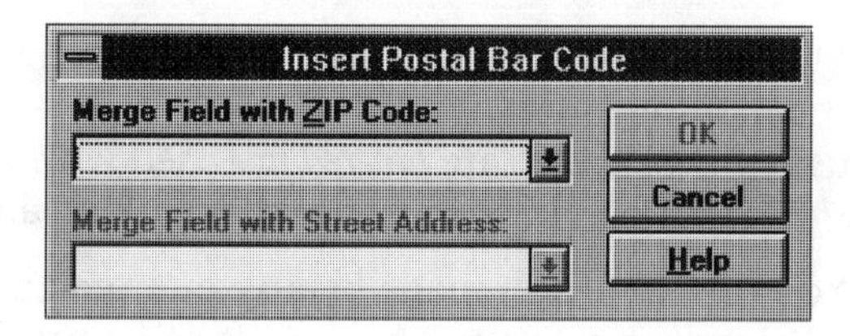

Tell Word which of your fields is the ZIP code and which is the street address.

After you choose the OK button, Word creates the envelope document, as shown in Figure 18-14. This is, in fact, a regular Word document. Save this as ENV1.DOC. You can use the View Merged Data button to see how the envelopes will look.

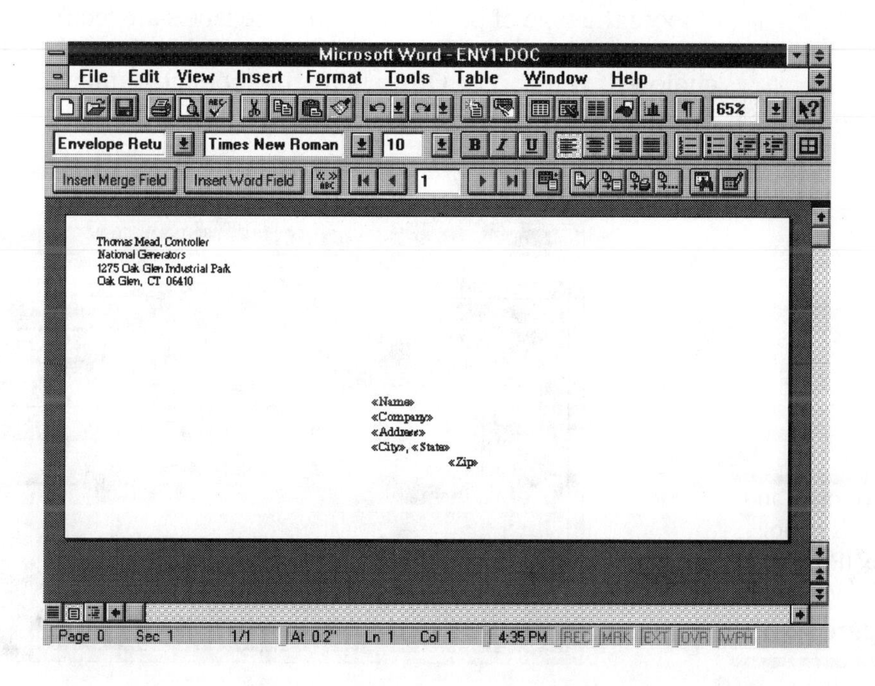

New envelope document created
Figure 18-14.

You can also use the same steps you learned earlier for printing out some or all of the envelopes. Before printing, however, choose the Envelopes and Labels command from the Tools menu and select the Printing Options tab, shown in Figure 18-15. The look of this dialog box will be different depending on the type of printer you have.

Mailing labels are similar to envelopes. However, you have to specify how the mailing labels are laid out on the page and what kind of printer you are using. Labels that are *pin-fed* are used with dot-matrix printers; labels that are *sheet-fed* are used with dot matrix, inkjet, and laser printers.

You can use labels made by any manufacturer with Word, but the largest label-maker is Avery. Thus, most other manufacturers make products that are compatible with Avery's numbering system. When you specify to Word the layout of your labels, you give the Avery product code. If you are using labels from other manufacturers, look for an indication of the Avery equivalent product. If there is none, Word may still know about the label layout.

To start making mailing labels, follow the same steps as you did for envelopes, but select Mailing Labels from the Create button in the Mail Merge Helper dialog box. Use the same data source, the PAYMENT1 document. The Label Options dialog box that appears is shown in Figure 18-16.

Choose the type of printer and how the labels are fed from the Printer Information choices. Choose the types of labels from the Label Products choices. If you choose Other here, the Product Number choices list labels

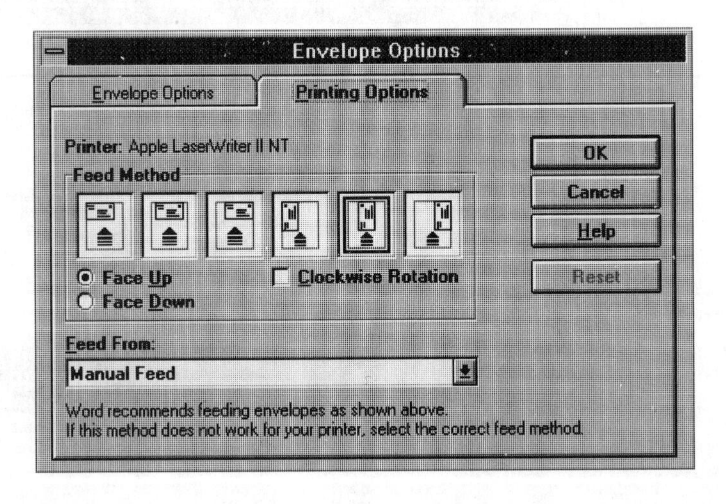

Envelopes and Labels dialog box (Printing Options tab)
Figure 18-15.

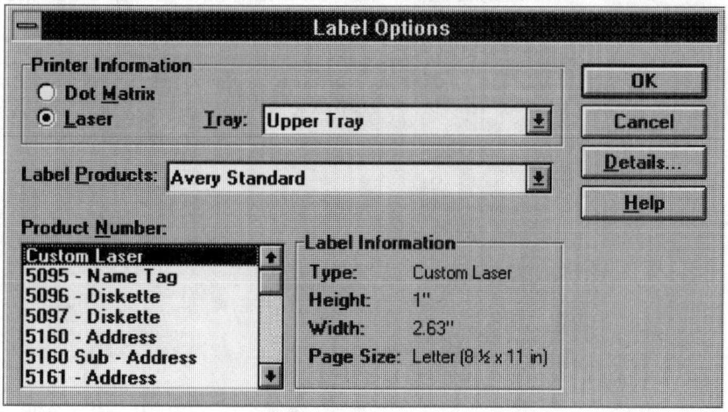

Label Options
Printer Information
Dot Matrix
Laser
Tray:
Upper Tray
OK
Cancel
Details...
Help
Label Products:
Avery Standard
Product Number:
Custom Laser
5095 - Name Tag
5096 - Diskette
5097 - Diskette
5160 - Address
5160 Sub - Address
5161 - Address
Label Information
Type:
Custom Laser
Height:
1"
Width:
2.63"
Page Size:
Letter (8 ½ x 11 in)

Label Options dialog box
Figure 18-16.

from manufacturers other than Avery. If you have a nonstandard label, choose Custom Laser or Custom Dot Matrix from the top of the Product Number list and choose the Details button to specify your label. That dialog box is shown in Figure 18-17. Enter all the sizes using the picture at the top of the dialog box as a guide. When you are finished, choose OK.

You then see the Create Labels dialog box, which is the same as the one you saw for envelopes. Use the Insert Merge Field button to complete your label and choose OK. Word creates the main document, such as the one shown in Figure 18-18. You then treat this document like your other main documents.

Custom Laser Information
Preview
Side Margins
Top Margin
Horizontal Pitch
Vertical Pitch
Width
Height
Number Down
Number Across
OK
Cancel
Help
Top Margin:
0.5"
Side Margin:
0.19"
Vertical Pitch:
1"
Horizontal Pitch:
2.75"
Label Height:
1"
Label Width:
2.63"
Number Across:
3
Number Down:
10

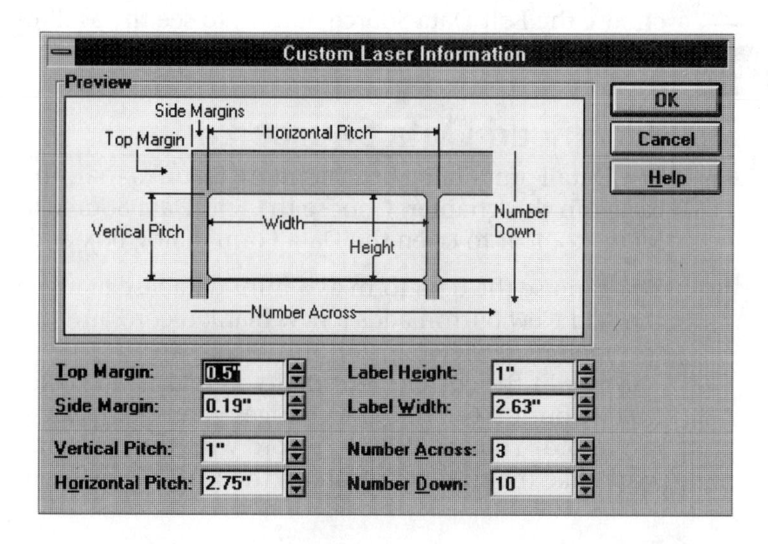

Details dialog box for specifying a label
Figure 18-17.

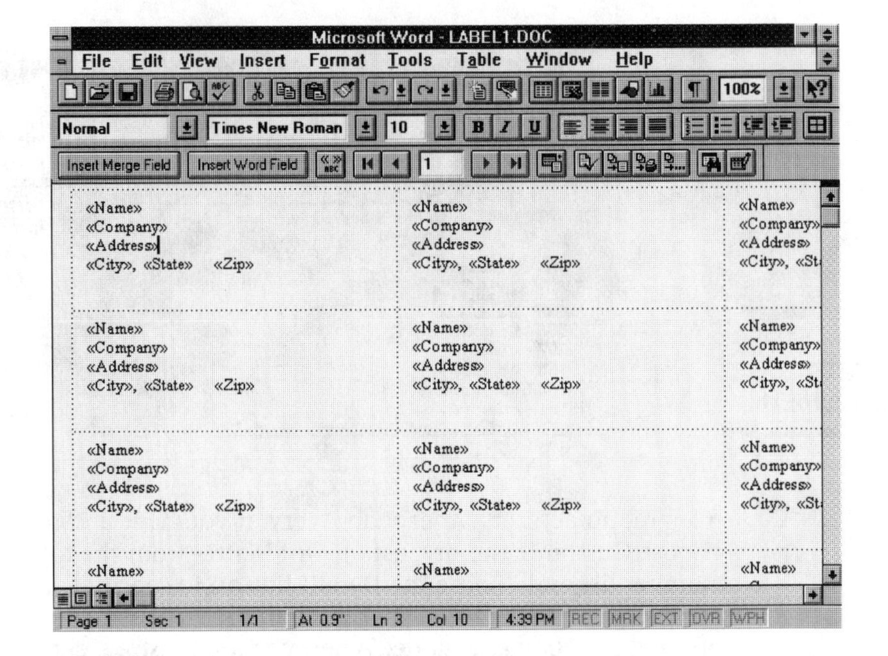

New mailing labels document created
Figure 18-18.

Lesson 114: Advanced Mail Merge Topics

The Mail Merge toolbar is your central control area for modifying, viewing, and printing your main document. It is also the jumping-off spot for modifying your data source. To add or change records in the data source, choose the Edit Data Source button; to see the Mail Merge Helper dialog box, choose the Mail Merge Helper button.

Advanced Data Source Editing

The Data Form dialog box has more features than the ones you explored earlier in this chapter. Choose the Edit Data Source button from the Mail Merge toolbar to open the Data Form dialog box and select PAYMENT1.DOC.

You can use the data form as a mini-database manager. You already saw how the Add New button adds a new blank record and how you can change the record you are viewing with the Record area at the bottom of the dialog box. As you edit the current record, if you make a mistake, you can choose the Restore button to undo the changes you have made since you brought up the record. You can delete a record with the Delete button. The Find button works like the similar button on the Mail Merge toolbar.

Because the data source is a Word document with a table, you can simply edit that document if you want. Choose the View Source button in the Data Form dialog box to see the document. Word also displays the Database toolbar:

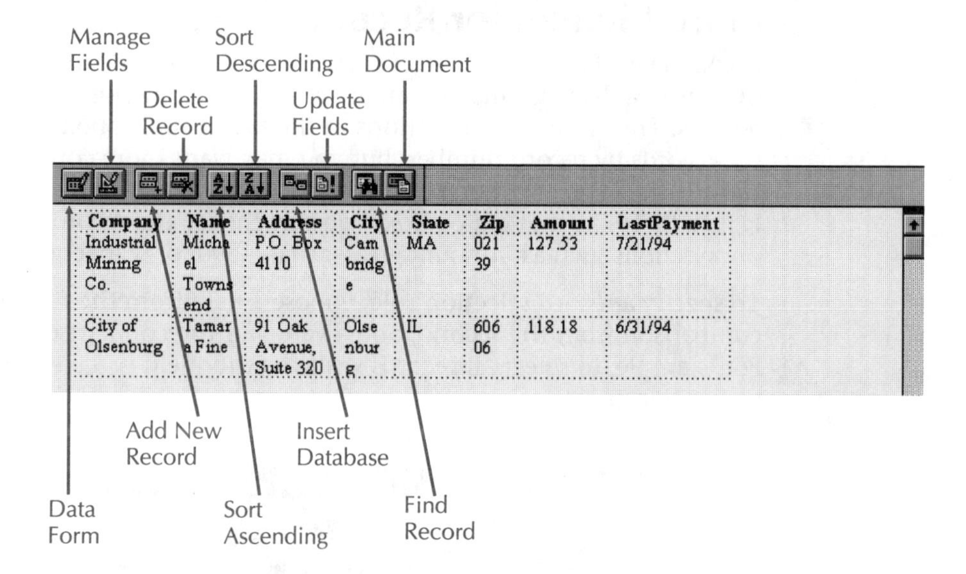

The Manage Fields button lets you add new fields, delete fields, or change the names of fields in the file. Its dialog box looks like this:

Manage Fields
Field Name:
Add >>
Remove
Rename...
Field Names in Header Row:
Company
Name
Address
City
State
Zip
Amount
LastPayment
OK
Cancel
Help

The Add New Record and Delete Record buttons work as you would expect, adding and deleting rows in the table. The Sort Ascending and Sort Descending buttons sort the table based on the currently selected column (sorting is described in detail in Chapter 25).

The Insert Database button is used if you do not have a table in the document, or if you want to change the data based on another database. The

Update Fields button is used if you are using fields in your database. These are both advanced options that are rarely used.

More Choices for Record Selection

If you have a large data source, particularly if you brought the data source over from a database management system, you may not want to print all the records. The From and To options in the Merge dialog box let you restrict the records by record number, but you may want more control. For this, you can use the Query Options button, which brings up the dialog box shown in Figure 18-19. In that dialog box, you can choose the records you want based on selections such as "Amount greater than 1500" or "City equal to New York."

To specify a record selection rule, choose a field from the first box, a comparison from the second, and a value for the comparison in the third. For example, to select all records with the City field equal to New York, you would select:

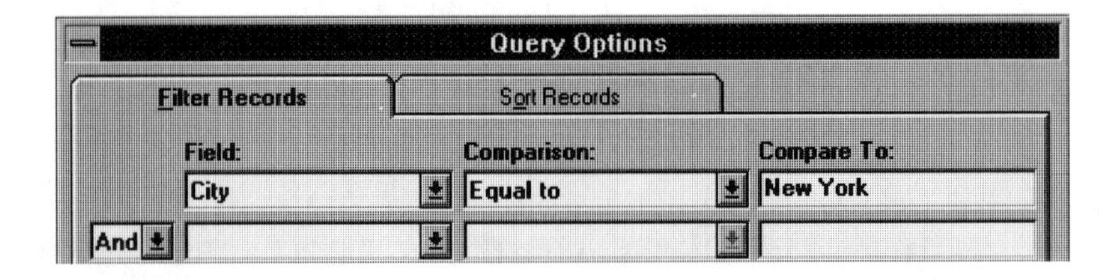

You can enter more than one criterion. For each additional row, you specify whether you want both of the criteria to be met (choose And in the first

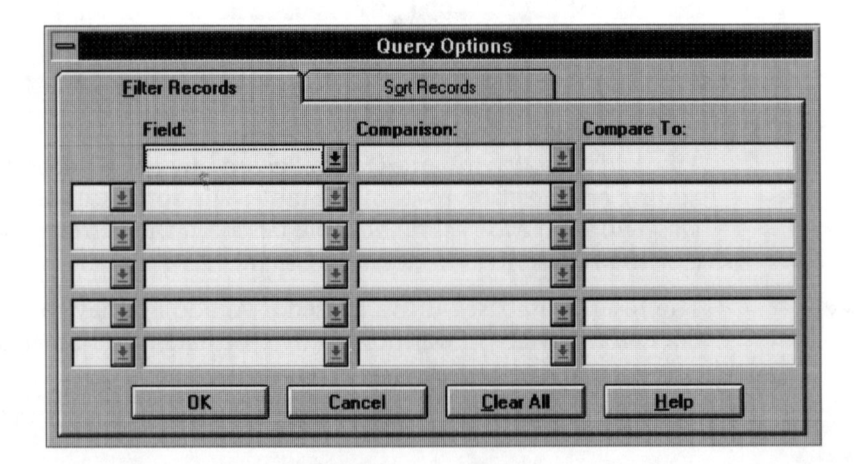

Query Options dialog box
Figure 18-19.

column) or if you want either of the criteria to be met (choose Or in the first column).

For instance, to find all the records for people in the city of New York who owe more than $1000, you would specify:

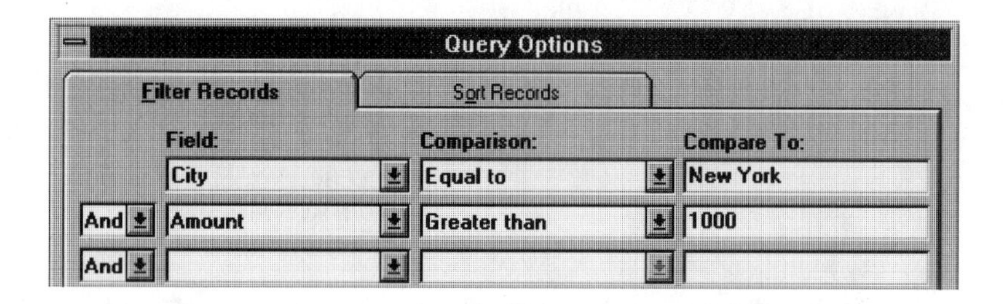

To find all the people in either New York or Chicago, you would specify:

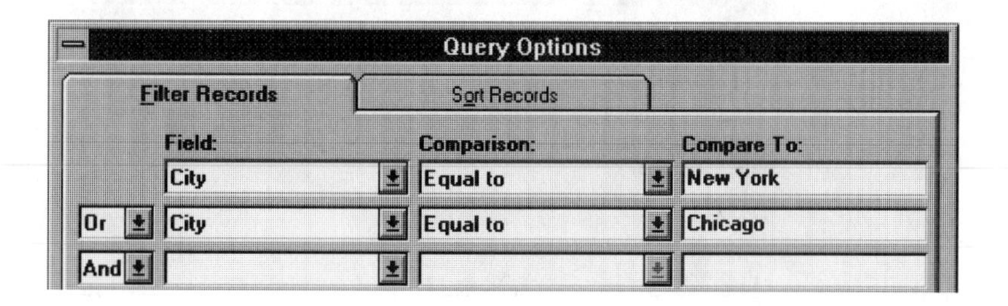

Conditional Insertion

The previous example showed a simple merge file with many fields. A unique feature of Word that makes letter writing even easier is *conditional insertion*. You can check the value of a field and insert different text depending on the value of the field. For example, if the information in the amount field is over 1000, you can insert a sentence describing the dire consequences of not paying promptly. Your data source can also have a field called "RegularCustomer" that contains a "Y" or "N", and you can use this to decide what type of salutation to use. You use *Word fields* to perform these tests.

The Word field feature has many instructions that you can use; some are described in this lesson, but the full use of merge instructions is beyond the scope of this book.

To enter Word field instructions, put the insertion point where you want the instruction in the main document and use the Insert Word Field button in the Mail Merge toolbar. The Word fields are listed on the drop-down list:

For example, when you choose If...Then...Else from the dialog box, Word displays the following:

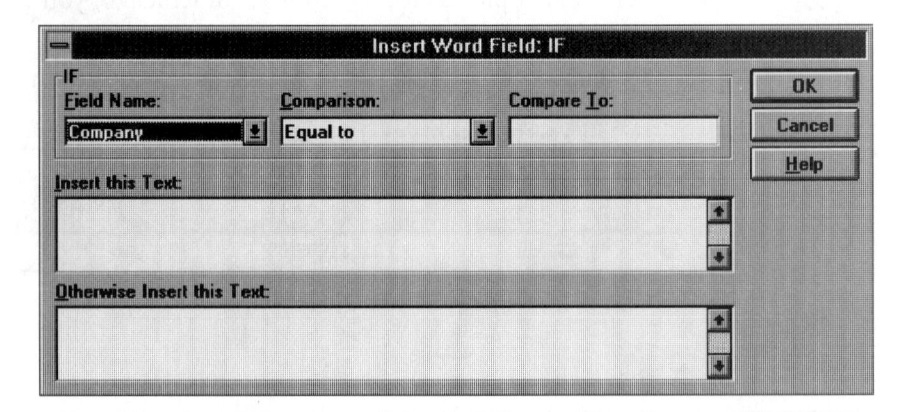

You need to fill in the correct fields and values in this instruction, as you will see in the next example.

The main document in Figure 18-20, BALANCE2, is similar to the BALANCE1 document except that it has an IF instruction used with a text field. The IF instruction checks the value of the "SalesRep" field and prints one of two possible sentences, depending on whether the information in the SalesRep field is "none" or some other value. The data source is also similar to the previous one but has an extra field called SalesRep added. Figure 18-21 shows the Insert Word Field dialog box.

You can also use the IF instruction with integer fields to test whether a number is greater than, less than, or equal to a field value. For instance, if your data source has a field named "CustYears", that is, the number of years a customer has been with your firm, you might include a sentence in a letter

August 15, 1994

«Name»
«Company»
«Address»
«City», «State» «Zip»

Dear «Name»:

Our records show that your outstanding balance is $«Amount», and that we have not received any payment from you since «LastPayment». Your sales representative will call you about this. If there is a disagreement about this amount, please feel free to call us about it.

Sincerely,

Sharon Myers
National Manufacturing

BALANCE2 main document with IF instruction
Figure 18-20.

that thanks customers who have CustYears over 10 for their long years of patronage.

The SET and ASK merge instructions allow you to enter information when you print. The SET instruction sets a field once for all letters, whereas the ASK instruction prompts you for a new value for each letter. You can include a string with which Word prompts you.

Review

Imagine you have an office supply business. Create a client order list including name, title, address, phone, item, and quantity purchased. Next, create a billing letter template and create customized bills for each client.

Think about how to use the information in the order list with the merge instructions. For example, think about how to thank a client for a large order.

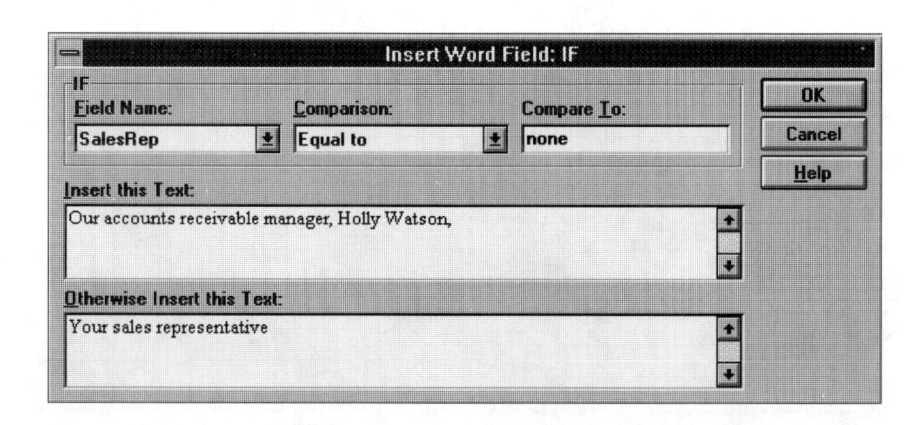

If...Then...Else dialog box
Figure 18-21.

Word For Windows

PART 3

ADVANCED FEATURES

C H A P T E R

19

EASIER TEXT EDITING

With Word's many formatting and document preparation features, it is easy to forget that most of your time in using Word is spent entering and editing text. The early chapters of this book showed you the basics of text editing, but there are many other features that make your most common word processing tasks go more smoothly.

Lesson 115: Easier Typing with AutoCorrect

Typing mistakes are common and frustrating. Many people can think much faster than they type and end up making many mistakes as they are typing in new material. This is particularly true when what you are typing isn't terribly interesting to you and your mind wanders. When you go back and read what you typed, you might find the same mistyped words over and over.

Word's AutoCorrect feature is an incredible boon to typists. Basically, it corrects your typing mistakes immediately after you make them. For example, a very common mistake is to type "teh" instead of "the". As soon as you press the Spacebar after "teh", Word changes it to "the" without any prompting from you. This is, of course, much handier than waiting until you check your spelling.

When you install Word, the AutoCorrect feature is normally turned on. You can configure AutoCorrect using the AutoCorrect command from the Tools menu. The dialog box is shown in Figure 19-1. If you decide you don't want to use AutoCorrect, simply deselect the Replace Text as You Type option. As you can see from the top of the dialog box, AutoCorrect can do much more than just correct simple mistypings.

The first option will change straight quotes to *smart quotes* (often called *curly quotes*).

Straight quotes: "leading edge"
Smart quotes: “leading edge”

Thus, when you type a quotation mark after a space, AutoCorrect changes it to a left curly quote:

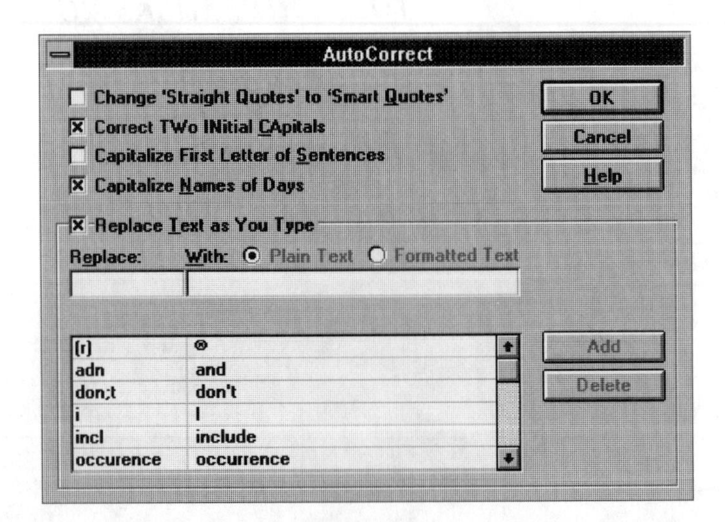

AutoCorrect dialog box
Figure 19-1.

He said that the product was on the "|

After that, when you type the next quotation mark after a character that is not a space, AutoCorrect changes it to the right curly quote:

He said that the product was on the "leading edge"|

The same rules apply to apostrophes, which are often used as single quotation marks. With this feature, all possessive nouns and contractions will automatically use the right curly quote:

He said that the product was on the "leading edge" of the technology. "I don't think that it is overstating our case to call this 'first-rate' technology," he concluded.

Another common typing mistake is to hold down the Shift key a bit too long when typing a capitalized word, causing the first two letters to be capitalized. AutoCorrect can fix this on words where you only capitalized the first two letters, such as changing "THere" to "There".

A less common mistake is to not capitalize the first letter of a sentence, and AutoCorrect can fix that as well. AutoCorrect can also make sure that the names of days are capitalized.

However, AutoCorrect's best feature is to correct your mistyped words as they happen. You can list as many incorrect-to-correct combinations as you want in the table at the bottom of the AutoCorrect dialog box. Word comes with a few corrections already in the list:

(r)	®
adn	and
don;t	don't
i	I
incl	include
occurence	occurrence

Note that some of these pairs are, in fact, not mistypings but shortcuts for phrases that you might commonly use in your writing. This is an easy way to create a typing shortcut; a more robust method is described in the next few lessons.

To add your own pairs, type the mistyped word in the Replace field and the correction in the With field, then select the Add button. The Replace field can be up to 31 characters long, although you will almost always use fewer than 10 characters.

You can also automatically fill the With field by selecting the corrected text in your document before choosing the AutoCorrect command. If you use this latter method, you can select whether or not to have the AutoCorrect entry retain the formatting of the selected text. Choose Plain Text to enter the correction in the document's current formatting or Formatted Text to retain the formatting.

For example, assume that you often mistype a client's name. In a document, type the name correctly, select it, and choose the AutoCorrect command from the Tools menu. Enter an abbreviation for that name in the Replace entry, choose Plain Text (because you don't know the kind of formatting that will be in effect when you next use the name), and choose the Add button.

AutoCorrect can also get its pairs from the Spelling command. As you are using the Spelling command, any correction that you make can also be added to the AutoCorrect list. Simply select the AutoCorrect button in the Spelling dialog box.

Lesson 116: Reducing Typing with AutoText

As you work more with a word processor, you will probably find that particular phrases or blocks of text are used over and over, such as the name of a company or a long product name. Typing this text many times in a report or memo is tedious, and copying it from another file each time can take almost as long as typing it.

Word eliminates this problem by using AutoText. AutoText is a set of names that correspond to longer phrases. Instead of repeatedly typing the longer phrase in the text, you simply type the AutoText name followed by pressing F3. Any phrase or block of text can be abbreviated. The name can consist of as many as 31 letters or numbers, if necessary, but keeping the names short makes this feature more useful. AutoText entries are kept in templates, so you can make global AutoText entries in the NORMAL.DOT file, as described in Chapter 11.

For example, in the SAMPLE1 file, Thomas Mead's name and address could be used as an AutoText name for those occasions when he types his address at the bottom of a letter. Chris Richford's name and address and the name "National Generators" could also be used. Some suggested AutoText entries are shown in Table 19-1.

AutoText can be a great time saver since it eliminates the typing of sections of text that you use often. It also prevents typing mistakes in commonly used terms and names, although you may want to use AutoCorrect for that. In addition, you can store graphics in an AutoText entry by using the same methods you use to store text.

Sample AutoText Entries
Table 19-1.

Name	Expanded Text
ng	National Generators
thomaddr	Thomas Mead, Controller National Generators 1275 Oak Glen Industrial Park Oak Glen, CT 06401
richford	Chris Richford, Vice President Manufacturer's Bank of the Northeast 1000 First Avenue Millerton, CT 06492

You can create an AutoText entry—a name and its associated text—by giving the AutoText command from the Edit menu. While editing a file, select the phrase or block of text for which you want to use a name. Then give the AutoText command, enter the name, and select the Define button. This creates the entry.

Now use the SAMPLE1 letter to see how to create entries. To store Chris Richford's name and address under the name "richford", select the text in the letter and give the AutoText command from the Edit menu. The AutoText dialog box appears, as shown in Figure 19-2. In the AutoText Name box, type **richford**. The first few words of the text you selected appear at the bottom of the dialog box. Select the Add button to define the entry and close the dialog box.

Also notice that the name is now in the list of names that appears under the AutoText Name box. To see what a name stands for, select it from the list.

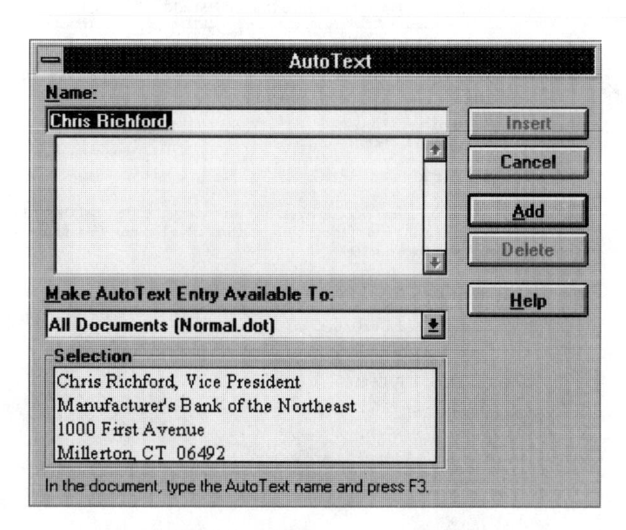

AutoText dialog box
Figure 19-2.

Select the Cancel button to close the dialog box.

When you want to expand a name, set the insertion point at the place where you want the text. You then have two choices:

- Type the name of the entry and press F3.
- Give the AutoText command, select the desired name from the list, and select the Insert button.

When you insert from the dialog box, you can select Formatted Text or Plain Text in the Insert As area. Use Formatted Text if you want to keep any character formatting you applied to the text of the entry, and use Plain Text if you want the text to be entered in the current character formatting.

To practice expanding names, include the three entries in Table 19-1 in your AutoText entries. (You have already created "richford".) Close the AutoText dialog box and the SAMPLE1 window, and give the New command from the File menu to start a new letter. Your finished text will look like the text in Figure 19-3, but you will use the AutoText names instead of typing the names and addresses or the company name in the body of the text.

Type **richford** and press F3. The AutoText name is expanded into the complete name and address. Continue the letter, using the AutoText names when you can. Save this letter as SAMPLE2.

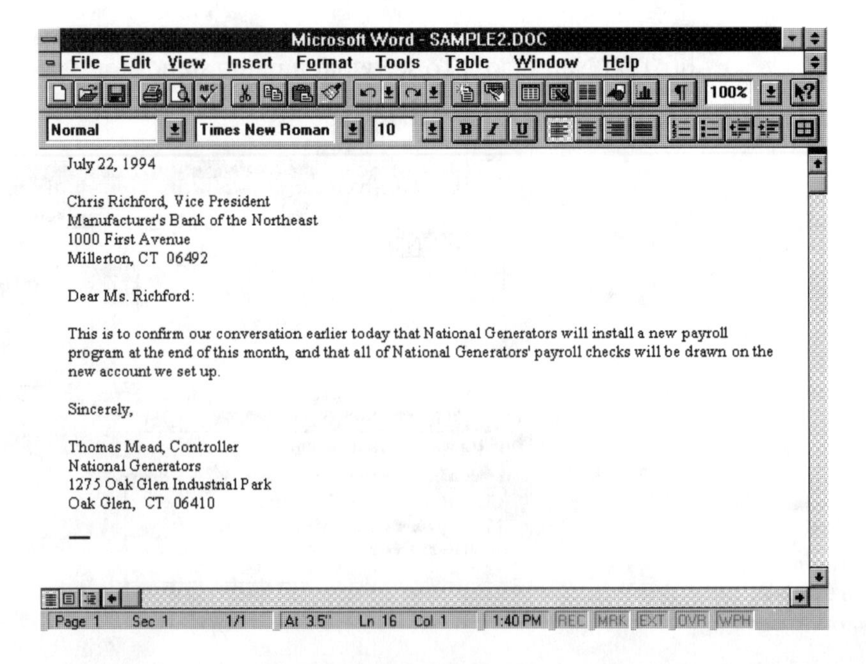

July 22, 1994

Chris Richford, Vice President
Manufacturer's Bank of the Northeast
1000 First Avenue
Millerton, CT 06492

Dear Ms. Richford:

This is to confirm our conversation earlier today that National Generators will install a new payroll program at the end of this month, and that all of National Generators' payroll checks will be drawn on the new account we set up.

Sincerely,

Thomas Mead, Controller
National Generators
1275 Oak Glen Industrial Park
Oak Glen, CT 06410

SAMPLE2 text
Figure 19-3.

If you want to remove some of the AutoText entries, give the AutoText command, select the entries, and select the Delete button. To replace the text of an AutoText entry, type the new text that you want for the name in the document and select it. Give the AutoText command, select the name from the list, and select Add, then choose the Yes button to redefine the entry.

As your list of AutoText entries gets larger, you may forget what is in it. To print out the entries for reference, choose the Print command from the File menu and select AutoText Entries from the Print What drop-down list.

AutoText can reduce typing and increase accuracy in many different applications. The following list should give you some ideas for using glossaries in your daily word processing.

- Complex scientific phrases, such as the names of chemicals, long theory names, process names, and the names of reactions
- Standard legal citations, case names, and legal jargon
- Long, nearly identical names, such as model numbers
- Phrases that are heavily used in a document

Table 19-2 shows examples of some of these uses.

Lesson 117: Inserting the Date and Time in Your Document

You may want to add the current date and/or time in your document. You already saw in Chapter 14 how to add the date and time in headers and footers, but you can add them to your normal text as well.

Name	Contents
13cb	anhydrous 1,3-dichlorobenzene, U.S.P.
rsae	Rivest-Shamir-Abel encryption
mcatcom	methyl-selenium catalytic combustion
yrox	Youngblood-Roberts oxidation
fiduc	34 N.E. 2d 68, 70
rw	Roe v. Wade
eqpro	equal protection of the laws
cl12	Colonial 12-422 Model S

Suggested AutoText Entries of Various Uses
Table 19-2.

To add the date, the time, or both, choose Date and Time from the Insert menu. You see the following dialog box:

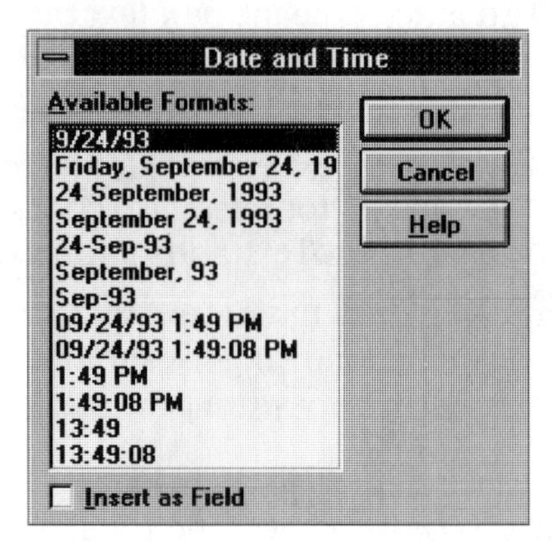

Select one of the formats and choose the OK button.

There are two ways you can enter the date and time: as actual text or as fields. Fields are described in Chapter 26 and are fairly technical. For now, you should understand that if you insert the date and time as a field, it will be updated each time you update fields (such as when you print). Thus, the date and time you enter now will change in the future. If that is what you want, select Insert as Field in the Date and Time dialog box.

Lesson 118: Multiple Levels of Undo

As you saw in Chapter 2, Word's Undo command from the Edit menu is very handy when you make mistakes or when you want to experiment with a change. The Redo command undoes the last Undo command. These two commands are common to many Windows programs.

Word has an advanced feature that makes these commands much more powerful. The Undo and Redo commands remember many edits that you made, not just the last one. In many programs (and in earlier versions of Word), you could only undo the last action you took. However, Word's Undo command can undo many steps, not just the last one.

To see this, open the SAMPLE1 file. Select the first few words of the first sentence and make them boldface. Select the next few words and make them italic. Select a few more and underline them.

I am pleased to send you the latest *update on the results* <u>of our expanded product</u> line. The enclosed summary documents our increased profit margin (7%) for the fourth quarter of our fiscal year (ending June 30), which is largely due to the successful introduction of our new model, the DC50. In the next year we expect to continue increasing our profitable inroads into this new area.

Clearly, these are changes you are going to want to undo before saving the letter.

Choose the Edit menu, and notice that the Undo command says "Undo Underline"; this tells you what action you are about to undo. Choose that command, and the underlining goes away:

> **I am pleased to send you the latest** *update on the results* of our expanded product line. The enclosed summary documents our increased profit margin (7%) for the fourth quarter of our fiscal year (ending June 30), which is largely due to the successful introduction of our new model, the DC50. In the next year we expect to continue increasing our profitable inroads into this new area.

Now look at the Edit menu again. The Undo command has changed to "Undo Italic", and the Redo command has become "Redo Underline". Choose the Undo Italic command, and the italic formatting disappears:

> **I am pleased to send you the latest** update on the results of our expanded product line. The enclosed summary documents our increased profit margin (7%) for the fourth quarter of our fiscal year (ending June 30), which is largely due to the successful introduction of our new model, the DC50. In the next year we expect to continue increasing our profitable inroads into this new area.

You can also use the Undo and Redo buttons from the Standard toolbar. Clicking on the buttons themselves is like giving the command in the Edit menu.

If you click on the associated arrows to the right of the buttons, you see a drop-down list of the actions that can be undone or redone. Using this list, you can undo or redo more than one command at a time.

For example, select part of the first paragraph of the letter and center it. Select part of the second paragraph and make it right justified. Now look at the Undo drop-down list from the Standard toolbar:

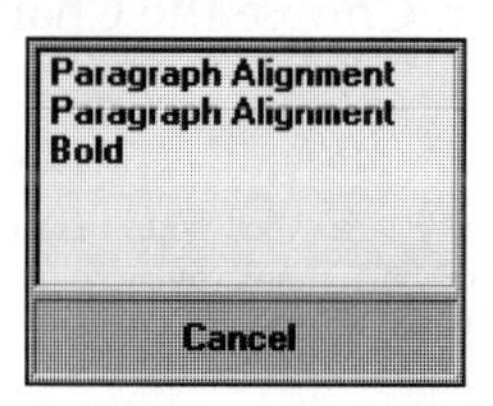

If you drag down this list, you can undo many of the actions in a single mouse action.

Note that you shouldn't rely too heavily on multiple levels of undoing and redoing. After you perform some actions, you can no longer undo certain other actions that you took earlier. However, if you discover that you have made changes in a document that you no longer want, feel free to see how far back you can go with the Undo command.

Lesson 119: Changing the Case of Text

Capitalization in the English language used to be very regular: the first letter of a sentence and the first letter of a proper noun. In the past few decades, however, the rules have become less clear. Many acronyms, like "IBM," appear in all capitals, but some acronyms like "UNIX" can also appear in just initial capitals (in this case, "Unix"). There are also times when you want whole sentences to appear in all capitals for emphasis (although using boldface usually has the same effect and makes the sentence easier to read).

You can change the case of text in your Word documents quickly with the Change Case command from the Format menu. The Change Case dialog box looks like this:

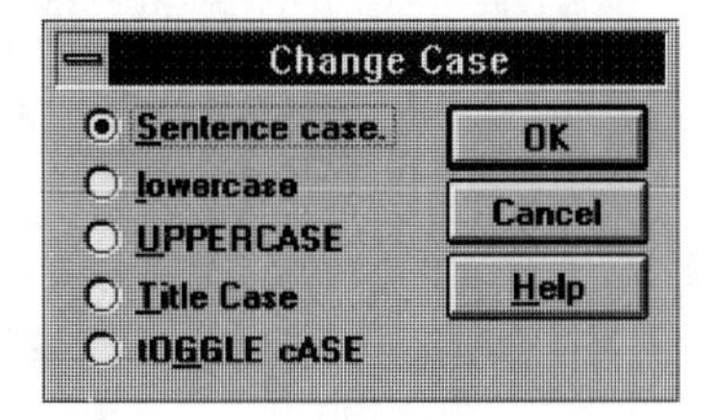

Sentence case only capitalizes the first letter of a sentence. Lowercase and uppercase change all of the letters in the selection. Title case capitalizes the first letter of each word, and toggle case changes all lowercase letters to uppercase and vice versa. Note that this command actually changes the case of the letters and is really not a formatting command.

For example, select the first sentence of the second paragraph of the SAMPLE1 letter. Choose the Change Case command and select the Title Case option.

> As You Can See, We Are Well Within The Projections We Outlined To You When You Helped Us Obtain Short-Term Financing. Thank you again for all your assistance. If you have any questions regarding this information, please feel free to call me.

Lesson 120: Seeing How Much You Have Written

Many writers have to know how much they have written on particular projects. There may be a maximum number of words allowed, or there may be a minimum that must be met by a particular deadline. Or you may just be curious as to how much work you've done in a document.

The Word Count command from the Tools menu gives you a quick set of statistics on the current document. Its dialog box looks like this:

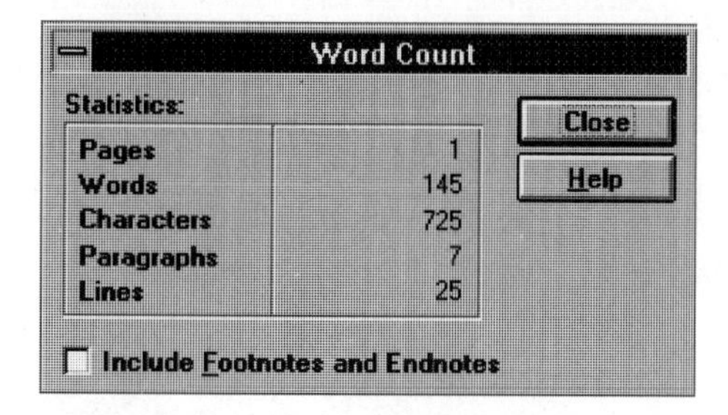

The Include Footnotes and Endnotes option tells Word whether you want to include these; most often you do.

Review

Look at some of the writing you are doing (or want to be doing) with Word. Determine which words and phrases would be good candidates for AutoCorrect and AutoText entries. Add a few of them to the NORMAL.DOT template. Start a new document and use these entries as you type some sample text.

As you work, start looking in the drop-down list under the Undo button. Think about how much of your work would be undone by each level of undo.

CHAPTER

20

DESKTOP PUBLISHING

In the past five years, word processors have become powerful and easy enough for most people to start performing real publishing tasks on their personal computers. Now, you don't need sophisticated (and usually complicated) desktop publishing programs to lay out brochures and newsletters. Word includes features that let you do a surprising amount of layout without a great deal of complexity.

Lesson 121: Creating Text with Newspaper Columns

You can use Word to print out newsletters and other material formatted with two or more columns on a page. These columns are called *newspaper columns* since they snake on the page, as in newspapers. When you use more than one column, Word adjusts whatever formatting commands you have given so that they work within the columns.

It is usually convenient to edit in page layout view if you are editing a section or document that has two or more columns and many headings. Using this view lets you see if a heading is falling near the bottom of a column and how the columns balance out.

The Columns command in the Format menu has the choices for producing multicolumn text. Figure 20-1 shows the dialog box. Number of Columns is the number of columns you want. The preset formats at the top of the dialog box let you specify how the columns will appear on the page. You can also specify whether you want a line between the columns.

Unlike many word processors (and earlier versions of Word), your columns do not need to be the same width. For example, choosing the Left option makes two columns, with the left column about half the width of the right column.

If you want your columns to be the same width, choose the Equal Column Width option. With this option selected, the Width and Spacing options are filled in for you automatically. If you want columns of different widths, deselect the Equal Column Width option and fill in the desired widths. You can change the amount of intercolumn spacing for each column as well.

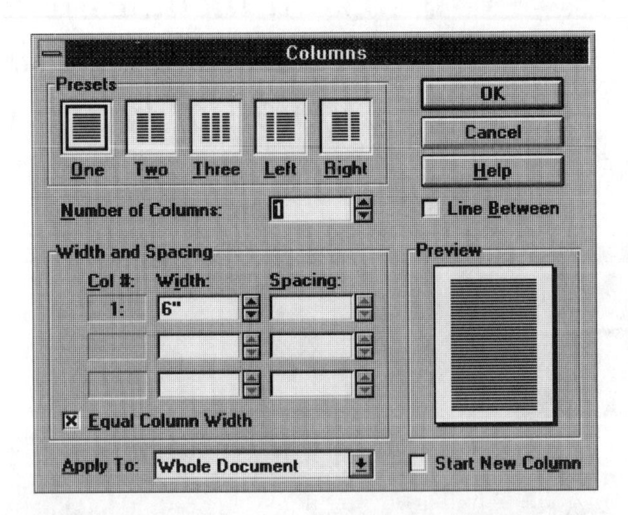

Columns dialog box
Figure 20-1.

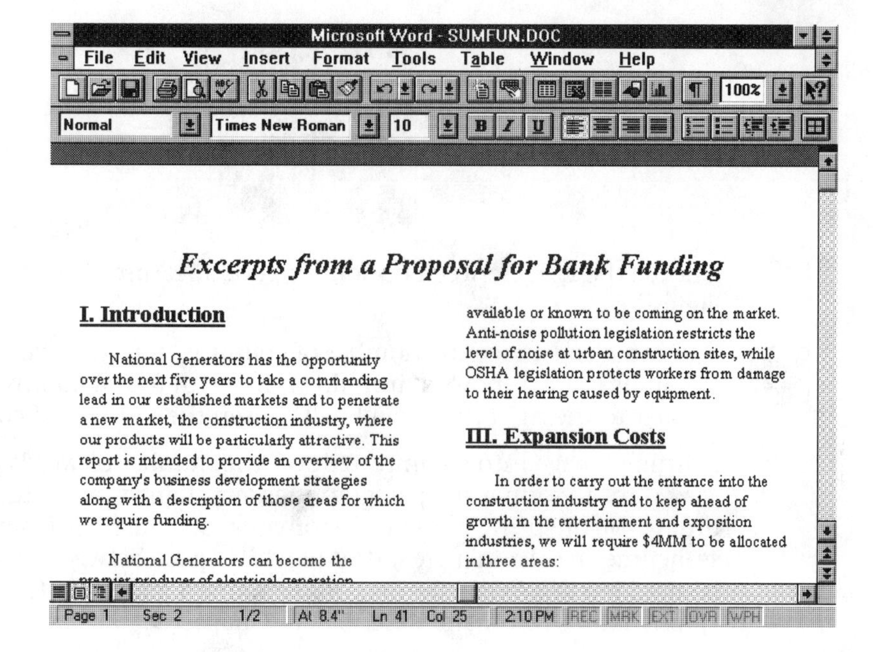

Two-column text under a single-column title
Figure 20-2.

The Start New Column option tells Word to insert a column break at the insertion point when you execute the command. You can also insert a column break at any time with the Break command from the Insert menu.

Remember that you will not see the multiple columns on the screen in normal view; you will see them only in page layout view or in print preview.

To see the effect of multiple columns, assume that you want the SUMFUN report in two columns. If you typed in the first few paragraphs of that report, open the document now; if not, you can experiment on another document.

Use page layout view so you can see the changes as you make them. In the report, put the insertion point at the beginning of the first heading (after the title) and choose the Columns command. Select the Two page from the Presets area, choose This Point Forward from the Apply To drop-down list, and select OK. You chose This Point Forward because you wanted the title to remain in one column across the top of the first page. The result is shown in Figure 20-2.

If you want, you can experiment with the result. For example, make the left column narrower than the right column, choose the Columns command again, deselect the Equal Column Width option, and enter the following for the widths:

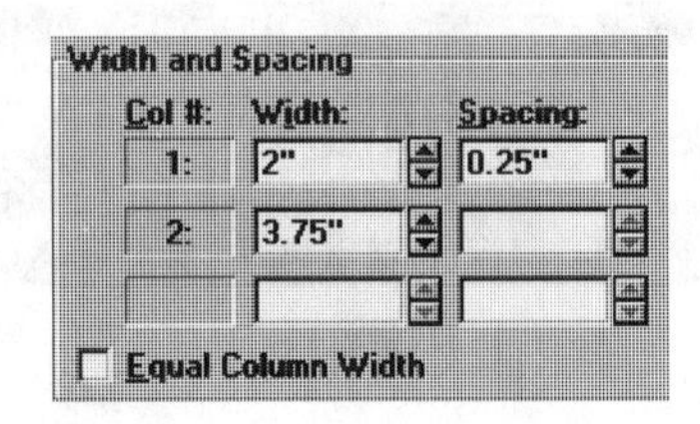

Choose the Line Between option for good measure. The result is shown in Figure 20-3.

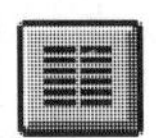

You can also change the number of columns from the Standard toolbar. The Columns button shows a drop-down list with four columns; drag the mouse pointer to the right until you have chosen the number of columns you want.

Splitting a page into columns reduces the number of words per line, so you may want to format the paragraphs as left aligned rather than as justified unless you are using a small size for your font. Justifying narrow columns sometimes results in a great deal of white space between words, which can be hard to read. With narrow columns, it is a good idea to use the Hyphenation command described in Chapter 9.

Even though multicolumn text is not often used in business documents, you may find that it enhances the appearance of some reports. If you design brochures with lots of text, you can select landscape mode in the Page Setup

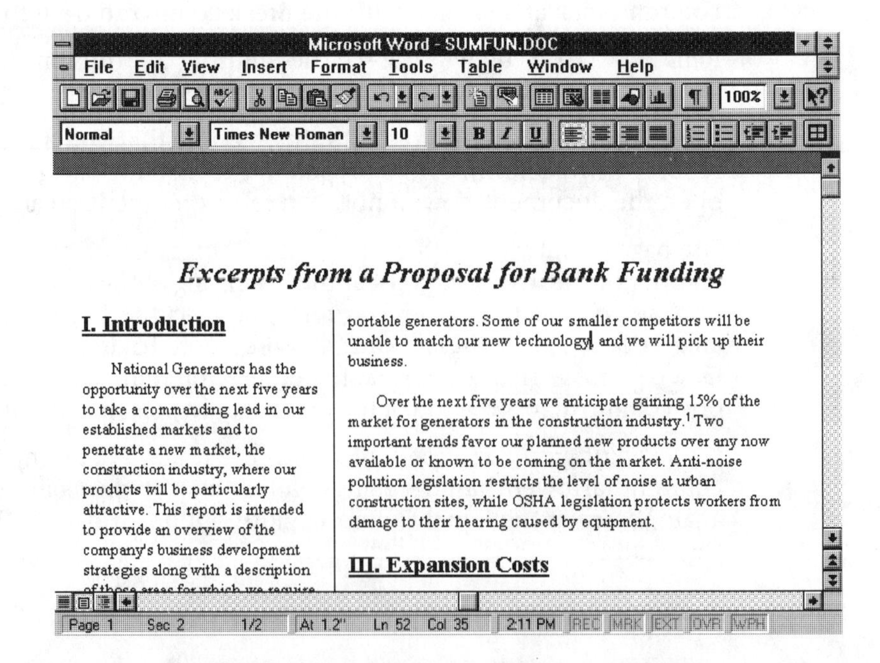

Two-column document with uneven widths
Figure 20-3.

command and use three columns of equal width with about an inch between the columns. Multiple columns are also useful for newsletters.

Lesson 122: Positioning with Frames

In a normal Word document, each paragraph appears on the page after the one that is before it. However, there are many times when you want a paragraph or a group of paragraphs to appear in a particular spot on the page and want other paragraphs to flow around this. That is, you want to specify the position for the paragraph (such as "in the middle of the page, 3 inches from the left margin and 4 inches from the top margin" or "at the bottom of this column"). To do this in Word, you insert a *frame* on your page and fill it with text, pictures, and so on. You can then move the frame to a desired location or specify the location exactly by using dialog boxes.

Frames are often used to add interesting layout elements, such as pictures or excerpts from your text. Figure 20-4 shows how a text excerpt in a two-column document can make the page look more interesting.

Few people use frames in their daily work. Although creating frames is easy, the results of editing a document with frames can be confusing to many Word users. Frames are mostly used by people doing desktop publishing or preparing highly designed documents such as sales brochures. Word's advanced framing features can match those of expensive desktop publishing

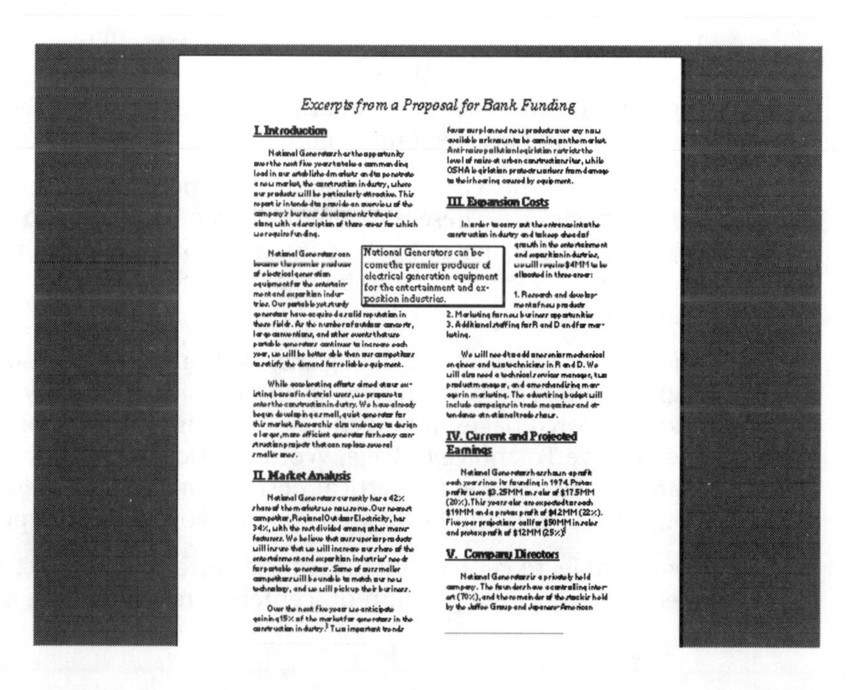
Excerpts from a Proposal for Bank Funding

I. Introduction

National Generators can become the premier producer of electrical generation equipment for the entertainment and exposition industries.

III. Expansion Costs

II. Market Analysis

IV. Current and Projected Earnings

V. Company Directors

Two-column document with a frame added
Figure 20-4.

programs such as Aldus PageMaker. These features are beyond the scope of this book but are covered briefly here so you can see their power in case you have need for them in the future.

You create a frame on a page by choosing the Frame command from the Insert menu. You have to start in page layout view or print preview. If you don't, Word asks whether you want to switch to page layout view, and if you don't, you can't create the frame. When you start a frame, Word prompts you at the bottom of the screen to draw the frame where you want it. Don't be concerned about the exact position or size of the frame because they are easy to change. Click one corner of the location you want and drag to the diagonally opposite corner. Word makes room for the frame by moving your text around.

Working with frames is best done in page layout view or print preview since that is the view where you can move and resize frames. If your frames are small, page layout view is just fine.

As an example, assume that you want to add a frame that will contain a picture in your SAMPLE1 letter. (Of course, it is unlikely that you would actually want to do this since pictures in letters almost always are placed after the text that describes them.) Open the SAMPLE1 letter and choose the Frame command from the Insert menu. Then click near the middle of the first line of the first paragraph and drag down and to the right. Word creates the frame and puts the insertion point in it, ready for you to enter text or paste in a picture. Figure 20-5 shows the result.

To position a frame and describe how the text will move around it, give the Frame command from the Format menu to display the Frame dialog box, shown in Figure 20-6. You can also bring up this dialog box by double-clicking on the frame's border.

When you define a frame's position, you specify both the horizontal and vertical positions. These measurements can be relative to the margin, to the edge of the page, or to the column if you have more than one column; the vertical position can also be relative to the paragraph to which the frame is anchored.

The choices in the Frame dialog box for horizontal position are Left, Center, Right, Inside, and Outside. Inside and Outside refer to even- and odd-numbered pages. If you choose Left, Right, Inside, or Outside and set the Relative To choice to Page, Word can position the object outside of the margins. The choices for vertical position are Top, Center, and Bottom. For both the vertical and horizontal choices, you can also type a measurement.

For example, to center a picture in the bottom of the text area, you could specify a horizontal position of "centered" relative to the margins and a

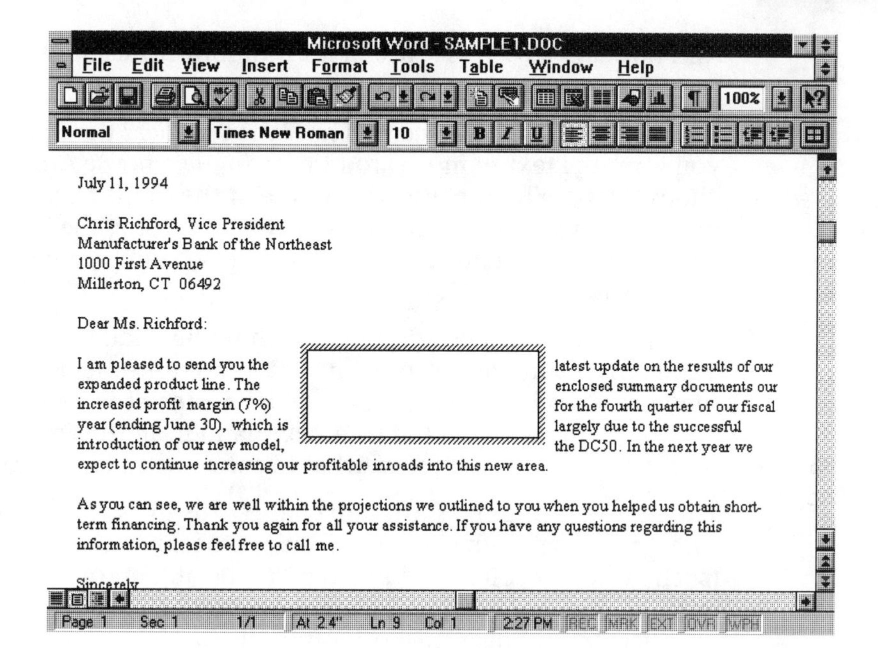

Frame inserted in SAMPLE1 letter
Figure 20-5.

vertical position of "bottom" relative to the margin. You can also specify a measurement for the position, such as "3.25 inches from the left margin" or "2 inches from the top of the page."

You can also specify the Move with Text option for vertical positioning. This tells Word to keep the frame with the paragraph it is next to when you view

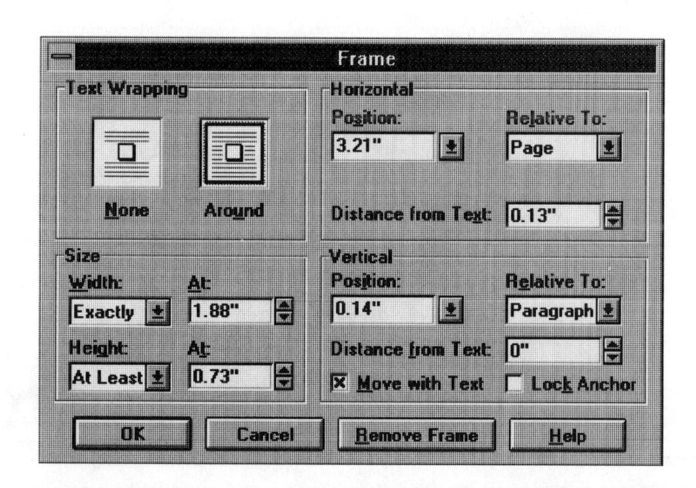

Frame dialog box
Figure 20-6.

it in normal view. This is useful for positioning headings with the associated text. The Lock Anchor command prevents the frame from moving.

The Text Wrapping choice tells how the text near the frame will appear. If you want the text to move around the frame, choose Around; otherwise, choose None. You can also set the size of the frame from the Frame dialog box. To change the size of the frame without using the Frame command, simply select the frame and drag one of the handles, as you learned for graphics in Chapter 12.

To experiment with positioning text in frames, add text to the frame in the SAMPLE1 document. With the insertion point in the frame, type the sentence **This is a large sentence in a movable frame.** Select the text and make it larger with the Font command from the Format menu. Your screen should now look somewhat like the one in Figure 20-7.

The default wrapping is Around; change this to None and note the result. Also, try changing the horizontal and vertical positions to relative positions (such as "top of column") instead of the default absolute positions. With every change, try adding text to the beginning of your document and see whether that changes the position of the frame.

Remember that frames do not need to hold just text: they are a great way to position graphics just where you want them on a page. If you anchor a drawing

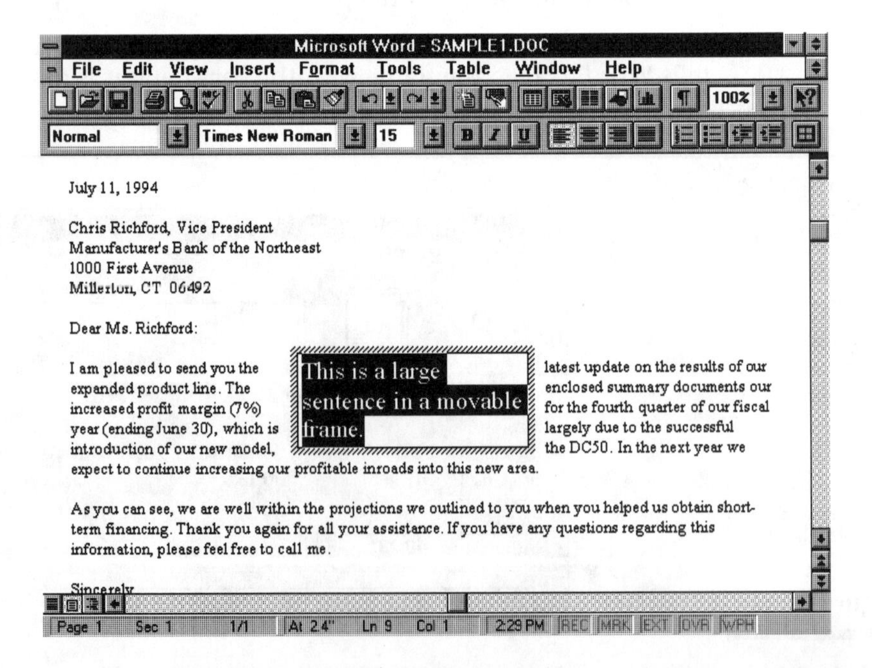

Text added to frame
Figure 20-7.

in a frame instead of to an unframed paragraph, the drawing only moves if the frame moves. This makes it less likely that a drawing will move without your knowing it, but it adds a level of complexity to laying out pictures.

As you can see, frames are a very powerful feature if you need to position text or graphics exactly in your text instead of having them flow in a normal fashion. Formatting frames is very much like formatting other items in Word, so feel free to experiment with them.

Lesson 123: Using Drop Caps for Emphasis

Using frames for text and graphics is fine, but the most common use for frames is for drop caps. A *drop cap* is a single letter that appears at the beginning of a paragraph, usually at the beginning of a chapter. Here is an example of a drop cap:

> As you can see, we are well within the projections we outlined to you when you helped us obtain short-term financing. Thank you again for all your assistance. If you have any questions regarding this information, please feel free to call me.

You don't need to use the Frame command to create a drop cap. Simply select the letter you want and choose the Drop Cap command from the Format menu. The dialog box looks like this:

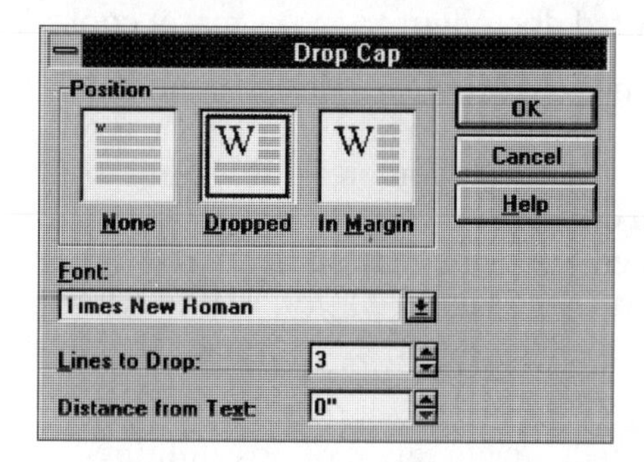

Choose Dropped from the position choices and select OK. You can change the default size of the drop cap from three lines to some other value; normally, you will choose two or three lines.

The In Margin choice puts the letter in the margin, but this is rarely used in publishing. You can select more than a single letter, but this is also rarely used.

The drop cap is just a frame with a paragraph of a single large letter. You can treat it just like a frame. As you can see in the dialog box for the frame, shown in Figure 20-8, the horizontal position is left relative to the column,

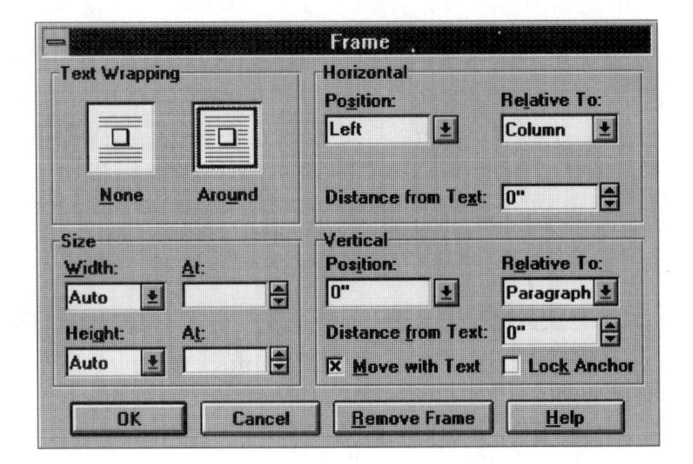

Frame dialog box for a drop cap
Figure 20-8.

and the vertical position is 0 inches from the top of the paragraph. Of course, the frame moves with the text.

Lesson 124: Creating Your Own Forms

For most people, the result of "desktop publishing" is paper. You design and edit a document, print it on a printer, and distribute it (or photocopy the printed document to make many copies of it). Someone reads it on the paper.

In the past few years, desktop publishing has taken many new directions. For example, you can add sound to a Word document, as you saw in Chapter 17. If you do that, you are "publishing" sound. Of course, any sound you attach to a document won't be available to someone reading the document on paper. Your publication is the document on the screen and the associated sound. In Chapter 21 you will see the kinds of things that can be included in a Word document, and some of them cannot be printed.

As you start to think of publishing as creating documents that might not be printed, a wide range of possibilities opens up. One area of nonprinted publishing that Word allows you to explore is that of interactive forms.

A form is anything that can be filled in. Business forms can take on a wide variety of features. A simple example is an invoice. On a paper invoice, you fill in the customer's name and address plus other customer-specific information. You then fill in what they ordered and the prices and determine a total, which you fill in near the bottom.

An interactive form replaces the paper form. In the case of the invoice, an interactive form could be a simple Word table in which you type the relevant information. When all the information is filled in, you save the form to disk and possibly print it to send to the customer.

If Word's interactive forms were just tables, they wouldn't be that much easier to use than paper forms. However, Word goes well beyond tables for its form features. Because most of these features are fairly advanced, this lesson only gives a brief overview of forms.

You can create a form that looks like a large dialog box. A form can have three types of data entry:

- Text fields
- Check boxes
- Drop-down lists

An example of a form with all three types of data entry fields might look like this:

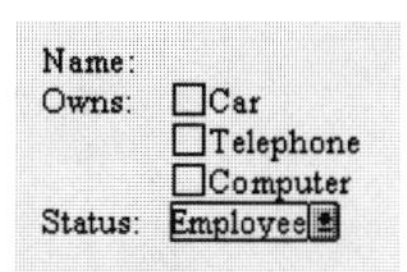

Again, because creating forms uses many advanced concepts, the methods used to create this simple form are not covered here.

Forms are stored in templates. To create a form, you open a new template and display the Forms toolbar:

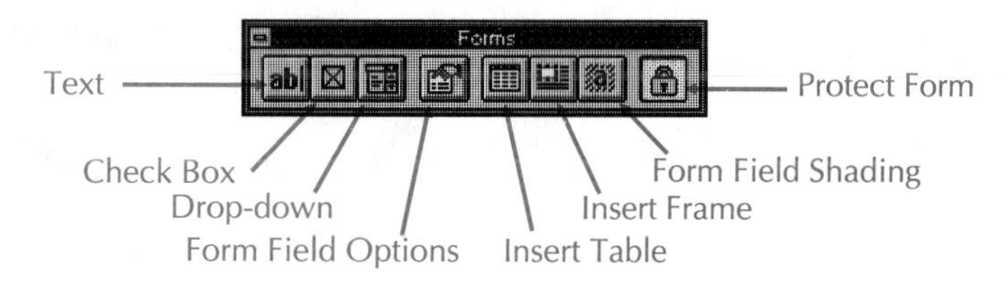

Form fields are inserted at the location of the insertion point, so most forms are based on tables that have the cells at the desired locations for the form fields.

After you design the form, you can add many advanced features to it. For instance, you can create help text for the form fields. You can also cause macros to be executed if particular fields are chosen.

Designing even a simple form takes a great deal of planning, but the result can be much better forms than their paper equivalents. For example, assume that your paper form has an area for a customer number. Someone filling that in could easily write in an incorrect number. In an interactive form with macros, you could check the customer number as it is entered to see whether or not it is valid.

Review

Look at some magazines, brochures, and promotional literature and notice how they use columns. Also, look for items that could be made as frames. Think about how you would specify their position both as absolute and as relative positions.

If you typed a great deal into your MAGAZINE file, make it into two and three columns and notice how the lines look in each. Change the font size and see whether a smaller font makes the text more readable with multiple columns. Add a few frames with simple pictures and move them around in the article.

Word For Windows
Word For Windows

CHAPTER

21 USING WORD WITH OTHER PROGRAMS

In Chapter 4, you learned how to use the Clipboard to copy and move text in a file within Word. Often, however, you want to incorporate a copy of an entire file created with another program into a Word file you are editing. For instance, you may keep important charts created with another program in separate files so you can include them in a variety of memos you write using Word.

When the other program you are working with is a Windows

program, the simplest way to bring information into Word or to pass information out of Word is to use the Cut, Copy, and Paste commands. You use these commands in other Windows programs just as you do in Word. For example, to copy a picture from a Windows graphics program into Word, you would create the picture, select it, give the Copy command, switch to Word, and give the Paste command.

There are a number of other ways you can interact with non-Word files. You can save Word files in ways that allow other programs to read them. (Most programs cannot read Word files.) You can also read files created by other programs.

You do not need to read or write files in order to work with other programs. Word can also create *links* to some programs' documents. A link is a way of getting the contents of a document in a way that, if the other document is later updated, the Word document gets the newest information.

Lesson 125: Using Text Files

It is unfortunate that there is no common standard for transferring files between programs. This is not to say that there are no standards: there are, in fact, dozens. However, unless a few major companies agree to a single standard, other companies won't adhere to it, and it languishes.

One enduring standard for transferring files between almost any kind of program is text files (sometimes called *ASCII files*). A text file contains all of the text from the original document but none of the formatting or graphics. Almost every word processor, spreadsheet program, database manager, and electronic mail program can read text files and save their documents as text files. Word handles text files better than other programs.

The Open command recognizes text files and opens them just like other documents. Many files that come with Windows are text files. For instance, Figure 21-1 shows the top of the WIN.INI text file that is in the same directory from which you run Windows.

Text files created on the Macintosh or Unix systems have a slightly different method for displaying the ends of lines. Still, Word can open them just as easily as it does text files you created on your PC.

Word's Save As command is quite robust with respect to text files. In the Save File As Type drop-down list, you have many choices for saving a text file:

- *Text Only* is the most common choice. This saves your file in a format that almost any program on any computer can read.
- *Text Only with Line Breaks* is similar, but it makes every line on your screen a separate paragraph in the text file. Use this choice when the

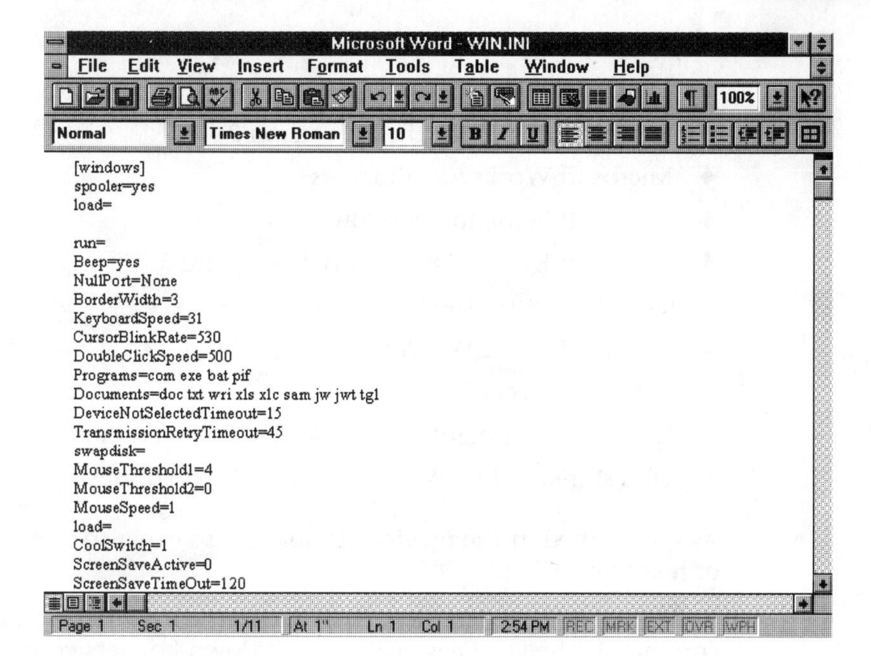

Editing a text file

Figure 21-1.

program you are using to read the file expects every line to end with a paragraph mark.

- *MS-DOS Text Only* is also similar, but it uses the MS-DOS character set, which has some characters that may not be readable by programs on other computers.
- *Text with Layout* attempts to keep the page layout of your document intact by putting spaces at the beginning and end of each line. This is only used when you are sending the file to a character-oriented printer or screen program, neither of which is common any more.

You may have to experiment with the different formats to find the one that works best with your desired application for reading the text files.

Lesson 126: Opening Documents from Other Word Processors

So far, you have used the Open command from the File menu only for Word files and text files. However, the Open command can perform other tasks as well. It can open the following types of word processing documents:

- Microsoft Word for Windows versions 1 and 2

- Microsoft Word for the Macintosh versions 4 and 5
- Microsoft Word for the PC versions 3, 4, 5.0, and 5.5
- Microsoft Works for the PC version 2
- Microsoft Works for Windows
- Microsoft Write for Windows
- Microsoft Excel BIFF versions 2, 3, 4, and 5
- WordPerfect for the PC version 5
- WordPerfect for Windows version 5
- Lotus 1-2-3 versions 2 and 3
- RFT-DCA documents from IBM DisplayWrite or compatible programs
- Files stored in Microsoft's RTF (Rich Text Format) specification

As you learned in the previous lesson, Word can also open a variety of forms of text files.

You can specify which files are visible in the list when you give the Open command. The List Files of Type drop-down box lets you specify the types of files that appear in the list. Word recognizes the types of files by their file extension, such as .TXT for text files. The choices are as follows:

Choice	Description
Word Documents	Only documents created in Word
Document Templates	Only templates (described in Chapter 11)
Rich Text Format	Only files created with Microsoft's Rich Text Format (text files that can save formatting characteristics)
Text Files	Only text files
All Files	All files, regardless of whether Word can open them

Note that Word does not rely on the extension when it opens a file. It looks in the file and tries to determine the format. If it cannot determine it easily, it asks you which format the file is in.

The File command from the Insert menu works like the Open command except that it puts a copy of the contents of the specified file in the current document at the insertion point. You can use this command if you want to read another file into your current file. The File command can read the same file formats as the Open command.

Lesson 127: Opening Graphics Files

In addition to word processing documents, Word can open many types of graphics documents. Instead of using the Open command, you use the Picture command from the Insert menu.

When you install Word, you specify which graphics converters you want installed. You can specify fewer graphics converters to save space on your hard disk. All of the graphics files you can open are listed here with the common file extension used for each file:

- PC Paintbrush (.PCX)
- Windows bitmaps (.BMP)
- Windows Metafile (.WMF)
- Encapsulated PostScript files (.EPS)
- TIFF files (.TIF)
- Lotus 1-2-3 graphics (.PIC)
- Computer graphics metafiles (.CGM)
- Hewlett-Packard graphic language (.HGL)
- DrawPerfect (.WPG)
- Micrografx Designer or Draw Plus (.DRW)

Many graphics programs can store files in at least one of these formats. For example, almost every graphics program can store documents in either .PCX or .WMF format.

Lesson 128: Saving Files in Non-Word Formats

Word lets you save files in different formats. This is useful for transferring formatted information to other word processing programs. The formats you can save in are the same as the ones you can open, except that you cannot save in Lotus 1-2-3 version 3 or Microsoft Excel BIFF version 4 formats.

When you save a Word document in another format, it is likely that some formatting information will be lost. For example, when you save a Word file in the format of another word processor, you lose the styles you may have attached. Word replaces the styles with direct formatting. Word features, such as tables, may also be lost. Remember that many of the formats you can save in do not have all of the capabilities of Word, so you almost always lose formatting information.

Lesson 129: Connecting to Documents from Other Programs

Word lets you add information from another Word document, a document from another word processing program, a spreadsheet, or a graphics program to your Word documents. This information is called *dynamic* because it can change outside of Word—for example, if you update it in the original program. When you add information from one of these files, Word keeps track of the file's name and the originating program. You can continue to update the file outside of Word and, with a simple command, have Word check the file to obtain the latest saved version.

Connecting to programs outside of Word is one of the most powerful features of Windows software. Almost every major Windows package uses *dynamic data exchange* (*DDE*). DDE allows two programs to send and receive requests for information. Many other programs use *object linking and embedding* (*OLE*), a more sophisticated form of DDE.

For instance, when you copy a part of a spreadsheet to a Word document and later want to update the figures in the document, Word can transmit that request to the spreadsheet program and get the new figures automatically. Instead of having to find the program and open it, you simply double-click on the linked object and Word starts the other program for you, opens the document, and selects the relevant information.

There are two ways of making a connection to another program:

- *Embedding* copies an object into your Word file but makes it easy to find the program that created that object. Embedding is not dynamic because the object is part of your Word document.
- *Linking* does not copy the object into your Word file; instead, it points to the file and the program that created it. Linking is dynamic because the file is kept separate from your document.

Embedding

In Chapter 12, you saw how to embed graphics in your documents. You can also embed other kinds of non-Word documents. Remember that you only want to embed objects that you do not want to be dynamic.

Embedding is very handy if you want to later edit the objects. To edit an object using the original program, you simply double-click on the object. For example, if you embed an Excel worksheet in a report and want to change some of the numbers in the worksheet, just double-click on the object in your Word document and Word starts Excel for you.

One drawback of embedding objects is that your Word documents can get quite large. This is particularly true of graphics files that can take up more than a megabyte of disk space. The advantage of embedding over linking is that you always know that the information in your documents will not change without you changing it yourself.

To embed an object, choose the Object command from the Insert menu. The Create New tab of that dialog box is shown in Figure 21-2, and the Create from File tab is shown in Figure 21-3. Use the Create New tab to create a new object; use the Create from File tab to embed an object that already exists on disk.

You can convert embedded objects to other types of objects with the Convert command under the Object command in the Edit menu. For example, you can convert some spreadsheet documents to other types. You can also convert many types of objects to pictures.

If you need to embed data directly from a database program, use the Database command from the Insert menu. This command embeds a database or part of a database in your document, depending on how you use the command. An advantage of using this command is that you can use a query language to specify which records to insert. Most people, however, would rather use the querying features in their database program to create a subset than to use Word.

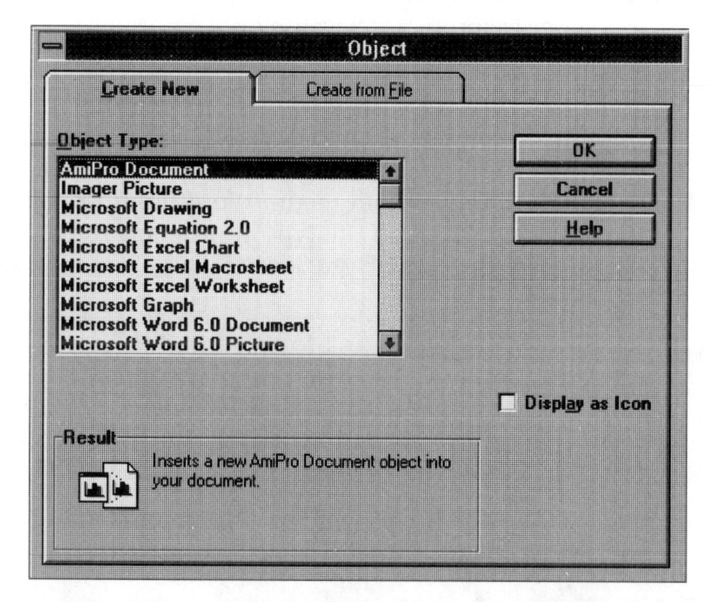

Object dialog box (Create New tab)
Figure 21-2.

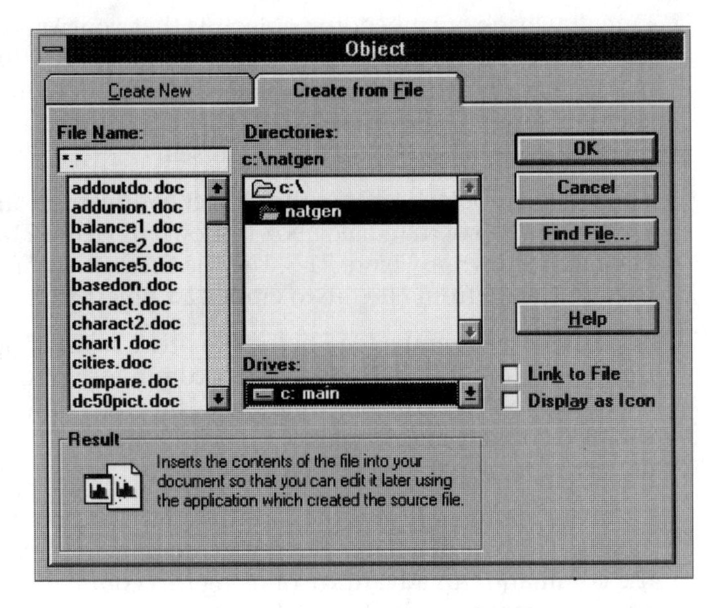

Object dialog box (Create from File tab)
Figure 21-3.

Linking

Linking has the advantage that others can update information in your documents without having to update the document itself. This can be particularly important in a company with a network because the linked files can be anywhere on the network. Also, documents with links do not have the same size problems because only a pointer to the information is kept, not the information itself.

To make a link, copy the information from the other program to the Clipboard using the Copy command in the other program. Switch to Word, set the insertion point, and give the Paste Special command (not the Paste command) from the Edit menu. Word prompts you for information about the link, depending on the type of program you are running. For example, Figure 21-4 shows the Paste Special dialog box for a selection from an Excel worksheet.

If you want to create a link to an entire file, you don't have to run the other program. Simply set the insertion point and choose the Object command from the Insert menu. Choose the Create from File tab, select the desired file, select the Link to File option, and select OK. You can link directly to an Excel worksheet with the Insert Excel button on the Standard toolbar.

You can see the files to which a document is linked with the Links command in the Edit menu. That dialog box is shown in Figure 21-5. You use this

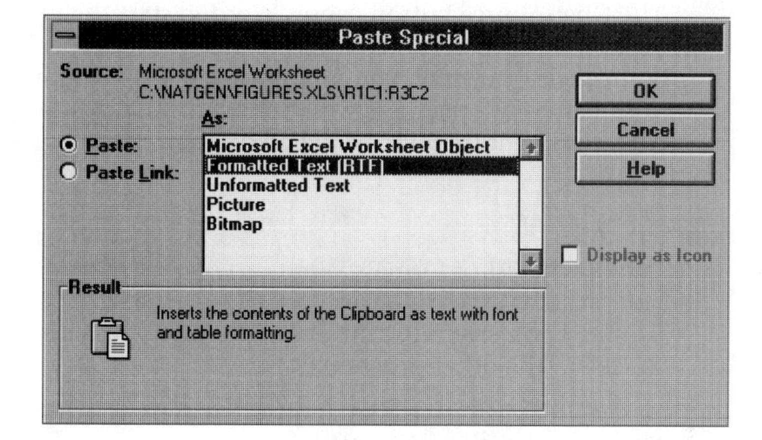

Paste Special dialog box for Excel worksheet
Figure 21-4.

dialog box to edit the links, update them, break them, and so on. To work on a single link, select it and choose the appropriate button. To work on more than one link at a time, select the first link, hold down the Ctrl key, and select the additional links.

Links can be updated automatically or manually, as specified at the bottom of the dialog box. Choosing Automatic means that the link is updated each time you open the Word document or when the other document is updated while the Word document is open. Manual updating only happens when you choose the Update Now button in the Links dialog box, or when you select the object and press F9. You can also update links before you print your document by selecting the Update Links option in the Print tab of the Options command.

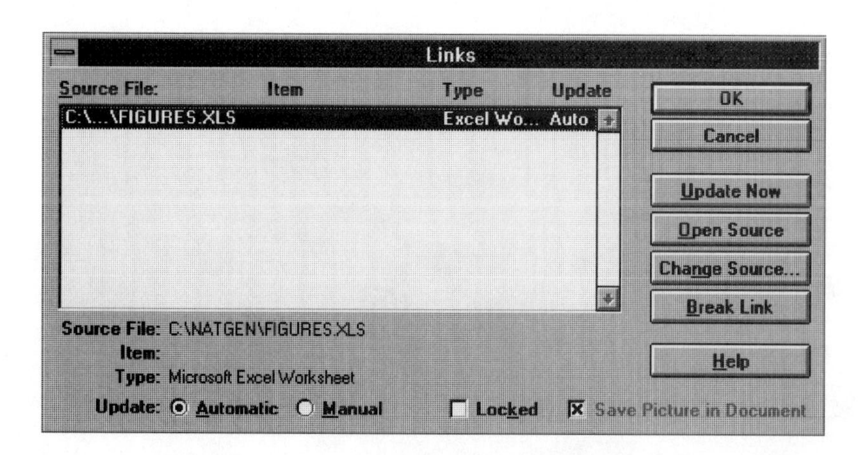

Links dialog box
Figure 21-5.

The Open Source button causes Word to start the program that will edit the linked object. You can change the link to that program with the Change Source button, which you might want to do if you move the program on your hard disk or get a newer version of the program. You can also break the link, causing it to never be updated again.

Review

Look at the list of formats Word can open. See if you have a program on your PC that saves in one of those formats and try opening a file in that format. Look carefully at the contents and compare them to the way the file looked in the other program.

Save a file in a format that another program can read and look at the results. Experiment with various Word features such as styles, tables, and graphics and see how they translate when Word saves the file.

If you work in an office that also has Apple Macintosh computers, find out how you can transfer files from your PC to a Macintosh. Save some Word files in formats that can be read by programs on the Macintosh and note the results.

Word For Windows
Word For Windows
Word For Windows

CHAPTER

22 RETRIEVING DOCUMENTS

You have probably noticed that the names of the files used in this book are somewhat descriptive of their contents. The name SUMFUN.DOC, for example, was used for a summary funding proposal. However, MS-DOS file-naming conventions severely limit how much you can indicate in a filename. If you have more than a few dozen files (as you are sure to after using Word for a few weeks), it is hard to remember what each file contains. When you have hundreds of files, opening and closing each one to find a particular file is really time consuming.

Since Word is designed for use in business, where efficiency is a primary concern, Microsoft has devised a method for scanning rapidly through a large number of files. Each Word file has a *summary sheet* where you can list information that is helpful when you search. For example, to search for a letter, you might include in the summary sheet the recipient, the subject, and a few keywords about the contents. Word automatically stores the dates when the letter was created and last updated, so you can also use those in your search.

When you search, Word scans the summary sheets of all the documents on the disks and directories that you specify. You can devise very specific searches (such as one for a file written after January 1 of this year that lists the keywords "timing" and "starter") or general searches (such as one for all letters to a certain person). This flexibility is very convenient when you are working with dozens or hundreds of files.

You can also have Word search for specific text in the files. For instance, you can locate every letter in which you mentioned "new manufacturing". Note, however, that searching for text in a file is slower than searching for words listed in the summary sheet, especially if you have long documents.

Lesson 130: Filling In Summary Sheets

To fill in summary sheets, you give the Summary Info command from the File menu. Note that this command works only on Word documents, not on the other files on your PC. Also, you can create summary sheets only for files saved with Word's formatting (not for text-only files). The Find File command from the File menu searches through summary sheets as well as through the text in files.

Open the SAMPLE1 file and give the Summary Info command from the File menu. You see:

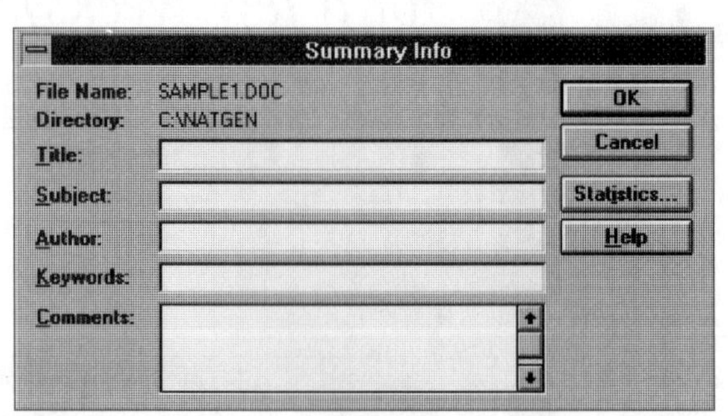

The options in the Summary Info dialog box are listed in the following table.

Field	Description
Title	A title for the document, such as "Request for information on new parts" or "Second notice on overdue accounts".
Subject	The document's subject. This is often similar to the title but might have additional information.
Author	The name of the person who wrote the document. It is good to use both your first and last name since the person searching the summary sheets may not know both. Word automatically uses the name you entered when you installed Word, but you can change the name if you wish.
Keywords	Words or phrases that are likely to be searched for. Examples are "accounts payable", "urgent", "third notice", and "final".
Comments	Remarks about the document. For example, you might use this option for a revision number or a note about what should happen next with the document.

You might use the field entries shown here for the SAMPLE1 document:

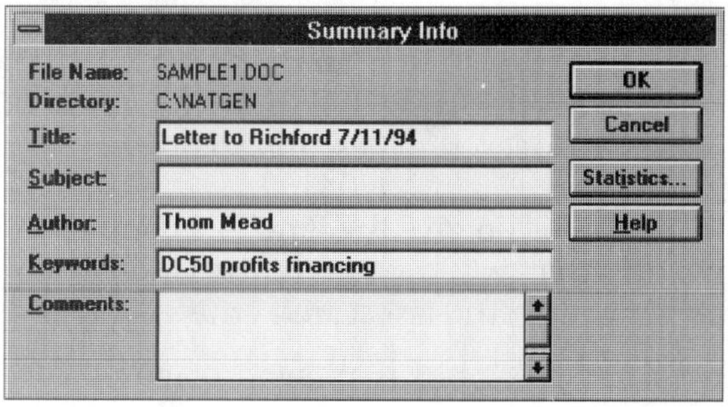

Selecting the Statistics button displays a dialog box like the one in Figure 22-1 that shows fixed information about the file. It also gives you information about the last time the file was edited.

If you find using summary sheets useful, you can have Word prompt you for the summary sheet information each time you create a new file. Select the Prompt for Summary Info in the Save tab of the Options command. Note that Word only prompts you the first time you save a file; to change the information in the dialog box, you must still use the Summary Info command.

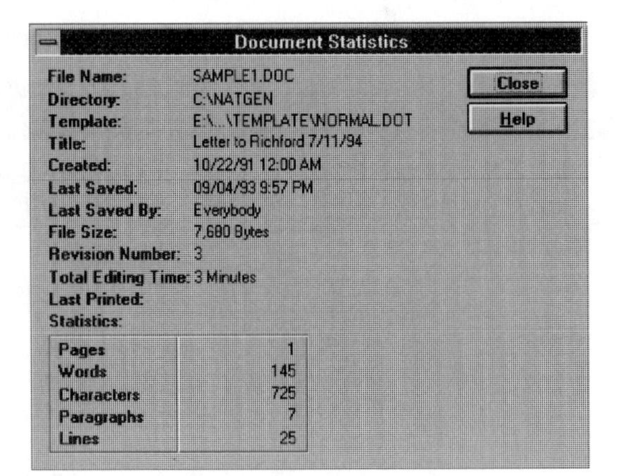

Statistics dialog box
Figure 22-1.

Lesson 131: Searching for Documents

The Find File command from the File menu lets you search for documents based on criteria you set, such as the drive on which to look and what to look for. This is very useful if you have many documents, or if you have to search for documents written by other people and you don't know where they may have stored them. You can also start this command by choosing the Find File button in the Open command.

There are two main dialog boxes for the Find File command:

- The Search dialog box lets you specify what you want to search for
- The Find File dialog box shows the result of the search, lets you preview the files, open the files, and so on

The first time you give the Find File command, you see the Search dialog box. After that, when you give the Find File command, you see the Find File dialog box with the last search criteria you gave.

The Search dialog box is shown in Figure 22-2. You use this dialog box for searching for all files in a directory. Choose the type of files (such as *.DOC for all Word files) from the File Name option and the location on which to search from the Location option. The Include Subdirectories option causes Word to search in all the levels lower than the one you specify. This is useful if you want to search a whole disk or through a complex hierarchy that is under a particular directory.

It is likely that you will want to search for more than just all the files in a particular directory. To narrow your search more, choose the Advanced Search button. That dialog box has three tabs: Location, Summary, and Timestamp.

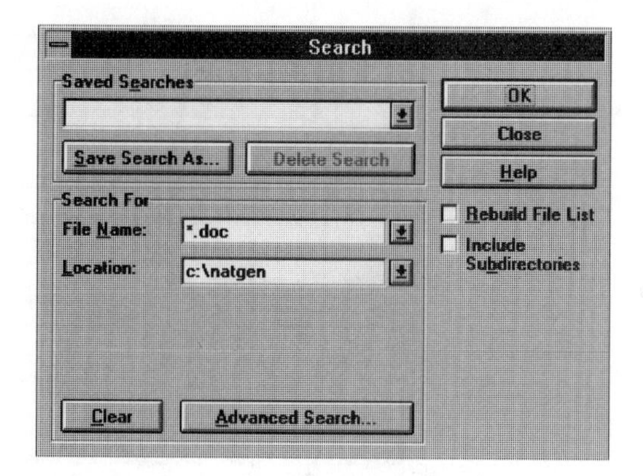

Search dialog box
Figure 22-2.

The Location tab is shown in Figure 22-3. Use this tab to change the Location option in the main Search dialog box. You can use it to add locations to the search. The Location option can have more than a single directory listed in it: you can have multiple directories separated by semicolons. For example, to search for files in C:\NATGEN and C:\THOMDOCS, you would enter **C:\NATGEN;C:\THOMDOCS** for the Location option. You can form these sequences in the Location tab by adding directories from the list on the right to the list on the left.

To specify files by the information in their summary sheet or by text in the file, choose the Summary tab of the Advanced Search dialog box. This is shown in Figure 22-4.

✦ Title, Author, Keywords, and Subject are the fields from the summary sheet.

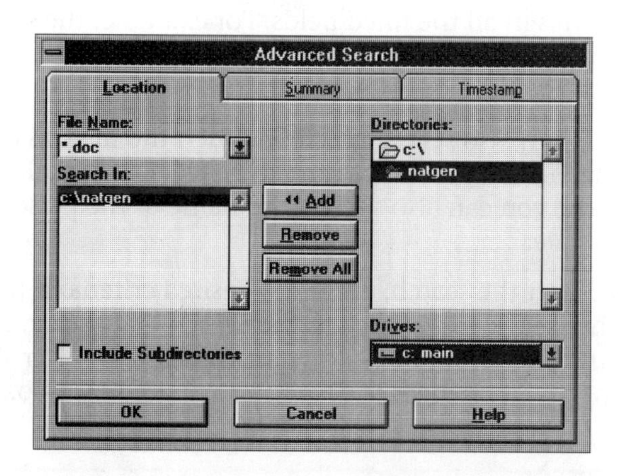

Advanced Search dialog box (Location tab)
Figure 22-3.

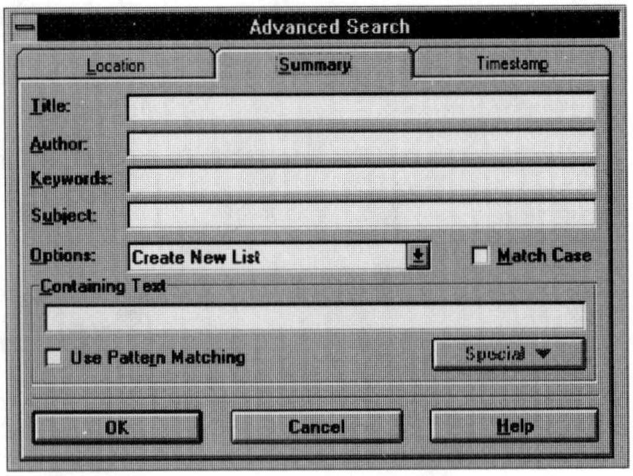

Advanced Search dialog box (Summary tab)
Figure 22-4.

- Options tells what to do with previous searches. Create New List ignores the results of the previous search. Use this option when you want to start over. Add Matches to List expands the previous search, adding files to the list of files found before. Search Only in List narrows the previous search. It looks for the new search criteria only in the files you already found.
- Containing Text is text to be searched for in the documents. This is slower than searching in the summary sheet, but it is very useful if you can remember only some of the content of the file you are looking for.

The Options list is useful if you perform a search and discover too many or too few files. For example, assume you searched for all letters from Thom to a particular customer. You discover there are 70 letters. You want to narrow the search by using a keyword. Enter the keyword in the Keywords field, and select Search Only in List to get a smaller list of files.

If you fill in more than one field, Word finds only files that match the entries in all the filled fields. For example, the set of entries shown in Figure 22-5 would find only documents for which the author field contains "Thom" and the Keywords field contains "loan".

You can also search based on when the file was created or last revised. Use the Timestamp tab of the Advanced Search dialog box, shown in Figure 22-6. Here, you can also specify the name of the person who saved or modified the file.

To start the search, enter the desired criteria in the Advanced Search options, choose OK to get back to the Search dialog box, and select OK. You see the Find File dialog box shown in Figure 22-7. After Word looks where you specify, it changes the list in the main dialog box.

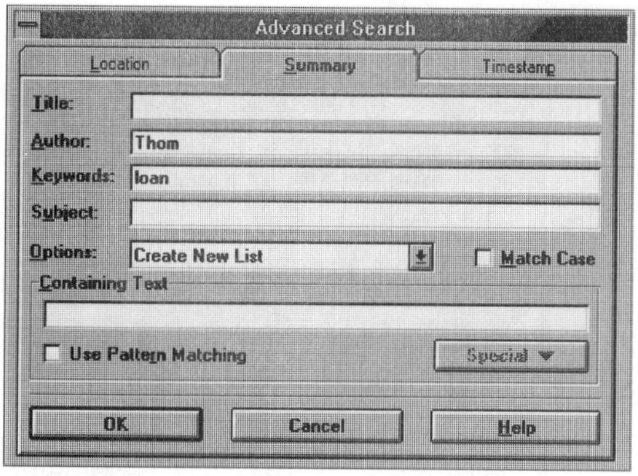

Searching for files that meet two criteria
Figure 22-5.

The buttons at the bottom of the dialog box let you decide what to do next. There are three possible views: Preview shows you the top of the contents of the file, File Info shows you the file statistics, and Summary shows you the summary info. The other buttons at the bottom of the dialog box give you many options, listed in the following table.

Button	Action
Search	Lets you search again
Commands	Gives you more commands (described in the next table)
Open	Opens the file. Use this after you find the file you want
Close	Closes the Find File dialog box
Help	Shows help for the dialog box

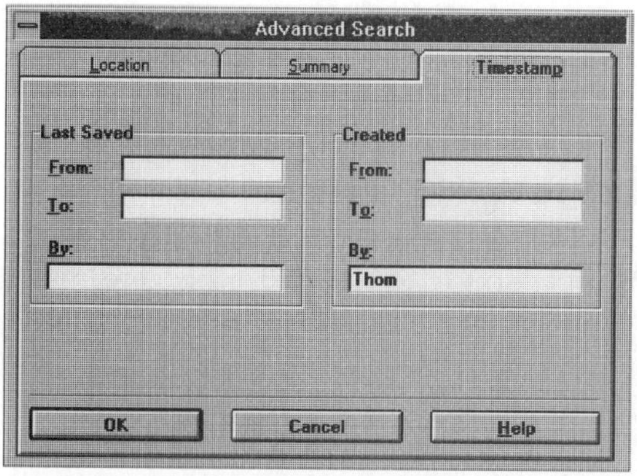

Advanced Search dialog box (Timestamp tab)
Figure 22-6.

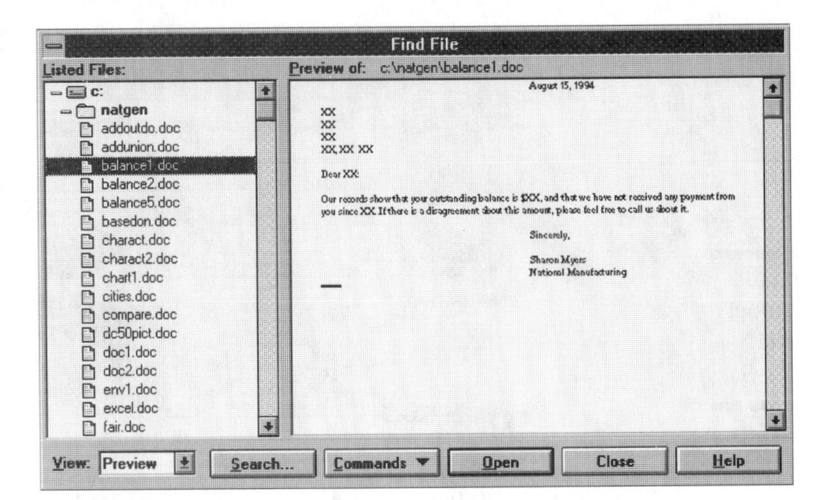

Find File dialog box
Figure 22-7.

The Commands button has a drop-down list that gives you more options:

Command	Action
Open Read Only	Opens the file in read-only mode
Print	Prints the file
Summary	Shows the summary information
Delete	Deletes the file
Copy	Makes a copy of the file on your disk
Sorting	Allows you to choose how the files at the left of the dialog box are sorted

You will find the Find File command useful for browsing through old files. If you select the Preview mode of the View choices, you can quickly see the top of each file in the list. You can also use the Delete command in the Commands list to cull out old files.

Review

Go back to the files you have already created and add better summary information to the files. With this new information entered, search for files by using different keywords and other criteria.

Word For Windows
Word For Windows

C H A P T E R

23 OUTLINING

There are many circumstances in which outlines help you organize your thinking. Writing an outline can assist you in determining how important thoughts relate to each other, and it is a good way to be sure you have covered all the topics that are relevant to your subject.

If you wish, you can use the features of Word you have already learned to make an outline. If you set the tabs for a document at half-inch increments, you can enter text in a standard outline format.

You can use Word's selection features to move groups of items around; you can even use a set of styles to specify a different emphasis for each level of your outline. However, Word's new outlining features allow you to do much more.

This chapter shows you how to create and modify outlines by using special outlining features. You can use these features to create new outlines or to display existing documents that have heading styles (described in Chapter 15) as outlines. If you are familiar with other outlining programs for the PC, you may see similarities between those programs and Word. Once you've learned how to outline with Word, you will find many situations in your daily work in which outlines are very useful.

Lesson 132: Introduction to Outlines

Every document in Word can also be viewed as an outline. Until now, you have used the normal and page layout views for editing; since you haven't used any of Word's outlining features, you haven't needed to see your document in *outline view*.

It is important to understand that outlines are regular Word documents. Word's outline features are simply a different way to view a Word document. In Chapter 3, you saw three different ways to view a document: normal view, page layout view, and print preview. Outline view is just a different, more streamlined way to look at a document that has an outline structure.

You use outline view and normal or page layout view for different purposes. You use normal or page layout view to edit and format text, as you have seen; you use outline view to review and change the structure of your text, in the same way you might decide to switch the position of two major ideas after writing an outline on paper.

When you move a heading in Word's outline view, all the text under that heading moves, too. In normal view, to move a heading and the text under it, you would have to select a large amount of text, delete it to the Clipboard with the Cut command, move your cursor to the new location, and insert the text there with the Paste command. In outline view, you just move the heading, and the associated text moves with it.

If you have a complicated and detailed outline, you may have dozens of subheads under a main heading. When you are working with this kind of outline, you can get lost in the lower level headings and miss the overall picture. Word lets you collapse an outline so that lower level headings are invisible.

Moving between normal view and outline view is very easy. You can switch between normal view and outline view by using the Outline command from the View menu. You can also choose the Outline button at the bottom of the document window, next to the horizontal scroll bar.

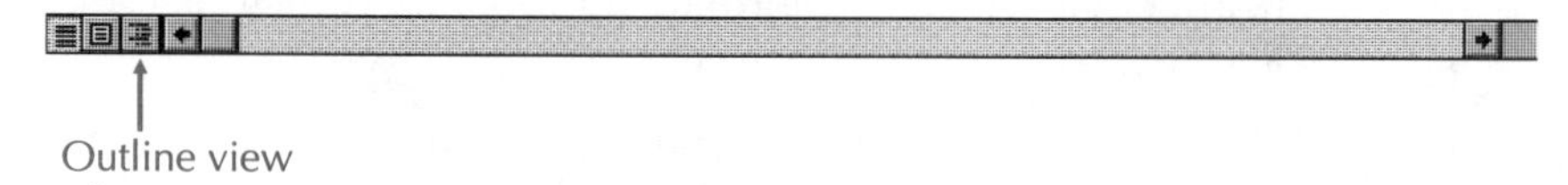

You can tell which view you are in by looking at the top of the window. In outline view, you see the Outlining toolbar at the top of the window, which looks like this:

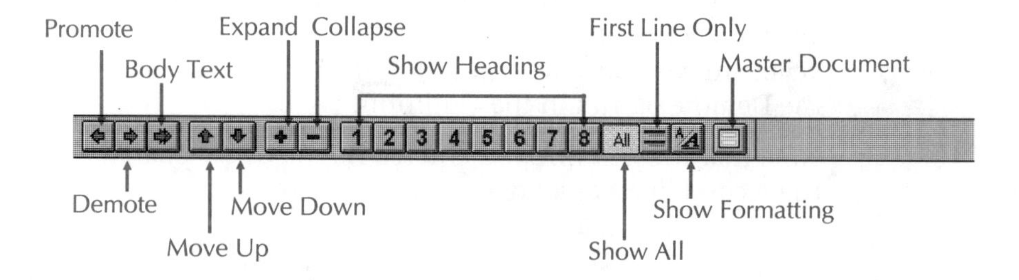

If you want, you can view a document in both outline view and another view (normal or page layout view) at the same time. Simply split the screen, as you learned in Chapter 3, select one pane, choose the view, select the other pane, and choose another view.

Outlines can have both *headings* and *body text.* (Body text is paragraphs that are not headings, like the regular text in a document.) Each heading has a level, starting with level 1. Body text does not have a level. As you make an outline, Word remembers the level of headings by saving a paragraph style with each one. These styles are Heading 1, Heading 2, and so on. Body text is formatted as Normal text. As long as you enter your outline in outline view, you do not have to add these styles; Word does it for you. (Styles are covered in Chapter 15.)

Many outlines are numbered. You can use the numbering commands you learned in Chapter 13 with outlines. When you add numbers to an outline, Word recognizes the different level of headings so that the numbering starts at 1 each time you go to a lower level.

Lesson 133: Creating an Outline

You can enter the text for a new outline in either normal view or outline view. It is usually better to enter and edit outlines in outline view because you can eliminate the heading formatting in outline view and it is easier to see the levels of headings.

Switch from normal view to outline view by choosing the Outline command from the View menu. You can see the level of the currently selected heading in the Style list in the Formatting toolbar. Your screen looks like the one in Figure 23-1.

Figure 23-2 shows the outline you will work with in this chapter. Begin by entering the first heading, **Contract preparation**, and press Enter. Word assumes you want to start at level 1.

Next, type the line **Use standard contract as basis**. However, you want this entry to be level 2, not level 1. To tell Word that this line is level 2, click the Demote button in the Outlining toolbar. Word indents the line, and the style indicator reflects the level you have chosen. If you prefer to use the keyboard, you can press the Alt-Shift-→ key combination instead of clicking the Demote button in the Outlining toolbar.

Note that the first line you entered has a hollow plus symbol next to it, and the second line has a hollow minus symbol:

Contract preparation
  Use standard contract as basis

The plus symbol indicates that the heading has a subhead beneath it, while the minus symbol indicates that the heading does not have any subheads.

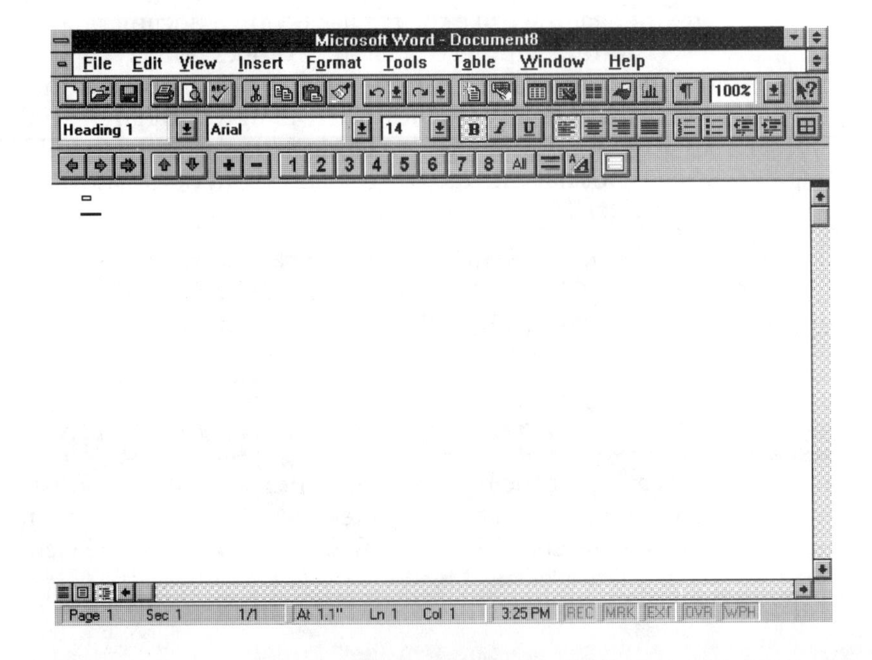

Outline view
Figure 23-1.

- Contract preparation
  - Use standard contract as basis
  - Add union work clause
    - Local 112 for installing
    - Local 112 and 427 for maintenance
  - Add outdoor setting clause
- Contract signing
  - Phillips at National Generators
  - Martinez and Washington at fair
- Site preparation
  - Verify space requirements
  - Erect shelters
  - Cable to main sections
  - 4 500' spans
  - Check with Martinez for exact locations
- Install generators
  - 2 30G's for main supply
  - 2 fuel tanks
  - 1 33G for backup
  - 1 extra fuel tank
  - Operations shack

Sample outline
Figure 23-2.

Continue by typing the next line, **Add union work clause**, then press Enter. Again, Word makes a new heading the same level as the previous one (level 2).

You can also specify the level of a new line before you type the text. On this new line, choose the Demote button again to tell Word that the new text, **Local 112 for installing**, is at level 3. After typing the text, press Enter, and type the second level 3 heading and Enter.

After you add the two level-3 lines, go back to level 2 for the next heading you type. To do so, click the Promote button or press Alt-Shift-←. You can see how the Promote and Demote buttons move the levels up and down. Finish entering all the text and save the file with the name FAIR.

So far, you have entered only headings. Many outlines contain body text, such as paragraphs under headings or a title. For this example, you might use body text to add a title to the outline or to fill in comments that are not headings. To tell Word that a paragraph is body text, select any part of the paragraph and choose the Body Text button.

You can insert a heading in the middle of an outline by moving to the beginning of a line, typing new characters, and pressing Enter. You can change the level of a heading by selecting any part of the heading and clicking the Promote or Demote button. You can change a heading into body text by selecting any part of the heading and clicking the Body Text button.

It is important to remember to use the Promote and Demote buttons or Alt-Shift-→ and Alt-Shift-← to shift headings. You should not use the Tab key to do this because Word does not recognize tabs as indications of outline levels.

Lesson 134: Collapsing and Expanding

A detailed outline can be very hard to follow, especially if it includes body text. When outlining a complex business report, for example, you can quickly lose track of the outline among all the text.

To avoid this problem, you often want to see only higher level portions of an outline. Word allows you to hide lower level heads and body text by collapsing them. To *collapse* the lowest level below a selected paragraph, simply select that heading (or any part of it) and click the Collapse button on the Outlining toolbar. To restore these headings, click the Expand button on the Outlining toolbar.

For example, put the insertion point in the first level-1 heading, "Contract preparation". Click the Collapse button in the Outlining toolbar twice to hide the two levels of subordinate headings. You can also press the Alt-Shift keys together with the - key on the numeric keypad. The result is shown here:

Contract preparation
Contract signing
Phillips at National Generators
Martinez and Washington at fair

When you collapse a heading, Word puts a gray bar where the collapsed material is, to remind you that there is more under that heading.

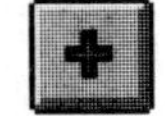

You can *expand* a collapsed heading by clicking the Expand button in the Outlining toolbar or pressing the Alt-Shift keys together with the + key on the numeric keypad. Expanding a heading shows only the level immediately below it. For example, if you collapse a level-1 heading and some of the level-2 heads below it have subheads, expanding the level-1 heading does not expand the subheads below the level-2 heads at the same time.

Contract preparation
Use standard contract as basis
Add union work clause
Add outdoor setting clause
Contract signing
Phillips at National Generators
Martinez and Washington at fair

If you have collapsed different levels of headings and want to expand them all at once, press Alt-Shift-A or click the Show All button in the Outlining toolbar. This expands all the headings.

- Contract preparation
  - Use standard contract as basis
  - Add union work clause
    - Local 112 for installing
    - Local 112 and 427 for maintenance
  - Add outdoor setting clause
- Contract signing
  - Phillips at National Generators
  - Martinez and Washington at fair

Note that the Collapse and Expand buttons on the Outlining toolbar collapse and expand the lowest level of heading under the selected paragraph. Thus, if you have an outline with three levels of headings and have selected a top-level heading, clicking the Collapse button on the Outlining toolbar hides the level-3 entries only.

It is likely that you will want to view your outline as a whole from various levels. To do this, choose the number buttons in the Outlining toolbar. For example, choosing the 1 button in the Outlining toolbar collapses everything except level-l headings.

- Contract preparation
- Contract signing
- Site preparation
- Install generators

Collapsing lower level headings in this way is useful when you are analyzing whether points in your outline are properly arranged and have equal weight. The keyboard equivalent for the number buttons is pressing Alt-Shift together with the number you want on the keyboard.

Lesson 135: Rearranging Your Outline

If you could write an outline correctly the first time you tried, there would not be much use for Word's special outlining commands. Because you use outlines to organize your thoughts, you need to rearrange headings as you decide to change their position or importance. The outline edit view makes these adjustments especially easy.

If you are moving a heading, it is likely that you also want to move all the ideas associated with it. Word lets you do this. In outline edit view, when you delete and send a heading to the Clipboard, all subheads and body text under that heading are included, so moving whole ideas is easy.

For example, suppose you want to move "Add union work clause" and its related subheads to follow "Add outdoor setting clause". To quickly select the head and its subheads, click the hollow plus symbol next to "Add union work clause":

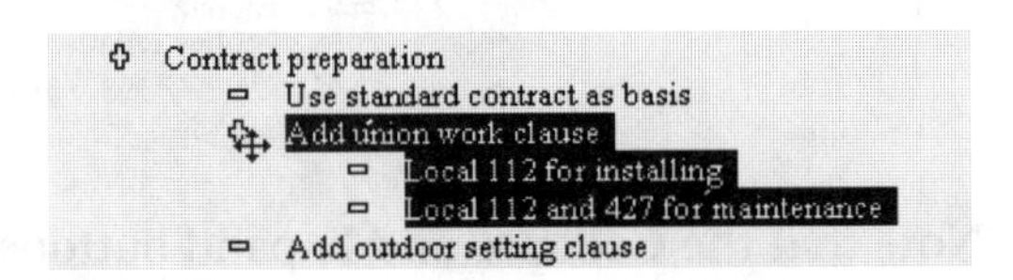

Click and drag the plus symbol down to the line after "Add outdoor setting clause". A dotted line appears, showing you where the selected text will move when you release the mouse button. The result is shown in Figure 23-3.

The ability to move a head along with the ideas associated with it is especially useful if you have a lot of body text. Instead of scrolling through many screens of text, you can simply select all the subordinate headings under the heading by clicking the hollow plus symbol.

Lesson 136: Creating a Master Document

Word's outline view is great for long documents because you can look at just one or two levels of headings in order to get an overview of the document. However, really long documents can be inconvenient in Word due to their size on disk. This is particularly noticeable when the file is stored on a busy network.

In this case, you may want to have a group of documents that combine into one large document. The three documents might even be worked on by

- Contract preparation
  - Use standard contract as basis
  - Add outdoor setting clause
  - Add union work clause
    - Local 112 for installing
    - Local 112 and 427 for maintenance
- Contract s[illegible]ning
  - Phillips at National Generators
  - Martinez and Washington at fair
- Site preparation
  - Verify space requirements
  - Erect shelters
  - Cable to main sections
  - 4 500' spans
  - Check with Martinez for exact locations
- Install generators
  - 2 30G's for main supply
  - 2 fuel tanks
  - 1 33G for backup
  - 1 extra fuel tank
  - Operations shack

Moving the heading down
Figure 23-3.

different people at the same time. You still want to view the combination of the documents in outline view. Each document is a separate document, but you can view the combination of documents as a single document, called a *master document.* A master document has links to the *subdocuments,* similar to the links you saw in Chapter 21.

Creating a master document is easy: you simply specify which headings you want to become subdocuments. Word pulls them out of the master document, creates a separate document for each, and then links these new documents back to the master document. Thus, you take a single document and convert it to many, all of which are linked in the original document.

With the Outlining toolbar open, choose the Master Document button. This displays the Master Document toolbar next to the Outlining toolbar:

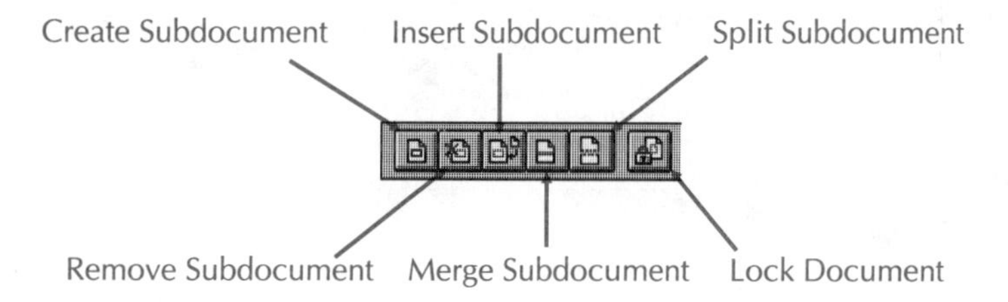

Next, select one or more headings that you want to become a subdocument and choose the Create Subdocument button. If you select more than one heading, Word will make subdocuments for all of them at the same level. Thus, if you choose some headings starting with a level-2 heading, each level-2 heading in the selection will become a separate subdocument.

You can see your subdocuments in outline view, as shown in Figure 23-4. The small icon at the upper left of each block indicates the part of your document that is a subdocument. Note that your master document can still have its own outline structure.

After you create subdocuments, Word assigns them filenames based on the first few letters of each document. You can open the subdocument file simply by double-clicking on the subdocument icon in the main document. If someone opens a subdocument, it becomes locked for all other people with access to the document, and you see a lock icon under the subdocument icon in the main document:

Use standard contract as basis

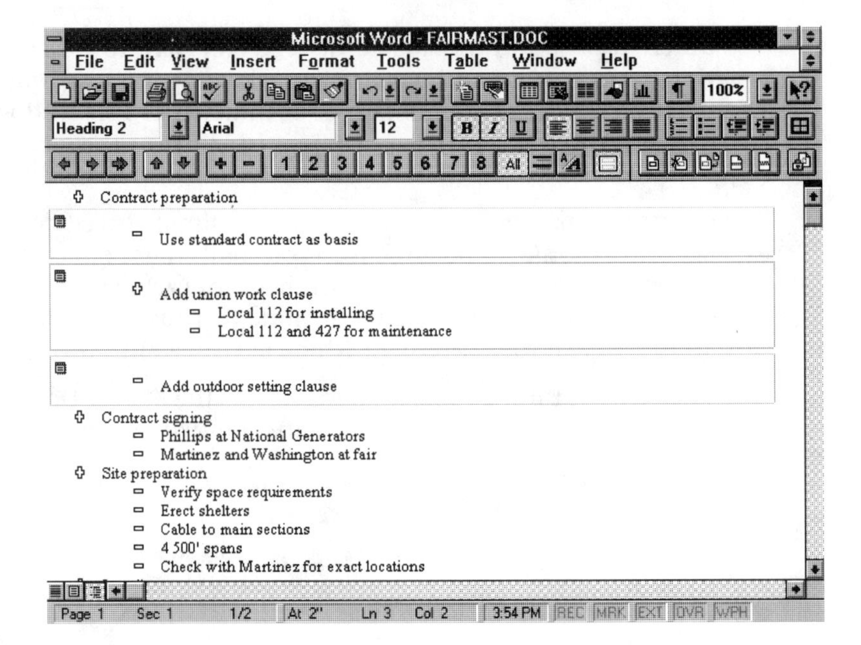

Master document with subdocuments
Figure 23-4.

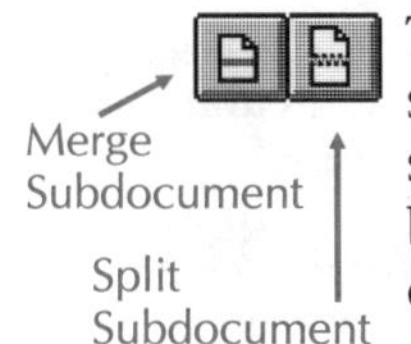

The buttons on the Master Document toolbar let you work with subdocuments while viewing the master document. You can merge two subdocuments by selecting them and choosing the Merge Subdocument button. To split a subdocument into two, put the insertion point at the desired location and choose the Split Subdocument button.

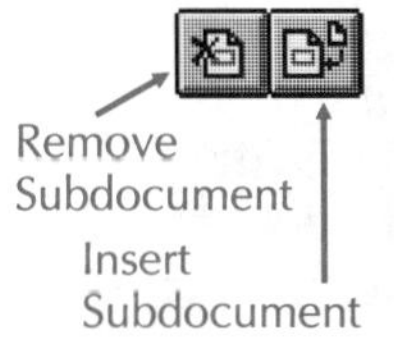

You might want to insert other Word documents into, or remove other Word documents from, your master document. For example, if you are working on an ongoing project and want to start a new master document, you would insert the current Word documents, possibly reformatting them as you insert them. Use the Insert Subdocument and Remove Subdocument buttons to add and remove subdocuments.

You will find that using subdocuments can really help in projects where more than one person wants to edit a document. You can keep everything organized using outline view and track which files are being worked on at any given time. In such an environment, you may want to consider using annotations (described in Chapter 17) to keep track of who is making what kind of changes.

Review

Make an outline that explains the advantages and disadvantages of three possible sites for an annual convention. First list the sites, then add the advantages and disadvantages as subheads, and add more detail under some of the advantages. Rearrange the order of the sites in the outline.

C H A P T E R

24 CUSTOMIZING WORD

If you use Word a great deal, you will probably want to change its appearance and actions to suit your personal preferences. Fortunately, that is fairly easy. You have already seen how to choose views and how to use the Options commands to set Word's options. This chapter shows you how to personalize three more types of settings: toolbars, commands in menus, and keyboard equivalents.

Lesson 137: Changing and Creating Toolbars

As you've seen throughout this book, Word uses toolbars to make your work easier. When you start Word, you have two default toolbars: the Standard toolbar and the Formatting toolbar. You have also seen the Borders toolbar, the Print Preview toolbar, the Drawing toolbar, the Forms toolbar, the Mail Merge toolbar, the Database toolbar, the Outlining toolbar, the Master Document toolbar, and others.

You can choose which toolbars you want to be visible in the Toolbars command from the View menu, as shown in Figure 24-1. Simply check all the toolbars that you want to be visible. Note that not all the toolbars are listed in this dialog box; some are only available if you are in particular modes. For example, the Print Preview toolbar is only shown in the Toolbars command if you are in print preview mode.

The options at the bottom of the Toolbars command let you customize the way that all toolbars are set up. You can choose whether or not you want colors on the buttons, the size of the buttons, and whether or not the name of the buttons appears after a few seconds if you put the pointer over a button. The Large Buttons option is only useful on high-resolution screens because it pushes many of the buttons off the screen at normal resolutions.

You can move the toolbars around the screen just by dragging them. To drag a toolbar, point at a space at the far left or right of the toolbar or between two buttons and press the mouse button:

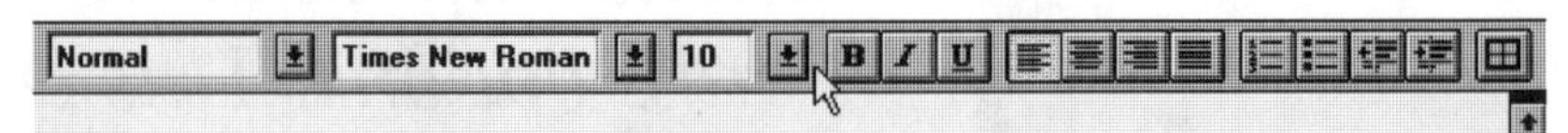

If you drag a toolbar away from the top or bottom of the screen, it becomes a *floating toolbar*. For instance, if you drag the Formatting toolbar down from its current position, it floats in the middle of the screen, as shown in Figure 24-2.

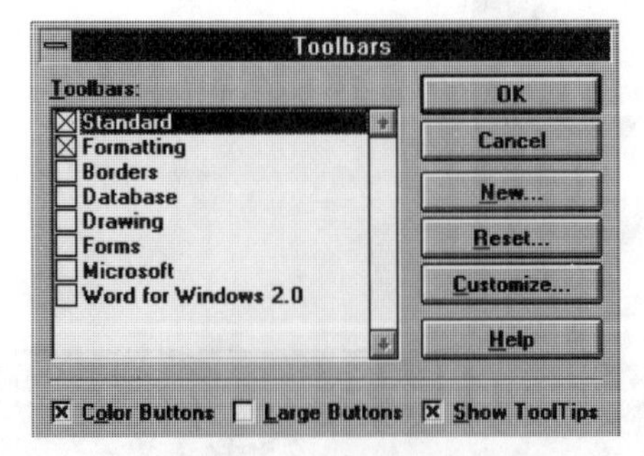

Toolbars dialog box
Figure 24-1.

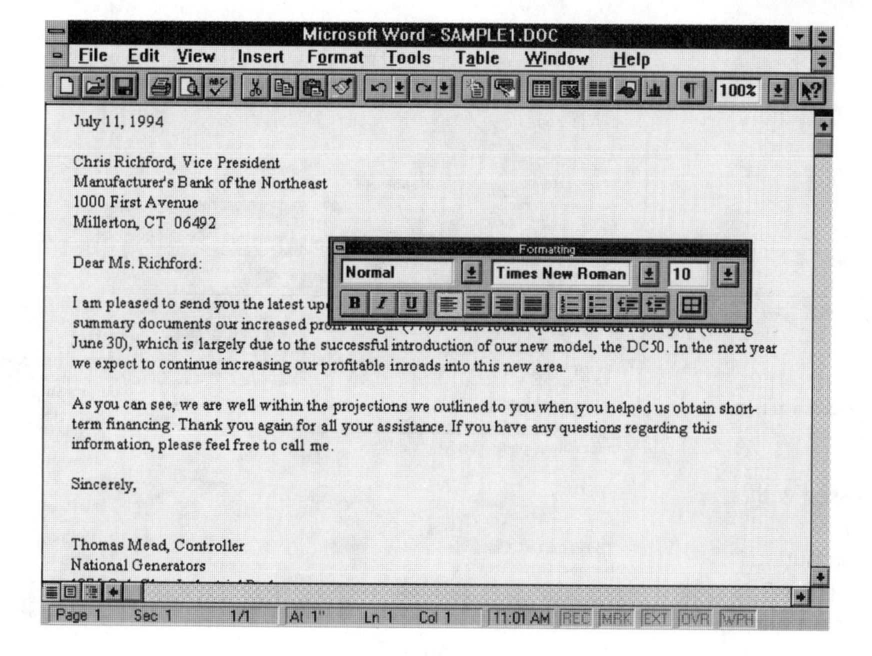

Formatting toolbar floating on a document
Figure 24-2.

Notice that Word sizes the toolbar so that it becomes two rows. You can reshape the toolbar by dragging on one of the edges. For example, you can drag the bottom down to make the toolbar square:

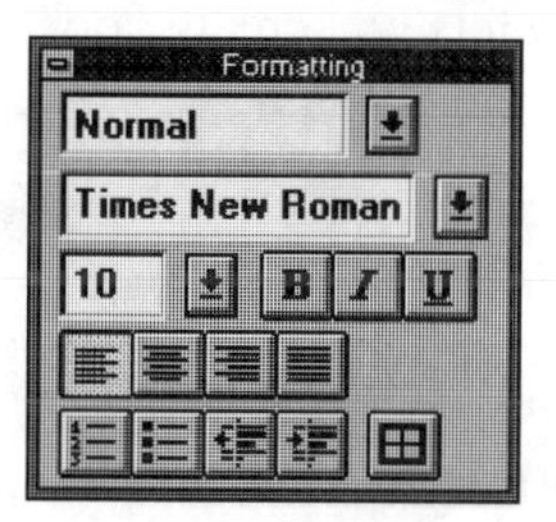

To put a toolbar back in its original position, simply drag it to the top of the window (not to the top of the screen). If you want a toolbar to reside at the bottom of the window, you can also drag it there. To close a floating toolbar, click on the close icon at the upper-left corner of its title bar.

You don't need to use the Toolbars command to specify which toolbars show: simply point at any toolbar and click the right mouse button. Word pops down a menu, as shown in Figure 24-3. Selecting a checked toolbar name causes that toolbar to disappear; selecting an unchecked toolbar name causes it to appear. The Toolbars command brings up the same Toolbars dialog box you saw before. The Customize command brings up the dialog box described next.

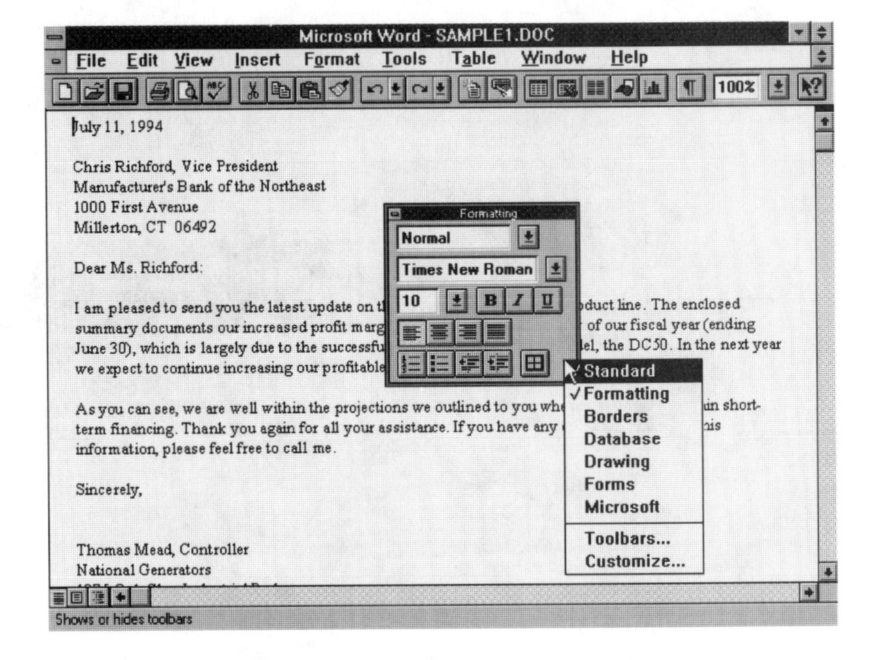

Toolbars menu accessed with the right mouse button

Figure 24-3.

You can not only specify which toolbars you want to see, but you can also specify what appears on a toolbar. You can even make your own toolbars that have exactly what you want on them. In the Toolbars dialog box, choosing New lets you create your own toolbars. You see:

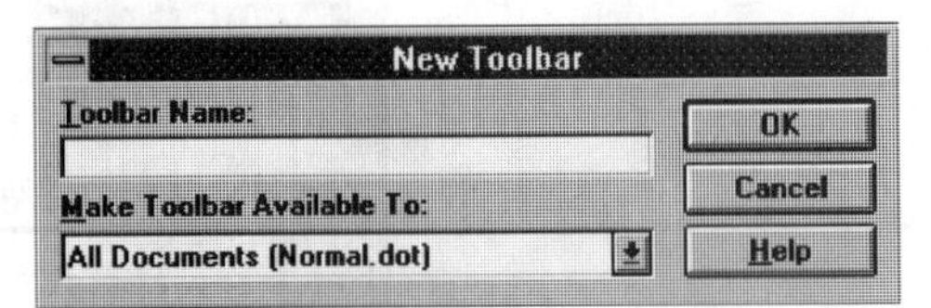

Enter a name for your new toolbar and choose OK. You now see the Customize dialog box for toolbars so you can add buttons to your new toolbar. This is the same dialog box you see when you choose the Customize button in the Toolbars dialog box. You can also get to this dialog box by choosing the Customize command from the Tools menu. It is shown in Figure 24-4.

Adding and removing buttons from toolbars is easy. In the Customize dialog box, choose the category that has the button you want, then drag the button to the desired toolbar. To remove a button, simply drag the button off the toolbar.

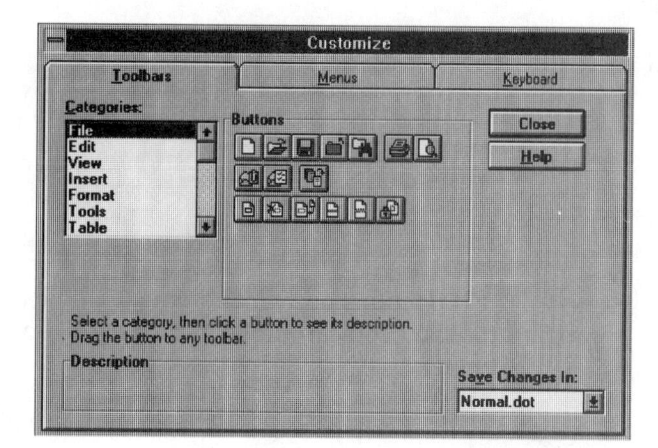

Customize dialog box (Toolbars tab)
Figure 24-4.

For example, assume you want to remove the New button from the Standard toolbar. With the Customize dialog box open, click on the New button and drag it to the main document area, as shown in Figure 24-5.

Next, assume you want to add the Find command to the Standard toolbar (now that there is some extra room). In the Categories list, choose Edit; the buttons to the right change to:

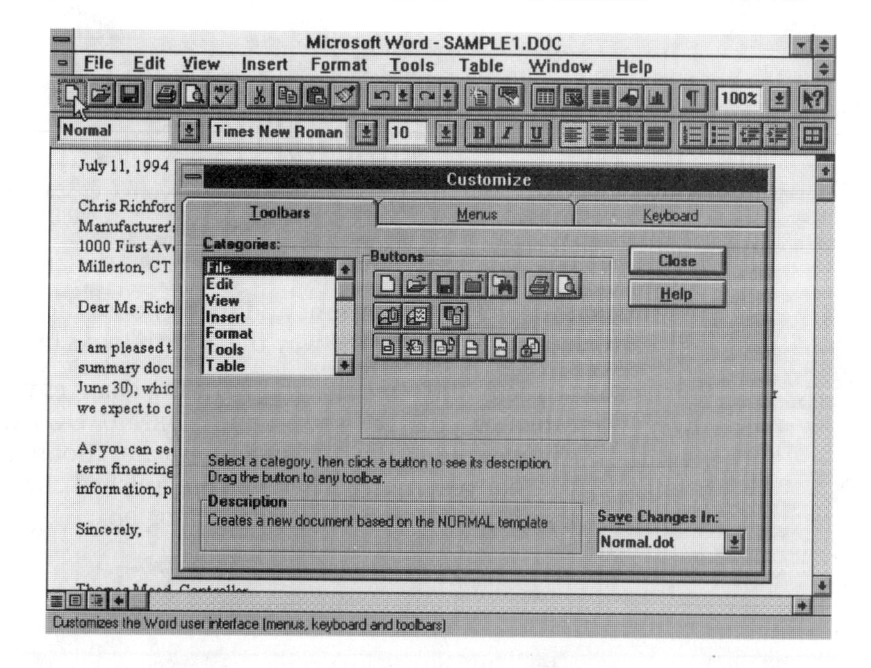

Removing the New button from the Standard toolbar
Figure 24-5.

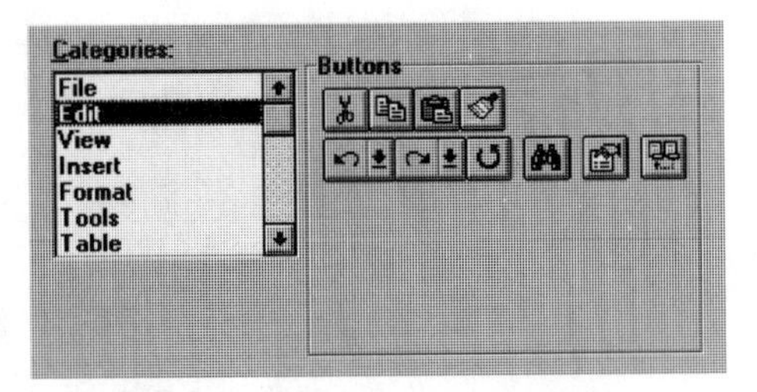

Choose the binoculars button and drag it to the desired position on the Standard toolbar. You can move buttons horizontally on the toolbar by dragging them.

Some of the choices in the Categories list bring up a list of choices on the right of the dialog box instead of buttons. If you choose a command that doesn't have a predefined button from the list and put the button in the desired place, you can choose the look of the button. Most of the choices don't have predefined buttons, and you then must use one of the unassigned buttons.

For example, the All Commands choice lists all of the actions possible in Word. If you choose a command from the list and drag it to a toolbar, you see:

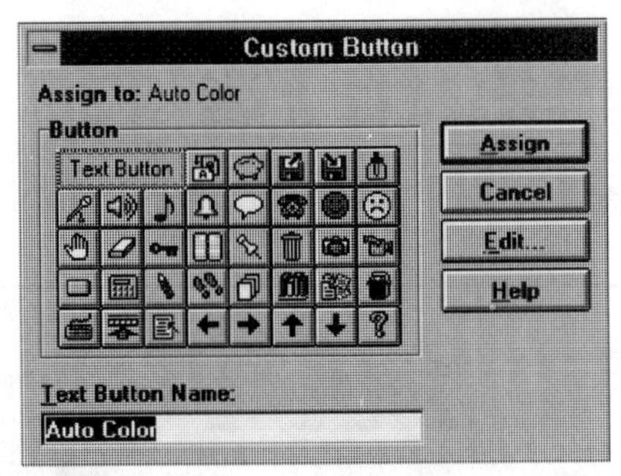

You can choose one of the buttons and then choose the Assign button. If you want, you can even edit the way the button looks by choosing Edit.

You can also specify the template you want the changes made in. If you always want the new changes, specify the NORMAL.DOT template. If you want these changes only for a particular template, choose that template from the Save Changes In list. When you are finished changing the toolbars, select the Close button in the Customize dialog box.

Lesson 138: Customizing Word's Menus

Use the Menus tab in the Customize command from the Tools menu to add items to menus and remove items from menus. This is a very powerful tool for customizing Word to your needs and for adding to the menus functions that you use often. The dialog box for the Menus tab is shown in Figure 24-6.

The categories and commands are the same as for the Toolbars tab except that the commands are listed by their names. These commands include all the commands normally found on the menus, as well as the names of dialog boxes directly available (such as the Tabs dialog box), all formatting commands (including those from the dialog boxes), and some actions that are usually accessed only through key combinations. The Commands list also has a separator, the line you see between groups of commands in many menus.

To add a command to a menu, choose the menu from the Change What Menu list, and choose a command. If that command already exists in the menu, the Remove button becomes available to remove it. The Position on Menu choice tells Word the command you want the new item to follow. You can also choose At Top, At Bottom, or Auto to let Word decide where to put the command for you.

Enter the desired name for the command in the Name on Menu choice. In the menu and command names, enter an ampersand (&) character to indicate which letter will be underlined and used as the speed selection character for that command.

For example, Figure 24-7 shows how you would add the Superscript command to the Format menu, just after the Drop Cap command.

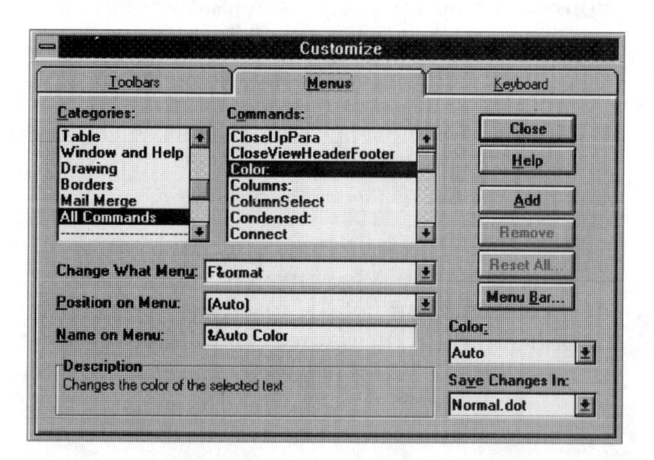

Customize dialog box (Menus tab)
Figure 24-6.

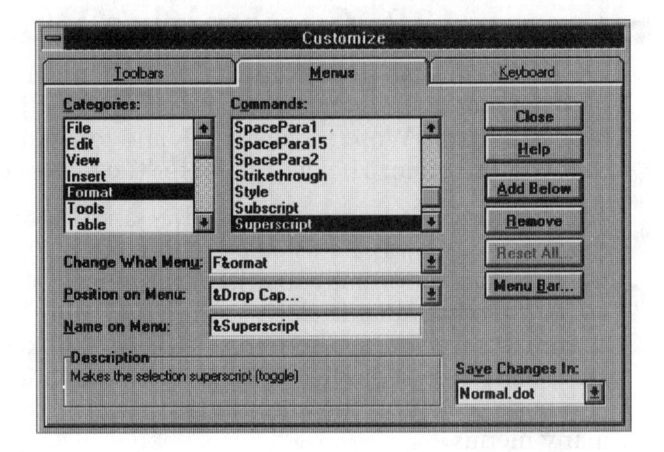

Adding the Superscript command to the Format menu
Figure 24-7.

You can rename or remove items by selecting them from the Change What Menu and Position on Menu options, then choosing Rename or Remove. The Reset All button resets your menus to the ones that come with Word. You can also specify the template in which you want the changes made.

The Menu Bar button lets you add or delete whole menus. Its dialog box looks like this:

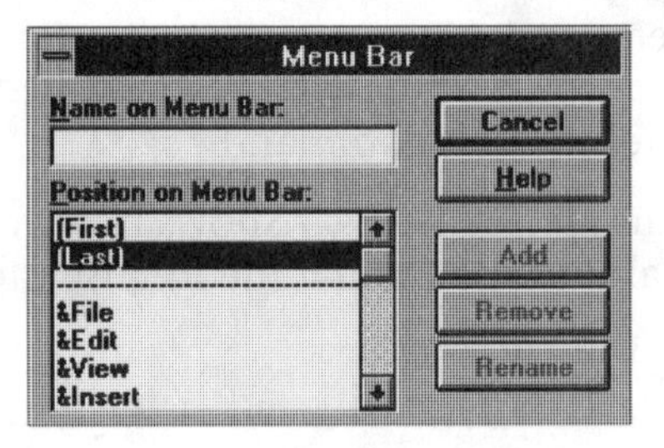

You use the options here in the same way you do in the Menus tab.

Lesson 139: Changing Keyboard Equivalents

You can add, remove, or change the key combination for a command in the same way that you change toolbars and menus, by using the Keyboard settings, shown in Figure 24-8.

After you select the desired command from the lists, the Current Keys section shows the key equivalents already used for the command. To add a new combination, put the insertion point in the Press New Shortcut Key option and press the desired combination. If that key is already selected for another action, Word tells you that in the Currently Assigned To option.

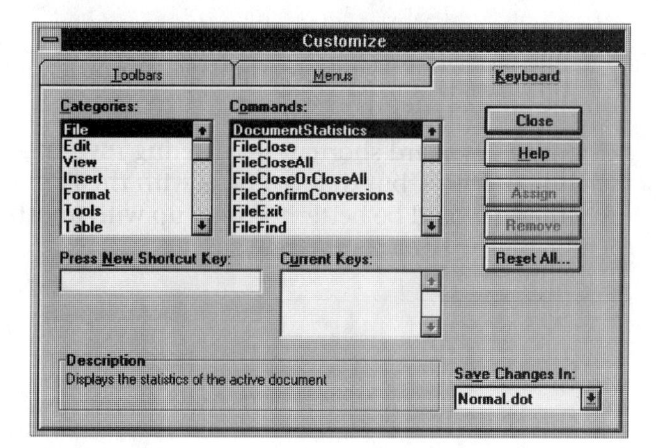

Customize dialog box (Keyboard tab)
Figure 24-8.

For example, to make Ctrl-B the Borders and Shading command from the Format menu, make the settings shown in Figure 24-9.

To remove a key combination, select it from the list, then select it from the Current Keys list, and select the Remove button in the dialog box.

Review

Think about which buttons you would put in a customized toolbar. Would all the buttons you commonly use from the Standard and Formatting toolbars fit into a single toolbar? If so, consider making your own and saving a line on your screen.

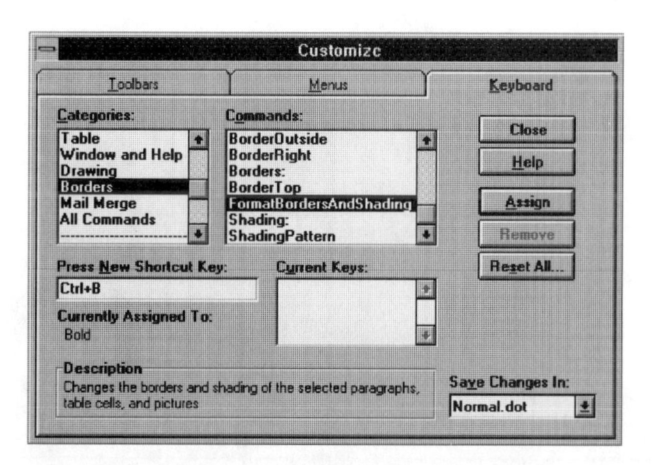

Adding the Ctrl-B equivalent for the Borders and Shading command
Figure 24-9.

Add the Subscript option (which normally is only available in the Font command) to the Format menu. Look for other actions that you might want on the Format menu.

Choose a keyboard shortcut for deleting rows in a table. A logical choice would be Ctrl-D, but that conflicts with the Font command. Think about whether it would be better to come up with another choice or whether you really use the Font command that much.

Word For Windows
Word For Windows
Word For Windows

CHAPTER

25 SORTING

There are often times when you want to sort a list inside one of your documents. If the list is only five or ten lines long, it is fairly easy to sort by hand, but sorting long lists by hand is extremely inconvenient. The Sort Text command makes sorting any list easy.

Word can sort both text and numbers. This distinction may seem trivial, but most word processing programs cannot sort numbers the same way they sort words.

Computers think in terms of numbers, not in terms of characters such as letters, punctuation, numerals, and so on. Early computer scientists got around this problem by assigning an internal numeric value to each character. Most computers use a specific system called ASCII to relate characters to internal numbers. The ASCII order, dating back to the 1960s, presents some problems, most of which Word overcomes.

The first problem is that sorting numerals is very different from sorting numbers. Look at the following list:

53
142
2

You would sort this list numerically as "2, 53, 142". However, in ASCII code, the number 1 comes before 2, and 2 comes before 5. Thus, an unintelligent sorter (the kind most word processing programs use) would sort the list considering only the first digit of each number:

142
2
53

Fortunately, Word can sort numerals as numbers rather than as ASCII characters. In fact, Word can also intelligently sort dates, a task that few word processors can do well.

A second problem is that upper- and lowercase letters are separated in the ASCII sorting sequence. Because of this, many word processors sort all words that start with uppercase letters before all words that start with lowercase letters. ("Zebra" would come before "aardvark".) Most of the time you want your lists sorted in alphabetical order, regardless of case. Word sorts upper- and lowercase words together.

A third, minor, problem is that not all punctuation comes before all numerals in the ASCII system. Some characters, such as the equal sign, fall between the numerals and the letters; others, such as the circumflex, fall between the upper- and lowercase letters; and some, such as the vertical bar, follow the lowercase letters.

Word sorts all paragraphs starting with punctuation first, then paragraphs with numbers, and then paragraphs with letters. In general, avoid sorting lists that include punctuation as the first character. The ASCII sorting sequence is shown here:

SPACEBAR
! " # $ % & ' ( ) * + , - . /
0 1 2 3 4 5 6 7 8 9
: ; < = > ? @
A B C D E F G H I J K L M N O P Q R S T U V W X Y Z
[\ ] ^ _ `
a b c d e f g h i j k l m n o p q r s t u v w x y z
{ | } ~

Word sorts international letters in with standard letters so that a word that starts with "ö" is sorted with words that start with "o".

You can tell Word whether you want to sort from "A" to "Z" (*ascending*), which is the default, or from "Z" to "A" (*descending*). For numbers, ascending is from lowest to highest. Most of the time, you will sort in ascending order.

Lesson 140: Sorting Text

Usually, you want to sort based on entire lines. The most frequent use for the Sorting command is sorting lists in which each item is formatted as an individual paragraph.

Using the Sort Text command from the Table menu is easy. Even though this command is in the Table menu, you can sort text in paragraphs even if they are not in a table. The Sort Text dialog box is shown in Figure 25-1.

First, select the range of paragraphs you want to sort. In text, Word sorts

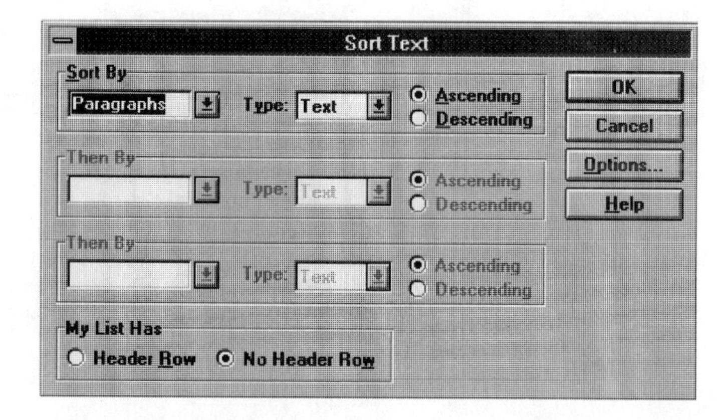

Sort Text dialog box
Figure 25-1.

only paragraphs, not lines separated by newline characters. In a table, Word sorts by rows. For this example, use the following list:

Chicago
New York
Detroit
Dallas
Houston
New Orleans
Buffalo

Select the paragraphs and give the Sort Text command from the Table menu. The default choices are Paragraphs, Text, and Ascending, which are the most common. Choose OK and Word sorts the list in the following order:

Buffalo
Chicago
Dallas
Detroit
Houston
New Orleans
New York

Choosing Descending produces the following list:

New York
New Orleans
Houston
Detroit
Dallas
Chicago
Buffalo

In addition to sorting lists in which each item is a separate paragraph, you can sort paragraphs that run many lines. Word simply sorts full paragraphs in this case, based on the first letter of each paragraph.

The Options button brings up the following dialog box:

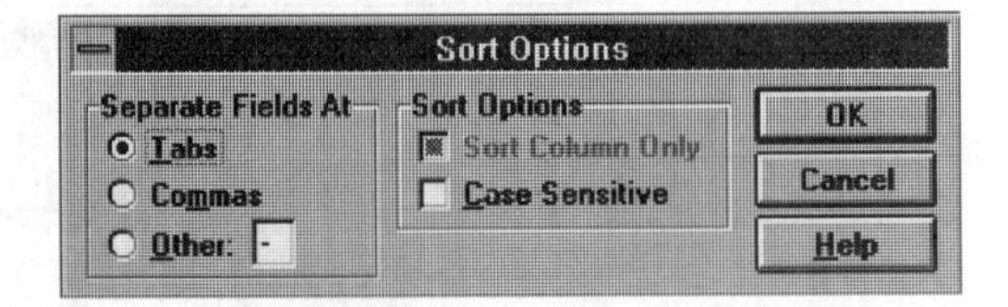

The Separate Fields At choices are only useful for tables that are separated by tab characters, commas, or other characters; you do not need this if you are sorting a table (sorting tables is described later in this chapter). The Case Sensitive option lets you sort the uppercase letters separately from the lowercase letters.

Lesson 141: Sorting Numbers

When you give the Sort Text command, you can specify how you want Word to sort. In the dialog box, the Type drop-down list lets you choose the type of data you are sorting. Your choices are Text, Number, and Date. If you are sorting based on numbers or dates, be sure to select the appropriate choice.

For example, use the Number choice to sort this list:

509
22.7
448
100
1000.
17

The result would be sorted as follows:

17
22.7
100
448
509
1000.

You can also sort numbers and dates in either ascending or descending order. Note that Word can handle many date forms such as "3/5/94", "March 5, 1994", and "5-Mar-94").

Lesson 142: Sorting in Tables

So far you have learned only how to sort based on the first letter in a paragraph. While this is usually what you want, there are some circumstances where you might want to sort a table by a column other than the first one. For instance, you may want to sort the following table on the Amount column:

Name	Age	Type	Amount
Terrence	88	Regular	88.00
Connors	150	Senior	125.00
Long	130	Regular	130.00
Yee	50	New	67.50

Word lets you sort a table by any column or a combination of columns. After selecting the rows in the table (but not the heading), give the Sort command (if a table is selected, Word changes the name of the command to Sort). Word changes the Sort By to Column 1.

For example, if you select the four rows, give the Sort command, and choose Column 4, it will produce the following table:

Name	Age	Type	Amount
Yee	50	New	67.50
Terrence	88	Regular	88.00
Connors	150	Senior	125.00
Long	130	Regular	130.00

If you select a single column and want to sort that, leaving the rest of the rows the same, choose the Options button in the Sort dialog box and select Sort Column Only.

Review

Create a list of names of people with whom you work. Sort it in both ascending and descending order.

Make a two-column table with the names of the same people and their ages. Sort the table by name, and then sort it by age.

Word For Windows
Word For Windows

C H A P T E R

26 OTHER ADVANCED WORD FEATURES

Word offers many features that are attractive to advanced users. Some of these features use programming and are thus only introduced briefly in this book. Others make long projects easier to manage.

The first three features explored in this chapter are fields, bookmarks, and cross-references.

- Word uses *fields* to mark special items that appear in documents. Although advanced use of fields is quite complicated, you can easily use fields without understanding all of their workings.
- *Bookmarks* make jumping around in your document much faster; you don't have to remember page numbers when you move within the document. Bookmarks are also handy for selecting sections or pages in your document quickly.
- *Cross-references* let you refer to parts of your document by pages or by numbers in a series. For instance, if you have a table you want to refer to, you can put a bookmark at the table and include a special cross-reference. When you print your document, the cross-reference will refer to the table's page.

Lesson 143: Introduction to Fields

Many parts of documents require a bit more treatment than regular text. Word handles them in special ways. For example, in Chapter 16 you learned how to insert entries for the index. These entries did not appear in your text; they were hidden in your document so when you later generated an index, Word knew what to include. Those entries were fields.

There are dozens of types of fields in Word. Some are fairly easy to understand, like index entries; others are very advanced and well beyond the scope of this book. The most important concept to understand about fields is that Word uses them to insert special text or hidden codes into a document. This lesson shows you how to handle fields so you can use them in the other lessons in this chapter.

Many Word commands enter fields into your documents. You have already seen some of these commands in Chapter 16, such as Index and Tables. When you used these commands, you saw the results of the fields, not the fields themselves.

To see the actual fields in your document, you use the Field Codes command from the View Tab of the Options menu. To see an example of a field, give the New command to start a temporary document. Type the words **This is a field:** followed by a space. Give the Field command from the Insert menu. You see the dialog box shown in Figure 26-1.

In the Categories list on the left, select Date and Time; in the Field Names list, select Time. Select OK to insert that field in your document, then type a

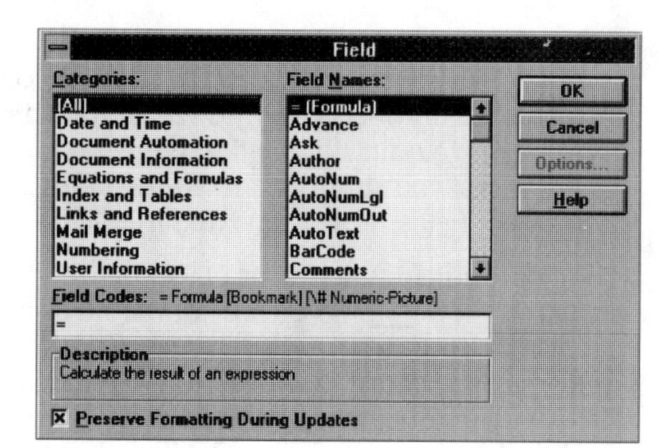

Field dialog box
Figure 26-1.

period followed by **That was a field.** Your window should look like this (but with the current time):

This is a field: 11:24 AM That was a field.

Now give the Options command from the Tools menu, choose the View tab, and select the Field Codes option. This causes Word to show fields as their *field codes,* not as the text that is produced by the fields. The window changes to the one shown here:

This is a field: { TIME * MERGEFORMAT } That was a field.

A field has three parts: field characters, field type, and field instructions. The field characters look like boldface left and right curly braces. (However, you cannot type a field simply by using these characters from the keyboard; you must use the field commands.) The field type is the first word after the left field character. This tells Word what the field is. In the case of the field you just entered, the field type is "TIME". Some fields will have *field instructions,* which further define how the field will be displayed, but others won't. In this case, "* MERGEFORMAT" constitutes the field instructions. You will probably not want to view the field codes very often.

Fields are *dynamic*—that is, they change constantly as you change your document. They have a displayed value when you first enter them in your document, but that value can change when circumstances change. For example, when you worked with tables of contents and indexes in Chapter 16, the page numbers changed when you edited or formatted your document. You did not need to write a new table of contents or index to see the changes; you simply updated the items that were already there. Those items were fields, so you updated the field values to get the new pagination.

To update a field, select it or place the insertion mark in the middle of the field and press F9. To update all the fields in your document at once, select the whole document and then press F9. This is useful if you have many fields, such as dates, that need to be updated at once. You can find all the fields in your document by pressing F11 or Alt-F1 to move forward from field to field and Shift-F11 or Alt-Shift-F1 to move backward.

Note that all fields are updated automatically when you open a file. You can also specify in the Print tab of the Options command that fields be updated automatically before printing.

At times you may want to prevent a field from being updated. For instance, you may not want the date to change each day. To lock a field's value (keep its current text value), select the field and press Ctrl-F11. To later unlock it, select the field and press Ctrl-Shift-F11. Unfortunately, there is no easy way to tell whether or not a field is locked.

The Field command from the Insert menu is the easiest way to enter most types of fields. For instance, you have seen how to insert the current time in your document. If you open the document at a later date and update the field, the value will change automatically to that of the current date. If you want to know more about fields, see your Word *User's Guide* for a complete list of fields available.

Lesson 144: Using Bookmarks

Bookmarks make jumping around a long document very easy. You don't have to remember page numbers (which might change when you edit your document) or search for specific text. Instead, you simply insert a named bookmark and jump to it by name. For instance, if you have a 250-page document that has 20 chapters, you might put a bookmark at the beginning of each chapter using a descriptive name instead of the chapter number. You might also put bookmarks at tables you refer to often.

Word's bookmarks can mark a selection of text, not just a location. For instance, if you create a bookmark for a table, when you give the Go To command from the Edit menu, the entire table will be selected. This is very handy for items that you copy often. When you move the selected text, the bookmark moves with it. A bookmark can be a single character if you wish.

To create a bookmark, select the desired text (or the single character) and give the Bookmark command from the Edit menu. You see the dialog box shown here:

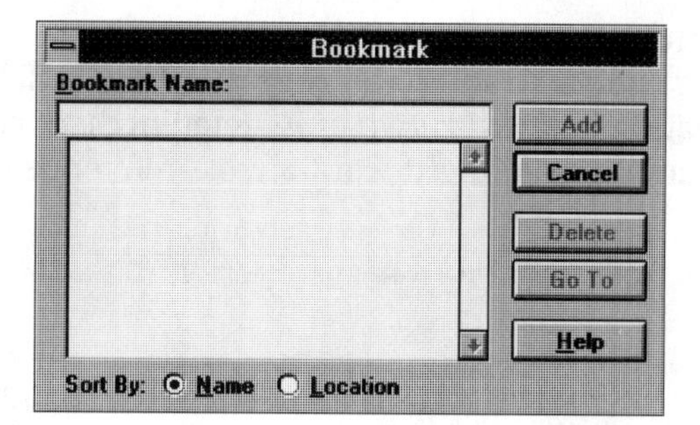

Enter the bookmark's name in the name field (from 1 to 40 characters, with no spaces), and select Add. To remove a bookmark, give the Bookmark command, select the bookmark you want, and select the Delete button. You can see the bookmark list sorted by name or by location in your document.

To jump to a bookmark, give the Go To command from the Edit menu, select Bookmark from the Go to What list, and choose the name of the desired bookmark from the list.

Lesson 145: Using Cross-References

Word can cross-reference any text or page number in a document. You use fields to refer to the chosen items and Word then replaces the fields with the numbers to which they refer. You usually cross-reference a bookmark.

For example, assume you want to refer to the page number of a specific heading in your document. The heading is "New Operations". You would want its reference to look something like this:

This is described in detail in the section called "New Operations".

To cross-reference a heading, put the insertion point at the place where you want the cross-reference for that section to appear and give the Cross-reference command from the Insert menu. You see:

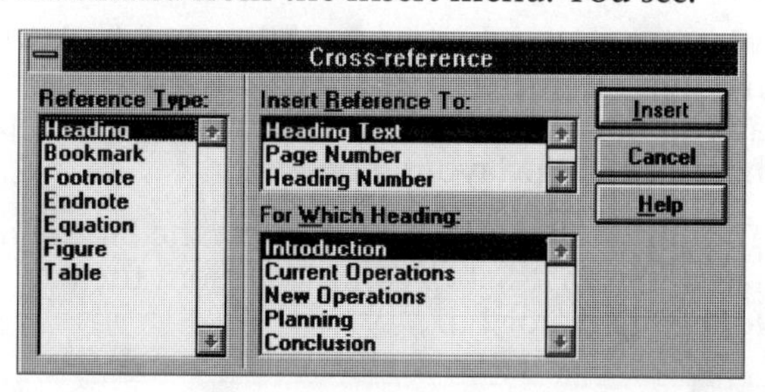

Choose Heading from the Reference Type list, choose Heading Text from the Insert Reference To list, and choose the heading from the For Which Heading list.

Note that you have three choices for what is shown in a cross-reference. You can choose to show the page number of the cross-reference instead of the heading text; with two cross-references, of course, you can show both. For example, you might want a cross-reference that looks like this:

This is described in detail in the section called "New Operations" on page 32.

The first part is a cross-reference to the heading text, the second to the page number. If your headings are numbered, you can also display the number.

You also have a wide variety of things that you can cross-reference. In the Reference Type list, you can also choose to reference bookmarks, footnotes, endnotes, equations, figures, and tables. For instance, you may have bookmarks for a quotation in your document. You could then refer to the page with that quotation.

Cross-references are stored as fields. If you repaginate your document after inserting a cross-reference, you should select the entire document and press F9 to update the page numbers in the cross-references. Similarly, if you cross-reference headings and later edit the headings, you have to update the cross-reference fields to get the new wording in them.

Lesson 146: Numbering Lines in Your Document

The legal profession often requires that line numbers be printed on documents such as pleadings and depositions. One method is to use forms with line numbers already printed on them. However, this limits the kind of text you can include, and it is difficult to line up the text and the paper in many printers. For example, footnotes (which are common in pleadings) do not line up with the numbers on preprinted forms. You can only see the line numbers in print preview mode and when you print your document.

Word's line-numbering capability enables lawyers (and anyone else who requires numbered lines) to edit and print documents easily. Line numbers appear only on the printed document and in print preview mode (not in normal or page layout mode).

To turn on line numbering, select the Line Numbers button in the Layout tab of the Page Setup command from the File menu. This brings up the following dialog box:

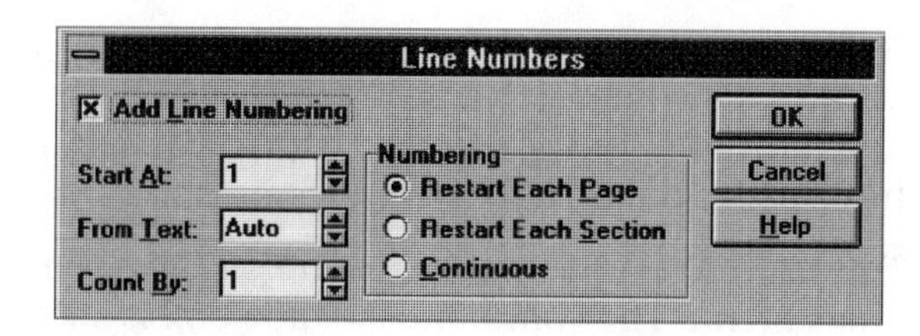

Select the Add Line Numbering option to start numbering.

You can specify what number to start at, how far from the text the numbers should appear, and whether to show every line number or only a few. For example, if you enter **5** for Count By, Word only prints every fifth line number.

The choices for the Numbering option tell Word how often to start the numbers. Generally, you want the numbering on each page to begin with 1, so you should select Restart Each Page. If, instead, you want the lines of your document numbered from beginning to end, choose Restart Each Section (for numbering in each section) or Continuous (for the whole document).

Lesson 147: Using Redlining for Revisions

When you change a document and save the changes, the previous version of the document is replaced by the new one. This is usually what you want when you edit documents. Sometimes, however, you may want to see the changes you are making in your document while you are working on it and have them take effect later. You can use Word's revision marks, called *redlining*, for this purpose.

Redlining is commonly used in law offices for making changes to standard forms and contracts. It is also useful for groups of people who work together editing one document. (Compare this to the Annotations feature described in Chapter 17, where each person made only comments, not changes, to a single document.) Redlining shows clearly any text added to or deleted from a document. It also adds a bar to one side of each changed line so you can quickly find where changes have been made.

For example, look at the SAMPLE1 letter. With Word's revision marks feature turned on, if you change "pleased" to "happy", the screen might look like this:

| I am happy~~pleased~~ to send you the latest update on the results of our expanded product line. The enclosed summary documents our increased profit margin (7%) for the fourth quarter of our fiscal year (ending June 30), which is largely due to the successful introduction of our new model, the DC50. In the next year we expect to continue increasing our profitable inroads into this new area.

Word's default is to show new or inserted text as underlined and to show deleted text as struck-through. The default also adds a bar to the left side of any line with a change in it.

As you edit, Word continually marks your inserted and deleted text in this fashion. Of course, at some point you will want to remove the underlining and delete the struck-through text so you can print the document and start fresh with no marks. The next lesson shows you how to do this.

To turn the revision marks feature on, give the Revisions command from the Tools menu. The command's dialog box is shown here:

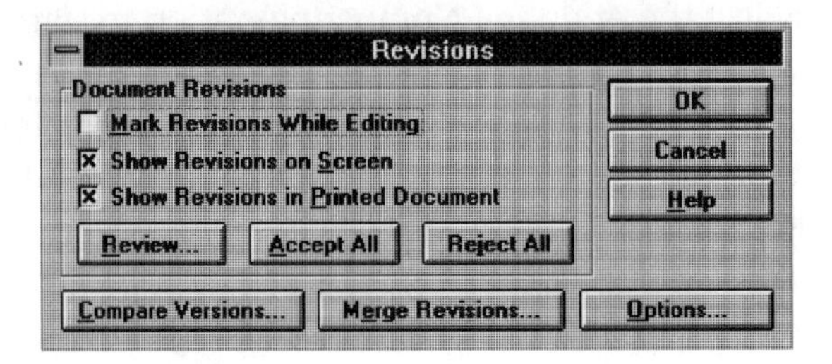

Select the Mark Revisions While Editing option and execute the command. When you are editing with revision marks on, Word displays "MRK" in the status bar near the right side of the window:

To see how editing with revision marks is different from the editing you have done up to now, start editing the second paragraph of the SAMPLE1 letter. Select "well" and press Del. Move the insertion point to after "projections" and type **that**. The result is shown here:

As you can see, we are ~~well~~ within the projections <u>that</u> we outlined to you when you helped us obtain short-term financing. Thank you again for all your assistance. If you have any questions regarding this information, please feel free to call me.

You can also change how Word shows revisions in the document window and on the printed page. Choose the Options button in the Revisions command (or the Revisions tab of the Options command from the Tools menu). The dialog box is shown in Figure 26-2. You can change the type of formatting used for inserted text and deleted text in their respective areas. You can also choose which colors are used (the default is to change color for each person).

Some people prefer the revision bars to appear on the right side of the page; in this case, choose Right Border for the Mark option in the Revised Lines area. Choosing Outside Border causes Word to put the revision bars on the outside margins if you are using odd and even pages. If you don't want to see the revision bars, choose None.

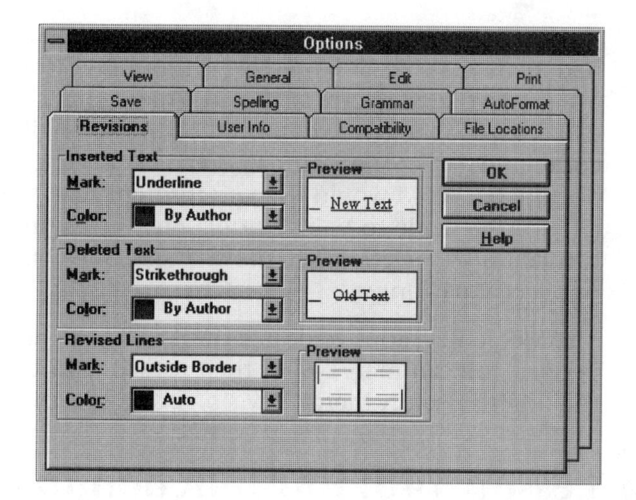

Options dialog box, Revisions tab
Figure 26-2.

When you save a document with redlining turned on, the revisions are saved with the file. Thus, if you leave Word and then come back to edit the file again later, your revisions are still there. This gives you the opportunity to edit your document as much as you want before you decide whether or not to implement the revisions.

When you are ready to accept the revisions, select the revised text, give the Revisions command, and select the Accept All button. You can also choose to accept the revisions manually. Instead of Accept All, choose the Review button. You see

Review Revisions
Description
No revisions selected. Use Find buttons or select a revision.
Hide Marks | Cancel
Undo Last | Help
← Find | Find → | Accept | Reject | Find Next After Accept/Reject

Use the Find buttons to move forward and backward in your document, choosing Accept or Reject for each revision. The Reject choice undoes the revision. Word deletes any text you have added since you started revising and retains any text you marked for deletion.

For example, assume that Valerie and Alex are working together on a report. After Valerie writes the report, she puts it on a disk and gives it to Alex. He turns revision marks on and edits the text. When he gives the disk back to Valerie, she can easily see what changes he has made. She chooses the Revisions command, goes through the document, and accepts or rejects each change.

You do not need to use revision marks to see changes in a document. If Alex had made his changes directly (without revision marks turned on), and if Valerie had kept a copy of the document that she gave to Alex, she could still compare the two. She would open the original, choose the Revisions command, select the Compare Versions button, then specify Alex's new document. Word would then go through Alex's document and make the changes he made to Valerie's document, this time with revision marks turned on so she could see the changes. She could also then decide to accept or reject the changes.

The Merge Revisions option is similar. If you hand out a document to many people, you can merge all of their revisions into a single document. Open the original, select Merge Revisions, and specify each of the newer files.

Lesson 148: Introduction to Macros

As you have seen throughout the book, Word gives you easy methods to produce complex parts of documents. For instance, imagine how hard it would be to create an index by hand each time you changed a document. By marking your index entries once, you can re-create a new index with a single Word command. Similarly, you can renumber a long list of steps in which you have added or deleted steps with a single command.

Some procedures, however, take more than a single command, and you may need to execute these procedures many times. For instance, you may want to excerpt certain parts of a long document into a smaller document that has a different format. Here are the steps you would use to do this:

1. Open both the long and short documents.
2. Select the long document's window.
3. Select a part to be excerpted.
4. Choose the Copy command from the Edit menu.
5. Change to the short document's window.
6. Put the insertion point at the end of the document.
7. Choose the Paste command from the Edit menu.
8. Repeat steps 2 through 7 as necessary.

If you have dozens of sections to copy, steps 2 through 7 could get tedious very quickly.

Macros offer many advantages over doing the steps yourself:

- Macros can make your work faster. Word zips through the actions in a macro many times faster than you could give the commands.
- Macros are more accurate than giving the commands yourself. In the preceding example, if you accidentally chose the Cut command instead of the Copy command in the long document, you may not notice it until it is too late. Running a macro would never make such a mistake.
- If you help other people use Word, you can create a macro for a procedure instead of listing all the steps in that procedure. This makes teaching much easier.

Word's macro feature lets you automate your work by grouping sets of steps into a single step that can be executed with a single keystroke or command. In the preceding example, you could create a macro (which is really a small computer program) that copies the current selection, switches to the next window, goes to the end of that document, pastes the selection, and switches back to the first window. Once you create a macro, you can make that macro available as a command on a menu, as a button on a toolbar, or as a keyboard equivalent.

Like other document settings, macros are saved in templates. Thus, when you create a macro, you can use that macro with any other document that uses the same template. Templates were discussed in detail in Chapter 11.

Because macros are like computer programming, they are only discussed briefly here. While the previous example shows you some of the power of macros to save you time and make your work more accurate, macros can do much more than this. However, in order to write such macros, you need a good understanding of programming concepts and a fair amount of patience with programming. If you work in an office with others who can program, they might use Word's macros to do a variety of tasks.

- Macros can intelligently look at text in a document. For instance, in the previous example, imagine that if the text in the long document is a list, you want to put it in one part of the short document; but if it is a regular paragraph, you want to put it in a different part. A macro can look at the type of text you select and put it in the correct part automatically.
- Macros can prompt you for information using standard dialog boxes. For instance, you might have five different standard formats for some documents. The macro could ask you which format you want to use.
- Many companies have designed macros to fill in forms. The macro asks questions and, based on the answers, asks other questions related to the first questions, all the time saving the information you enter. It then fills out the form for you. Word's forms feature, described briefly in Chapter 20, works best when the fields are associated with macros.

If you are comfortable with programming, you may want to learn more about macros from Word's manual.

Review

Think about how you would use annotations in your office to have your coworkers comment on work. Consider how they would suggest insertions, deletions, and changes.

In the documents you have created by using Word, think about where cross-references would help refer the reader to another part of the document. Would this add to the readability or make it more confusing?

PART 4

APPENDIXES

APPENDIX

KEYBOARD REFERENCE

The following tables list all the actions you can take in Word using the keyboard. Some keyboard equivalents are listed as "keypad"; in this case, you use the keys on the numeric keypad on the right of the keyboard. Be sure that you are not in "Num Lock" mode when using the numeric keypad.

Moving in a Document

Command	Keys
Character left	←
Word left	Ctrl-←
Character right	→
Word right	Ctrl-→
Beginning of line	Home
End of line	End
Line up	↑
Line down	↓
Paragraph up	Ctrl-↑
Paragraph down	Ctrl-↓
Top of window	Ctrl-Pg Up
Bottom of window	Ctrl-Pg Dn
Window up	Pg Up
Window down	Pg Dn
Page up	Alt-Ctrl-Pg Up
Page down	Alt-Ctrl-Pg Dn
Beginning of document	Ctrl-Home
End of document	Ctrl-End
Previous frame or object	Alt-↑
Next frame or object	Alt-↓

Moving in a Table

Command	Keys
Cell left	Shift-Tab
Cell right	Tab
First cell in row	Alt-Home
Last cell in row	Alt-End
First cell in column	Alt-Pg Up
Last cell in column	Alt-Pg Dn
Previous row	↑
Next row	↓
Previous column	Ctrl-↑
Next column	Ctrl-↓

Selecting

Command	Keys
Start selecting a column	Ctrl-Shift-F8
Extend in direction	Shift-Direction (use arrow keys)
Select entire document	Ctrl-A
Turn extend on	F8
Reduce selection	Shift-F8
Select table	Alt-5 keypad

Windows

Command	Keys
Previous window	Ctrl-Shift-F6
Next window	Ctrl-F6
Previous pane	Shift-F6
Next pane	F6
Move window	Ctrl-F7
Split window	Alt-Shift-C
Close window	Ctrl-F4 or Ctrl-W
Resize document window	Ctrl-F8
Maximize document window	Ctrl-F10
Restore document window	Ctrl-F5
Maximize Word's window	Alt-F10
Restore Word's window	Alt-F5

Deleting

Command	Keys
Delete character left	Backspace
Delete word left	Ctrl-Backspace
Delete character right	Del
Delete word right	Ctrl-Del

Clipboard

Command	Keys
Cut	Ctrl-X
Cut to spike	Ctrl-F3
Copy	Ctrl-C
Paste	Ctrl-V
Paste from spike	Ctrl-Shift-F3
Copy formatting only	Ctrl-Shift-C
Paste formatting only	Ctrl-Shift-V
Move	F2

Special Characters

Command	Keys
Line break	Shift-Enter
Page break	Ctrl-Enter
Column break	Ctrl-Shift-Enter
Optional hyphen	Ctrl--
Nonbreaking hyphen	Ctrl-Shift--
Nonbreaking space	Ctrl-Shift-Spacebar
Tab character in table	Ctrl-Tab

Character Formatting

Command	Keys
Bold	Ctrl-B
Italics	Ctrl-I
Underline	Ctrl-U
Word underline	Ctrl-Shift-W
Double underline	Ctrl-Shift-D
Hidden text	Ctrl-Shift-H
Small caps	Ctrl-Shift-K
Subscript	Ctrl-=
Superscript	Ctrl-Shift-=
Plain characters for style	Ctrl-Shift-Z or Ctrl-Spacebar
Symbol font	Ctrl-Shift-Q
Change font	Ctrl-Shift-F
Change size	Ctrl-Shift-P
Increase font to next size	Ctrl-Shift->
Decrease font to next size	Ctrl-Shift-<
Increase font by 1 point	Ctrl-]
Decrease font by 1 point	Ctrl-[
Change case	Shift-F3
All capitals	Ctrl-Shift-A

Paragraph Formatting

Command	Keys
Single space	Ctrl-1
Double space	Ctrl-2
1.5 space	Ctrl-5
One line before	Ctrl-0 (zero)
Left align	Ctrl-L
Center align	Ctrl-E
Right align	Ctrl-R
Justify	Ctrl-J
Indent	Ctrl-M
Unindent	Ctrl-Shift-M
Hanging indent	Ctrl-T
Reduce hanging indent	Ctrl-Shift-T
Plain paragraph for style	Ctrl-Q

Styles

Command	Keys
Change style	Ctrl-Shift-S
Normal style	Ctrl-Shift-N
Heading 1 style	Alt-Ctrl-1
Heading 2 style	Alt-Ctrl-2
Heading 3 style	Alt-Ctrl-3
AutoFormat	Ctrl-K

Outline View

Command	Keys
Promote	Alt-Shift-←
Demote	Alt-Shift-→
Make body text	Alt-Shift-5 keypad
Move heading up	Alt-Shift-↑
Move heading down	Alt-Shift-↓
Expand	Alt-Shift-+ keypad
Collapse	Alt-Shift-− keypad
Show level	Alt-Shift-1 through Alt-Shift-8
Show all	Alt-Shift-A
First line	Alt-Shift-L
Show formatting	/ keypad

Fields

Command	Keys
Insert field	Ctrl-F9
Update field	F9
View this field code	Shift-F9
View all field codes	Alt-F9
Unlink field	Ctrl-Shift-F9
Update link	Ctrl-Shift-F7
Previous field	Shift-F11
Next field	F11
Lock field	Ctrl-F11
Unlock field	Ctrl-Shift-F11
Insert date field	Alt-Shift-D
Insert time field	Alt-Shift-T
Insert page field	Alt-Shift-P

Form Letters

Command	Keys
Check merge	Alt-Shift-K
Merge to document	Alt-Shift-N
Print merge document	Alt-Shift-M
Edit data source	Alt-Shift-E

Menu Commands

Command	Keys
Edit menu	
Undo	Ctrl-Z
Redo	F4 or Ctrl-Y
Cut	Ctrl-X
Copy	Ctrl-C
Paste	Ctrl-V
Clear	Del
Select All	Ctrl-A
Find	Ctrl-F
Replace	Ctrl-H
Go To	F5 or Ctrl-G
Bookmark	Ctrl-Shift-F5
Update Link	Alt-Ctrl-U
File menu	
New	Ctrl-N
Open	Ctrl-O
Close	Ctrl-F4 or Ctrl-W
Save	Ctrl-S
Save As	F12

Menu Commands

Command	Keys
Print Preview	Ctrl-F2
Print	Ctrl-P
Exit	Alt-F4
Format menu	
Font	Ctrl-D
Change Case	Shift-F3
Bullets and Numbering	Ctrl-Shift-L
AutoFormat	Ctrl-K
Style	Ctrl-Shift-S
Help menu	
Contents	F1
Insert menu	
Page Numbers	Alt-Shift-P
Annotation	Alt-Ctrl-A
Date and Time	Alt-Shift-D or Alt-Shift-T
Footnote	Alt-Ctrl-F
Endnote	Alt-Ctrl-E
Mark Index Entry	Alt-Shift-X
Mark Citation Entry	Alt-Shift-I
Mark TOC Entry	Alt-Shift-O
Table menu	
Select Table	Alt-5 keypad
Tools menu	
Spelling	F7
Thesaurus	Shift-F7

Menu Commands

Command	Keys
View menu	
Normal	Alt-Ctrl-C
Outline	Alt-Ctrl-O
Page Layout	Alt-Ctrl-P
Window menu	
Split	Alt-Ctrl-S

Other

Command	Keys
Display nonprinting characters	Ctrl-Shift-*
Insert AutoText	Alt-Ctrl-V
Insert index entry	Alt-Shift-X
Repeat Find or Go To command	Shift-F4

APPENDIX

B

WORD COMMANDS

Figure B-1 shows Word's menus and their commands.

File
- New... Ctrl+N
- Open... Ctrl+O
- Close
- Save Ctrl+S
- Save As...
- Save All
- Find File...
- Summary Info...
- Templates...
- Page Setup...
- Print Preview
- Print... Ctrl+P
- 1 CHARACT.DOC
- 2 SUMFUN.DOC
- 3 SAMPLE1.DOC
- 4 CITIES.DOC
- Exit

Edit
- Undo Typing Ctrl+Z
- Repeat Copy F4
- Cut Ctrl+X
- Copy Ctrl+C
- Paste Ctrl+V
- Paste Special...
- Clear Delete
- Select All Ctrl+A
- Find... Ctrl+F
- Replace... Ctrl+H
- Go To... F5
- AutoText...
- Bookmark...
- Links...
- Object

View
- • Normal
- Outline
- Page Layout
- Master Document
- Full Screen
- Toolbars...
- Ruler
- Header and Footer
- Footnotes
- Annotations
- Zoom...

Insert
- Break...
- Page Numbers...
- Annotation
- Date and Time...
- Field...
- Symbol...
- Form Field...
- Footnote...
- Caption...
- Cross-reference...
- Index and Tables...
- File...
- Frame
- Picture...
- Object...
- Database...

Format
- Font...
- Paragraph...
- Tabs...
- Borders and Shading...
- Columns...
- Change Case...
- Drop Cap...
- Bullets and Numbering...
- Heading Numbering...
- AutoFormat...
- Style Gallery...
- Style...
- Frame...
- Picture...
- Drawing Object...

Tools
- Spelling... F7
- Grammar...
- Thesaurus... Shift+F7
- Hyphenation...
- Language...
- Word Count...
- AutoCorrect...
- Mail Merge...
- Envelopes and Labels...
- Protect Document...
- Revisions...
- Macro...
- Customize...
- Options...

Table
- Insert Cells...
- Delete Cells...
- Merge Cells
- Split Cells...
- Select Row
- Select Column
- Select Table Alt+Num 5
- Table AutoFormat...
- Cell Height and Width...
- Headings
- Convert Table to Text...
- Sort...
- Formula...
- Split Table
- ✓ Gridlines

Help
- Contents
- Search for Help on...
- Index
- Quick Preview
- Examples and Demos
- Tip of the Day...
- WordPerfect Help...
- Technical Support
- About Microsoft Word...

Window
- New Window
- Arrange All
- Split
- ✓ 1 CHARACT.DOC
- 2 SAMPLE1.DOC
- 3 SUMFUN.DOC

Word's menus
Figure B-1.

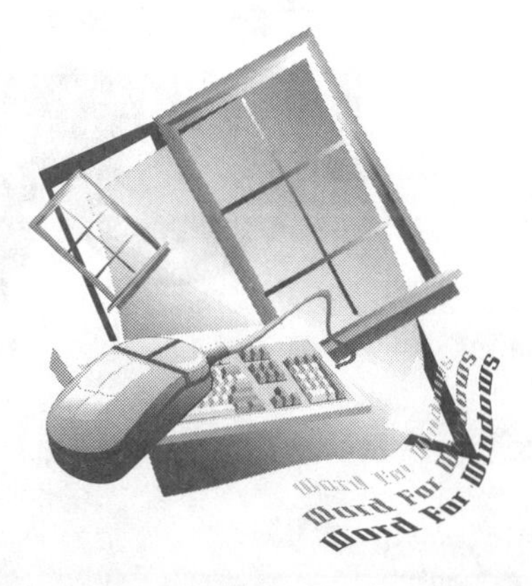
Word For Windows
Word For Windows
Word For Windows

APPENDIX

PROCEDURE REFERENCE

This appendix lists the procedures for actions in Word, in alphabetical order. For many procedures, there is more than one possible action that would produce the same result. If there is more than one action, the procedure given here is the simplest. Many of the procedures assume that the Standard toolbar and Formatting toolbar are showing on your window.

Adding

See Inserting

Addressing Envelopes

1. Select the address in your document.
2. Choose Envelopes and Labels from the Tools menu.
3. Choose the Envelopes tab.

Aligning Text

   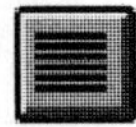

1. Select the paragraph(s) that you want to align.
2. Choose the Left, Center, Right, or Justify buttons from the Formatting toolbar.

Alphabetizing Lists and Text

See Sorting

Annotations, Inserting

1. Put the insertion point at the place where you want the annotation to appear.
2. Choose the Annotation command from the Insert menu.
3. Type in the annotation pane.
4. If you want (and your PC is able to), click the tape recorder icon to include a voice annotation.

Annotations, Viewing

1. Put the insertion point near the annotation you want to see.
2. Choose Annotations from the View menu.

AutoCorrect

1. Choose AutoCorrect from the Tools menu.

AutoFormat

1. Open the document you want formatted.
2. Choose the AutoFormat command from the Format menu.

AutoText, Defining

1. Type the definition you want for a new AutoText entry.
2. Select the definition text.
3. Choose the AutoText button from the Standard toolbar.
4. Enter a name for the definition.

AutoText, Inserting

1. Type the name of the AutoText entry.
2. Choose the AutoText button from the Standard toolbar or press F3.

Backup Copies

1. Choose the Options command in the Tools menu.
2. Choose the Save tab.
3. Select the Always Create Backup Copy option.

Bold

1. Select the text you want to format.
2. Click the Bold button on the Formatting toolbar.

Bookmarks

1. Select the text you want to identify or place the insertion point at the desired location.
2. Choose Bookmark from the Edit menu.

Borders

1. Select the paragraph(s) you want the border on.
2. Choose the Borders button from the Formatting toolbar.
3. Choose the type of border(s) you want from the Borders toolbar.
4. For more options, choose the Borders and Shading command from the Format menu.

Bulleted Lists

1. Select the paragraphs you want in the list.
2. Choose the Bullets button from the Formatting toolbar.
3. For more options, choose Bullets and Numbering from the Format menu.

Calculations in Tables

1. Put the insertion point in the cell where you want the calculation.
2. Choose the Formula command from the Table menu.

Capital Letters

See Case of Letters

Captions

1. Put the insertion point where you want the caption.
2. Choose the Caption command from the Insert menu.

Case of Letters

1. Select the characters whose case you want to change.
2. Choose Change Case from the Format menu.

Centering Text

1. Select the paragraph(s) that you want to align.
2. Choose the Center button from the Formatting toolbar.

Charts

1. Put the insertion point where you want the chart (probably in a paragraph by itself).
2. Choose the Insert Chart button from the Standard toolbar.

Checking Grammar

1. Put the insertion point where you want to start checking.
2. Choose the Grammar command from the Tools menu.

Clipboard

1. Choose the Run command from Word's application menu.
2. Enter **clipbrd** for the Command Line option.

Closing Documents and Windows

1. Be sure the window or the document you want to close is the top window.
2. Choose the Close command from the File menu or press F4.

Color

1. Select the text you want to change the color of.
2. Choose the Font command from the Format menu.

Column Breaks

1. Put the insertion point where you want the column break.
2. Choose Break from the Insert menu or press Ctrl-Shift-Enter.

Columns

1. Put the insertion point in the section in which you want to adjust the columns.
2. Choose Columns from the Format menu.

Combining Documents

1. Activate the first document.
2. Choose Select All from the Edit menu or press Ctrl-A.
3. Choose the Copy button from the Standard toolbar.
4. Activate the second document.
5. Put the insertion point where you want the contents of the first document.
6. Choose the Paste button from the Standard toolbar.

Converting Documents

1. Choose the Save As command from the File menu.
2. In the Save File As Type drop-down list, choose the type of file you want to convert to.

Converting Objects

1. Select the object you want to convert.
2. Choose the Convert subcommand from the Object command in the Edit menu.

Copying Documents

1. Choose the Save As command from the File menu.
2. In the File Name option, enter the name you want for the copy of the file.

Copying Formatting and Styles

1. Select the text with the format you want to copy.
2. Choose the Format Painter button in the Standard toolbar.
3. Choose the text to which you want to copy the formatting.

Copying Text and Graphics

1. Select the text and/or graphics you want to copy.
2. Choose the Copy button from the Standard toolbar.

3. Put the insertion point at the place you want the copied material.
4. Choose the Paste button from the Standard toolbar.

Counting Characters, Words, Lines, and Paragraphs

1. Set the insertion point to count the whole document, or select the text you want to count.
2. Choose Word Count from the Tools menu.

Creating Documents

1. Choose the New button from the Standard toolbar.
2. If you want to create a document using other than the NORMAL.DOT template, choose the New command from the File menu.

Cropping Graphics

1. Select the graphic.
2. Hold down the Shift key while dragging one of the handles.

Cross-references

1. Put the insertion point where you want the cross-reference to appear.
2. Choose Cross-reference from the Insert menu.
3. Choose the type of reference, the kind of text you want inserted, and the object (such as a heading or bookmark) you want to refer to.

Cutting Text and Graphics to the Clipboard

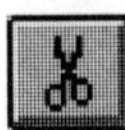

1. Select the text and/or graphics you want to copy.
2. Choose the Cut button from the Standard toolbar.

Dates

1. Put the insertion point where you want the date.
2. Choose Date and Time from the Insert menu.
3. Choose the format of the date you want.
4. Decide whether or not you want the date to be a field (meaning that it will be updated when you open or print the document).

Deleting Cells

1. Select the cell(s) you want to delete in the table.
2. Choose the Delete Cells command from the Table menu.
3. Specify how you want the rest of the table to move relative to the deleted cells.

Deleting Columns

1. Select the column(s) you want to delete in the table.
2. Choose the Delete Columns command from the Table menu.

Deleting a Document

1. Choose the Find File command from the File menu.
2. Using the Search dialog box, create a search criterion that includes the file that you want to delete.
3. In the Find File dialog box, choose the desired file from the list.
4. In the Commands drop-down list, choose the Delete command.

Deleting Rows

1. Select the row(s) you want to delete in the table.
2. Choose the Delete Rows command from the Table menu.

Deleting Tables

1. Choose the Select Table command from the Table menu.
2. Choose the Cut button from the Standard toolbar.

Deleting Text and Graphics

1. Select the text and/or graphics you want to delete.
2. Choose the Clear command from the Edit menu or press Del.

Dictionaries

1. Choose the Options command from the Tools menu.
2. Choose the Spelling tab.
3. Select the desired dictionaries from the Custom Dictionaries list.
4. To create a new dictionary, choose the New button.
5. To add an existing dictionary to the list, choose the Add button.
6. To edit a dictionary, select it and choose the Edit button.

Displaying Nonprinting Characters

1. Choose the Show Paragraph button from the Standard toolbar.

Double-spacing

See Spacing Within Paragraphs

Drag-and-Drop Moving

1. Select the text you want to move.
2. Click in the middle of the text.
3. Drag the selection to the desired location and release the mouse button.

Drawing

1. Choose the Drawing button from the Standard toolbar.
2. Add drawing elements to your document using the buttons from the Drawing toolbar.

Drop Caps

1. Select the letter at the beginning of the paragraph you want to make into a drop cap.
2. Choose Drop Cap from the Format menu.

Editing Graphics

1. Double-click on the graphic.
2. Use the drawing tools to add to or modify the graphic.
3. Choose the Close button from the Picture toolbar.

Embedding New Objects

1. Choose the Object command from the Insert menu.
2. Choose the Create New tab.
3. Choose the desired type of object from the list.
4. Use the tools in the object's program to create the object.
5. Choose the Exit command from the other program's File menu.

Embedding Objects from Files

1. Choose the Object command from the Insert menu.
2. Choose the Create from File tab.
3. Choose the desired file from the list.
4. Be sure that the Link to File option is not checked.

Envelopes

See Addressing Envelopes

Equations

1. Choose the Object command from the Insert menu.
2. Choose the Create New tab.
3. Choose Microsoft Equation from the list.

Excel Range

1. In Excel, select the desired range.
2. Choose the Paste command from the Edit menu.
3. Switch to Word.
4. Put the insertion point where you want the Excel range.
5. Choose the Paste Special command from the Edit menu.
6. Choose how you want the range pasted into the document.

Excel Worksheet

1. Put the insertion point where you want the Excel worksheet.
2. Choose the Insert Microsoft Excel Worksheet button from the Standard toolbar.
3. Specify the worksheet you want to insert.

Exiting Word

1. Save all changed documents.
2. Choose the Exit command from the File menu.

Fast Saves

See Saving, Fast

Fields, Inserting

1. Put the insertion point at the place you want the field.
2. Choose the Field command from the Insert menu.
3. Choose the type of field and add any additional options to the field code.

Fields, Updating

1. Select the field to be updated (to update all fields in a document, select the entire document).
2. Press F9.

Fields, Viewing Codes

1. Press Alt-F9 to switch between viewing codes or results.
2. To switch between viewing codes or results for just one field, select it and press Shift-F9.

Finding Files

1. Choose the Find File command from the File menu.

2. Make your choices in the Search dialog box. You will probably need to use the Advanced Search button for specifying criteria.
3. Choose the OK button to see the found files in the Find File dialog box.

Finding Formatting

1. Choose the Find command from the Edit menu.
2. Enter text if you want to find specific text with formatting, otherwise leave the Find What field empty.
3. Choose one or more types of formatting from the Format drop-down list.
4. Fill in the dialog boxes with the desired formatting to find.

Finding Special Characters

1. Choose the Find command from the Edit menu.
2. Choose the special characters you want to find from the Special drop-down list.

Finding Text

1. Choose the Find command from the Edit menu.
2. Enter the desired text in the Find What option.

Fonts

1. Choose the Font list in the Formatting toolbar or press Ctrl-Shift-F.
2. Choose the desired font from the list.
3. Choose the Size list in the Formatting toolbar or press Ctrl-Shift-P.
4. Choose the desired size from the list.

Footers

1. Choose Header and Footer from the View menu.
2. Type the desired footer in the footer area.
3. To specify that a section has different odd and even footers, or a different footer on the first page, choose the Layout tab of the Page Setup command from the File menu.

Footnotes, Inserting

1. Put the insertion point at the place where you want the footnote to appear.
2. Choose the Footnote command from the Insert menu.
3. Type in the footnote pane.
4. Choose the Close button when you are finished typing the footnote.

Footnotes, Viewing

1. Put the insertion point near the footnote you want to see.
2. Choose Footnotes from the View menu.

Form Letters

1. Start a new document using the New command from the File menu.
2. Choose the Mail Merge command from the Tools menu.
3. Follow the steps for creating a main document, creating a data source, and merging the two.

Formatting Characters

1. Select the character(s) that you want to format.
2. Choose the Font command from the Format menu.
3. You may also want to use the Style command from the Format menu for character formatting.

Formatting, Copying

See Copying Formatting

Formatting, Finding

See Finding Formatting

Formatting Paragraphs

1. Select all or part of the paragraph(s) that you want to format.
2. Choose the Paragraph command from the Format menu.
3. You may also want to use the Tabs, Borders and Shading, and Style commands from the Format menu for paragraph formatting.

Formatting Sections

1. Choose the Page Setup command from the File menu.
2. You may also want to use the Columns command from the Format menu for section formatting.

Formatting with Styles

See Styles

Formatting Tables

1. Select the cells you want to format.
2. Choose the Font command or the Paragraph command to apply character or paragraph formatting in the selected cells.

Forms

1. Activate the document you want to make into a form.

2. Choose the Form Field command from the Insert menu.

Formulas

See Calculations in Tables

Full Screen

See Viewing in Full Screen View

Getting Help

See Help

Going to Locations

1. Choose the Go To command from the Edit menu.
2. Select the type of location you are going to and the desired location.

Grammar Checking

See Checking Grammar

Graph

See Charts

Grid Lines

See Borders

Gutters

1. Select the section(s) in which you want to change the gutters.
2. Choose the Margins tab of the Page Setup command from the File menu.

Hanging Indents

1. Select the paragraph(s) that you want to have hanging indents.
2. Press Ctrl-T.
3. If you need to change the indentation on these paragraphs, choose the Paragraph command from the Format menu.

Headers

1. Choose Header and Footer from the View menu.
2. Type the desired header in the header area.
3. To specify that a section has different odd and even headers, or a different header on the first page, choose the Layout tab of the Page Setup command from the File menu.

Help

1. Choose the Help button from the Standard toolbar.
2. The pointer becomes a question mark and an arrow. Choose the item you

want help on. You can choose buttons, commands from menus, or parts of the screen.

Hidden Text

1. Select the text you want to format.
2. Press Ctrl-Shift-H.

Hyphenating

1. Put the insertion point at the position you want to start automatic hyphenation.
2. Choose Hyphenation from the Tools menu.
3. To insert an optional hyphen, press Ctrl-−.
4. To insert a nonbreaking hyphen, press Ctrl-Shift-−.

Indenting

1. Select the paragraph(s) you want to indent.
2. Choose the Increase Indent button from the Formatting toolbar.
3. To unindent, choose the Decrease Indent button from the Formatting toolbar.

Index

1. Put the insertion point at the place where you want the index.
2. Choose the Index and Tables command from the Insert menu.
3. Select the Index tab.

Index Entries

1. Select the text (if any) that you want included in the index.
2. Press Alt-Shift-X.

Inserting a Cell

1. Put the insertion point where you want the new cell.
2. Choose the Split Cells command from the Table menu.

Inserting Columns

1. Select the column that will be to the right of the new column.
2. Choose the Insert Columns button from the Standard toolbar.

Inserting from a Database

1. Put the insertion point where you want the data to appear.

2. Choose the Database command from the Insert menu.

Inserting Documents

1. Put the insertion point where you want the new document to appear.
2. Choose the File command from the Insert menu.

Inserting Frames

1. Put the insertion point in the paragraph where you want the frame to be anchored.
2. Choose the Frame command from the Insert menu.

Inserting Objects

1. Put the insertion point where you want the object to appear.
2. Choose the Object command from the Insert menu.
3. You can edit an object by double-clicking on it.

Inserting Rows

1. Select the row that will be below the new column.
2. Choose the Insert Rows button from the Standard toolbar.

Inserting Special Characters

1. Put the insertion point where you want the characters to appear.
2. Choose the Symbol command from the Insert menu.

Inserting Tables

1. Put the insertion point where you want the table to appear.
2. Choose the Insert Table button from the Standard toolbar.

Italics

1. Select the text you want to format.
2. Click the Italic button on the Formatting toolbar.

Jumping

See Going to Locations

Justifying Text

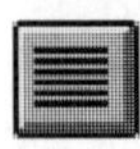

1. Select the paragraph(s) that you want to align.
2. Choose the Justify button from the Formatting toolbar.

Keeping Lines Together

1. Select the paragraph(s) that you want to keep together.
2. Choose the Paragraph command from the Format menu.
3. In the Text Flow tab, select the Keep Lines Together option.

Keeping Paragraphs Together

1. Select the paragraph(s) that you want to keep together.
2. Choose the Paragraph command from the Format menu.
3. In the Text Flow tab, select the Keep with Next option.

Kerning

See Spacing Between Characters

Keyboard, Changing

1. Choose Customize from the Tools menu.
2. Choose the Keyboard tab.

Landscape Orientation

See Orientation

Languages

1. Select the text for which you want to specify the language.
2. Choose the Language command from the Tools menu.

Leader Characters

1. Select the tab stops to which you want to add leader characters.
2. Choose the Tabs command from the Format menu.

Leaving Word

See Exiting Word

Line Breaks

1. Put the insertion point where you want to add a line break.
2. Press Shift-Enter.

Line Numbering

See Numbering Lines

Line Spacing

See Spacing Within Paragraphs

Linking Objects from Files

1. Choose the Object command from the Insert menu.
2. Choose the Create from File tab.
3. Choose the desired file from the list.
4. Be sure that the Link to File option is checked.
5. You can see the links in the current document with the Links command from the Edit menu.

Lists

See Bulleted Lists or Numbered Lists

Loading Documents

See Opening Documents

Locking Documents

See Read-only Documents

Lowercase Letters

See Case of Letters

Macros, Creating

1. Choose Macro from the Tools menu.
2. Choose the Record button.
3. When you are finished recording, choose the Stop button in the Macro toolbar.

Macros, Running

1. Choose Macro from the Tools menu.
2. Select the desired macro and choose the Run button.

Magnifying the Page

See Viewing Magnified Pages

Mail Merge

1. Choose the Mail Merge command from the Tools menu.

Mailing Labels

1. Choose the Mail Merge command from the Tools menu.
2. In the Main Document drop-down list, choose Mailing Labels.

Margins

1. Put the insertion point in the section in which you want to change the margins.
2. Choose the Page Setup command from the File menu.
3. Select the Margins tab.

Master Documents

1. View a document in outline view.
2. Choose the Master Document button from the Outline toolbar.

Mathematical Formulae

See Equations

Measurements

1. Choose the Options command from the Tools menu.
2. Choose the General tab.
3. Specify the units from the Measurement Units drop-down list.

Menus, Changing

1. Choose Customize from the Tools menu.
2. Choose the Menus tab.

Moving Between Panes

1. Press F6 or Shift-F6.

Moving Between Windows

1. Press Ctrl-F6 or Shift-Ctrl-F6.

Moving Text and Graphics

1. Select the text and/or graphics you want to move.
2. Choose the Cut button from the Standard toolbar.
3. Put the insertion point at the place you want the moved material.
4. Choose the Paste button from the Standard toolbar.

See also Drag-and-Drop Moving.

Multilevel Lists

1. Select the paragraphs you want in the list. The list must use the Heading styles.
2. Choose the Bullets button from the Formatting toolbar.
3. For more options, choose Bullets and Numbering from the Format menu.

New Documents

See Creating Documents

Nonbreaking Hyphens

1. Press Ctrl-Shift--.

Nonbreaking Spaces

1. Press Ctrl-Shift-Spacebar.

Nonprinting Characters, Inserting

1. Put the insertion point where you want the characters.
2. Choose the Symbol command from the Insert menu.

Nonprinting Characters, Viewing

See Displaying Nonprinting Characters

Normal View

See Viewing in Normal View

Numbered Lists

1. Select the paragraphs you want in the list.
2. Choose the Numbering button from the Formatting toolbar.
3. For more options, choose Bullets and Numbering from the Format menu.

Numbering Headings

1. Select the headings you want numbered. The list must use the Heading styles.
2. Choose the Heading Numbering command from the Format menu.

Numbering Lines

1. Put the insertion point in the section in which you want the numbered lines.
2. Choose the Page Setup command from the File menu.
3. Choose the Layout tab.
4. Choose the Line Numbers button.

Numbering Pages

1. Put the insertion point in the section in which you want the numbered pages.
2. Choose Page Numbers from the Insert menu.

Objects

See Inserting Objects

Opening Documents

1. Choose the Open button from the Standard toolbar.

Optional Hyphens

1. Press Ctrl-- (hyphen).

Orientation

1. Put the insertion point in the section in which you want to change the page orientation.
2. Choose the Page Setup command from the File menu.
3. Choose the Paper Size tab.

Orphan Lines

1. Put the insertion point in the paragraph(s) in which you want to change the widow and orphan control.
2. Choose the Paragraph command from the Format menu.
3. Choose the Text Flow tab.

Outlines

See Viewing in Outline View

Overtyping

1. Press the Ins key.
2. When you are finished overtyping, press the Ins key again.

Page Breaks

1. Press Ctrl-Enter.

Page Layout View

See Viewing in Page Layout View

Page Setup

1. Choose the Page Setup command from the File menu.
2. Choose one of the four tabs (Margins, Paper Size, Paper Source, and Layout) and make changes.

Paginating Documents

See Repaginating Documents

Paper Settings

See Page Setup

Paragraph Marks

See Nonprinting Characters

Passwords

1. Select the document for which you want to set passwords.
2. Choose the Options command from the Tools menu.

3. Choose the Save tab.
4. Enter the passwords in the File Sharing Options area.

Pasting

1. Choose the Paste button from the Standard toolbar.

Point Size

See Fonts

Portrait Orientation

See Orientation

Positioning Text

See Frames

Print Preview

See Viewing in Print Preview

Printing

1. Select the document that you want to print.
2. Choose the Print command from the File menu.
3. Choose what you want to print from the Print What drop-down list.

Quitting Word

See Exiting Word

Quotation Marks

1. Choose the AutoCorrect command from the Tools menu.
2. Select the Change Straight Quotes to Smart Quotes option.

Read-only Documents, Creating

1. Select the document for which you want to set passwords.
2. Choose the Options command from the Tools menu.
3. Choose the Save tab.
4. Enter a password in the Write Reservation Password option.

Read-only Documents, Opening

1. Choose the Open command from the File menu.
2. Select a document.
3. Select the Read Only option.

Removing

See Deleting

Repaginating Documents

1. Choose the Options command from the Tools menu.
2. Choose the General tab.
3. Select the Background Repagination option.

Repeating Actions

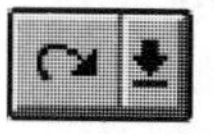

1. Press F4 to repeat the previous action.
2. To repeat sets of actions, drag down the Redo drop-down list to select the group of actions you want to repeat.

Replacing Text

1. Choose the Replace command from the Edit menu.

Resizing

See Sizing

Revision Marks

1. Choose the Revisions command from the Tools menu.
2. Select the Mark Revisions While Editing option to start marking revisions.
3. When you are ready to incorporate revisions, select the Review button.

Ruler

1. Choose the Ruler command from the View menu.

Running Heads

See Headers

Saving, Automatic

1. Choose the Options command from the Tools menu.
2. Choose the Save tab.
3. Select the Automatic Save Every _ Minutes option.

Saving a Document

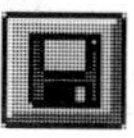

1. Select the window of the document you want to save.
2. Choose the Save button from the Standard toolbar.
3. If you want to save all the open documents and templates, choose the Save All command instead.

Saving, Fast

1. Choose the Options command from the Tools menu.
2. Choose the Save tab.
3. Select the Allow Fast Saves option.

Scroll Bars

1. Choose the Options command from the Tools menu.
2. Choose the View tab.
3. Select the Horizontal Scroll Bar and Vertical Scroll Bar options.

Searching

See Finding

Selecting an Entire Document

1. Press Ctrl-A.

Selecting Tables

1. Put the insertion point anywhere in the table.
2. Press Alt-5 on the keypad.

Selecting Text

1. Put the insertion point at one end of the desired selection.
2. Press F8.
3. Use the cursor keys to extend the selection to the other end.

Shading Text

1. Select the paragraph(s) you want shaded.
2. Choose the Borders button from the Formatting toolbar.
3. Choose the type of shading from the Shading drop-down list in the Borders toolbar.
4. For more options, choose the Borders and Shading command from the Format menu.

Single-spacing

See Spacing Within Paragraphs

Sizing Columns

1. Select the column(s) you want to resize.
2. Choose the Cell Height and Width command from the Table menu.

Sizing Frames and Graphics

1. Click on the edge of the frame to activate its border.
2. Drag any of its handles.

Sizing Rows

1. Select the row(s) you want to resize.
2. Choose the Cell Height and Width command from the Table menu.

Sizing Text

See Fonts

Sizing Windows

1. Drag the size box in the lower-right corner of the window to the desired location.

Small Caps

1. Select the text you want in small caps.
2. Choose the Font command from the Format menu.

Sorting

1. Select the paragraphs (in text) or the rows (in tables) you want to sort.
2. Choose the Sort or Sort Text command from the Table menu.

Spacing Between Characters

1. Select the text in which you want to change the spacing.
2. Choose the Font command from the Format menu.
3. Choose the Character Spacing tab.

Spacing Between or Within Paragraphs

1. Select the paragraphs you want to change.
2. Select the Paragraph command from the Format menu.

Special Characters, Finding

See Finding Special Characters

Special Characters, Inserting

See Inserting Special Characters

Spelling

1. Put the insertion point at the point where you want to start checking.
2. Choose the Spelling button, the Spelling command from the Tools menu, or press F7.

Spike

1. Select the text you want to cut to the spike.
2. Press Ctrl-F3.
3. Continue selecting and cutting the desired text to the spike.
4. Put the insertion point at the place you want the collected text.
5. Press Ctrl-Shift-F3.

Splitting Tables

1. Select the row that you want to be the top row of the second table after splitting.
2. Choose the Split Table command from the Table menu.

Splitting Windows

1. Point to the split icon in the desired window.
2. Click and drag the icon to where you want the split.

Spreadsheets

See Excel

Starting

See Inserting

Statistics

See Word Count

Status Bar

1. Choose the Options command from the Tools menu.
2. Choose the View tab.
3. Select the Status Bar option.

Strikethrough

1. Select the text you want in strikethrough formatting.
2. Choose the Font command from the Format menu.

Styles

1. Select the paragraph for which you want to change the style.
2. Choose the Style command from the Format menu.

Subscripting Text

1. Select the text you want in subscript.
2. Choose the Font command from the Format menu.

Summary Information

1. Select the document for which you want to edit the summary information.
2. Choose the Summary Info command from the File menu.
3. To see the summary information for many files, use the Find File command from the File menu.
4. To have Word always prompt you for summary info the first time you save a file, select the Prompt for Summary Info option in the Save tab of the Options command.

Superscripting Text

1. Select the text you want in superscript.
2. Choose the Font command from the Format menu.

Symbols

See Inserting Special Characters

Synonyms

See Thesaurus

Tables of Contents

1. Put the insertion point at the place where you want the table of contents.
2. Choose the Index and Tables command from the Insert menu.
3. Select the Table of Contents tab.

Tabs

1. Select the paragraph(s) for which you want to change the tab settings.
2. Choose the Tabs command from the Format menu.

Technical Support

1. Choose the Technical Support command from the Help menu.

Templates

1. Create the document you want to store as a template.
2. Choose the Save As command from the File menu.
3. In the Save File as Type drop-down list, choose Document Template.
4. Enter a name for the new template.
5. You can also manage templates with the Template command from the File menu.

Thesaurus

1. Select the word (if any) for which you want to find a synonym.
2. Choose the Thesaurus command from the Tools menu.

Time

1. Put the insertion point where you want the time.
2. Choose Date and Time from the Insert menu.
3. Choose the format of the date you want.
4. Decide whether or not you want the time to be a field (meaning that it will be updated when you open or print the document).

Toolbars, Changing

1. Select the Customize command from the Tools menu.
2. Choose the Toolbars tab.

Toolbars, Viewing

1. While pointing at an empty space in any toolbar, hold down the right mouse button.
2. Drag down the menu to select the desired toolbar.

Underlining

1. Select the text you want to format.
2. Click the Underline button on the Formatting toolbar.
3. For other types of underlining, choose the Font command from the Format menu.

Undoing Actions

1. Choose the Undo drop-down list from the Standard toolbar.
2. Drag down through all the actions you want to undo.

Unit of Measurement

See Measurements

Uppercase Letters

See Case of Letters

Vertical Alignment

1. Select the section(s) for which you want to change the vertical alignment.
2. Choose the Page Setup command from the File menu.
3. Select the Layout tab.
4. In the Vertical Alignment drop-down list, choose the type of alignment you want.

Viewing in Full Screen View

1. Select the document that you want to view.
2. Choose the Full Screen command from the View menu.

Viewing Magnified Pages

100%

1. Select the level of magnification from the Zoom list from the Standard toolbar.

Viewing in Normal View

1. Select the document that you want to view.
2. Choose the Normal button from the bottom left of the document window.

Viewing in Outline View

1. Select the document that you want to view.
2. Choose the Outline button from the bottom left of the document window.

Viewing in Page Layout View

1. Select the document that you want to view.
2. Choose the Page Layout button from the bottom left of the document window.

Viewing in Print Preview

1. Select the document that you want to view.
2. Choose the Print Preview button from the Standard toolbar.

Widow Lines

See Orphan Lines

WordArt

1. Choose the Object command from the Insert menu.
2. Choose the Create New tab.
3. Choose Microsoft WordArt 2.0 from the Object Type list.

WordBasic

See Macros, Creating

Word Count

1. Put the insertion point anywhere in the document if you want to count the whole document, or select the text for which you want a count.
2. Choose Word Count from the Tools menu.

WordPerfect Keys

1. Choose WordPerfect Help from the Help menu.

Zooming Views

See Viewing Magnified Pages

INDEX

The page numbers in boldface indicate entries in the Procedure Reference (Appendix C).

B

C

E

F

G

J

K

L

M

N

O

P

Q

R

S

T

U

V

W

Z